RE-MODELING

THE MIND:

PERSONALITY

IN BALANCE

RUTH A. JOHNSTON

Re-Modeling the Mind: Personality in Balance
Copyright 2015 by Ruth A. Johnston.

Pannebaker Press
Gibsonia, PA

This book is not intended as a substitute for the medical advice of physicians. The
reader should consult a physician in matters relating to his/her health and particularly
with respect to any symptoms that may require diagnosis or medical attention.

ISBN 978-0-9831810-2-6

Library of Congress Control Number: 2015913030

Contact:
Pannebaker Press
3945 Gibsonia Road
Gibsonia, PA 15044
www.pannebakerpress.com

Cover design and illustrations by Streetlight Graphics, LLC.
www.streetlightgraphics.com

OTHER BOOKS BY RUTH A. JOHNSTON:

A Companion to Beowulf, 2005
All Things Medieval, 2010
Excavating English, 2013

ACKNOWLEDGEMENTS

I would like to thank many friends and family for their support and input into this book. Writing began at the request of Jed Arkin, who believed in its value when I was not sure and supported my work in many ways.

My late mother, Connie Johnston, listened patiently and read my first draft. My father David Johnston, my niece Paula McHenry, and my friends Rob Crutchfield and Amber Baker have helped with many hours of discussion over several years. Jeremy Lauer read all of the drafts, providing key encouragement and insights. Anna Macdonald copyedited the final manuscript.

Many other friends have shared stories and reactions to my ideas, too many to remember and thank them all by name; I hope they know who they are. The book would not exist without these hundreds of conversations.

Thank you to *everyone* who has been involved.

Table of Contents

INTRODUCTION

This book began as many years of conversation among family and friends. I'm neither a psychologist, a neuroscientist, nor an expert on Carl Jung. But I was facing some very complicated human problems, ones that would take years to solve, if it was even possible. Friends and I began to talk about the Myers-Briggs personality framework: have you read about this? What have you heard? How was it helpful? The key question: how many chronic problems could be clarified if we saw them as stemming from *personalities*, not situations?

Books about personality types present sixteen different profiles and some basic explanations. They are usually written to aid in self-understanding, or perhaps understanding how spouses or children may be different from yourself. Sometimes they're written to help with understanding people at work. They're not written to help with the level of human complexity and dilemma I was facing. It looked like I could find at least some clarity with this system, but I would need to understand the theory, beyond mere profiles. I had to push the framework to its limits and experiment with it.

I read Isabel Myers' book *Gifts Differing* (1980) and David Keirsey's *Please Understand Me* (1978), comparing the ways they framed the theory. I also looked for logical alternatives: were there other important dimensions to personality? How could we be sure this simple framework was a complete system? I read about some alternative theories, especially the trait theory most used in psychology research, often called the Big Five. I also read a number of books about personality disorders and mental illness.

From reading contrasting ideas about human personality theory, I saw something that felt increasingly important: human personality should be seen as an interacting, self-balancing system. Living creatures, both plants and animals, are interactive, self-balancing systems. Human personality, above all, must be modeled in a way that's as alive as nature. While a list or chart of traits can help to organize academic research, it's not a model for living beings. And a list of traits was not going to help solve my puzzles: I had to know why things came to be and how to predict further changes. I needed a dynamic, life-like model.

Within Myers-Briggs theory, there appeared to be the foundations of a living system, but its parts were explained only in specialty books intended for Jung enthusiasts and Myers-Briggs professionals. Even there, nobody laid it out as the kind of self-balancing model I was seeking. After picking up some clues, I decided to go back to Jung's *Psychological Types* (1921), the original source. The book was excruciatingly difficult to read, but I found some fresh approaches in it. Jung appeared to present his ideas in a different order from modern interpretations.

As I thought about Jung's system, I was reading neuroscience books to find out the most current view on many things. How do emotional systems work in the brain? What is the "unconscious" in modern terms? What can studies show us about disease processes and their effects on personality? A startling fact became clear: Jung's personality system had leapfrogged over some of the 20th century psychological assumptions that are now being discarded. His model had been rejected by academic psychology long ago, but it actually suited the new neuroscience ideas very well.

I could see how to update the model in a few important ways. I could also see that by presenting it in the same order and with some of the same emphases that Jung did, I could lay it out as a moving, self-adjusting model instead of a table of traits or preferences. It was this three-dimensional, dynamic model that began to solve some of my puzzles. I had a working model now; in a sense, I could turn the crank and watch it move, or tinker with the parts and see how it changed. Chiefly, the model demonstrated how personalities normally form to help us live with the greatest efficiency.

My dynamic model suggested ways to see how early life stresses can shape our personalities in ways both good and bad. In a sense, it bridged the divide between Nature and Nurture; it allowed for both genetics and environment. It included elements of both determinism and free will. I could also see how more extreme stresses, such as mental illness, can influence personality. It's not easy to separate someone's mental illness from their core person, but here was a model that suggested ways to do it. It could help someone set realistic goals in recovery.

The dynamic model also provided explanations for which kinds of interpersonal problems might be solved easily and which ones might prove to be the Titanic's iceberg. Prediction of this type can be very powerful when we're making key relationship decisions. There are so many dilemmas in marriage and parenting; while nobody can tell what the future will bring, this model could at least suggest which decisions might be most consistent with who the child or spouse—or yourself—will become.

This book is an attempt to lay out the reasoning behind my model, its parts and pieces, the way the model is put together, and how it works when we look at real lives and relationships. It takes a lot of reading patience to get through all of this material, but absorbing even some of it can help clarify human conflicts and dilemmas. I know that the book could have been a page-turner, had I included the stories in which I was living. I wasn't free to do so, nor did I feel the model needed their support. It stands on its own and every reader can support it with examples from life. My words, however, are based in my life and the book is built from its bones.

Ideally, reading the book will build a model in your mind that will take you beyond the suggestions I have here.

PART ONE:
LIVING SYSTEMS

CHAPTER 1

What Is Personality?

M OST OF LIFE IS SPENT finding out who you are, chiefly by trial and error. When you're a child who finds himself in the wrong club or sport, the error is easy to undo: you just quit. During the years of childhood, these trials and errors are supposed to lead to a good understanding of what you can do, what you like to do, and what you do particularly well.

Past a certain age, trials lead to errors that are much harder to undo. Many people major in a program in college that leads to an impossible, unworkable or otherwise just wrong career, so they end up abandoning their huge financial investment to do something else. Others follow through with the work plan they prepared for, but a decade or two later, they're depressed and frustrated by work they dislike and can't do easily. At the middle of their lives, instead of coasting into old age on the strength of a long career, they may find themselves starting over to learn optometry or sheep farming.

People make the same mistakes in forming personal relationships. Friendships are easily left behind when they prove problematic, but when a relationship has committed you to a house and children, it's hard to break it off. Many people reach middle life aware that in spite of good intentions all around, they are married to spouses with whom they just can't work or be happy. Marriage therapists usually try to tell the couple how they can change to be more what the other needs. The advice always sounds sensible and it may even sound possible, but few people can actually bring about such changes in themselves, since it would mean changing their own needs. It's one thing to make up sentences about changing your needs and abilities, but it's quite another to actually change them in important ways.

In the middle of life, people can feel themselves stuck in a life that doesn't feel like it's really theirs. Looking back, it's clear that they made mistakes, but at each point, the career and friendship choices seemed to make sense. For a while each decision seemed right, but something changed. What changed? "Did I change, or did everyone else change?" they wonder. Sometimes people are aware of feeling like they changed, but it rarely feels like true change. Usually, it feels like a process of changing back to what they always were. In these cases, they can see that they made these wrong decisions at a time when they were not, in some sense, being their real or best selves.

In order to know how you're changing, you have to know who you are. Do you have to guess again about how to change? What if you make more mistakes? Learning more about who you actually are, based on both the past and the present, can help you make more accurate predictions and smarter decisions.

The process of learning who you are means both learning the plain facts about yourself and understanding how you are different from (or the same as) other people. The facts about yourself are learned as you try new things. How do you react when challenged to a fight? Are you good at planning large parties? Some people know answers to these questions by late childhood, because they've had those experiences or very similar ones, but many others do not. If someone is looking at a career path that might lead to managing large organizations, he'll have no way of knowing whether he's good at that kind of management if he's never done anything like it.

Understanding how we compare to others is often more difficult than just getting some basic events behind us. We tend to assume that people are mostly much alike, and that they are mostly similar to us. Even people who have always been aware of feeling different may assume that their thought processes are mostly universal. Shy people know that others are not shy, but being shy may feel like a defect amid a general similarity. Men and women see differences between the sexes, but then there are exceptions to these generalities, and there are many traits that boys and girls can have in common. Overall, we tend always to assume that everyone sees the world just as we do.

Our experiences in life are subjective. We perceive and remember experiences in ways that make it almost impossible to have an objective, outside view of what happened. Only later in life do we start to understand that someone else's experience of the same events was radically different. It may not be until the middle of life that we come to realize how very different it would feel to live in someone else's perspective and sensations.

When we do come to understand these differences, it is eye-opening. We say things like, "You mean that's why other people aren't bored at movies?" "So that's why he voted for that candidate!" "No wonder she didn't want to go to college; I see it now, but I never understood it at the time." Over and over, we find that we mistakenly assumed that people were too much alike, thinking either that we ourselves were defective versions of everyone else, or that everyone else must feel the same way we do about things.

Seen in a broad way, like turning a telescope on the stars, all human beings have certain motivations in common: they want to survive, form relationships and avoid rejection. If we are all alike (a common focus of psychology research), then there is no way to specify what would be wise for this individual to do. At that level, we have only general truths which can be about as useful as knowing that your destination is somewhere to the west (but should I turn right or left at this Y?).

But at the other extreme, the narrowest view, each human being is perfectly unique. Nobody will ever again be born in this place and time to this parent, and nobody will ever again read the exact same set of books or live in the exact same set of circumstances. If we are all entirely unique, then there is no way for us to learn from other people's experiences. At that level of individuality, we have to rely on trial and error, since what worked for one has no bearing on a different individual.

Somewhere between these opposite poles, both true to an extent, we can find a way to group individuals in ways that allow them to see how they are alike and to learn from each other. The study of personality type is exactly this effort: a way to look at features of individuals and group them so that we gain some wisdom about predicting what will work for them.

I define "personality" as **the recognizable pattern of how an individual processes and responds to the world**. People respond to events differently because their way of perceiving and evaluating the event was different from another person's. By and large, people react in ways that make complete sense to them. Usually, their reactions and decisions seem (to them) like the only possible ones, even if other people would do something different.

In order to understand why people do certain things, we must understand how they process the world. This is especially true of our own selves, because in no other way can we start to get an objective view of who we are and why we do what we do.

CONSCIOUS AND UNCONSCIOUS BRAIN PROCESSES

First, we need to understand that personality is rooted deeply in neural patterns in the brain. It is not something we plan or choose; it's a function of the unconscious mind that we can't control.

The concept of the "unconscious mind" is key in modern psychology. For the last century, the unconscious mind has indicated a small part of ourselves, deep and hidden, that can control our conscious actions. Conscious actions are the ones we choose for reasons we understand, and they seemed to be the majority. But we have to redefine these terms when looking at brain processes; first, we can't go on viewing the unconscious as either small or hidden. The conscious mind is the part of our thinking that pays attention, so it seems very big. But it turns out that nearly every brain process is, in fact, unconscious.

This means we have to reassess what we mean by "unconscious." When it was viewed as a small, hidden part of the mind, there was a sort of mythology of the unconscious. It was thought to operate in cloaked, unexpected or even undetectable ways. It was like a secret self, at times like an "evil twin," undercutting what the conscious self did. In Freud's time, they thought that dreams could be used like x-rays to examine this hidden mind. Psychiatrists thought they could treat the unconscious mind using dreams for diagnosis and suggestions as surgical instruments.

It's observably true that people often do not pay attention to emotional motivations, doing the opposite of what they claimed they would do. So far, so good. But this doesn't work now as the way to define the "unconscious" mind. Beginning with studies of subliminal images, neuroscience experiments have come to define "consciousness" in terms of speed. When an image is shown to the eye for more than one-quarter of a second, the mind is conscious of seeing it. Other neurological perceptions or events can be measured too, and it turns out that 250 milliseconds, one-quarter of a second, is an approximate threshold of consciousness in things other than vision.

So in the new way of defining consciousness, **conscious thought takes place when processing goes on for longer than 250 milliseconds.**[1] This means that by the time we're conscious of something, it is in the just-barely-gone past. By this definition, "unconscious" means any part of the brain that can process faster. As it turns out, that's nearly everything.

Nor are the conscious and unconscious brains located in separate places. Any action or thought that we're conscious of is really made up of many unconscious actions and parts. Although we consciously choose to speak words, word selection and comprehension turn out to be handled by an unconscious process. Commands to our tongue, lips and breath control to make sounds are also too fast for the conscious mind. When we listen to speech, we consciously understand it, but all of the sounds were handled by faster, unconscious actions. In the same way, we are conscious of what we see, but all aspects and tasks of vision are handled faster, outside or below consciousness. The same turns out to be true of every sense, movement and memory. Our use of them is conscious, but the actual sensation, motion control and bits of memory are not.

Consciousness seems to be a summing-up of many unconscious brain functions. What we're conscious of is what we're *paying attention to* at some level. An infinite array of information streams through our brains every day. At every moment, some part of your brain is monitoring your body temperature and the room air temperature; your hunger, thirst, and other sources of physical comfort; every sound wave that meets your ear drum, colored light that reaches your eyes, breeze of air or crawling insect on your skin; and a million memories and primary feelings designed to keep you secure. It isn't possible to pay attention to all of it.

Consciousness feels to us like a movie we're watching; it assembles what we see, feel, hear and remember into a narrative. It seems to be, primarily, a means of assessing our experiences as we go along. We compare what we remember with what we're experiencing at the moment so that we can make decisions.

There is no one single brain part that handles conscious awareness and comparison. Every brain part suspected of being the movie-screen of consciousness has turned out to do something else. Conscious thought may be a group effort of several brain regions, or it may be the effect of many brain cells communicating electrically and chemically, so that while these brain cells are primarily doing some unconscious business, they are also signaling to each other in a way that produces the experience we call being conscious.

At the electrical level, conscious and unconscious thought are identical. All brain actions can be described as either exciting or inhibiting an impulse. Each impulse goes from one neuron to another, within the same brain organ or crossing over to other regions of the brain. Impulses can be described in terms of chemicals, but they are also electrical signals that switch on the neural stations they pass through. At each junction, impulses are inhibited or amplified: either not passed on, or passed on with greater power to the next neural station.

1: Jeffrey Gray, *Consciousness: Creeping up on the Hard Problem* (New York: Oxford University Press, 2004), 7.

Attention to sensory detail amounts to inhibiting or amplifying a signal about sight, sound or touch. As attention to a detail grows, related emotions may be amplified or inhibited; these emotions filter through parts of the brain that inhibit or increase action. Brain cells that often receive impulses from each other create strong habitual electrical pathways. Groups of neural cells that interact frequently begin to work together in a systematic way. By the time a baby reaches his first birthday, his brain has formed many alliances and working groups. When a baby reaches his hand out to touch a toy, he is training processes of sight and motor coordination; he gets faster and better at it when the neural processes become strong and habitual.

Even with so much going on below the surface of consciousness, we still casually assume that our conscious decisions are more important than unconscious ones. Freud's generation was correct about that aspect of the unconscious: it does seem to be the fundamental generator of decisions and motivation. We aren't even close to understanding how super-fast unconscious decisions relate to conscious perception of the same decisions. In 1985, one study suggested that it's possible we "make decisions" at the super-fast level before we know we've actually made the decision. In the study, the decision was just whether to move one's hand or not. Brain-wave monitoring showed a pre-movement impulse that may have occurred before the conscious awareness of the choice.[2]

When we make conscious decisions about how to handle danger, much of the work has already been done at the faster unconscious level. Studies of the hippocampus have suggested that one role for this deep brain structure is in mediating between conflicting goals.[3] Part of the brain wants to move forward, but another part flashes fear of some bad thing that might happen. The hippocampus, a structure not directly related to verbal or visual thought, strikes a balance and helps inhibit either the fear or the wish to move forward. We have no awareness of the hippocampus's process of choosing whether to inhibit fear or not. Conscious decision-making isn't involved at this level and can't control how the balance is struck.

In Freud's time, it was fine to talk about fears and desires in the unconscious mind. But if we think of the mind as emerging from the brain's electrical activity, we need to look first at the laws of natural systems. After we understand how living systems organize themselves, we can start to put emotional or other uniquely "human" labels on what we see. The physical brain and what we call "mind" or "personality" are not exactly the same; the brain is made of cells. Neuroscience often says that the mind is an "emergent property" of the brain. This means it's our perception of how the brain works; it's an idea that we've constructed.

Think of the difference between a symphony and the actual orchestra that produces it. The symphony began as an idea in the composer's mind; knowing his craft, he broke it down into individual parts and wrote out the score. Each musical instruments operates on the rules of physics: vibrating strings, pipes and reeds; saliva-laden breath blown across holes and into tubes; horsehair catching silver-bound gut and leaving pine-resin dust all over varnished wood. It's very physical, very material, and every instrument plays a different musical line. No single piece of this is the symphony. The symphony exists as something that emerges

2: Benjamin Libet, "Unconscious Cerebral Initiative and the Role of Conscious Will in Voluntary Action," *The Behavioral and Brain Sciences*, 8 (1985), 529-526.

3: Jeffrey Gray and Neil McNaughton, *The Neuropsychology of Anxiety: an Enquiry into the Functions of the Septo-Hippocampal System* (Oxford: Oxford University Press, 1982).

from the concrete activity, blending in the air as vibrations that work together. It exists in our minds, as we perceive the symphony in the blended sounds we hear. The symphony, as a product of the mind, is conveyed to our minds.

The symphony concept is very similar to the concept of mind itself. The brain is working at a physical level, using electrical signals, chemicals and cell actions. No single one of these things produces the human mind as we perceive it. But out of them all, there's an emerging "thing" that we recognize as a unified body of thought and action. Our minds perceive other minds and their products. The mind is tied to the brain as the symphony is tied to the instruments; they can't be separated, but we can see the difference between them. Just as the symphony has to be shaped around the physical traits of musical instruments, the human mind mirrors and parallels many of the physical laws of the brain. The brain is part of the natural world, but the mind is not; just as you can touch a violin but not a symphony.

ORDER AND CHAOS IN LIVING SYSTEMS

We learn fundamentals of the mind by studying the physical brain. It's part of the natural world, like any living thing. While it has some unique properties, some of its rules are the same as those we can see around us. First and most importantly, we can see how chaos is organized into order. It's visible in the natural world, where gravity, friction, evaporation and other basic processes are constantly organizing.

For example, water falls as raindrops, landing on many objects at random. Gravity immediately begins to organize the water by drawing it away from higher points, toward lower ones. As water collects into a stream, it presses against rocks, leaves and other things. Depending on their mass relative to the water, they move or stay still. At the surface, water turns into vapor again. When these processes have been completed, water may have re-organized the landscape by cutting new canyons and moving boulders. The organization was carried out by a blend of unpredictable, chaotic events (how much rain and where it falls) and highly predictable natural laws.

A similar set of processes happen in our minds, but we can't see them. Like the natural world, the brain has a certain low level of chaotic activity going on at all times. Its activity is electrical: neurons receive random signals from other neurons in light background murmur the way leaves constantly move in the wind. Scattered electrical activity keeps all options open. But then, through the senses, some real information comes in. Neural connections made before get reinforced; memories are stored.

It begins at the level of the individual neuron. The neuron can fire a signal or not; it is always just on the threshold of firing, when it's in a resting state, and sometimes it just randomly fires. This is an unpatterned signal, as if for practice. Individual neurons become parts of neural networks, which have the same trait. In a resting state, the neural network sends unpatterned, apparently meaningless electrical signals. But as soon as the network is called into action by an outside stimulus (like a sound), it halts unpatterned signaling and becomes very orderly. Patterns that have been used before get strengthened: more and more neurons are devoted to amplifying these signals. These develop into habitual networks with better connections than others.

Without these network patterns we could not learn, remember or carry out complex actions. But as soon as organized networking is done, the system begins a light murmur of unpatterned signaling again. Why? Why is it important for the network to practice chaos when it's not doing orderly work?

In the first experiment that established the role of chaotic electrical connections, rabbits were conditioned to recognize certain smells that would win them a drink of water if they licked the control button.[4] The rabbits' brains were monitored at a minute level during the experiment; learning a new smell could be tracked as it went from something new, to a repeated pattern, to a memory. The experiment's development was difficult; it took place over twelve years, published in 1987. During most of these years, other researchers were suggesting that a computer closely modeled the way the brain worked: data comes in, it is subjected to rules, it is sorted into results. At first, it looked like that's what the rabbits were doing, too; smells appeared to be data input that were sorted into remembered results. However, when the experimental goals had finally been completely achieved, something very different emerged.

Between tests and even when they exhaled (and therefore were not actively smelling), the rabbits' brains reverted to unpatterned olfactory signaling. "Unpatterned" means it was not orderly; instead it was chaotic and random, like raindrops. The unpatterned signaling seemed to prepare the rabbit for the next intake of breath, the next opportunity to smell. It erased the orderly, patterned memory of a half second before. In a sense, the olfactory nerves were daydreaming about smells that might not exist, smells the rabbit had never encountered. Just in case.

A computer model might suggest that rabbits could be seen as odor-detecting robots. A robot designed to sort out chemical smell signatures would rest quietly when not actively receiving a signal. Its patterns are pre-set. The living rabbit, by contrast, had a function that seemed to deliberately disrupt patterns. Each brief period of chaotic signals kept its smelling system primed to move in new directions. Of course, those new directions followed the patterning rules; an actual new smell was quickly organized into the rabbit's memory system. But on exhaling, the rabbit's brain would again generate some disruptive signals.

In their paper, researchers James Freeman and Christine Skarda argued that chaos was necessary for learning. It kept the rabbit's brain always on the brink of tipping into increased chaos; they called it "an 'I don't know' state of mind" that easily led to a searching mode.[5] The searching mode permitted faster learning responses.

The "I don't know" state is like a baseball team that throws the ball around to random positions when nobody is up at bat. As soon as there's a batter and a hit, they only throw the ball in ways that respond directly to what's happening on base. But during pauses, the team might practice tossing the ball from left field to right, to shortstop, to first base, to third base, and so on. There's no meaning in "playing catch," but it keeps the team flexible for any

4: Christine A. Skarda and Walter J. Freeman, "How brains make chaos in order to make sense of the world," *Behavioral and Brain Sciences* (1987) 10, 161-195. Posted online at Freeman's archive: http://sulcus.berkeley.edu/freemanwww/manuscripts/IC8/87.html

5: Skarda and Freeman, 4.6 "The sensory-motor loop."

unusual plays that might be needed. They can practice doing what hasn't yet been needed, but might be needed, instead of just standing still or redoing what's already been done.

What Freeman and Skarda were seeing in their rabbits was not a strict rules process as in a computer; it was a self-organizing system that oscillated between order and chaos. Systems in the natural world generally move between these states, like the example of a rain storm falling on land. Rain and wind are chaotic, random and disorganizing, but then gravity, friction and evaporation re-organize the system.

There is a key difference between the chaos and order of a non-living system (like a rain storm) and a living one. Skarda and Freeman made this an explicit comparison as they considered what their rabbit experiment might mean. In a non-living system, the parts do not influence each other. A rainstorm and a seacoast are both part of an ecological system, but they're not pieces of the same living system. The storm won't modify itself to avoid damaging the coast, nor will the coastline move to keep from weakening the storm.

Living systems must adapt and balance within themselves, unlike the storm and the land. This is true of all cells, but it's especially so in animals with neuron systems. What is apparently "random" signaling in a neural network is actually an adaptive partner with orderly signaling. Skarda and Freeman noted that the partnership within a living system takes place at a deep level, "long before there is any reason to refer to 'consciousness' or 'beliefs.'"[6] Balancing within the brain's living system is not consciously intentional. It's also not optional.

The mind is a living system. It has a unified, cooperative way of switching between patterned behavior and unpatterned potential. It sorts impulses into patterns at a level below our conscious choice, but it also spontaneously generates thoughts, reactions and choices that may be outside our usual habits. Like the rabbit's olfactory system, the human mind stays ready to adapt and change, while at the same time being efficiently organized for memory and learning. It's the patterns that provide us with personality—but it's the unpatterned spontaneity that prevents personality from being a rigid shell that controls every action.

In physics, a system is a group of parts that interact with each other in predictable ways. There are static systems that don't change and adapt (like the air conditioning system in an office building); there are also dynamic systems that change and adapt over time. While most dynamic systems are living, some weather systems, landforms, and complex machines also count as dynamic. Some systems are self-organizing; their parts influence each other so that they maintain an overall balance even when the parts shift and change. Non-living systems can be self-organizing, but living systems are always both self-organizing and dynamic.

Personality is a self-organizing, dynamic system, because it emerges from the brain, which is a living, cell-based organism. Instead of talking about personality in terms of fears and desires, we can start with how it's organized around the physics of systems. When we use human-based words like "fear," we may mistakenly assume that the system is easy to change, for example by learning not to be afraid. When we talk about core personality organization in terms of physics, we can see more clearly how little choice has to do with its most fundamental patterns.

Systems become organized by moving toward some states and away from others. The

6: Skarda and Freeman, 4.6 "The sensory-motor loop."

state the system tries to avoid is called a repeller, while the state it's drawn to is an attractor. Attractors are always states that require little or no energy to maintain. It's easiest to look first at a non-living system that organizes itself. We can see a simple, visible attractor and repeller system at work with a ball on a hill.

Fig. 1-1

Unless something is keeping the ball in place, we know that it will move to the bottom of the hill. It gains energy as it rolls downward and almost certainly it will pass the lowest point and begin rolling upward. But moving upward, toward the top of the hill, requires more energy. That's why we can call the top of the hill a repeller state. It isn't intentionally repelling the ball, but without some counter-force holding the ball in place, the ball will always leave the hilltop. When the ball rolls partway up the other side, its forward energy runs out so it reverses. Now it falls back toward the bottom again, the point where no energy at all will be needed. It may pass this point another time, but sooner or later, with its momentum gone it will stop at precisely the lowest point of the hill. There it will stay. For this simple system, that is the state of least energy maintenance. The hill itself is a system that organizes rocks, balls, water and other things with basic forces like gravity, friction and momentum.

We can see another simple system visibly "attracting" toward a minimum state of maintenance energy when we watch a pile of sand growing. On a small scale at the beach, or on a large scale in industry, sand falls steadily in a small stream onto the pile. As more sand goes on top, the hill gets taller and its angle steeper. Suddenly, there is a landslide. Sand shifts from the top of the pile to the bottom so that the hill's angle is less steep. If you set up an experiment with a slow continuous dribble of sand landing on top of a pile, you would see a regular pattern in which the hill grows taller and steeper, readjusts with a landslide, grows again, and readjusts again.

When the sand pile settles after a landslide, the hill's angle is called the "angle of repose." Every material can be measured for its angle of repose. Wet and dry sand are different, as every kid at the beach knows, and different sizes of gravel or coal are also different. As a matter of safety, industries that plan to store big piles of things must plan for each material to be stored at its angle of repose. Otherwise, it would take added energy to keep the stones or grain at a steeper angle, so the pile would automatically slide to the level that does not require energy.

All systems have a very strong tendency to move toward whatever arrangement takes the least energy to maintain. Neural networks strongly follow this rule, organizing themselves whether we like it or not. Whatever is high maintenance will soon be abandoned; whatever is most efficient will become more frequent.[7] In a neural network, high maintenance states

---

7: Jim Grigsby and David Stevens, *Neurodynamics of Personality*, (New York: Guilford Press, 2000), 120.

include the chaotic "I don't know" state of unpatterned signaling. The brain's equivalent of the bottom of the hill, or the angle of repose, is organized, patterned, habitual signaling. This state requires the least electrical signaling energy.

While sand piles and balls settle into the state of greatest repose, living systems continue to alternate between attractors and repellers. There is always a move to push things back toward the repeller point, like when the rabbits' brains "rested" between breaths by returning to chaos. Living things must do this because their greatest survival and efficiency is not in the angle of repose, but right at the brink of the repeller state.

Think about sitting in a chair, knowing that you're probably going to be asked to stand up quickly at any moment. In order to be ready to move, you sit on the edge, where your weight is resting on the chair, but not fully. Part of your weight is ready to shift into standing motion. Your muscles are tensed, ready to move. You are not at rest; this will be a tiring state to keep up for very long. But in this position, right on the brink of motion, you have greatest flexibility to make a change.

The heart is constantly moving between attractor and repeller states. Electronic signals are always preparing one of the chambers to contract, while another is relaxing. If the heart didn't keep an equal exchange between being about to move (a state of tension and high energy) and having just moved (a state of rest) it would stop beating. Living systems are most efficient when they are balanced like this. They don't maintain the high-energy state longer than necessary, but they swing back around to being ready, again, to meet it. This is the most efficient state for a living system: a constant flux between high and low energy. It always moves toward lower energy, but it is always pushed back toward high energy potential again.

Habitual patterns are attractors in a brain system; they are the low energy maintenance states. Disrupted habits, unpatterned signaling, and dilemma are repeller points. The mind, as we perceive it in brain patterns, has the same set of attractors and repellers. It moves toward habit, resolution, certainty and action. Thought is needed to prompt action, so after we act, our minds are at rest. Indecision, dilemma, uncertainty and inaction are repellers.

PERSONALITY: DYNAMIC SYSTEM IN THE MIND

So we could say that "personality" is a set of organizing principles that move us away from indecision, uncertainty and inaction. Remaining in a state of dilemma and confusion is too energy-consuming a state to maintain for any longer than we absolutely must. Life brings difficult new information and nobody can avoid states of dilemma and confusion. But everyone moves away from these states as quickly as possible, falling back into habitual patterns. It's not a choice; it's built into the brain at the neural level.

So far this discussion has seemed academic, but here we see the first practical conclusion. People often wish that they could change their personalities, and if personality is described as a list of traits, it seems reasonable that someone could just "develop" some new traits. In a limited way, it may be possible. But at base, your personality is too deeply rooted in neurological patterns laid down since infancy. It's a self-organized system that cannot be changed at will from the outside. Its organizing rules are as imperative as the angle of repose on a sand pile or snowy mountain.

Here is the inherent challenge of this book: personality is much easier to understand when it's seen as a list of traits. Traits may not capture the dynamic way that a living system behaves, but a list is not hard to understand. Personality as presented in this book is based on the Myers-Briggs framework, but we will look at it as a self-organizing dynamic system, not as traits. Presented as a system, it takes many more pages to explain and grasp.

The usual explanation is that there are four categories of traits, and each one has two options. You are extroverted or introverted; sensing or intuiting; thinking or feeling; judging or perceiving. Your personality type is the sum of four trait preferences, and it's named by four letters that stand for these preferences.

One benefit of the typical presentation is that it's easy to understand. We could picture a cafeteria line; each personality goes through the line with a tray, selecting one of two meats, breads, vegetables and desserts. You can select beef or turkey; mashed potato or a dinner roll; carrots or beans; cake or pie. There are sixteen possible meals: beef, potato, carrot and cake, or beef, dinner roll, carrot and cake, or beef, potato, beans and cake, and so on.

These sixteen different meal combinations are parallel to the sixteen different personality categories in the Myers-Briggs system. Each one is a combination of "preferences" among the four pairs of options. In the analogy to a cafeteria line, there is nothing preventing someone who has chosen turkey from taking a dinner roll, or someone who chose beef from eating pie. Each preference is separate from the others. For understanding the meaning of the letter codes used to name personality types, it works pretty well.

But we've already established that while a mind or personality can be described this way, it can't really be understood in such terms. Living systems aren't like cafeteria lines with separate choices. They are more like recipes in which flour and butter have to coordinate with each other, or like machines whose gears have to fit and move together. They are most of all like living cells or ecological systems, whose parts modify each other. So while the presentation of four preferences is easy to understand, it can't be an accurate model of what's really happening.

Another typical aspect of the Myers-Briggs personality types is that they are all described in positive terms. We all know that many people, including ourselves, are not entirely positive. We also see pretty clearly that the idealized type descriptions don't perfectly capture ourselves or other people. When we use the types as dynamic models, we can better understand why sometimes we're less than ideal and happy.

First, if we're viewing personality descriptions as just the most ideal form that a dynamic pattern can take, we can understand better how real individuals may differ. An ideal hill with a ball isn't much like a real hill with a real ball, although we can clearly see that they are the same. Any real living system has unique features, just as any tree in a forest is shaped only like itself, even if it's a maple among thousands.

Second, we know that systems can become imbalanced; even simple washing-machines start to rattle and walk when too many towels are on one side. If personality is a dynamic system, we can see how it can slip from correct balance into imbalance, so that an actual person's "traits list" may not match up well with balanced systems. To take another machine analogy, if cars aren't supposed to make the squeaking noise your car makes, we don't conclude that your car is not a car (perhaps it's a tractor or a motorcycle? perhaps machines can't be named?). We understand that your car is behaving in a way that isn't ideal, and we look at the ideal car model to see how your car is different. In other words, the ideal pattern can help diagnose a problem and how to improve it.

We can do the same thing with personality descriptions when they stand for living patterns. However, living systems are so much more complicated than basic machines that in order to understand what we're up against, with personality, we should look at an imbalanced living system. It's not always clear that it's imbalanced, not in the way that a washing machine is. Living systems are so complicated that they re-balance into new patterns, instead of clunking or squeaking. Imbalance may create patterns that look natural, and in those cases, it's only by seeing the ideal model that we can understand the nature of imbalance.

Yellowstone National Park demonstrated how changing one element in a living, self-organizing ecosystem can change it at every level, so much that it's hard to recognize what its original systems model was. In the 1920s, wolves became extinct in the park; they were re-introduced in 1995. For seventy years, the mountain ecosystem slowly adjusted to the loss of wolves. Most visibly, grazing animals had no predators; mule deer, bison and elk herds grew, but especially elk. At first, this probably looked like a purely good change. Visitors to the park in 1990, near the end of the no-wolf period, would still have seen a beautiful park with lots of elk. Valleys were less likely to have logs lying about, since fewer brushy trees grew taller than the elk. Elk were free to graze and live where it was easiest.

It was only when wolves came back that naturalists could see the full impact of their past loss. Of course, first the wolves preyed directly on elk, so the herd was reduced. Elk moved higher into the hills, avoiding river valleys, and they stayed at the edges of tree stands. Bison increased; they had competed with elk for grazing, but were apparently harder for wolves to catch. Fast-growing trees such as aspen, cottonwood and willow began to grow back in valleys and along riverbanks, where previously the elk had eaten them as shoots. Plants not only draw from the soil, they also change it by releasing minerals and other chemicals. So as over-grazing stopped, microbes and mineral balance in the soil itself shifted, encouraging different plants to grow.

Coyotes, which had to compete with wolves for small prey, shifted out of the park. The coyotes' former prey, like rabbits and mice, moved into the new green cover in valleys that were no longer bare. Before wolves, there had been one beaver colony in the northern range of the park, but as willow and aspen grew back, beavers increased to a dozen colonies with dams and ponds. In these new ponds, more swimming animals like muskrats and otter could live. Erosion of riverbanks stopped as mature tree roots stabilized them. More birds moved in too: hunting birds to catch mice, and songbirds to live in the willows. The bear population grew, perhaps because young bears can clean up elk meals left behind by wolf packs.[8]

Naturalists call these changes a "trophic cascade," in which some part of the food chain gets deleted. The loss forces changes all the way up and down the system, in this case even changing the mineral composition of the soil. Cascades of change and adjustment are part of

8: William J. Ripple and Robert L. Beschta, "Trophic Cascades in Yellowstone: The first 15 years after wolf re-introduction," *Biological Conservation*, 145 (2012): 1, 205-213.

being self-organized and alive; we see them in all living things, from very simple plants and animals to complex systems like endocrine balance. It's not possible to make just one change without many other things shifting.

So if personalities are alive like ecosystems, we can expect that life stresses can nudge the system into adaptive changes that may amount to a tropic cascade. It's especially true of stresses that last a long time, forcing adaptation. When "predators" or "plants" are removed from a personality's system, it has to self-organize in a new way.

Self-organizing doesn't mean that the resulting system is always the best it could be. Personality self-organizes along lines of least energy maintenance; in your own life context, this could be very good or very bad. The time when your personality settled its patterns might have been special: perhaps you lived in a stressful family or needed to act unlike your true self. Staying out of trouble pushed your balance a little bit out of its ideal pattern. Now you don't live in the same conditions, but the adaptive patterns remain in your personality. They were formed because they required less energy to survive at the time, but they aren't fundamentally best for your brain, and they aren't helping in your current life.

If you can accurately identify the fundamental patterns of how you process and react to the world, you can then accurately spot which of your personality habits is a misfit. Sometimes it's not the ones you think, and it's usually not the ones that everyone keeps complaining to you about. Too controlling? You might need to exercise more, not less, control. Too outgoing? Maybe you're not outgoing enough. Too indecisive? Maybe you're focusing on dilemmas that your personality isn't set up to handle. Few habits or traits are objectively bad; they're good or bad for you in the context of how else you manage life.

A dynamic, living model of personality helps in another way. It's very hard to define the word "normal" as applied to human beings. We crack jokes about this, usually denying that "normal" has any meaning. At the same time, anyone who has been around truly abnormal behavior knows that the word "abnormal" does have significant meaning. How do we define it? How can we tell when we're dealing with unpleasant behavior or truly abnormal behavior? How should we change our reactions if we suspect it's abnormal? Can someone be a blend of normal and abnormal? What would this look like, and what causes it? How can we understand it? When you have a flexible model based on processes, not traits, these questions can be addressed.

Finally, many people are uncomfortable with personality type systems because not only do they seem too simple, they also appear to restrict human potential. Naming personality "types" seems to put people into boxes, perhaps to deny that growth is possible. This is a very uncomfortable idea if you want and need to make big changes in your life. It's also worrisome when personality type is described in a rigid, prescribed way. It sounds as though free will isn't possible, as though your life is determined by this pattern.

However, with a living model, we don't have to get stuck in these worrisome traps. Personality has patterns, but it's not a box, because in a living system habit is always being challenged by unpatterned chaos. In the rabbits' smelling systems, unpatterned signals kept habits from becoming inflexible. We see the same exchange of pattern and non-pattern at the level of the neuron, the neural network, the personality and even larger groups of individuals: families, societies, nations. While most of life is handled by habit, everyone generates unpatterned thoughts and decisions to disrupt habits. You may drive to work on the same streets every day, but there will come some day when you decide to take a different road. It doesn't really mean anything; it's unpatterned behavior. If it means anything, it's just a reminder that habits never completely constrain us. There are always potential actions and spontaneous changes alternating with strong habitual patterns.

New ideas and trials are quickly integrated into patterns, for example, you may learn that your usual route to work is the one to keep, when the new route makes you late or puts you in danger. Without the spontaneous trial, you couldn't test and reinforce your patterns. But the unpatterned, spontaneous trials also open the door to different potential. Your mind daydreams, you say something out of character, you do something unexpected. Sometimes you end up going in a new direction. This too is part of personality, since it's how a living system organizes itself.

The barrier to having a system like this as a tool is that it's initially difficult to learn. How many of us would learn to drive if we had to understand, first, everything about the mechanism of the car? Most of us know people who understand the inner workings of the cars they drive; clearly there are times when this deeper knowledge helps them with the actual driving, such as in bad weather or when the brakes fail. It would be great if everyone had this kind of grasp of driving, but most of us don't, and we feel (perhaps wrongly) that we just can't understand at that level.

This book is asking you to understand human personality by first setting aside practical use and learning to observe some patterns that probably aren't visible to you yet. You can skip ahead to Chapter 12, where there is a full explanation of the sixteen Myers-Briggs personality types, if you want to. Most books about personality focus on these types, so that once you've identified your type, the goal has been met. My goal is different. I'm asking you to understand the parts, how they fit together and influence each other, and what kinds of patterns they form together. If you are patient with the early chapters and learn to see how the system works, nothing in the profiles will be mysterious to you, any more than types of cars can surprise a mechanic.

The fully-understood dynamic system becomes a diagnostic tool that is able to do much more than simply put a label on someone. If you can understand exactly how you are like and unlike the best-match personality model, you may gain insight into some stubborn problems you can't solve. Being somewhat out of balance can cause far-reaching effects. Even when the imbalance isn't negative in itself, such as when someone has more gifts and talents than usual, there are losses and changes that can become negative.

If you have a problematic family relationship, you may be able to get some insight on it by understanding how each person's personality is balanced, not just in theory but also in their individual patterns. In each relationship, our personality balances interact with the other person's. We can see how the theoretical model personalities would react, but when we understand them as moving parts, not as static lists, we can also see how the individual patterns may increase the pressures.

The power of the tool isn't available if you don't learn to see the system's parts, how they move together, and how they blend as a whole. My book explains these things as clearly as possible, but it requires patience to learn each piece and slowly build the working model.

Once you can see the parts, you may start to see practical insights into your own life even if the book doesn't actually explain the issue you're dealing with. With the model built in your own mind, you can use it as your own tool.

So at the outset, I must ask patience and trust from readers. If you want to have the system as a working tool, you may need to read slowly, put up with a great deal of theory, and then go back to re-read some parts. The pay-out when you really understand it should go beyond the book's two covers. In the meantime, as the ideas are built, I'll try to be both clear and interesting. You may find some practical uses for even the early, theoretical ideas.

CHAPTER 2

Basic Processes in Personality

O UR THEORY'S ROOTS GO BACK to Carl Jung's 1923 work, *Psychological Types*. It is
a dense, difficult book that appears to ask and answer questions that no 21st century
writer would consider important. The book was read by many psychiatrists and readers of
early psychology, in its time, but it has little influence on academic and research psychology
today. Why did this book fall out of the mainstream, and why go back to it now?

In the 1920s, Carl Jung and Sigmund Freud were both very influential. Freud was
about twenty years older, had trained originally as a neurology researcher, and now practiced
psychiatry in Vienna. Jung (born in 1875) lived in Switzerland, and all of the German-
speaking psychiatrists formed a fairly cohesive community. Freud met Jung in 1909, when
they were both invited to lecture at Clark University in Massachusetts. They began to share
and collaborate on ideas, with Freud always taking the lead.

The turn of the 19th to the 20th century was a time of rapid scientific discovery. Between
Freud's birth in 1856 and the two men's 1909 meeting, the science of medicine had been
transformed from medieval to modern. When Freud was born, stethoscopes were a new
invention, and doctors were still developing methods for how to use them. A British doctor,
Walter Gaskell, discovered most of the secrets of heart function between 1869 and 1908. He
also mapped the autonomic nervous system and described the effects of pH imbalance on
heart tissue. The function of many organs was determined during this period, too.

As laboratory experiments proved how the organs worked, medicine followed quickly
with improvements in care. For example, an experiment with dogs, in 1889, determined
the role of the pancreas. Early microscopic studies of kidney tissue were published during
the 1860s, and in 1878, a surgeon developed a new technique for removing kidney stones.
At the same time, experiments with morphine and derivatives of cocaine began to develop

general and local anesthetics for these improved surgeries. Development of the first x-ray machine began around 1895.

Louis Pasteur progressed from studying wine spoilage in 1866 to testing the first rabies vaccine in 1885. Hand-washing was not an accepted medical practice until Pasteur and Joseph Lister proved that bacteria could be kept out of wounds with basic antiseptic practices. Robert Koch isolated the Tuberculosis bacillus in 1882; this disease had been the great mystery disorder of "consumption" for centuries, and science could now prove that it was caused by a microorganism, not by bad air. Koch's students went on to isolate and name the microorganisms behind the diseases that most concerned the 19th century: typhoid, pneumonia, leprosy, diphtheria, syphilis and tetanus, among others. They were no longer mysteries, after centuries of superstition and guesswork.

Other branches of science made huge progress during this time, too. Darwin's Theory of Natural Selection moved from controversial theory to wide acceptance. At the same time, there were great discoveries in paleontology. The first Tyrannosaurus Rex tooth turned up in Colorado in 1874, while the first partial skeleton was found in 1900, in Wyoming. Other dinosaur and fossil discoveries that we now take for granted were big news during that period. In 1869, the first modern periodic table of the elements was published; it organized a staggering number of individual discoveries about physical properties of minerals and gases. Between 1856 and 1870, there were several different methods to determine the speed of light, but in 1888, Heinrich Hertz measured it definitively using electromagnetic waves. In 1879, Thomas Edison announced that he would make electricity so cheap that only rich people would burn candles; the 1893 World's Fair in Chicago glowed with electric light. The Wright brothers' first heavier-than-air flight took place in 1903, and in 1905, Albert Einstein introduced his Theory of General Relativity.

In these exciting years, it seemed there was nothing that science couldn't discover or do, and the pace only accelerated going into the 20th century. What game-changing discoveries could be made in the area of the human mind?

Neurology and psychiatry were not clearly distinguished in this time. When head trauma caused emotional and behavior problems, neurologists could not determine that there really was a brain injury, as we can today. Epilepsy wasn't well understood, either. Neurologists saw patients who had memory problems and strange phobias but they did not have any way to diagnose a physical cause. Psychiatry began as an offshoot of neurology. Freud and others looked for "psychological" causes of strange behavior in their patients—that is, causes that appeared to have no visible physical injury or disease at the root.

Freud had trained in medical research and wanted very much to contribute some great discoveries as others were doing. When he began a private psychiatric practice, he used his patients' cases to publish papers that proposed a model of the mind. It was the first mechanical model that didn't involve any religious beliefs about the soul, that instead tried to show cause and effect in a scientific way. He proposed three forces in conflict: an animal-like force that was mostly driven by sex, called the Id; the Super-Ego as a moralistic, philosophical force; and the Ego, which acted as a referee and was more conscious than the other parts. He believed that dreams could be used like x-ray imaging to understand the Id.

Carl Jung, one generation younger, had a different perspective. His father had been a minister, and although Jung was not religious, he was interested in the spiritual idea of the mind. He did not believe that enough was yet known about the brain to permit scientific discoveries. Eventually, he published a paper that questioned Freud's doctrine about dreams. Until then, he had been the favorite to carry on Freud's work. After he publicly questioned Freud, they were rivals and antagonists.

The break with Freud isolated Jung in two key ways. First, the emotional tide of the second World War moved Freud's work into greater popularity after his death in 1939. Freud, a Jew, was evacuated from Austria by English friends, only a few months before he died in London. Jung remained in Switzerland during the war, and he also continued to publish papers in German-language psychology journals. To the post-war world, contact with Germany (even from neutral Switzerland) was an unfavorable sign suggesting sympathy with Hitler. Freud's work was carried on in England and America, in some cases by Jews who had survived the Holocaust. The continuing bitter feelings between Freud's disciples and Jung made it convenient to allow post-war emotion to discredit him.

Second, Jung had explicitly stepped away from the science of his time, seeking to understand the human mind by looking at what it produced. Although he valued science and considered himself a doctor, he believed that it would be many years before medicine really knew much about the mind. In the meantime, he thought, the only way to study the mind was to look at art and stories, especially when certain ideas and themes seemed to persist across time and around the world. As he got older, he was increasingly interested in folklore, art and Renaissance-era alchemy.

In 1950s university research and clinical psychiatry, two approaches were seen as scientific. Freud's case-study approach was still accepted, and his ideas were dominant through the 1970s. The other gold standard was the double-blind placebo study, the only accepted standard in physical medicine. In such a study, participants don't have any way to know whether they are taking the target medicine or a substitute, so their unconscious ideas can't influence how their bodies react. Psychology began doing similar studies of behavior, finding ways to disguise the true point of the study. This was also the time when the "blank slate" theory of a baby's mind was most dogmatic. In this theory, the neural cells of an infant's mind were not pre-assigned to tasks, so that all later traits were shaped solely by the way the baby was raised. In the debate between "nature" and "nurture," nurture was the clear winner.

During the last decades of the 20th century, there has been some research on inborn personality, but its goal was restricted to determining whether double-blind studies could prove that some traits existed. Five trait categories have been the central focus of worldwide research on humans and animals, across ages and cultures. Gradually, mainstream opinion has shifted to accepting the idea of innate personality traits.

In the 21st century, we're quickly moving toward genetic definitions of personality. Beyond genetic, even more surprising, is the evidence of epigenetic inheritance. Some non-genetic exposures and experiences in parents and grandparents may influence how their genes develop in offspring. In a sense, it's like inheriting memories, without the actual memories. Each link in our DNA contains directions for developing an individual, but some of the possibilities are limited by epigenetic influences. A gene for aggressive behavior may turn out differently in an individual based on whether the gene was on the mother's or the father's side. Genes are further changed by substances that one of the parents was exposed to, or even by traumatic experiences in the grandparents' generation.[9]

The inheritance of experience was one of Jung's most important ideas. It seemed ridiculous during the blank-slate years, but the clear line between "nature" and "nurture" is gone. Jung's core ideas do not seem as unscientific as they once did.

In fact, Jung's breakdown of the basics of human thought works pretty well with contemporary ideas of the brain. Instead of positing forces locked in eternal conflict, as Freud did, he outlined a model of co-operation and balance. Instead of focusing mainly on dreams and the "unconscious," he tried to describe holistically how people function as they face decisions, goals, setbacks, and aging. He did this by defining a small set of logical divisions of thought, based on observation. We can't map his "functions" directly to lobes of the brain as defined by MRI and PET scans, but imaging-based notions of how brain regions work together are easily compatible. Jung couldn't map the brain, so he mapped the mind (the symphony emerging from the orchestra), and he got it very close to right.

Psychological Types became the basis for the Myers-Briggs Type Indicator® (MBTI), which has remained commercially popular. Its enduring popularity with business and individual readers is testament to how much truth the system captures. Although university psychology research ignores Jung's work on personality, basic college classes on psychology often explain or even use the MBTI test. There are many books written about Myers-Briggs types, but they are almost always at the popular level, showing how personality typing can be useful in different settings. They assume its truth and seek to make it easy to understand and use. Of course, commercial success has a price: the ideas seem even more discredited in the eyes of academic researchers and clinical psychiatrists.

All of these factors—his personal politics with Freud, our ideas of science, and the attitudes of universities to anything popular—mean that Jung's original book is largely unfamiliar. Moreover, *Psychological Types* is difficult to read even in English. It doesn't pose and answer the same questions a modern reader is asking, and it's disorganized by our standards. Insights and observations are scattered within long discussions of medieval philosophy or the poetry of Schiller and Goethe. When Jung finally lays out his own framework, his writing is more focused on creating technical terms than on explaining them well. We're stuck with his terms; they've been used in both Jungian philosophy and Myers-Briggs testing so much that we can't easily substitute easier words.

Let's look at his key terms and framework now. I'll capitalize words that have carefully defined technical meanings, to distinguish them from ordinary use of the same words. I'll do this throughout the book, though when I'm developing my own ideas, usually the only technical terms will be these same ones inherited from Jung.

9: Tabitha M. Powledge, "Behavioral Epigenetics: How Nurture Shapes Nature," *Bioscience* (2011) 61: 8, 588-592. Posted online at http://bioscience.oxfordjournals.org/content/61/8/588.full

JUNG'S FRAMEWORK OF MENTAL PROCESSES

Jung divided the mind's fundamental processes into **Perceiving** and **Judging**. Perceiving means receiving, processing and experiencing all kinds of information. It isn't just one part of the brain, of course, rather the category is a summary of how we can observe the mind taking in the world. Perceiving is about learning: recognizing, classifying, paying attention to details. Because there is really too much information going on around us, Perceiving selects what we'll pay attention to.

The selective attention of Perceiving takes place at the unconscious level. Babies are probably already wired to pay attention to some things more than to others. Living with their built-in preferences for a few years confirms tendencies into patterns. Eventually, patterns can become conscious beliefs and worldview. But they start as neural nets that happen to be better at some kinds of attentiveness than others.

Judging functions take what the Perceiving functions are collecting and passing on; they put it in order and handle decisions about what action we'll take, considering this information. The ways the brain handles Judging are among the better-known facts of popularized neuroscience. We know that many decisions, called "executive functions," are handled in the frontal lobe. We know that executive functions in the left hemisphere tend to be about logic and math, while Judging functions in the right hemisphere tend to be about emotion.

This general background is good to have, in order to understand Judging. However, we can't stay tied to hemisphere and lobe distinctions. There will be huge discoveries about these brain functions in the coming years, perhaps invalidating much of what we think we know now. Jung observed "Judging functions" in the mind long before science had suggested left-right hemisphere roles. His observations are still more complex than brain studies can support with detail.

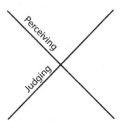

Fig. 2-1

Perceiving and Judging should not be seen as personality traits in this context. They are basic elements of thought, completely different but working together like two hands. To represent their relationship, we can show them (in figure 2-1) as lines that go in different directions but cross:

Together they form an X. At the point where they cross, we could imagine that they're working together on learning and sorting the same information. Otherwise, they are different trajectories, different actions, two separate motions in the brain.

Perceiving can pay attention to what the senses report directly; it can also pay attention to studying connections between things and events. When Perceiving pays direct attention to real things that are seen, heard, felt and known, Jung called it **Sensing**. When it pays attention to connections, which cannot be directly seen, he called it **Intuition**. You might say that where Sensing sees nouns, Intuition sees prepositions that tell how nouns are related: because, between, beyond, and so forth. Connections are invisible and can't be detected by any of our senses, but our lives may depend on being able to "see" them, so Intuition should be considered equal to Sensing.

In the figure 2-2 below, I represent Sensing and Intuition as balls on each end of a Perceiving axis.

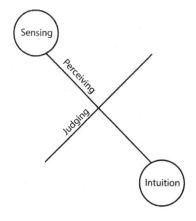

Fig. 2-2

Judging is also divided into two kinds. Sometimes Judging priorities are derived from numbers and logic, but alternatively, they may be based on the impact our actions have on relationships. When Judging is done by logic, Jung called it **Thinking**. Decisions made with an eye to human relationships were called **Feeling**.

It's important to notice from the start that these four words have a narrow, technical meaning when used this way. Usually, when we use the word "thinking," it just refers to all mental processes: "Wait a bit, I'm thinking about it." When we use the word "feeling" in daily speech, it means consciously experiencing emotion: "Are you feeling sad?" However, in the context of this book, Thinking will always mean "Judging by logic," and Feeling will always mean "Judging by relationships." The technical meanings of Sensing and Intuition are not as different from their everyday meanings. Sensing usually means using the five physical senses, and indeed we do use them to understand facts, nouns and concrete realities. However, Sensing can also work with somewhat abstract, invisible things like rules. You can't see or smell a rule, but knowing rules is part of Sensing's technical definition. Similarly, the everyday meaning of Intuition is knowing something without being able to explain why, like having a hunch. The technical meaning of Intuition is broader than this, but it includes it. Hunches are still part of Intuition, but so are other things like imagination and idealism.

In the diagram 2-3, Thinking and Feeling are balls on each end of the Judging axis.

Now both axes have been separated further into two different actions. Representing the subdivisions as balls on opposite sides of each axis suggests that they're not really working together; they don't intersect the way the Judging and Perceiving axes do.

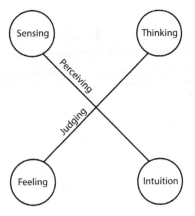

Fig. 2-3

There's one more division to complete the system. Jung saw our responses to the world as primarily rooted either in a pragmatic view of our environment or an instinctive, inborn sense of how things should be. For the moment, I'll use "E" to stand for **e**xternal **e**nvironment, and "I" for **i**nborn **i**nstinct. Each of the four basic functions can be divided in these two ways in figure 2-4:

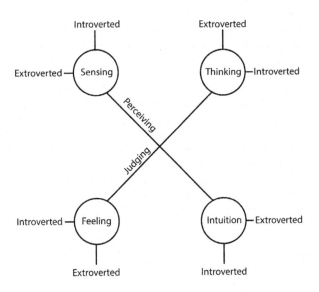

Fig. 2-4

I just did a sleight of hand trick with words, of course. For those familiar with personality psychology, "E" and "I" also stand for Extroverted and Introverted, and these are the more familiar terms. Of course, I also mean these words too, but in some ways, it's a problem that they are so familiar. "Extroverted" usually means outgoing and liking to be around people. "Introverted" usually means that you're occupied with thoughts in your head and don't like to be around people for long. However, as with words like thinking and feeling, we're going to use them only in a restricted, technical meaning. If you read one of these words in a sentence and assume that it means its usual everyday sense, chances are the sentence will make no sense. In this book, **Extroverted** will always mean that a mental function is pragmatic, flexible, and optimistic as it searches the outside world. **Introverted** will always mean that a mental function is inborn, innate, idealistic, stubborn and scanning for problems and anomalies as it compares the outside world to an inner ideal. Chapter 3 will discuss these meanings in great detail, and later passages will often include context and synonyms to make the new meanings clear and memorable.

The diagram 2-4, above, shows all eight of Jung's technical terms for mental processes, organizing how they relate to each other. If you've read books about Myers-Briggs personality typing, my diagram may seem puzzling. I'm proposing a major shift in how we see these familiar terms. Some readers may be willing to accept this and move on, while others want to know why I think my diagram is a good representation of Jung's ideas. This next passage is for those readers. If you're not familiar with or interested in Jung's writing, please feel free to skip along to the next section, "Rules for Stable Balance."

The first really big shift in explanation is that I drew four basic mental functions (Sensing, Intuition, Thinking, Feeling), while using the words "Perceiving" and "Judging" only as categories for these four. Usually, Perceiving and Judging are given their own category as a dimension of personality. A person is described as "preferring" either Judging or Perceiving, meaning they tend to do one or the other more. They're considered traits of personality: you like to make decisions (Judging) or you don't like to make decisions (Perceiving). But here, I use them simply as categories to organize the other words.

I believe that Jung's original understanding was along my lines. In the "Definitions" appendix to *Psychological Types*, he refers more than once to the "four basic functions" of Sensing, Intuition, Thinking and Feeling.[10] He groups Thinking and Feeling together, saying for example, "In the same way that thinking organizes the contents of consciousness under concepts, feeling arranges them according to their value... Feeling, like thinking, is a rational function."[11] His definition of "rational" is unusual, and it will not be part of this book; but to understand why it equates to the word "Judging," which Jung used in other places, we need to know what he meant. For Jung, "rational" meant a thought process that was "decisively influenced by reflection."[12] In other words, it was part of a decision-making process, Judging. Thinking and Feeling are both "rational," decision-oriented, reflective, therefore Judging processes.

He called Sensing and Intuition "irrational" functions,[13] but he was careful to say that this didn't mean they were opposed to reason. It meant, rather, that they were separate from reason; they were not on an anti-reason mission, but they were on a completely different sort of mission, one that has nothing to do with reflection and decisions. Jung included in

10: C. G. Jung, *Psychological Types* (Princeton: Princeton/Bollingen, 1971), 723, 770, 792, 830.
11: Jung, *Psychological Types*, 727.
12: Jung, *Psychological Types*, 787.
13: Jung, *Psychological Types*, 776.

the idea of "irrational," plain facts, events that happen by chance,[14] and our mind's direct perception "of the flux of events."[15] In other words, the things and events that we learn about are "irrational," and so is the learning process. We perceive facts, events, and changes from our senses. We also perceive connections and meanings. So the "irrational" functions are really kinds of Perceiving.

Jung's meanings for "rational" and "irrational" are not used further in this book. One reason Jung's works can be so difficult to read is that he created many special terms, and then he used alternative versions of them. Isabel Myers chose "Perceiving" and "Judging" from among his terms, probably guessing correctly that "rational" and "irrational" were just not going to be comprehensible.

If you're used to working with the Myers-Briggs personality ideas already, shifting Perceiving and Judging away from a stand-alone trait category may seem like a loss. You may be used to seeing people as either "Perceiving" or "Judging." But the reality captured by these terms remains in the system. My explanation is more difficult, but I believe the change in difficulty is justified by greater nuance and insight.

The second big shift is with Extroverted and Introverted. I have made two changes here: first, they are usually given their own separate category to describe personality; second, they are not usually defined in anything like my terms. How do I justify not only making the words into adjectives, but also changing their definitions?

First, this is actually how Jung used the words. He does speak of "extroversion" and "introversion," and he describes them in terms of energy. But when he begins to present his own ideas of what Thinking, Feeling, and the others mean, they are always described as two kinds: Extroverted and Introverted. Using them as adjectives is a consistent pattern all through the last section in *Psychological Types*. He talks about "extroverted thinking" and "introverted thinking," "extroverted sensing" and "introverted sensing." He speaks sometimes of an extroverted or introverted person, but he spends far more time using the words to describe the four basic kinds of mental functions.

The second reason is more compelling: we can shift these words from psychology jargon into useful words with a stronger link to our experience of life. By their Latin roots, extroverted means "turned outward," and introverted means "turned inward." Jung defined them as inward and outward turning of "libido," by which he meant something like "life energy." He also said that introversion is a "negative relation of subject to object,"[16] while extroversion is positive movement from subject toward object. Both of these definitions are not only technical to his field, but also obscure and hard to understand in daily life. Sometimes they are further defined as "gaining energy from" or "losing energy to" people and the outside world. This is easier to understand, since many people do feel a loss or gain of energy in being around people. But it doesn't make sense to describe logical decisions as gaining or losing energy from people. The energy gain/loss definition doesn't help at all with describing kinds of Perceiving, either.

To explain how I'm going to use these words, I want first to bring in one of Jung's well-

14: Jung, *Psychological Types*, 774.
15: Jung, *Psychological Types*, 776.
16: Jung, *Psychological Types*, 769.

known and equally obscure concepts: the "collective unconscious." To modern readers, it may sound like he was talking about Star Trek's "Borg," a sort of shared consciousness among many individuals. It sounds mystical or supernatural. But Jung actually meant the part of the human mind that's least like a "blank slate," the part that may have hereditary structures of thought. We inherit a certain ability to think and understand, and these inherited abilities are shared among all humans; that's all he intended to convey by "collective unconscious." In the Computer Age, we'd say "it's what's *hard-wired* into the human brain at birth."

Sometimes he used this phrase interchangeably with the word "introverted." For example, in *Psychological Types*, he wrote, "The introverted attitude is normally oriented by the psychic structure, which in principle is hereditary and is inborn in the subject… The psychic structure is the same as… what I call the 'collective unconscious.'"[17] What's inherited and inborn is introverted. When our mental processes are rooted in these hard-wired structures, they are introverted.

The hard-wired, inborn structures are "possibilities of ideas,"[18] in Jung's words. He called these possible ideas "**archetypes**." They aren't full-blown ideas; when people believe that "past lives" provide them with foreknowledge or recognition of people and places, that's not what Jung meant. He was talking about the most general outlines of ideas, and based in comparing art and folklore around the world and through time. His reasoning was that if we have innate "possible ideas," these forms will repeatedly show up. Therefore, if some motif keeps showing up, it might be an inborn possible idea, an archetype.

For example, we see artistic designs based on circles all over the world; they often show a mandala, that is, a group of balanced designs enclosed in a circle. The mandala and the circle are considered inborn ideas that people come up with, even without having seen other circle art; the circle may also have some concepts and feelings associated with it. Jung believed that most of the possible ideas were collected and inherited from long-past generations; some of them recall the experience of becoming civilized.[19] Others are universal and help us understand family and social structure.

If we define "Introverted" to mean "rooted in inborn possible ideas," then "Extroverted" means the opposite, not-inborn. Extroverted functions are more like a blank slate, waiting to be filled in by the outside world. With these meanings, it makes more sense to say that Thinking, Feeling, Sensing and Intuition are Introverted or Extroverted. When they are Introverted, they are shaped by inherited possible ideas; when Extroverted, they are not.

Our understanding of inherited possible structures of the mind doesn't need to rest on art and literature now. Since Jung's time, there have been many studies of inborn knowledge in both animals and human babies. It's hard to know what babies and animals know, since they can't talk. It's also very hard to pick apart what is already known at birth from what is quickly learned soon after birth. Some animal and infant studies have tried hard to create situations in which learning could not have been possible. We'll look at this kind of research in Chapter 3, to build a useful picture of the "possible ideas" that may be involved in Introverted functions. It isn't possible to achieve anything like the sophistication that Jung

---

17: Jung, *Psychological Types*, 623-624.
18: Jung, "Concerning the Archetypes, With Special Reference to the Anima Concept," *The Archetypes and the Collective Unconscious*, 136.
19: Jung, "On the Psychology of the Trickster Figure," *The Archetypes and the Collective Unconscious*, 466.

assumes from his folklore and art studies, but at least we can get a sense of what's possible among "possible ideas."

RULES FOR STABLE BALANCE

In *Psychological Types*, Jung wrote as though a personality has only one or two of these functions, but the Myers-Briggs system correctly includes all four (Sensing, Intuition, Thinking, and Feeling) in every personality type. As a psychiatrist, Jung had much opportunity to talk to unhappy people. He was most interested in what happens when one of these functions becomes imbalanced and takes over too much of someone's personality. Writing for other psychiatrists, he focused on imbalance and unhappiness, but he also set out some rules for correct balance. When his rules are worked out logically, they imply that a normal, balanced personality has all four mental processes; the Myers-Briggs descriptions are based on these rules.

Personality is a living system, balanced between settled habits and flexibility. Jung's rules fit neatly into this idea by suggesting how mental functions that could be in conflict can, instead, self-organize into patterns of balance. Efficiency for brain, mind and personality mean being able to act with minimal dilemma. It's more efficient to be either right-handed or left-handed than to be ambidextrous (which can be associated with learning disabilities). It's more efficient to have one standard way of doing things, assuming that it works, than to have to decide every time.

So the first rule is that **it's most efficient for personality to use one of the mental functions to solve most problems**. Some kind of Perceiving or Judging has the greatest neural strength in early childhood, so it becomes stronger with each successful use. By adulthood, this top mental function has been used in so many different scenarios that it can handle almost anything. Because it is the habitual leader, it has "clear and unambiguous aims," (Jung's words) which allow for quick, efficient action.[20]

The other parts of personality act as lesser team members, usually coordinated with the strongest part. Occasionally, an unusual situation pushes personality to draw from a less-practiced function. But most of the time, the other mental functions develop in partnership with the strongest one. They feed in extra observations and double-checks; they help fine-tune its attentiveness.

Jung observed that usually there is a second-strongest mental function that has formed a very close partnership with the strongest one. However, the constraints of brain energy rule out a few kinds of close partnerships. What if the two strongest were both Judging functions, Thinking and Feeling? The "clear and unambiguous aims" of logic are often completely different from the aims of relationship needs. Such a partnership would be constantly stuck in dilemmas. It isn't natural for the brain to gravitate toward a partnership like this because such dilemmas use up a lot of mental energy. Life brings real dilemmas, but we need them to be rare, not something we face every hour and minute of every day. That would be just too inefficient.

20: Jung, *Psychological Types*, 667.

It would also not work well for the two strongest mental functions, working as partners, to be the two Perceiving functions. They direct our unconscious and conscious attention to observing and learning. There is so much to perceive and learn that trying to take in all of it would mean standing still or going in circles. If most of a personality was taken up with Sensing and Intuition, there would always be more to observe, feel and learn before a decision could be made. That's highly inefficient for surviving in life; we've got to get on with decisions and actions. Too much Perceiving could also overload the brain with sensory processing and ambiguity.

Jung's second rule makes sense, then: **When a Judging function is the strongest, its close partner must be a Perceiving function. When a Perceiving function is the strongest, its close partner will be a Judging function.**[21] The strongest part of personality could be Sensing, a Perceiving function, and then it would need to partner with either Thinking or Feeling as the second strongest. It could also be Thinking or Feeling, but not both; strong Judging would need one of the Perceiving functions in partnership.

The third rule says that **when the strongest mental function is oriented to inborn, instinctual knowledge, the second one must be focused on flexible learning about the outside world.** If the strongest one is Extroverted, the next strongest must be Introverted, and the other way around.[22] The reasons for this balance will become clearer in later chapters.

All three of the rules start by observing an inefficient state that the mind can't sustain. The first rule provides that personality must have a clear hierarchy of strength, while the second and third rules are conditionals to avoid conflict. It's a very minimal set of organizing principles, allowing for a number of ways for strengths to play out. Although Jung explained them only in terms of the two strongest functions, it's also clear that people need all four of them, so the balancing rules can be extended to a complete set of four.

The four mental functions, governed by these minimal rules, are a sort of closed system. Each part influences and conditions the others, so that you can't make a change in one place without affecting the whole system. That's why I call it "dynamic," not to suggest continual change and growth over time, but because there is interaction between the parts. They self-organize according to these minimal rules.

The first and most important implication of this interaction is that each mental function is influenced by its place in the system. In the following chapters, I'll define and describe the purest, clearest forms of Extroverted or Introverted Thinking, Feeling, Sensing and Intuition, eight different kinds of mental processing. To describe each one, I must treat it as though it's the sole mental function and show its purest state. But when it's placed into a real personality, it's rarely as pure as the description.

Thinking, for example, has both mathematical and moral components. When it's influenced by other parts of personality that balance, modify and limit it, it may show up as primarily mathematical or moral, or it may have parts of both, sometimes in inconsistent patterns. Real humans are inconsistent, above all. But that's what this closed, interactive system predicts: that as each part influences the others, they will become individually and sometimes uniquely tailored.

21: Jung, *Psychological Types*, 668.
22: Jung, *Psychological Types*, 670.

Extroverted or Introverted Thinking has a different character when it's the top mental function rather than an assisting one. The description of its purest, most theoretical form is often very close to reality in people who do have it as the strongest. When it's moved into any of the lesser, assisting roles, it may come out as mathematical talent, sarcasm, an ability to handle conflict, or just willingness—or unwillingness—to make a moral judgment. The pure, theoretical description is still correct, but the function itself may be so modified, limited and influenced by stronger ones that it's only partly recognizable.

Every description in this book should be seen as a model or paradigm, not dogma about what a real person must be like. The model is true as a model, even if not a single individual is precisely, entirely described by it. Models and paradigms explain what things mean and how they work; if there's a counter-example among individuals, this example doesn't mean the model isn't true, unless it's a rare case that really does invalidate the model. Usually it means that there's a personal history of development. The model exists in our minds, while individuals exist in real, unique forms in life. The model should be able to explain why the individual developed this way by showing patterns of interaction and influence. If it can do that, it doesn't need to be exactly like any individual, nor any individual exactly like it.

The second implication of interactive flexibility is that personalities can adapt in the moment to stresses. If personality were rigid, it would be constructed to work one way and no other; it would be like a steel-girded building that's vulnerable to shaking apart in an earthquake. All of us get into situations where our strongest habitual functions are completely wrong and could be disastrous, if we had no way to flex and find some back-up abilities.

It's because personality is adaptive in the moment that it can be so stable over time. To lean on another analogy about rigidity and motion, it's like standing on the deck of a large boat that is constantly moving in the waves. "Getting one's sea-legs" means learning how to adapt the inner ear to constantly shifting weight and balance while somehow perceiving ourselves as upright and stable. Sailors never stop moving in order to stand still.

In a child's personality, what works well gets reinforced, so whatever helps best with coping in the family and at school becomes habit. At the same time, having four quite different personality strengths to draw on allows the child to create combinations that are better for school or home, better for one or another type of person or situation. Personality isn't just the main list of strengths, it's the entire pattern of flexibility and habit that allows maximum efficiency in the brain while still surviving life's new problems.

This is why a dynamic model of personality can be described as stable across a lifetime. We see people adapt to different situations, but these are not personality changes, there are just subroutines of the same personality pattern. The pattern is complex enough to handle a wide variety of problems, so it doesn't need to recreate something new for every new situation. Flexibility among the interacting mental functions is already very responsive to these things.

When we do see change in personality, it's safe to say that the root cause is always some very serious stress that seems to threaten survival. Generally there was an early, long-lasting stress in these cases. It forced the child's personality to develop not exactly as it would have, without the stress. When survival is at stake, the brain can develop inefficient patterns just to stay alive. Even mild, chronic stresses feel like survival threats to a young child, so it's very common to grow up with this sort of pressure.

There's an underlying pattern of neural strengths that we can consider the natural personality pattern. It's like the original food chain of the Western mountains, the one that included wolves. The role that a child needs to play forces some adaptive habits, ones that push personality out of its original balance. Sometimes weaker parts of personality have to become main strengths, while other times, strengths become too strong. The rest of personality adapts to these new needs, being flexible like someone standing on the deck of a ship.

This adapted personality arrives in adulthood as, supposedly, the actual personality. It's the only way this individual knows how to live. Later in life, a new set of stresses may come along. They are not ones that the adapted, imbalanced personality can handle. It's possible that the original neural strengths can help, and if so, the adapted personality may appear to change. The change is only going back to what was already there.

In either case, adapting to stresses or adapting back to an original pattern, self-organizing flexibility allows the individual to survive. The alternation of habit and unpatterned options allows old patterns to be tested and reshaped. Whether we're in the stage of Yellowstone without wolves—or a building under earthquake attack, or a sailor shifting his balance—or going back to original strengths, in some ways it's all one to the living brain. It's doing no more or less than what every living system does.

CHAPTER 3

Inborn Knowledge

IN THE EARLY 20TH CENTURY, science generally worked on the assumption that all neural cells were blank slates in both people and animals. Neural cells looked different from blood, skin or muscle cells, but they all seemed to resemble each other. So neurons in the brain and throughout the body were assumed to be all-purpose workers, trained to particular tasks through early learning. They were like electrical wires that could be shifted from wiring in light fixtures to wiring in outlets. However, around 1950, lab experiments began to show that this wasn't true. Neural cells could not be switched to another task and expected to learn it; they didn't.[23] It also turned out that animals couldn't learn just anything; there was a set range of possible learning.

Learning turns out to be a luxury accessory in nature. Simpler brains, like those of insects and fish, have no capacity or only a little capacity for learning. Nobody believes that Monarch butterflies or eels *learn* (from other individuals) where to migrate for breeding; these simple creatures appear to have it programmed that they'll fly or swim very long distances to central, traditional locations. We can't imagine how they know it, but inborn knowledge turns out to be the default state in nature. Learning, on the other hand, requires an unusually complex brain.

I want to start out by looking at this default state in the simplest animals. Although we cannot begin to do justice to the whole field of what insects know, we can begin to discern the basic question of what kind of inborn knowledge insects need to have in order to survive. There should be overlap with what higher animals and humans need, too. We can begin to see the purpose, scope, nature and even tone of inborn knowledge by starting at the bottom.

23: Michael Gazzaniga, *Who's In Charge?: Free Will and the Science of the Brain* (NY: HarperCollins, 2011), 11-17. Gazzaniga's personal history of being part of the shift away from "blank slate" doctrine is worth reading.

We don't know if all insects can communicate with each other. If really simple creatures like earthworms can communicate, we don't even know what that means. But let's start with a well-studied social insect that visibly and obviously can communicate: the ant.

Social insects like ants and bees communicate so much that they almost can't be considered individuals. Their own lives, point of view, and direct knowledge have no meaning except as communicated to the colony. Social insects depend on communication for their survival; their lives are better described not as the life of a bee or ant, but as the life of the colony. No bee or ant will remember tomorrow where it found food today, but that information, quickly passed along, sustains the colony's life. How do they learn information from each other if they don't "learn"?

Deborah Gordon, professor of entomology at Stanford University, has been studying colonies of red harvester ants in Arizona since 1981. Years of close observation led her to conclude that an individual ant begins its life deep inside the nest, where it carries out its first work assignments, and that the ant gradually ages into tasks closer to the surface and finally outside the nest. The same ant, working in and out of the nest, may switch tasks when the colony has a sudden need for more workers for a crisis or opportunity.

There's no evidence for learning among the ants; experiments proved them to be very set in their ways, like robots. And yet most ants go through a cycle of tasks over the space of a full year. Most of these tasks require picking up and carrying things, but the ant has to know what to carry where: stray dirt out of tunnel doorways, seeds back to the nest, seed husks out of the nest to a trash pile, food to the queen, and so on. Not only that, but during the course of a day, one ant may switch tasks, suddenly turning aside to join in digging out a tunnel or carrying newly-found seeds. It was hard, at first, to see how the ants knew when to join other work groups. Ants have only the most primitive vision and hearing.

The key was a discovery that ant communication takes place through chemicals that they perceive with their antennae. The ants recognize familiar and unfamiliar chemicals from plants, insects and locations nearby. Their detection of chemicals goes beyond simple avoidance or attraction: the *same* chemical can prompt them to do *different* things when it appears in different contexts.

After many years of painstaking study, Dr. Gordon learned that harvester ants have an outer coating that changes its composition ("smell") by age and by contact with the outside air. Ants know by touching antennae whether they are meeting a young or an old ant, an outdoor or an indoor worker. There appears to be a counting machine built into the ant's brain, so that it keeps track of how often it meets types of ants. If a young ant is working deep in the nest and begins to meet more older ants that have recently been in contact with air, the ant is drawn to go into higher tunnels and join the older ants. By this means, indoor workers start working outside part of the time; eventually after a year, they are mostly outdoor workers. That's ant communication: the literal concrete passing of chemical signals from antenna to antenna.[24]

The same system works to warn ants of danger: counting a higher number of ants who are exuding a certain chemical triggers an alarm to make some ants swarm to fight, while

24: Deborah Gordon, *Ant Encounters: Interaction Networks and Colony Behaviors* (Princeton, NJ: Princeton University Press, 2010), 49.

others work to move eggs. The way they react is conditioned by how much they have been exposed to air. Ants who have the chemical changes associated with the outdoors experience a different reaction to the same chemical. Survival and communication can't be separated in ants, because no single ant "knows" anything in particular. The nest survives by a sort of corporate chemical database.

We still don't know how ants interpret the chemical reactions. The chemicals involved can be defined, but why does this reaction make the ant speed up its walking or drop what it's carrying? There must be a sort of template for chemical reactions built into the ant's simple neural net. While its outer coating keeps changing, the template is already prepared to interpret new signals. The ant's "brain" is nothing but this template for translating chemical signals to behavior responses.

TEMPLATES OF COMMUNICATION

Because humans are so conscious of learning, it's hard for us to imagine how a template might exist without learning. One of the groundbreaking studies in the limits of learning— and of inborn knowledge—came in 1964. Peter Marler and Miwako Tamura, zoologists at the University of California at Berkeley, published a short paper in the journal Science that outlined the limits of learning in bird song transmission.

Their paper came at a time when biologists were just beginning to believe that animal brain cells were not all "blank slates," but official doctrine still emphasized that all knowledge came through learning, especially rewarded learning. That's what this team set out to study. Marler and Tamura chose a common bird in the Berkeley area, the white-crowned sparrow. Using audio recordings of sparrow populations in Berkeley and to the south and north, they captured young sparrows at different ages and tried to train or retrain—or even derail—their singing ability.[25]

Sparrows are hatched in the early spring and spend up to 100 days listening to adult male sparrows singing. All of the white-crowned male sparrows within a few miles' radius sing the same song, but sparrows 20 or 30 miles away sing the song a little bit differently. Marler and Tamura referred to these different songs as dialects: all recognizable as white-crowned sparrows, but each region distinctly different in intonation. Within the three months that fledgling sparrows are sitting in the nest listening, they must learn the regional pattern, because later in the summer, all of the birds stop singing.

When they start again, the following late winter, the young sparrows are now adults, and as they start to sing for the first time, they join in the regional song dialect. Of course, they haven't heard it for a number of months, and there's no evidence that they could practice it as fledglings. This presents a good opportunity to experiment and find out whether the young birds can learn other songs.

Experiments soon showed that after the 100-day singing season is over, the young sparrows can't be retrained in the laboratory. If they are caught as fledglings (just out of the

25: Peter Marler and Miwako Tamura, "Culturally Transmitted Patterns of Vocal Behavior in Sparrows," *Science*, New Series, Vol. 147, No. 3650 (December 11, 1964), 1484.

nest) and kept till adulthood in a room where a different dialect-song is played every day, come spring they will still sing the song they heard in the nest. Then the Berkeley team raised some newly-hatched sparrows in isolation, hearing no songs at all. At the right young adult age, the birds still began to sing, but their song did not have any regional pattern. It was a very generic, simple white-crowned sparrow song. This suggested that the birds were somehow born knowing the basic pattern.

Further tests showed that birds in the same window of time, about 30 to 100 days old, could be taught either the song dialect they had been born to or a different one. But when they were exposed only to some other species of sparrow's singing, they acted like the birds who had been raised in silence. They still sang the white-crowned sparrow song, but in the simple, generic, innate way.

The young birds were clearly very impressionable in the early window of time. Even if their father had sung a dialect for three weeks before the nestlings were captured, they could be taught a different dialect song. But they could not be taught a song that didn't belong to white-crowned sparrows, nor could they be taught not to sing. Sing they must, and it could only be a white-crowned sparrow variation.

Marler and Tamura were further puzzled because until then, biologists believed that baby animals only learned behavior patterns through social relationships that gave them rewards for learning. But when fledging sparrows were raised in isolation, hearing impersonal recordings, they still learned. No reward was needed.

It turned out that the only way to stop a white-crowned sparrow from singing his native song was to damage his hearing during the period when the bird himself was starting to sing. Each bird needs to hear his own voice and match it to his memory. If a bird became deaf later in life, he could still sing by rote; but if he lost his hearing before he had learned to make the song himself, he could not form pure whistles, but instead vented his instinct for song on broken patterns and random noises.[26]

The knowledge of white-crowned sparrow song was clearly embedded in each bird's brain, without any need for learning; it existed almost like an mp3 file. Learning only tuned the bird to his regional dialect, which must have made communication among his flock easier. But learning was only possible if he was listening to a variation on the pattern that came with his brain. He was born knowing how to communicate with his own kind; learning made him better at it but could not teach him something else.

That's an important principle. When we talk about inborn knowledge in a higher animal or human being, we may be looking at some behavior that includes learning. To talk about inborn knowledge, we don't have to rule out learning. But the inborn template restricts and channels potential for learning, as with the white-crowned sparrows. If no learning was added, the template was sufficient on its own to produce the right song. On the other hand, the template could not be overcome. It allowed songs that were in the right pattern to stick but interpreted other bird songs as unlearnable noise.

Of course, we can also apply some of these lessons to human communication. In the early 1960s, around the same time that the Berkeley scientists were learning that sparrows

---

26: Peter Marler and Miwako Tamura, "Culturally Transmitted Patterns of Vocal Behavior in Sparrows," *Science*, New Series, Vol. 147, No. 3650 (December 11, 1964), 1485.

have a built-in sense of sparrow song, linguistics professor Noam Chomsky challenged blank-slate orthodoxy by suggesting that human infants are born with universal, generic grammar already programmed. By 1980, he had developed a full theory known as Generative Grammar: babies' brains have a structure for words and adapt this structure to the languages they are actually exposed to. Most people today accept some version of this idea.

At first, it may sound like "inborn language" suggests that babies are born with the ability to learn particular languages, as white-crowned sparrows can only learn their own species' songs. Of course that isn't so. The real point is that all human languages, however different they seem to us, are no different at the brain level than the white-crowned sparrow dialects were. We need words to name things, actions, time, people, and relationships between things (over, under, etc.). We need questions, demands, and ways to negate. All human languages use these things. These are the template concepts we're born with, not language but the possibility for it.

The sparrow experiment raises an interesting speculation. Are there languages that human minds can't learn? Sparrows can only learn a certain range of sparrow songs, so perhaps *human* minds can only learn *human* languages. We already know that any human baby can learn any human language that it's exposed to during early years—comparable to the 100 days that sparrow chicks are in the nest. And we know that deaf signing works the same way that spoken language does. So what's excluded: whale songs, bee dancing, radio frequencies, and bar codes?

Chomsky's recent research directions are toward defining exactly what it is that babies inherit. What's the human equivalent of the basic sparrow song? This turns out to be one of the most difficult questions to answer. We define language in terms of grammar, but grammar varies so much in world languages that this doesn't work beyond a basic level. At this time, we really can't define the internal structure that babies are born with.[27]

TEMPLATES OF SAFETY AND DANGER

Jung's idea of inborn templates went far beyond language. As we'll discuss in later chapters, he believed that moral and aesthetic ideas could be inborn. Myths and legends suggest that our ideas of danger are usually linked with ugliness, safety with beauty. Babies' early, simple responses to the world show them mirroring back the beauty and ugliness that they perceive, such as smiling back at smiling faces. Not only do they have template notions of what the world should be like, they have inborn behaviors to help link them into the system, seeking beauty and safety and avoiding ugliness and danger. Moral and aesthetic templates may have a very real place in safety instincts.

We don't have any evidence that animals have moral or aesthetic ideas at all, but if we generalize a step further we can find a bridge to animal studies. Animals do seem to be born knowing what danger looks like; they have instinctive fears of situations, appearances, and faces. Studies of human infants show that pre-verbal babies also have ideas about safety and danger.

27: Noam Chomsky, *On Nature and Language* (New York, Cambridge University Press: 2002), 93-97.

So what inborn knowledge do higher animals have about danger? One research method is to find animal populations whose environments have changed in the last century or even millennium—if not longer. In these animals, it is certain that their ancestors used to cope with certain challenges, but the current population can't possibly have faced these challenges for many, many generations. If these living animals seem to "remember" the past conditions and know how to cope with those challenges, the knowledge of danger must be inborn. It isn't possible that any of the parents or grandparents of the living animals could have taught them, if none of them have been exposed to these things for a hundred or more generations.

Researchers can find animals like this on islands, where they have been isolated from the mainland for a long time. We can also identify some places where other animals (like predators) appear in the fossil record but have been extinct for a very long time. In other places, humans have recently accidentally changed the environment by importing European animals. In this last case, the newcomer is in a new environment, but the native animals also face a new challenge caused by the intruder's presence.

There are two important studies of island animals which suggest that these living animals had inherited inborn knowledge about predators that were not at all relevant to their own lives. Not all islands are isolated enough to conduct such studies, but both Kangaroo Island, off Australia, and the Galapagos Islands off South America clearly have isolated animal populations.

Kangaroo Island once had predator animals, but they became extinct and appear only in fossils. In the Galapagos chain, it's even more interesting, because the islands are somewhat isolated from each other. A few of them have unique traits: Pinta Island has no snakes, while tiny Wenman Island has no predators at all. Other islands have either owls or snakes, finch predators who are common to the South American mainland.

So on Kangaroo Island, researchers can test to see whether the native wallabies know that some animals are predators, while in the Galapagos chain, they can test finches for fear of owls and snakes. In both cases, they can be sure of one thing: that the wallaby or finch they are testing has never actually seen the predator, nor did its ancestors for many generations back, possibly for thousands of years.

Nobody knows how long finches have been living on the Galapagos Islands, but the original finch population must have migrated from the mainland. On the South American mainland, finches needed to dodge both snakes and raptor birds, such as owls and hawks. Researchers, led by Dr. Richard Coss (University of California-Davis), took test birds from Pinta and Wenman Islands, as well as from other sample islands. They exposed them to models of owls and snakes.

As expected, the finches who lived with owls and snakes instantly showed fear. Finches from Pinta Island, who had never seen snakes, were not as immediately fearful. But finches from Wenman Island were afraid of owls, a bird they had never seen. Researchers tried showing them parts of owls to determine which feature caused fear. Finches who had encountered real owls were afraid of any portion of an owl, but the Wenman Island finches didn't recognize the model as fearful if its eyes were missing. An owl's whole head was scary, and an owl's eyes were scary; but not an owl's body or head minus the eyes.[28] It seems that

28: R. G. Coss, "Effects of relaxed natural selection on the evolution of behavior," in S. A. Foster and J. A.

the birds had inherited some kind of template for owl eyes, and this persisted even when they had long forgotten to fear owl ears, talons or wings. (Even in human art, owls are known by their distinctive eyes. A graphic artist can suggest an owl with the same minimal features that the finches remembered.)

Kangaroo Island has an inbred population of wallabies that have been isolated from the mainland, and from predators, since the Ice Age. As Kangaroo Island, once a peninsula, was separated from the mainland by rising ocean levels, the wallabies were trapped and slowly became their own breed, now called tammar wallabies. Humans then crossed the water to live on Kangaroo Island, but they were never crazy or careless enough to give any large predators a lift on their boats. In modern times, Australian immigrants have carried domestic cats over to Kangaroo Island, but so far, the cats have not turned into feral populations; they are still house pets, and are now strictly regulated. House cats are the only predator animals on the island.

Ten thousand years seems plenty of time for tammar wallabies to forget that other animals could ever present danger. In 1999, a team from Macquarie University, in Sydney (Australia), tried to find out whether tammar wallabies still had any ancestral memory of the sights or sounds of mainland predators. They carefully exposed a small group of wallabies to recorded cries of Australian predators and, separately, to visual sightings of predator animals.[29]

The wallabies didn't seem to react to the recorded sounds; they were no more or less startled by eagle cries than by magpies. But they did show fear when shown taxidermy models of predators. The researchers put models of cats (probably unknown to the wild test wallabies, since cats must be kept indoors), red foxes (which never set foot on the island), another wallaby, and an extinct predator shown in Australia's fossil record, the thylacine wolf (or tiger). The extinct animal couldn't be a real taxidermy model, so it was molded by an artist.

Seeing cats and red foxes made the wallabies stop eating, look around, and foot-thump alarms to other wallabies in the area. They didn't specially react to the thylacine model, but that may have been because it had no animal smell and didn't seem truly real. However, they were clearly troubled by taxidermy cats and foxes.[30] Something about the eyes and bodies of predators still connected with a dim visual template in the wallaby brain.

What if humans are born with some instinctual knowledge of danger signs? There is some evidence that snakes, for example, are instinctively feared. We react to images of snakes at an unconscious level: quickly, with autonomic fear response.[31] Are babies born with this instinctive knowledge, or do humans learn the fear as they acquire memories?

Since babies cannot talk, we can only guess at what they know. But when they grow into stages where they can show and tell us, some months and years have passed and learning has

Endler (Eds.), *Geographic variation in behavior: Perspectives on evolutionary mechanisms* (New York: Oxford University Press, 1999), 182.

29: D. T. Blumstein, J. C. Daniel, A. S. Griffin, C. S. Evans, "Insular Tammar Wallabies (Macropus eugenii) Respond to Visual but not Acoustic Cues from Predators," *Behavioral Ecology* (2000) 11 (5): 528-535.

30: D. T. Blumstein, J. C. Daniel, A. S. Griffin, C. S. Evans, "Insular Tammar Wallabies (Macropus eugenii) Respond to Visual but not Acoustic Cues from Predators," *Behavioral Ecology* (2000) 11 (5): 532.

31: Arne Öhnen, "Of Snakes and Faces: An Evolutionary Perspective on the Psychology of Fear." *Scandinavian Journal of Psychology*. December 2009. Vol 50, issue 6, pp 543-552.

taken place. By then, we can no longer be sure that their knowledge was inborn; it's much more likely that other people or bad experiences have caused their fears. This is the inherent difficulty in tests of infant knowledge.

Experiments with babies often rest on watching their faces and eyes. Sometimes the baby's face changes, but other times they can track eye movement enough to show that the baby consistently stares at some things longer than at others. When an experiment is carefully designed, we may be able to detect infant reactions that could not have been learned.

For example, in one study, babies were shown movies and still photographs of snakes while the researchers played tapes of adults talking. In some audio segments, the adults sounded happy and relaxed, in others frightened and tense. Most babies who are six months or a year old have not encountered real snakes, and if they have, the snakes were certainly harmless or were presented without any scare factor (behind glass in a zoo). The youngest babies in the test didn't seem to react much to the snake images. But when babies between 7 and 18 months old heard a tape of an adult's voice sounding scared, they paid more attention to the snake films than they did when the recording was of an adult sounding happy and unafraid.[32]

The babies didn't know why the adults sounded tense, but they had a sense that the snake in the movie might have something to do with it. They didn't pay as much attention to the snake photos when the adults sounded confident. Did the babies have an innate sense that fear and snakes have something to do with each other? If so, that would have to be from an inborn template.

Other studies have shown that both snakes and spiders are more easily learned as objects of fear than other things. In a 2009 study, they taught 11 month old babies to look at pictures of objects (spiders, snakes, flowers and mushrooms) paired with happy faces or scary faces. Sometimes the flower or mushroom was next to a happy face, and sometimes it was next to a scary face. The spiders and snakes, similarly, could show up with happy or scary faces. They followed the infants' eyes to see how long they studied pairs of pictures, on the assumption that when a baby sees what it expects, it looks away sooner than if it sees something strange or mystifying.

All of the babies generally expected the flower with the happy face and acted surprised if it came with a scary face. But in this study, baby girls in particular quickly picked up on the pairing of snakes or spiders with scary faces and began to expect that pair. They were clearly surprised when they were shown snakes or spiders next to *happy* faces. Baby boys didn't show as much surprise; it took them longer to learn that the snakes and spiders typically came with frownies.[33]

There is one part of this study that is very suggestive for snake and spider knowledge being inborn: the fact that the infant girls seemed to learn the fear association faster than boys did. Girls did not just learn to pay attention to faces better than boys. Their learning was no better than the boys' learning when the pictures were neutral. It wouldn't be surprising if some individual babies more quickly learned what to expect; perhaps they were just more

32: J. S. Deloache and V. Lobue, "The Narrow Fellow in the Grass: Human Infants Associate Snakes and Fear." *Developmental Science*, 2009 Jan; 12 (1): 201-7.

33: David H. Rakison, "Does Women's Greater Fear of Snakes and Spiders Originate in Infancy?" *Evolution of Human Behavior* 2009 November 12; 30 (6): 439-444.

easily frightened or quicker to learn. But instead, one group of infant brains all responded the same way: when a spider or snake was in play, the girls appeared surprised that anyone could pair these scary creatures with a happy face. Even if they had never seen snakes or spiders before, the association of dangerous animals and scary faces apparently made sense.

It's possible that their parents had already shown them simple books about animals, but most baby books leave out snakes and spiders. We can't really form a theory about why girls learned the fear association faster, but we know that especially in infancy, male and female brains are not identical. There may be a stronger danger template for scary (long, thin, leggy, slithery) animals in girls' brains.

There's at least one more animal study that can help flesh out our picture of these "what the world is supposed to look like" templates. In this case, birds were able to remember across many generations how to deal with the behavior of other birds. There was no fear factor, but the behavior was indeed a danger.

In the 18th century, village weaver birds were accidentally carried by slave traders from Africa to Hispaniola (the island shared by Haiti and Dominican Republic). Back in their homeland, village weaver birds faced the challenge of African cuckoos who laid cuckoo eggs in village weaver nests. If the village weavers sat on their own eggs and the cuckoo's egg, they might hatch and begin feeding both kinds of chicks. Both cuckoos and cowbirds use a strategy like this; their own chicks are often larger and eat more than the chicks who really belong to the nest. As the smaller parent birds try to keep up with feeding their infants and the baby intruder, their own infants may get weaker and die. So to protect their own young, African village weavers long ago developed the instinct to scan their eggs every day, looking for eggs that look different. When they spotted intruders, they pushed the eggs out of the nest onto the ground.

When African weaver birds were carried into the New World, they found themselves on an island with no nest intruders. Hispaniola had no cuckoos or cowbirds. For about two centuries, they didn't have to check their nests for intrusive eggs. But then humans changed the environment again: within the last 40 years, cowbirds were accidentally brought to Hispaniola from the South American mainland. The intruder cowbirds immediately began laying their eggs in African village weaver nests, just as African cuckoos had done. Researchers noticed the situation and wondered whether the weaver birds would still know what to do. If they still had the instinct to knock eggs out, then it would seem that they were still using ancestral, inherited knowledge, not fresh learning.[34]

As it happened, the village weavers still remembered. They weren't as good at the task as their African relatives, who had never seen a generation go by without cuckoo intrusion. The Hispaniola weavers missed a few cowbird eggs in early years. In 1982, Alexander Cruz and James Wiley began placing intrusive eggs into the Hispaniola weaver nests so that they could study what the birds were noticing (or failing to notice): was it different size, color, spots, or something else?

It seemed that the birds had a basic instinct to inspect eggs frequently, perhaps practiced fruitlessly and carelessly for 200 years. Once they had a little experience with actually finding

---

34: A. Cruz, J. W. Prather, J. W. Wiley, and P. F. Weaver, "Egg Rejection Behavior in a Population Exposed to Parasitism: Village Weavers on Hispaniola." *Behavioral Ecology* (2008) 19 (2): 398-403.

intrusive eggs, they grew skilled at noticing any and all differences. The inborn, inherited knowledge was the sense that *eggs in one's nest could not be taken for granted.* They did not know what intrusive eggs looked like; but in Jung's phrase, they had the "possibility of an idea" that eggs must be inspected and compared. Learning had to happen, but it came only by building on this existing potential.

TEMPLATES FOR HUMAN DANGER

If humans are born with any sort of template that tells them what to expect in the world, it must have some suggestions about human relationships. Unlike any animal species, we are our own greatest predators. Part of the story of civilization has been how people have found ways to create predator-free environments and cheat fatal diseases, but they have never found a way to really protect us from each other. Human personalities can have as much variation among them as among different animal species—but without visible markers like long, slithery shape or owl eyes.

If there's one life-saving skill for a baby to have, it's not running from wolves or even avoiding spiders, it's placating or avoiding an angry person. Babies know far more about human behavior than they do about physical threats, and for good reason: the most dangerous threat to a baby human is an adult human. The baby can't know if it's been born into a loving family or a crack house; it will take years for the baby to learn to understand his context. Its father may be gentle or he may be violent; its mother may be deeply attached, or she may need help learning to put the baby's needs first. Innate instinct about human behavior is the most important inborn knowledge a baby can have.

Carl Jung suggested that a baby is born with a template for "mother" and "father." There's not an actual idea, but there's a possibility of an idea. As the baby sees his own mother and father, he begins to fill in the idea with details. But the idea never becomes completely particular: he always has a sense of "mother" and "father" as ideals, and as he grows up, he can compare his own parents to the ideal.[35]

The ideal is somewhat drawn from the actual parents, but it's also independent. If it were purely learned, a persistent ideal of "mother" seems unlikely, because for many other things such as food, clothing and weather, children take what they know as the only possible way. They are shocked or even disbelieving when they see a climate or manner of dress that they'd never imagined. However, if they see a mother who acts more maternal than their own mother, they seem to connect it with a known ideal. They know that this new vision is more correct than the image they've been living with.

A typical or normal baby is an active participant in shaping adults into "parents." The baby's unlearned, instinctive behavior, beginning less than a month after birth, creates a powerful tie with caretaking adults, and most especially with her mother. This begins a cycle of instinctive behavior and learning. As the child grows older, the template for human

---

35: Jung, "Concerning the Archetypes and the Anima Concept," *The Archetypes and the Collective Unconscious,* 137.

behavior may have many more possibilities than just mother and father. But at birth, this is what matters most.

We sometimes wonder why animals like horses can walk and run within an hour of birth, while human babies need more than a year to reach that point. Of course, the animals who can walk and run so quickly are born in the open, where the ability to run may be lifesaving within a very short time after birth. Human babies have the equivalent life-saving ability: they know how to smile within days and weeks of birth. For a human baby, that's as good as running from a predator.

When a first-time mother sees her baby's smile, her brain responds involuntarily with activation of dopamine reward circuits. These are the same circuits that are active in cocaine addiction; the drug produces a rush of dopamine, and the brain is built to need and want to have that reward repeated. With a baby, the reward circuit is doing its proper work, so the word "addiction" here is just the chemical side of love. The mother feels a solid, warm joy when her baby smiles, and she wants to feel it again by making her baby smile again. One study found that the baby's smile is much more effective in eliciting a brain response than the baby's crying. All maternal brains reacted with distress to a photo of a crying baby, but although the researchers expected the mother's brain to distinguish her own baby from a stranger, they didn't see any difference with a crying face. The difference came only with smiles. Any baby's smile is nice, but a mother's own baby's smile is the one that hits her with dopamine rewards.[36]

The mother's system is also flooded with oxytocin, the bonding chemical, when she interacts with her baby. Oxytocin and dopamine together form a very strong, addictive attachment to this baby out of all other babies in the world. Oxytocin may also be the signature chemical of the "mother" ideal. All people have some amount of oxytocin, but its influence on behavior is characterized by the way it influences mothers to put their babies first, even at great cost.

The bond of the new baby and mother may be conditioned by the mother's own experience as a baby. If she had a happy infant experience herself, she may have a stronger sense of the archetype of a mother, and that sense may be more deeply integrated. One study looked at the distressing effect of a baby's crying to see how well mothers could handle the negativity.

When her baby cries, the mother's brain response shows activation in the anterior insula; this signals to neuroscientists that she may be feeling some seriously negative emotions like disgust and unfairness. She may not consciously call what she feels "unfair" or "disgusting." But a persistent baby's cry can be a skin-crawling experience for a mother. When the baby has a problem that causes frequent, long crying, the mother may be pushed into serious negativity by the anterior insula. She may find herself looking frantically through the telephone book, wondering which stranger to call to "come take this baby away." (That's the story a new mother told me once. It was funny after the fact, not funny at all during the panic attack.)

The mother needs to feel emotional rewards strongly enough that they carry her through

---

36: Lane Strathearn, Li Jian, Peter Fonagy, and P. Read Montague. "What's In a Smile? Maternal Brain Response to Infant Facial Cues," *Pediatrics* 2008; 122, 48.

these distressing times. When that's true, she can remain in a positive frame of mind toward her baby. The study that took into account how positive the mother's own infancy had been discovered that there was a startlingly real correlation. Mothers with secure attachments to their own mothers experience a larger boost of oxytocin than mothers who (through no fault of their own) had insecure maternal attachments. Baby girls raised by secure mothers become secure mothers: their brains don't register as much negativity, and they get more dopamine out of the baby's smile.[37]

Science can't prove or disprove the idea of an inborn ideal of "motherhood," of course. We only know the bare facts of the study. But we can say that the facts cooperate with the concept of an inborn ideal. The fact that the brain's chemistry correlates during infancy and motherhood, in spite of the time gap between, suggests that something quite real is happening at the physiological level. Learning is reinforcing instinct, altering the brain.

A baby girl raised by a mother who comes close to matching the "archetype" of a mother has less inner conflict about what it means to be a mother. Her brain knows at a deep level—both inborn and learned—what it means. When she is an adult and becomes a mother, the role feels organic and not voluntary or assumed. There's not much struggle between her personal identity and the archetypal role.

Babies appear to have inborn templates for understanding human danger, too. We can clearly see a steady progression in their understanding of face reading though early childhood. However, certain instinctive responses show up so early in life that they really could not be learned.

For the first six months of life, the baby looks at his mother's face a lot, and he studies other faces. Mostly he looks at the eyes, with wandering gaze to take in mouth, nose and other parts of the face. He sees smiling faces more than anything else, usually. By four months, researchers have found that babies avoid looking at angry faces. They look at the eyes, as usual, but then they avert their gaze.[38] [39] It seems likely that infants have an instinctive sense that staring at an angry face is uncomfortable and a bad idea.

A baby can't know this, but it's true that angry adults, especially men, often get angrier when someone stares back at them. They feel challenged and even insulted. Nobody who knows about babies would dream that a baby is actually challenging an angry man, but angry men often know very little about babies. Some really do imagine that a baby could be insulting them. It's very good for the baby to have this avoidant instinct about anger.

Then, in her second half year, the baby's visual patterns change. Already at this young age, she begins to scan faces with the same eye movement patterns that adults use. Instead of

37: Lane Strathearn, Peter Fonagy, Janet Amico, and P. Read Montague, "Adult Attachment Predicts Maternal Brain and Oxytocin Response to Infant Cues," *Neuropsychopharmacology*. 2009 December, 34(13), 2666.

38: Mikko J. Peltola, Jukka M. Leppänen, Silja Mäki, and Jari K.Hietanen, "Emergence of Enhanced Attention to Fearful Faces Between 5 and 7 Months of Age." *Scandinavian Journal of Psychology* (2009) 4,134–142.

39: Sabine Hunnius, Tessa C. J. de Wit , Sven Vrins and Claes von Hofsten, "Facing threat: Infants' and adults' visual scanning of faces with neutral, happy, sad, angry, and fearful emotional expressions." *Cognition & Emotion*, 2011, 25:2, 193–205.

looking mainly at a face's eyes, the baby also glances at the mouth and nose, and back to eyes. For the rest of her life, that will be her pattern of taking information about faces.[40]

A baby in the second half-year also begins to notice a new face pattern that he didn't see at younger ages. Instead of knowing only happy and angry faces, the baby starts to notice and study faces that convey fear. His gaze lingers over these faces a little bit longer.[41] [42]In fact, further research shows that the baby is definitely noticing far more than fear-filled, dilated pupils in eyes. He is paying attention to the entire face, searching for unifying clues.[43]

Most babies this age have not been in true danger. For them, fear means being alone. But there seems to be an inner instinctive knowledge that it's critically important to recognize when adults are afraid. The baby's brain pays attention, storing up memories. He may only understand the reasons for fear much later, but by then, recognizing fearful faces will be instant and automatic. His memory has stored up thousands of face images even before his first birthday.

These facts may suggest that the baby's brain comes with strong templates for trouble, rather than peace and happiness. Although the baby has an instinct to smile, his other possible ideas are pessimistic. Babies come into the world crying, after all. They begin to notice anger and fear long before they have felt these emotions in any real way.

If the strongest template is for the possibility of danger and fear, then it would be in a sense the default setting. Unmodified, it would mature into general caution, fear and mistrust. The effect of secure comfort from the infant's mother may be to help *turn off* the trouble sensors, allowing the baby to feel that the world might be okay some of the time. During later years, as a toddler, the baby begins to learn the difference between a secure environment in which he can stop searching for trouble, and an insecure one that reverts to the trouble-searching patterns.

An inborn trouble template could be part of the problems we see when attachment isn't secure. Perhaps children who are not securely attached to their mothers are closer to a state of nature and make more use of their inner templates for anger and danger. Their worlds really are more dangerous, maybe not even because they've experienced danger. Their worlds are more dangerous because they haven't experienced enough peace.

A study of securely and insecurely attached babies retested the same babies when they were six years old. The children were shown an array of simplified drawings of faces: a smiley face, a frowny face, a mean face, a sad face, and so on. They were asked to name the emotion shown. Children who were insecure babies were not as good at identifying complex feelings. They tended to guess too readily that the faces were negative; the cartoon face for

40: Mikko J. Peltola, Jukka M. Leppänen, Vanessa K. Vogel-Farley, Jari K. Hietanen, and Charles A. Nelson, "Fearful Faces But Not Fearful Eyes Alone Delay Attention Disengagement in 7-Month-Old Infants." *Emotion.* 2009 August ; 9(4): 560–565.

41: Mikko J. Peltola, Jukka M. Leppänen, Silja Mäki, and Jari K.Hietanen, "Emergence of Enhanced Attention to Fearful Faces Between 5 and 7 Months of Age." *Scandinavian Journal of Psychology* (2009) 4, 138.

42: Jukka M. Leppänen, Margaret C. Moulson, Vanessa K. Vogel-Farley, and Charles A. Nelson, "An ERP Study of Emotional Face Processing in the Adult and Infant Brain," *Child Development*, 2007 ; 78(1): 232–245.

43: Mikko J. Peltola, Jukka M. Leppänen, Vanessa K. Vogel-Farley, Jari K. Hietanen, and Charles A. Nelson, "Fearful Faces But Not Fearful Eyes Alone Delay Attention Disengagement in 7-Month-Old Infants." *Emotion.* 2009 August ; 9(4): 560–565.

surprise was not supposed to look angry, but these children perceived it as angry.[44] They couldn't understand or label a cartoon face that showed angry eyes and a happy mouth; by contrast, half of the securely attached children understood that it meant someone who wanted to do mischief. The insecurely attached children seemed to assume the worst, instead of understanding that many human situations contain some negative factors but are not actually dangerous.

By a year old, babies have figured out the most important things about the world, the foundation for the rest of their lives. Babies who did not receive a secure enough first year may struggle with unexplained negativity when they are children and adults. In the above-cited study of six year old children, a third study came five years later, when the same children were eleven. The insecure children had made great gains in understanding faces, by then. They could recognize the complex emotions as easily as secure children.[45]

We don't remain prisoners of our infant knowledge forever. But the studies of maternal brains and babies' faces showed that insecure attachments can reach far into the future and cause involuntary negativity. It's hard to believe that the children who guessed "anger" too readily didn't still carry that reflex, even if they had learned more about cartoon faces.

INBORN AND ARCHETYPAL KNOWLEDGE

Let's summarize what science can tell us about the "possibility of ideas" that human babies are born with. Although we still don't know much, we can sketch the basic nature of an inborn knowledge template.

We know that human babies are born with the innate ability to learn human language; further, they're born with a desire to learn and use language. It's not just that they can learn it, they start actively trying long before they're actually able to. The most powerful reward in learning is to get what you want, and most babies learn quickly that if they look at something and make certain sounds, the adults will guess correctly and put it into their hands.

To go with this, we know that babies have inner templates about faces and voices. It's part of communicating with their own kind, since most basic communication takes place visually, without words. They are born knowing that they must look at eyes and listen to voices. Like white-crowned sparrow chicks, they begin to store up memories of these patterns long before they can put them to significant use.

When a baby uses his inner template and he sees something that doesn't fit the right pattern, he's surprised. Things that fit are learned quickly; things that don't fit have to be repeated many more times before the baby will accept them. Snakes naturally fit with scary faces. It's possible to train babies not to have these natural fears, but it's uphill work. It's very likely that if researchers worked hard to teach babies to expect spiders/snakes and smiley faces,

44: Howard Steele, Miriam Steele, and Carla Croft. "Early Attachment Predicts Emotional Recognition at 6 and 11 Years Old." *Attachment & Human Development*, Vol. 10, No. 4, December 2008, 387.

45: Howard Steele, Miriam Steele, and Carla Croft. "Early Attachment Predicts Emotional Recognition at 6 and 11 Years Old." *Attachment & Human Development*, Vol. 10, No. 4, December 2008, 387.

it would take only one experience of associating the animal with fear for all that progress to be undone. The template resists learning whatever doesn't fit its possibilities.

Last, we know that the template of inborn knowledge tends to focus on danger and negatives. As unpleasant as this idea is, it makes sense for survival. Babies have all the time in the world to learn about goodness, truth and beauty. But if anger and danger come along, they may have only one chance to react in a way that placates it. Staring at an angry man's face in a "challenging" way could turn out to be the last look the baby ever takes. So the inborn template of possible ideas has a lot more information about fear and danger than about love and peace. Love can be learned; survival must be inborn.

When Carl Jung wrote about the "collective unconscious," he meant exactly this template of possible ideas. Each "possibility of an idea" was termed an archetype. When asked to list the archetypes, Jung grew uncomfortable. They were not, he insisted, actual ideas. Ideas are something we're conscious of; possibilities of ideas can only be observed in action. An individual whose ideas are restricted by those possibilities is truly not conscious of either the possibilities or the restrictions.[46] We just observe that individual by individual, people keep coming up with the same kinds of ideas.

Jung compared the archetypes to the way scientists grow crystals. Rubies, for example, can be grown artificially. They have no value as jewels when grown in a laboratory, but they can be used in industry, for example in lasers. The molecules are dissolved into a liquid, so that they are freely moving past each other. Gradually, they begin to connect and attach. Because of the way the molecules are structured, they will form into lattices; at high magnification, you can see that the molecules form the same shapes over and over. When the molecules have not yet formed into crystal lattices, the shape they will take is only possible, not actual. We know by experience and theory that each material will form its own type of lattice. We can encourage it to grow without defects by putting it in contact with the same lattice; it attaches and begins to build itself like Legos, sometimes rapidly and visibly.

This is how possible ideas work, wrote Jung. "The archetype itself is empty," but it is a form that will use our experiences to build a crystal. Continuing the analogy with growing crystals, he pointed out that the form only specifies what the lattice structure will look like.[47] The actual crystal might grow to be large or small; it might be perfect or defective; it might be pure or mixed with the molecules of another material.

Of course, a pure concept like this is not very useful to us without developing some content. It's important to understand that we don't mean a human infant is born already knowing about folklore and mythology. But when we want to know what possibilities they are born with, we can look at the typical repeating "lattices" of ideas. We see them in all cultures, and sometimes we can feel that they're ideas we know innately. Let's look at some of the obvious ones.

First, there is the idea of a mother. We've already suggested that babies have some innate potential idea of a mother, such that as they grow up, they can see sameness and difference between their particular, individual mother and the idea of a mother. We know that this ability to abstract the idea of "Mother" from a particular mother persists into adult life. It

---

46: Jung, "Psychological Aspects of the Mother Archetype," *The Archetypes and the Collective Unconscious*, 155.
47: Jung, "Psychological Aspects of the Mother Archetype," *The Archetypes and the Collective Unconscious*, 155.

allows us to compare the mothers we see to an ideal, so that as adults we try to imitate the ideal, sometimes deliberately avoiding the actual mother models we have observed. The idea of a mother also seeps into emotional, philosophical and religious ideas around the world. One of the most common mythological ideas is that the earth is a mother to all living things. Then we give the physical earth the emotional attributes of a mother.

Another obvious one is the pairing of opposites, primarily male and female. (Jung called this the "syzygy," which just means a pair of opposites.) Although individual men can come in many forms and types, around the world there is a general agreement on what's "manly" in behavior and appearance. We abstract the idea of "male" from men, and also the idea of "female" from women. As with the idea of mother, the abstract idea of a man or father can be transferred to other things. The sky as the "universal father" is one of the most common religious ideas. When the sky is envisioned as the father, the earth is always its opposite pair, the mother. The two ideas always go together. Male contrasts with female; they only have meaning when they're in this opposite pair. This is the essence of the "possible idea," the archetype of male and female. It's universal around the world, both as applied to human beings and also as transferred to other concepts.

The concept of God is another universal archetype. It can be blended with the archetype of father or mother, but it has its own meaning. The idea of God means a spirit existing outside of our time, with the ability to create and destroy. Even when folklore believes in many gods who aren't much different from humans, there seems always to be an older, perhaps more secret or ancient story of a supreme God who created even the gods. The archetype of God also includes some sense of the Creator spirit's judgment, whether for failing to give correct sacrifices or for being morally wrong.

The idea of a king is another "possible idea." Strong, tough-fighting leadership is a practical necessity, since we are our own worst predators. But people don't look at the local gangster and assume he's the best that a leader can be. As with mothers and fathers, there seems to be a pre-existing concept of what a king should be like. The king must be fair, and he must never act out of fear or hurt feelings. The king must be able to recognize what's good for the community or nation and reward it, even at times when it goes against his personal wishes.

There's another interesting detail: according to the archetype, a king is tall. It's in the Bible, where the Israelites' first king, Saul, was tall enough that his head was completely above the heads of other men in a crowd (I Samuel 10:24). Not long after, the prophet Samuel is sent to the family of Jesse to choose the next king, and he automatically prefers the tallest (I Samuel 16:7). While we could argue that in ancient times, a taller man had a real advantage in battle, we can't account for the persistence of this preference for height into our time, when the brain matters much more than stature. Successful presidential candidates in the United States are typically taller than unsuccessful ones. Even more significantly, any nominee for President is typically taller than average. Men who are tall tend to think of themselves as leadership material, and others perceive them that way.[48] Since we know very well that great inventions, books, musical compositions, art, and other achievements can be

---

48: Gregg R. Murray and David Schmitz, "Caveman Politics: Evolutionary Leadership Preferences and Physical Stature," *Social Science Quarterly* (2011) 92:5, 1215-1235.

made by men and women who are not tall, our continuing preference for height can't be conscious or logical. It appears, instead, to support an unconscious preference based on what a "king" looks like.

There are books that draw from folklore and mythology to name many other archetypal ideas about roles in human society. But I want to stop here, with just four archetypes of role or images. As Jung feared, it quickly starts to sound like we're suggesting that babies are born with the ideas completely in place. At the same time, there are non-image, non-role facets of inborn knowledge to explore. Archetypes aren't just about people or even God.

Philosophers have long suggested that people are born with innate understanding of moral and aesthetic ideas. In Plato's *Meno* dialogue, Socrates made this point so strongly that he included the suggestion of reincarnation (which would explain how the soul knew things, since it had lived already). Virtue isn't a fact or science that can be taught, he argued, and yet the soul appears to know what virtue means. In fact, the less concrete and more abstract the idea of "virtue," the more clearly we know it.

Plato suggested in many of the dialogues that our thought is based in some fundamental, innate concepts. We can compare things: larger or smaller, same or different, one or many, part or whole. Geometry, the mathematics of the Greeks, was constructed from these basic logical ideas. In the *Meno* dialogue, Socrates uses questions to lead an uneducated boy to "prove" a complex idea in geometry. At each point, the boy is answering only by using his innate sense of shape and relationship. Did he really "know" the geometry, as Socrates insists? Not really. But he did not need to be taught the elements of visual comparison and reasoning, and these were enough to follow each step of a geometry proof.

It would be fair to include these logical concepts among the archetypal seeds, ideas like a whole made up of parts, things that are similar or different, and even some basic shapes. We don't have them as full ideas at birth, but we have the crystal lattice of the idea. Learning about numbers, shapes and logic trains the archetypal possibility. But these archetypes aren't human roles, they are something completely different. Although in popular use, "archetype" refers only to a human role, we need to include basic abstract ideas among archetypes. They're universal and innate.

There's also a universal concept of what "beauty" means. It has something to do with proportion, something with color contrast. Our experiences with seeing daylight in all its shades also help build our idea of beauty; so do our experiences of observing nature in motion. What each person sees depends a lot on where and how he lives, but the concept of beauty is much the same everywhere. So here is another possibility of an idea: an archetype of beauty.

We have universal concepts of morality, such as goodness, truth and courage. People vary in how they think these concepts should be applied. Should you be merciful to everyone or only to the deserving? Or perhaps only to members of your own family? Are there cases when it's good not to tell the truth? But at the same time, we can all see the same moral tension in such questions; we all see that a concept can be universal, while its concrete embodiment maybe can't be. The most abstract version of each idea is the most universal, the most innate. It's easy to see the universal principle among the particular problems, and everyone in the world identifies the same principles.

So let's consider all of these concepts as possible archetypes, each an idea grown from a possibility that's inborn: social roles; divinity; morality; logic; beauty. Now remember the purpose of inborn knowledge: to keep you safe from danger. This poses a challenge: can we integrate these two ideas about the inborn template of knowledge?

FOLK STORIES REINFORCE ROLES AND MORALS

Although these two facets of the mind's template may sound logically unconnected, they are closely connected in human perception and behavior. We associate what's expected with what's safe. When people look the way they *should* look, we assume that everything will go the way it ought, without danger. This may be an incorrect assumption, but most people feel it to be profoundly true. Its converse also feels true: that when someone looks wrong, things might go wrong. Behavior or appearance that's out of place may signal that things are about to go off the rails. That's dangerous.

Social roles are a big part of conditioning our expectations. When people know their proper social roles and stay in them, we know what to expect. Someone who dresses properly is more likely to be cooperating with society's expectations. With proper social roles, we expect and watch for moral rules to be followed. When people signal that they are behaving according to the moral principles we know, we relax. Someone who tells the truth is less likely to do something dangerous. Someone who's kind to a child or animal is also less likely to be dangerous. We even feel that someone who's properly dressed is more likely to be good.

We don't usually think about it consciously. In fact, most people rarely stop to parse in words why they feel safer when people look, speak and act precisely as they're expected to. You're most likely to dig out the truth—that it makes them feel unsafe—when you see them respond to a non-dangerous but very eccentric, unusual person. People who look odd or do things that are out of place are perceived as extremely dangerous, even if there is no possibility of violence or other threat. Most people will avoid speaking to them and will move away physically.

As we look at the connection between social roles and safety, we can start to see why Jung may have been correct that mythology and legends were shaped by our inner templates. Folk stories reinforced connections between good behaviors and the roles people play in society. For every good king, there's a bad one who shows what dangerous behavior looks like. Every good mother is matched by a wicked stepmother, every good wizard with a bad one. We often see the importance of a social role by its loss: when the poor woodcutter died, his children were unprotected. Fathers, then, mean protection. Wicked stepmothers don't feed little children, which reinforces the idea that real mothers (ones who live up to the archetype) certainly do.

Modern children's books teach roles, too, though without the medieval elements of the folk tale. We want everyone to understand what is proper, expected behavior for mothers, fathers, teachers, students, doctors, policemen, and so on. Knowing what typical, patterned behavior looks and feels like helps us know when things are off the rails.

Beauty is also connected, though in an ambivalent way. Think about how innate ideas of beauty come through in folk stories: the good people are generally very beautiful, unless they are very ugly as a disguise for their goodness. Mythic archetypes usually associated ugly faces with evil intention and danger. In folk stories, elements of darkness, mismatching details, and dirt always mean danger. When we listen to the stories, the lesson is clear: it's safer to avoid ugliness, disorder and darkness than to rush naively into them. Remember how you felt, when you were a child, the first time you saw Oz's Wicked Witch, whose wickedness and ugliness can hardly be separated.

On the other hand, ugliness does not always mean wickedness, and many folk stories seem designed around this tension. We don't want children to think that everything ugly is bad. In fact, this simple mistake could be quite dangerous. Beauty can be a disguise for evil, whereas good people or places could be ugly. Folk stories addressed this question head on.

There is a typical folk story motif in which the hero or heroine is walking on a country road, sees a very old, unappealing, poverty-stricken person, and responds to a request for help. Often, several others have already passed by the ugly old crone or dervish, only to fall into great danger. The hero or heroine is the one who knows that it's wrong to refuse to help someone; when he or she follows the moral rule of kindness or mercy, in spite of the aesthetic instinct of disgust, it turns out to save the day. The ugly old crone or dervish passes on a magic item or secret knowledge. Without having cut the old dervish's hair, or without having split the last piece of bread with the old crone, the folk-story hero would have been turned to stone or killed by an ogre, just like the others.

The message seems to speak directly to our ambivalence about beauty. Our instinctual sense is that beautiful things and people are good. We want to find beauty and avoid darkness and ugliness. The folk story doesn't want to completely discourage this idea, but at the same time, it wants to point out a huge exception to the rule: Beauty is good, *except when it isn't*. Ugliness is dangerous and bad, *except when it isn't*, either. Sometimes you need to look past appearances. And how do you know you should look past appearances? By resolving your doubt through *moral*, not aesthetic, rules. The folk stories teach us to put our fears and concerns in proper order: a moral rule is more important than the aesthetic taste that loves beauty and fears ugliness.

As Jung suggested, these often-told stories really do provide instruction in the deepest forms of inborn knowledge. Our inborn "possible ideas" may conflict or be hard to interpret. The stories often tackle such conflicts head-on: it's right to obey your stepmother, but what if she commands you to do something suicidal? It's right to keep a promise, but what if the promise turns out to require you to be cruel? And which is more important, beauty or goodness?

INTROVERTED AND EXTROVERTED
PARTS OF THE MIND

Inborn knowledge, in Jung's theory, comes in four modes. We can have inborn, instinctive knowledge of logic and order; of relationships and love; of appearances and roles; of meaning and connections. (The following chapters will go through each of these modes in great detail.) Each personality has some of these modes as inborn, instinctive knowledge, and others as pragmatic, open, learning and exploring knowledge. The way they are balanced is what gives each personality its essential way of processing and responding to the world.

All inborn knowledge has a certain signature mood: it's very, very sure of itself. What we know based on an innate template doesn't feel "learned." It doesn't feel optional or open to question. It feels as true to each person as the white-crowned sparrow song feels to the sparrow. It's as unlearned as fear of owls or snakes to a finch who's never seen one. It doesn't even feel like it's part of our own minds. It feels like we're just perceiving an absolute truth about the outside world. It feels as certain as the law of gravity.

There's an area of the brain specialized for processing what we might call "sacred values." It is the junction between the temporal and parietal lobes, especially on the left. A very clever 2012 study at Emory University used fMRI imaging to capture the brain's switching from handling decisions in a pragmatic, cost-benefit analysis way to activating inborn sacred values in the left temporo-parietal junction (TPJ). Participants in the study negotiated a list of statements while they were in the fMRI scanner; at the end of the negotiation, they'd have to sign their name to the truth of the statements.[49]

Some of the statements were about preferences, such as "You are a dog person" or "You like Pepsi." When these statements weren't factually true, participants could negotiate how much money it would take to accept them as true. Questions about Pepsi and Coke, or dogs and cats, showed up as brain activation in the frontal lobe, where questions of utility and comparison are handled. Is it worth $10 to say you're a dog person when you really like cats? The question is evaluated just as we'd evaluate whether to buy the color of balloon we'd prefer or a less expensive one. It doesn't create any emotion.

However, when the statements had to do with purely ethical and belief matters, bargaining for cash activated no pragmatic activity. Instead, the left temporo-parietal junction was activated. Belief in God, killing, stealing and lying are all about sacred values. Even for just signing a statement, not for actually committing actions against their sacred values, bargaining for cash felt like an offense against the sacred. When we say "sacred values," we mean beliefs that feel like they have reality outside our minds. We all know that preference for dogs or cats is strictly our own personal feeling, but we believe that the wrongness of murder is larger than what's in our heads. That's how inborn knowledge feels; its certainty of right could come from closer or richer connections to the TPJ.

When negotiating over sacred values used the left TPJ, the fMRI also picked up activation in the amygdala. The amygdala is our warning system for threats. Its role is to flood the brain with fear and resistance to moving forward. Even though the Emory study was only asking people to sign their names to statements like "You believe it's okay to kill an innocent person," or "You would lie to your spouse," continuing pressure to sign (offering higher amounts of money) made the amygdala flare up. The person in the fMRI, refusing higher offers, felt indignation. To the amygdala, the idea was a real threat.

Inborn knowledge seems to be rich in connections to the TPJ and amygdala. It feels solid, real and sacred, not mere preference. We can't evaluate inborn knowledge as if it's a

49: Gregory S. Berns, E. Bell, C. M. Capra, MJ Prietula, S. Moore, B. Anderson, J. Ginges, S. Atran, "The Price of Your Soul: Neural Evidence for the Non-utilitarian Representation of Sacred Values," *Philosophical Transactions of The Royal Society* B, 5 March 2012, 367: 1589, 754-762.

cost-benefit trade-off. Instead, something higher is at stake: something that exists regardless of cost, something that may exist outside of the mind itself.

Inborn knowledge tends to resist change very deeply. Although it feels like we're just seeing a truth about the world, the fact is that an inborn function nearly refuses to learn contradictory information. It isn't really gathering facts about the world. It feels that it already knows, and it is attracted only to facts that match. It isn't interested in checking out facts that clash. This tendency is so strong that it can lead to complete denial of validity to whatever might prove it wrong.

Inborn knowledge also tends to be somewhat negative. We've already seen that its purpose is to help us comprehend our world as quickly as possible, but mainly in terms of its dangers. An innate sense of morality carries a strong taboo against breaking moral rules. We may compare it to the weaver birds who continued to check their eggs for 200 years without any real need; they didn't know what danger they were avoiding, but the feeling of urgency must have never quite left. Without knowing exactly what sort of predator is going to swoop, we feel that something disastrous is looming if we don't cooperate with the inborn template. It's probably the same amygdala activation that the Emory study observed.

Inborn knowledge is idealistic. It is formed by an abstract lattice; it's as pure as Plato's best ideas. It believes in true love, perfect circles, the Golden Mean, pure beauty and all that is best. It's not based on the messy world outside us, which certainly is not filled with those things. A child in the dirtiest, poorest slum could still have an innate sense of beauty, having only glimpsed it here and there. An abused child may somehow, against all odds, still believe in true love. People in a dictatorship may still dream of freedom and good government. Idealistic images of love, beauty, truth and rightness are dead set against compromise with reality.

So that is the nature of the innate, archetypal knowledge we're born with: idealistic, stubborn, absolutely confident, and a bit negative. What about the other side of the mind? I've spent a great deal of time building up a profile of the inborn parts of the mind, and so far none at all on anything else. This is not because it's unimportant, but because it's easier to see and understand.

There is a huge part of the mind that isn't based on an inborn template, and we use it most in our everyday lives. What we learn from the outside world is definitely based on what we see and experience. A part of the mind that can learn this way isn't idealistic. It takes things at face value and doesn't expect anything to be better than it is. At the same time, it isn't negative or danger-oriented the way inborn knowledge is. It's just pragmatic, generally cheerful, and ready to be flexible. It can be even relentlessly optimistic.

What we learn from the outside world feels like a set of tools that we can use. When there's a tool missing, this part of the mind immediately begins exploring to find it. It has learned by experience that if you keep looking, you'll find what you need. And you can probably use something else you already have. If there's a will, there's a way, and we just need a little time. Everything will be fine, and we'll figure it all out.

Since "extroverted" means "turned to the outside," it simply refers to this part of the mind. **An Extroverted mental function is pragmatic, flexible, positive, exploring and expansive**. It's willing to take whatever it finds and make use of it. It's not put off by dirt or disorder; it doesn't sink into negativity on finding out that nothing is ideal. By this definition, "extroverted" does not mean anything about how much we like people. There are times when an extroverted part of the mind can feel very positive and pragmatic about people, but that's only one part of the range of meaning. It can also mean learning about machines, numbers, or how to do things. If it's friendly and sociable, that's actually secondary to being pragmatic and flexible.

"Introverted" means "turned to the inside," so **Introverted refers to the part of the mind that is focused on the inborn template**. Of course, the mind has to take outside information into account. But an introverted part of the mind is a bit stubborn and resentful about new information that doesn't fit the template. It may refuse to believe. It will always refuse to modify the template, in any case. If part of your introverted mind "knows" what true beauty or love is, it will refuse to write an exception clause saying that bad behavior and dirt are also okay.

While an Extroverted mental function would take an anomaly in stride, the Introverted function puts the disturbing fact in quarantine. It thinks something like this: "while it may be, unfortunately, true that *right now* we live in ugliness or have bad friends, those facts can't be allowed to dim the light of the ideal. It is possible—it must be possible!—for things to be different. We may have to live with badness for a while, but we must use every ounce of strength trying to force the world to become like the ideal. If we have control over nothing else, at least our own behavior: if nobody else exhibits true love, beauty or goodness, at least we can do it ourselves. We'll take back a bit of territory for beauty, love and truth."

So the Introverted part of the mind becomes the root of conscience. As we'll see in later chapters, conscience is not the same in every personality. The best reason to spend so much time establishing the nature of the Introverted mind—inborn idealistic knowledge—is because it is the most profound shaping influence on personality. It's what we puzzle over and study in each other's behavior, and it's what we focus on most in ourselves. And yet we have very little satisfactory framework to actually see why we make the decisions we do, let alone why others do. Once we see how to identify the roots of conscience, much of this will become plain.

The Introverted part of the mind also defines what we find difficult to learn. The Extroverted part learns new facts and habits pretty easily. It's the Introverted part of the mind that can only learn what already matches its template. We have to understand the nature of the template so that we know why we gravitate to some things and simply cannot cope with others. At some level, the Introverted mind feels that whatever doesn't match the template is dangerous, bad, and invalid. It doesn't want to learn those things, any more than it wants to walk in a dangerous place at night. What is easy and natural to one personality can be precisely what another personality cannot accept. That's why we have blind spots. It's often why we can't resolve conflicts.

In the next three chapters, we'll look at the Judging functions: Thinking and Feeling. What are they like when they're oriented to inborn idealism or outward-looking pragmatism? How does each form part of conscience, and how are they different? We'll leave the Perceiving functions for later, because although they come first logically (they control the mind's input), they are harder to talk about. It will be easier to understand Sensing and Intuition when you can compare them to the material on Thinking and Feeling.

PART TWO:
PARTS OF PERSONALITY

CHAPTER 4

Thinking

WE START WITH THE JUDGING function of Thinking, though not because it comes first in the brain's processing order. Of course, information must be Perceived before it can be Judged. However, Thinking is easier to understand, partly because its technical meaning (Thinking) is not that different from its daily meaning (thinking). Understanding how Thinking can be Introverted or Extroverted allows us to move to Feeling, then to the more difficult concepts involved in the types of Perceiving.

At its simplest, Thinking is the application of logic and order. It is a rule system that compares numbers and logical outcomes. It compares sizes, such as cost or distance. It evaluates goals and the actions needed to reach them. At a more complex level, Thinking creates sets of rules to help us choose which of two goals is more important at this moment. There might be competing sets of logical priorities, so logical Thinking has to figure out which one to follow, and which to set aside.

Thinking pays a lot of attention to numbers, since numbers are the best way to compare and rank things. Thinking cares a lot about words like "first" and "last." The more someone leans on Thinking in his personality, the more he cares about being first. To look at it another way, any time someone's competitive spirit gets going, it's an expression of Thinking in their personality.

We all need to navigate the world and make decisions, so to some extent, we all need to use logic to think about outside facts. But when we talk about Thinking *as a mental function*, it's not about the simple act of having to decide if it's logical to buy your socks at Walmart or at Macy's. We all make those choices at times. Thinking in a broader sense means logic and numbers as part of how we experience and evaluate the world, even when we aren't making simple logical choices. It's a preferential way to make those—or any—evaluations.

When Thinking is oriented in an inner, idealistic way, its character is very different from pragmatic, flexible Extroverted Thinking. As an Introverted function, it expresses an inborn template that tells about ideal order and perfect logic. As an Extroverted function, it is a tool for pragmatic order and sharp, even caustic logic.

AMORAL EXTROVERTED THINKING

Extroverted Thinking focuses on the facts of the outside world, the problems presented by the outside world, and efficient solutions to these problems. It isn't primarily about right and wrong, it's about practical comparisons like cheapest, best, and fastest. It begins by looking at all of the facts, especially facts that can be measured by numbers. These numbers include size, cost, time, distance, age, and quality. What matters most to Extroverted Thinking is getting the best outcome.

There are specific areas of the brain that handle pragmatic questions of utility. They don't answer the question, "what's right?" but only "what would be more useful and effective?" They work out cost-benefit analysis. To some extent, utilitarian decisions are most often tied to numbers and logic. As we'll see in later chapters, there's evidence that utility can be neurally connected to other things, too. But in this case, Extroverted Thinking definitely uses utility as its goal.

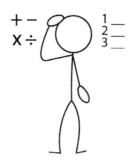

Fig. 4-1

The cartoon here symbolizes Thinking when it's focused on the outside world. Logical methods like mathematics and putting things in priority order are applied to facts and rules in the world. The four arithmetic symbols and the numbered list symbolize logical use of numbers. For the stick man, who symbolizes some part of the human mind, these things are outside of him. He learns about them as he goes through life and he doesn't take them personally.

We all use Extroverted Thinking for certain tasks, like when we make choices about what to buy. We compare the measurable qualities of shoes, cars or houses. When Extroverted Thinking is part of personality, it is very open-minded when looking at a complex problem such as buying a house. It is also strictly unsentimental. If a person who mainly used

Extroverted Thinking had to choose between buying the house he grew up in or a completely different one, he would not count his fond memories of the house as part of the real decision. Extroverted Thinking would be able to look past sentimental reasons and family pressure, and would make the decision based entirely on measurable factors like the conditions of the roof and the driveway.

The clearest example of Extroverted Thinking as applied in real life is the increasing use of numerical data to make decisions that used to be made with "gut feelings." Modern life is full of data on all kinds of things; using this data to find predictive patterns is called "data mining." Big internet companies, like Google and Amazon, use our searches and purchases to link interests that tend to go together. Dating websites use numbers collected on current and past members to make better predictions about who you might like to date. Weather statistics can predict which wine vintages will taste better.[50]

Perhaps the most famous example of objectively processing numbers to influence human decisions comes from baseball. Bill James had a degree in economics and an obsession with baseball, and there are few sports that generate numbers as much as baseball. On his own, in the 1970s, James began playing with baseball statistics to answer questions about how to predict which players would do well. He published an annual book, *The Bill James Baseball Abstract*, which used statistics to show things like which pitchers were more likely to walk batters, and many more complicated questions. He developed a mathematical formula for predicting which players could best help their teams to win. The formula took a player's total on-base number and divided it by his at-bat times and walks, then multiplied it by the sum of his hits and walks. This gave him a number that told how many runs the player had contributed to winning a game.[51]

James was already well known among baseball insiders when Michael Lewis wrote *Moneyball: The Art of Winning an Unfair Game* in 2003. Lewis told the story of how the Oakland A's built a winning team using one of the lowest budgets in either baseball league. After *Moneyball* became a movie, everyone was talking about James's theories and their influence on the sport. Lewis explained that baseball scouts had always believed in their ability to spot future great players by just watching them. James, and the teams who based their hiring on his theories, showed that his formula for evaluating a player's ability to score runs in any way possible mattered more. The movie shows how the A's manager made many decisions that seemed (to onlookers) completely wrong, but as his assistant says, "Numbers don't lie."

This line is a neat statement of the fundamental belief of Extroverted Thinking: people can fool you, guesses can go wrong, and even experience doesn't always predict what will happen. But *numbers* themselves don't lie. If the numbers are right and you're using them correctly, then your conclusion can't be wrong, even if it goes against what everyone thinks. People who use Extroverted Thinking a great deal can become obsessive about finding the purest source of the most accurate numbers, and they often prefer to handle evaluating the numbers themselves.

Legal arguments are traditionally based in Extroverted Thinking. In criminal law, a

---

50: Ian Ayres, *Super Crunchers* (New York: Bantam, 2007), 1-6.
51: Ian Ayres, *Super Crunchers* (New York: Bantam, 2007), 7.

murderer may have some point of the law on his side, even if he was wrong to kill someone. It's the lawyer's job to make the most of every legal point his client has going for him, not to judge him morally. Commercial law looks at contract provisions, not at whether a company will go bankrupt if these provisions are enforced. If a company broke its contract or made foolish investments, bankruptcy and sale are the logical consequences. Legal thinking cares a lot about procedure, since skipping a logical step may change everything, even if other people think the step appears trivial.

Extroverted Thinking is applied in American daily life whenever a club or committee meets. People with no formal schooling or legal training know to begin a meeting with a motion to read and approve the minutes of the last meeting. Our culture of civic participation ensures that we all know the line, "All in favor, say 'aye'." Rules of procedural order often seem fussy, and it would be just as easy to run meetings without them. But Extroverted Thinking long ago convinced most people that these logical rules are a protection from later allegations or disputes, especially when a dispute can't be imagined or anticipated. When you least expect it, that's when you most need logical procedural rules.

We all use some Extroverted Thinking, of course, even if it's only for simple tasks like price comparison or choosing the lower-calorie food. But when we say that a *personality* uses this kind of logic, we mean that Extroverted Thinking is innately part of the mind's way of making decisions about life. It can be a dominant part of the personality, or it can be a much lesser, but still important, part. In later chapters, we will look at how mental functions like Thinking can be balanced in a personality type. For now, when we call someone an "Extroverted Thinker," we mean that this type of logic is an observable part of their personality. If we say that Extroverted Thinking is "dominant," we mean that it is a very important part of the personality. When it's dominant, Extroverted Thinking may take care of most decisions. If you know someone who has dominant Extroverted Thinking, you are probably aware of cool, legal, pragmatic logic as part of who he or she is every day.

Like anyone who practices some skill to the point of mastery, dominant Extroverted Thinkers can become very good at using logic in the most complex cases. Comparing prices alone is almost too simple for them after the age of 12. They will tend to compare many aspects of a purchase, and they often like to research consumer reports. They don't just go for what's cheapest or fastest. Instead, they have ways of considering which factors are most important in this particular decision, and how this decision fits into a strategy of other decisions. Extroverted Thinking at its strongest can balance out rules, risks, strategy and numbers, and it can calculate importance as situations change over time.

There's a certain amount of competition in many Extroverted Thinking tasks. Extroversion is focused on the world outside; most of the Thinking skills are engaged in negotiations with other people. Being the best Extroverted Thinker in the room may mean winning the best deal, getting the task done fastest, or some other form of coming out on top. Winning is the ultimate real-world test. In some situations, winning is the only measure of whether the Extroverted Thinker did his best. The world is filled with financial competitions on which real results and fortunes hang: buying and selling real estate, buying and selling companies and their shares, negotiating legal settlements.

Extroverted Thinking is probably the mental process most strongly associated with men.

While it's true that more men than women have it as a major part of personality, we must not blind ourselves to how often Extroverted Thinking can show up in women. There's a great example that you can watch on the internet.

In January 2013, Cameron Russell, who is an international model, gave a TED talk about the ways appearances are manipulated.[52] She explained how photographers set up shots, and she showed home photographs from the same periods of her life to contrast with the professional ones. Further, she had researched statistics about the unfair benefits of having white skin; she presented parallel statistics about how many non-white young people get stopped by police. The juxtaposition of her cold logic and beautiful, feminine appearance made her talk one of the most-watched of the year.

A beautiful woman who's known for modeling clothes isn't the person we first think of when we talk about Extroverted Thinking. If that's how we insist on looking at it, we'd be wrong: in addition to her modeling work, Russell has a degree in economics.[53] The whole point of Extroverted Thinking is to cut through prejudices and reduce what we believe we know to what we actually know. It's fitting that we must use Thinking to understand Russell's talk and block out the prejudicial idea that a woman must be emotional, not logical, since that's the kind of blind spot Extroverted Thinking loves to expose.

We're going to take this point from Extroverted Thinking and apply it through the rest of the book. It's easy to assume that men or women have certain mental functions, but in fact, most of them are distributed equally among men and women. We should not consider Thinking as a male trait, nor Feeling as a female one. While describing kinds of Thinking, I may give an example with "he" and "him" in one paragraph, and "she" and "her" in the next, without meaning that those details are relevant to men or women. I'll follow this pattern in later chapters, too. If it's relevant that I'm talking about men or women, the context will make it very clear. I've chosen not to use the grammatical use of "he" to mean any person, because when we talk about personality, it's important for the text to use words that disrupt our patterns of expectations, to dispel blind spots.

Extroverted Thinking is one of the most important functions in the world of business and government. Everyone who succeeds at top levels has some degree of skill with it, and most of them have it as a dominant mental function. Extroverted Thinking is good for academic success, too, especially in fact-based fields like science. Children with Extroverted Thinking can usually find a way to do well in all of their school subjects, though if Thinking is dominant, they may dislike assignments that demand creativity. They are usually comfortable with arithmetic, since it is about learning logical rules. But in any school subject, even a creative or emotion-based one, as long as there is a structured way to succeed, they will find it.

We should also emphasize the expansive, positive nature of Extroverted Thinking. Not just in school, but in anything, Extroverted Thinking is optimistic about finding a way. The answer may be more research or gaining new skills. It's logically possible for the answer to be "no, this won't work," but Extroverted Thinking won't admit this until the bitter end

---

52: http://blog.ted.com/2013/01/16/model-cameron-russell-gives-the-real-story-behind-six-of-her-stunning-photos/
53: Dwyer Gunn, "Cameron Russell, a Model, Puts Looks Aside," *New York Times*, July 10, 2013.

when all else has failed thoroughly. Strong Extroverted Thinkers tend to be fundamentally optimistic when they look at their lives and futures. The burden of proof is always on the negative side to prove that no solution exists. Until that is proven, the solution is assumed to exist.

There can be a certain amount of rule-breaking involved in pragmatic, optimistic problem-solving. If Extroverted Thinking sees a way to solve a problem, but the solution means breaking the law or a promise, it's not necessarily ruled out. Instead, logic asks, how important is the law or promise? What consequences would result from breaking it? Are the consequences less dire than the consequence of failure to solve this task? Faced with a situation without a clear win, the Extroverted Thinker will choose the smaller loss. This could mean paying legal fines; it could mean risking a small lawsuit. Both choices might appear "wrong" in some way, but logic forces one of them to go forward. In that case, it's logical to choose the smaller loss.

Extroverted Thinkers are not usually much afraid of being sued or kicked out of churches or clubs. Social consequences are not as real as financial and legal ones. The group's purpose matters as an element of logical factoring: is this a group that will have some impact on a numbers question? If so, then it's a priority to succeed in the group; if not, then it isn't. Extroverted Thinking can often do pretty well for a while as the manager of group relationships. Socially, the Extroverted Thinker is optimistic, efficient, and often funny. Humor is the most common way of handling groups of people.

The function of Extroverted Thinking is much less successful when it is applied to personal relationships and emotional decisions. Extroverted Thinkers who are very skilled at logic may try using the same rule set for other areas of life. It is obvious to other people that these rules won't work, but it's not at all obvious to the strong Extroverted Thinker. If she could figure out how to get an A in art based on Thinking, then surely she can use the same skills to choose friends or even a spouse. It rarely works well.

In logic, making an apology should be based on who is at fault, not whose feelings are hurt. Of course, in relationship situations, logical decisions can be far from appropriate. People who lean on Extroverted Thinking most of the time can find it very, very difficult to absorb the need to just apologize to make a relationship better. If they succeed at handling the problem, it's probably by stepping out of Extroverted Thinking for a little while. Love isn't about numbers or winning.

EXTROVERTED THINKING IN LITERATURE

In each section explaining one of the mental functions, we will look at some snips from classic literature that demonstrate this kind of thinking. Sometimes, the passage talks about someone using the function, while other times, the passage is itself an example. In this first passage, Benjamin Franklin's *Autobiography* tells how he reacted to a great preacher's visit (in 1739) to Philadelphia. While massive crowds were listening and weeping, Franklin used Extroverted Thinking to make a practical calculation:

[Mr. Whitefield] had a loud and clear voice and articulated his words and sentences so

perfectly that he might be heard and understood at a great distance, especially as his auditors, however numerous, observed the most exact silence. He preached one evening from the top of the courthouse steps, which are in the middle of Market Street and on the west side of Second Street, which crosses it at right angles. Both streets were filled with hearers to a considerable distance. Being among the hindmost in Market Street, I had the curiosity to learn how far he could be heard, by retiring backwards down the street towards the river; and I found his voice distinct until I came near Fourth Street, when some noise in that street obscured it. Imagining then a semicircle of which my distance should be the radius and that it were filled with auditors, to each of whom I allowed two square feet, I computed that he might well be heard by more than thirty thousand. This reconciled me to the newspaper accounts of his having preached to twenty-five thousand people in the fields and to the ancient histories of generals haranguing whole armies, of which I had sometimes doubted.

René Descartes, a philosopher and mathematician, is one of history's most famous Extroverted Thinkers. In 1637, he wrote *A Discourse on Method*, the work that contains his most famous line, "I think, therefore I am." Here he explains the most important rule of Extroverted Thinking, to accept only what can be absolutely proven:

…as for the opinions which I had up to that time embraced, I thought that I could not do better than to resolve at once to sweep them wholly away, that I might afterwards be in a position to admit either others more correct, or even perhaps the same when they had undergone the scrutiny of reason. I firmly believed that in this way I should much better succeed in the conduct of my life, than if I built only upon old foundations, and leaned upon principles which, in my youth, I had taken on trust… The first [rule] was never to accept anything for true which I did not clearly know to be such; that is to say, carefully to avoid precipitancy and prejudice, and to comprise nothing more in my judgment than what was presented to my mind so clearly and distinctly as to exclude all ground of doubt.

Perhaps the most famous Extroverted Thinker in literature is Sherlock Holmes. In the first story about Holmes, *A Study in Scarlet* (1887), Arthur Conan Doyle introduces the detective by showing his optimism about the use of scientific logic to solve crimes. When a mutual friend introduces Watson to Holmes in a chemistry laboratory, Watson is astonished at the optimistic joy that Holmes evinces about his use of logic:

This was a lofty chamber, lined and littered with countless bottles. Broad, low tables were scattered about, which bristled with retorts, test-tubes, and little Bunsen lamps, with their blue flickering flames. There was only one student in the room, who was bending over a distant table absorbed in his work. At the sound of our steps he glanced round and sprang to his feet with a cry of pleasure. "I've found it! I've found it," he shouted to my companion, running towards us with a test-tube in his hand. "I have found a re-agent which is precipitated by hoemoglobin 4 and by nothing else." Had he discovered a gold mine, greater delight could not have shone upon his features.

"Dr. Watson, Mr. Sherlock Holmes," said Stamford, introducing us.

"How are you?" he said cordially, gripping my hand with a strength for which I should hardly have given him credit. "You have been in Afghanistan, I perceive."

"How on earth did you know that?" I asked in astonishment.

"Never mind," said he, chuckling to himself. "The question now is about hoemoglobin. No doubt you see the significance of this discovery of mine?"

"It is interesting, chemically, no doubt," I answered, "but practically —"

"Why, man, it is the most practical medico-legal discovery for years. Don't you see that it gives us an infallible test for blood stains. Come over here now!" He seized me by the coat-sleeve in his eagerness, and drew me over to the table at which he had been working. "Let us have some fresh blood," he said, digging a long bodkin into his finger, and drawing off the resulting drop of blood in a chemical pipette. "Now, I add this small quantity of blood to a litre of water. You perceive that the resulting mixture has the appearance of pure water. The proportion of blood cannot be more than one in a million. I have no doubt, however, that we shall be able to obtain the characteristic reaction." As he spoke, he threw into the vessel a few white crystals, and then added some drops of a transparent fluid. In an instant the contents assumed a dull mahogany colour, and a brownish dust was precipitated to the bottom of the glass jar.

"Ha! ha!" he cried, clapping his hands, and looking as delighted as a child with a new toy. "What do you think of that?"

"It seems to be a very delicate test," I remarked.

"Beautiful! beautiful! The old Guiacum test was very clumsy and uncertain. So is the microscopic examination for blood corpuscles. The latter is valueless if the stains are a few hours old. Now, this appears to act as well whether the blood is old or new. Had this test been invented, there are hundreds of men now walking the earth who would long ago have paid the penalty of their crimes."

"Indeed!" I murmured.

"Criminal cases are continually hinging upon that one point. A man is suspected of a crime months perhaps after it has been committed. His linen or clothes are examined, and brownish stains discovered upon them. Are they blood stains, or mud stains, or rust stains, or fruit stains, or what are they? That is a question which has puzzled many an expert, and why? Because there was no reliable test. Now we have the Sherlock Holmes' test, and there will no longer be any difficulty."

His eyes fairly glittered as he spoke, and he put his hand over his heart and bowed as if to some applauding crowd conjured up by his imagination.

"You are to be congratulated," I remarked, considerably surprised at his enthusiasm.

While people with Extroverted Thinking may not always be optimistic, they tend to be more enthusiastic and determined to find answers when they are actively using this Extroverted function.

In *Out of Africa* (1937), Baroness Karen Blixen (writing as Isak Dinesen) narrates how the Somali manager of her Kenya coffee farm once responded to hearing, for the first time, the plot of Shakespeare's *The Merchant of Venice*. To her surprise Farah, unlike most European audiences, shows a keen Extroverted Thinking interest in figuring out some way that Shylock could have taken a pound of flesh.

Farah gave his full attention to the affairs of Antonio, Bassanio and Shylock. Here was a big, complicated business deal, somewhat on the verge of the law, the real thing to the heart of a Somali. He asked me a question or two as to the clause of the pound of flesh: it obviously seemed to him an eccentric, but not impossible agreement; men might go in for that sort of thing. And here the story began to smell of blood,—his interest in it rose. When Portia came upon the stage, he pricked his ears; I imagined that he saw her as a woman of his own tribe, Fathima with all sails set, crafty and insinuating, out to outman man. [Africans] do not take sides in a tale, the interest to them lies in the ingeniousness of the plot itself, and the Somali, who in real life have a strong sense of values, and a gift for moral indignation, give these a rest in their fiction. Still, here Farah's sympathy was with Shylock, who had come down with the cash; he repugned his defeat.

"What?" said he. "Did the Jew give up his claim? He should not have done that. The flesh was due to him, it was little enough for him to get for all that money."

"But what else could he do," I asked, "when he must not take one drop of blood?"

"Memsahib," said Farah, "he could have used a red-hot knife. That brings out no blood."

"But," I said, "he was not allowed to take either more or less than one pound of flesh."

"And who," said Farah, "would have been frightened by that, exactly a Jew? He might have taken little bits at a time, with a small scale at hand to weight it on, till he had got just one pound. Had the Jew no friends to give him advice?"

Without getting bogged down in generalizations about Somalis, Africans or Jews, the passage shows us how easily Extroverted Thinking can set aside moral considerations. Farah isn't interested in whether it would be *right* to remove bits of flesh with a red-hot knife, he is only interested in whether it would be possible so that the contract doesn't need to be made void. He sees what looks like the legally correct side being put in the wrong, and he doesn't like this logical outcome.

MORAL INTROVERTED THINKING

In Chapter 3, we looked at how archetypes may include logical and mathematical concepts, as well as moral ones. When Thinking is rooted in concepts of inborn knowledge, it takes on a different character. Extroverted Thinking is a conscious application of logic to find the best pragmatic solution, but Introverted Thinking is an unconscious, innate understanding of archetypal logic.

Logical archetypes include many concepts of comparison and numbers; we find some of them written out formally as fundamentals of geometry. Things can be equal in size, or they can be greater or smaller. If A is greater than B, and B is greater than C, A must be greater than C. A part is not larger than the whole that it's part of. Logic is not only about size and number, it's also about time and causation. If A happened before B, then B could not have caused A to happen. Numbers also tell us about putting things in order: first, second, last. These mathematical and logical concepts are universal, and of course they are indisputably true.

When personality has Thinking as inborn archetypal knowledge, logical concepts extend beyond basic math. They are ideals of what's right, part of the inner template of safety and danger. In Extroverted use, logical concepts are value-neutral and pragmatic, but as part of the Introverted mind, they're idealistic and moral. They are an image of ideal order in the world; if the world could be this orderly and logical, it would be safe. If your behavior is guided by logic and order, you'll be safe. Logical moral principles are right and good in themselves; they feel like an absolute, inviolable moral truth.

The morality of Introverted Thinking is about maintaining strong boundaries and orderliness in behavior. It is more connected to the logic of machines and mathematics than to emotion. In fact, the morality based in Introverted Thinking believes that not all kinds of happiness are important. You could break a rule to make someone happy, like letting a child onto an amusement park ride when the rules say he is too short.

But to Introverted Thinking, rules exist for a reason, and that reason is to keep things orderly so that everything goes smoothly. Making a child wait another two years to grow isn't happy for the child at the moment, but being able to ride that rollercoaster will mean more if he has to be patient. It teaches him to respect the orderly flow of logic in society, and in the long run, that will make him happier. Introverted Thinkers believe that lasting happiness comes only when everyone follows moral logic and keeps life in order.

Fig. 4-2

The cartoon shows us that the Introverted Thinker's sense of logic and order doesn't come from the outside world. The arithmetic symbols and number list still stand for numbers and logic, but they are now inside a book, inside the mind. When this personality sees numbers and logic in the outside world, he just recognizes them as true because they were already true inside.

Like all inborn knowledge, Introverted Thinking is stubborn, idealistic and often a bit negative. Even when things break down in the real world, the Introverted Thinker knows how it all ought to be, how it really should be. Inner logic is very good at critiquing failure. It's especially good at noticing when a failed outcome results from wrong procedure or breaking rules. Because inner logic has such a high ideal for proper order and behavior, it's not surprised by logical flaws. An Introverted Thinker expects a lot of herself, and realizes her own failures. Having no control over what others do, she expects to see a lot of failure. Introverted Thinking senses danger and feels pessimistic.

Introverted Thinking cares a lot about basic moral logic. We can see some of these rules clearly by noticing what seems "fair" to very young children. First, the principle of fairness: nobody should get something better than another person unless there's a logical reason. Every two year old knows that the other child should not get a bigger cookie, or worse, two cookies when he got only one.

Fairness means equal application of logical rules to everyone. If someone gets more of something now, there may be a logical reason. This reason matters very much, because it must be fairly applied to everyone. If it's about age, then the younger child expects to get the treat on reaching the right age. If it's about turns, there should be a reasonable chance at its being "my turn" soon. If someone has the first turn at choosing and takes the best prize, it's very annoying but it's still fair as long as I can have a chance at first turn, when I'll get the best prize.

Introverted Thinking applies the same principles to adult life. If someone is in charge, he gets to make the rules, and everyone else has to listen. But that's only because it's rightfully his turn to be the leader, whether he's a club president or a King. Seizing power is wrong because it disrupts order and turns. Most of formal law through history is a matter of spelling out specific cases of fairness or order. As long as a law seems to reflect this inner principle of fairness, people feel it's fair.

Challenging authority seems unfair to Introverted Thinking, unless there's a very good reason to do it. If someone earned the right to be the leader, then it's fair to respect the turn. When they are in authority, Introverted Thinkers create some orderly way for people to politely question, but not challenge, their power. Both respecting and wielding rightful authority are seen as the bedrock of a fair society. On the other hand, if the authorities are not observing logical fairness, they have lost the right to respect. Introverted Thinkers respect the rules, not the individual, so they can participate in a rebellion if they feel there is no other way to uphold true logic.

The other inborn moral principle known by young children is that the outcome of your actions should match the goodness of your actions. If you try really hard, follow rules, be kind to others, and mean well, you should have a good outcome. Conversely, if you don't try but break rules and act in mean ways, you should have a bad outcome.

Law tries to maintain this principle, but its power is limited. We see the outcome principle even more clearly in stories, where people can impose ideals through fiction. The most enduring stories tend to be ones that show good triumphing over evil. If a story ends with a bad person unpunished and a good person feeling sad and wronged, little children won't accept the ending. It feels completely wrong to leave things that way, even if it's the way it really happened. Folk stories from around the world reliably shows us a proper moral order and suggest how the world ought to operate. Good always wins in the end, and evil loses.

Introverted Thinking is strongly oriented to the basic principles of moral logic. If the world were a better place, things would be numerically fair and people would reliably get what they deserve. Introverted Thinkers certainly try to make these things happen in their own lives and actions. When something unfair or undeserving happens, it feels so wrong to the Introverted Thinker that it's almost unreal. What should happen is real at a deeper level than what does happen. Inborn knowledge rejects messy facts that don't fit, refusing to modify its image of right and wrong to fit what happens.

You can find the rules of Introverted Thinking in much of the world's "wisdom literature," like the Bible's *Book of Proverbs* and *Ecclesiastes*. Traditional proverbs are about what *should* happen; sometimes they even admit that the real world doesn't follow their rules. In *Ecclesiastes*, "the Preacher" states confidently that, "Though a sinner do evil an hundred times, *and his days be prolonged*, yet surely I know that it shall be well with them that fear God, which fear before him: but it shall not be well with the wicked, *neither shall he prolong his days…*" (Ecclesiastes 8:12) In other words, his own eyes tell him that bad people live as long as good people, but he refuses to accept it.

The proverbs and wisdom of many cultures and languages express the same ideas: don't believe your eyes when they tell you that the real world is a messy place. Instead, believe the proverbs and live by their rules; their reality is more profound, therefore more real.

The rules of Introverted Thinking can be applied to some external decisions, because the basic logical rules are the same. Introverted Thinkers who have well-developed Thinking may be equally good as Extroverted Thinkers at facts, business, and school. They may be drawn to science, especially physics and chemistry, because science explores the internal logic of a chaotic world. Science makes sense of the messy real world. Engineering can be even more attractive, because it helps put things into order. Engineers look at opposing mechanical forces, like wind shear and gravity, and figure out how to balance them to make things work. Most appealing of all to the strongest Introverted Thinkers, mathematics is the most logical world, a place where reality does not intrude on ideals.

Introverted Thinkers are usually neat and dutiful. The stronger this function is in an individual, the more reliable and orderly she will be. The Introverted Thinker can't see any other way to behave. Leaving chores unfinished or failing to clean up after herself would be illogical and wrong. They have a strong sense of duty.

Introverted Thinking can be very competitive, too. Part of dealing with numbers is putting things in order: first, second, third, last. There are at least two different ways that even idealistic Thinking focuses on competition. Like all Thinking, it wants to be first: the winner. Introverted Thinkers usually care very much about winning competitions in sports or in their profession. When the idea of "first" is part of an inborn ideal, it may cause an even deeper competitive spirit than when it's a conscious strategy.

Alternatively, there's a silent competition for being morally best. It may exist only in the Introverted Thinker's mind, but it's quite real there. Most of the time, the two types of "winning" don't conflict, but occasionally they do. When an Introverted Thinker finds out that winning (or even entering) a competition means breaking a principle of behavior or religion, she's very likely to set aside literal winning for the moral win. It's a clear choice, but setting aside the competitive win may be harder than she lets on.

Introverted Thinkers are most at a disadvantage when they find themselves in a chaotic time of life with a lot of changing facts. Extroverted Thinking applies logic to the facts as they are, so when the facts change, they change their decisions and behavior. Introverted Thinkers resist this kind of change. A hero of Introverted Thinking is the Marine guard marching stiffly past the Tomb of the Unknown Soldier while a hurricane drenches him with rain and threatens to blow tree limbs down on his head. It doesn't matter to these Thinkers if it might be safer to stop guarding a post, because their logical decisions and orderly behavior were not based on external facts in the first place.

In fact, since an Introverted template feels like it's about detecting danger, Introverted Thinking lends a sense of urgency to sticking with the rules. It can be very hard to make a strong Introverted Thinker change his mind. Unless one of the inner rules permits a change, he's not likely to listen to "irrelevant" facts. The stranger and more chaotic the facts seem, the more the Introverted Thinker will resist. Fundamental pessimism suggests that there may not be a good outcome possible. In that case, believe only the inner compass.

INTROVERTED THINKING IN LITERATURE

The Wisdom of Ptah-Hotep is an ancient Egyptian work of proverbs. Here, in "Maxim 5, On the art of being a leader while respecting the Rule," Ptah-Hotep explains that becoming a leader is not about making rules, it's about following them.

If you have the responsibility of leadership, are in charge of setting guidelines for a large number of subordinates, seek every opportunity to be effective so your behavior is irreproachable. Great is the Rule—its effect on both great and small is complete and long-lasting. The Rule is illuminating and practical and has not changed since the time of Osiris. Those who break the law must be punished—something the greedy fail to understand. Wrongdoers can achieve material gain, but evil never leads to good. It is wrong to say, "I want only to take things to enrich myself," rather than, "I want my actions to benefit the position entrusted to me." Whenever anything reaches its due term, it is the Rule which endures.[54]

The Rule (natural moral law and tradition) is more important than what any individual ruler wants. It isn't felt as a rule inside the mind, but rather as its own independent reality in the outside world. That's how inborn knowledge always seems.

Jane Austen lived most of her life in a time that admired the steady values of Introverted Thinking. Her novel *Sense and Sensibility* (1811) contrasted two sisters, one who lived for her romantic feelings, and the other who lived by inner rules. Elinor, the Introverted Thinker, here reflects on how to keep her promise not to tell a secret; if she appears at all unhappy it would be like giving away the secret, and she must not break her promise.

Supported by the conviction of having done nothing to merit her present unhappiness, and consoled by the belief that Edward had done nothing to forfeit her esteem, she thought she could even now, under the first smart of the heavy blow, command herself well enough to guard every suspicion of the truth from her mother and sisters... The necessity of concealing from [them] what had been entrusted in confidence to herself, though it obliged her to unceasing exertion, was no aggravation of Elinor's distress... She was stronger alone, and her own good sense was so well supported that her firmness was as unshaken, her appearance of cheerfulness as invariable, as with regrets so poignant and fresh, it was possible for them to be.

Notice how Elinor feels she will be "stronger alone," a clear indication of the Introverted root of her behavior rules. Austen's *Pride and Prejudice* (1813) shows another character with Introverted Thinking. Mr. Collins is less successful in his use of logic, since he is trying to use it to manage a proposal of marriage.

"My reasons for marrying are, first, that I think it a right thing for every clergyman in easy circumstances (like myself) to set the example of matrimony in his parish. Secondly, that I am convinced it will add very greatly to my happiness; and thirdly, which perhaps I ought to have mentioned earlier, that it is the particular advice and recommendation of the very noble lady

---

54: Christian Jacq, trans., *The Wisdom of Ptah-Hotep*, (London: Constable & Robinson, 2004).

whom I have the honour of calling my patroness…[The] fact is that being, as I am, to inherit this estate after the death of your honoured father… I could not satisfy myself without resolving to choose a wife from among his daughters, that the loss to them might be as little as possible."

To Mr. Collins, the proposal is about doing what's fitting and right, not about feelings. He expects logic to have the same persuasion with the girl that it has with him.

George Eliot's novel *Middlemarch* (1872) depicted characters with many different personality traits. Here, Mrs. Garth discusses whether her young adult daughter, Mary, was correct in refusing to destroy a will because no attorney was present. Later, it turned out that her refusal made a good friend lose an inheritance. But for both Mary and her mother, correct reasoning is based in Introverted Thinking, which doesn't care about outcomes:

"Mary could not have acted otherwise, even if she had known what would be the effect on Fred," said Mrs. Garth. "And she was quite ignorant of it. It seems to me, a loss which falls on another because we have done right is not to lie upon our conscience."

In Walter Scott's *Rob Roy*, a Scottish town official reacts to the hero's sudden duel to near death with the story's villain, his cousin. (Scots dialect has been modified in both passages for easier reading.)

When I came to the account of the rencounter… Mr. Jarvie broke in upon the narration with "Wrong now—clean wrong—to draw a sword on your kinsman is inhibited by the laws of God and man; and to draw a sword on the streets of a royal burgh is punishable by fine and imprisonment."

His first reaction leans on an inner sense of primal law, followed closely by reference to the city's authorized laws. The circumstances don't matter to him, since his judgment of wrongness is absolute by an inner rule. Later, Mr. Jarvie has just witnessed a murder, but the Highland Scottish woman who ordered the death demands him to say it was justified.

"And were I to set you at liberty," said the imperious dame, "what name could you give to the drowning of that Saxon dog?"

"Ahem!" said the Bailie, clearing his throat as well as he could, "I should study to say as little on that score as might be—least said is soonest mended."

"But if you were called on by the courts, as you term them, of justice," she again demanded, "what then would be your answer?"

The Bailie looked this way and that way, like a person who meditates an escape, and then answered in the tone of one who, seeing no means of accomplishing a retreat, determines to stand the brunt of battle—"I see what you are driving me to the wall about. But I'll tell you it plain, kinswoman,—I behoved just to speak according to my own conscience; and though your own husband can tell ye that Nicol Jarvie can wink as hard at a friend's failings as anybody, yet I'se tell ye, kinswoman, mine's ne'er be the tongue to belie my thought; and sooner than say that yonder poor wretch was lawfully slaughtered, I would consent to be laid beside him—though I think ye are the first Hieland woman would mint such a doom to her husband's kinsman but four times removed."

Mr. Jarvie's Introverted Thinking is so stubborn and idealistic that he can't become pragmatic even for a "white lie" to get himself out of danger.

CHAPTER 5

Feeling

Parallel to Thinking, there is a completely separate system for making value judgments. Feeling is about understanding human relationships and how to take care of them. It certainly includes an important role for emotion, because our emotions give us information about relationships. When Feeling is a stronger function in someone's mind, emotion becomes a source of fact and insight. The better these emotional facts are understood, the better decisions Feeling can make about how to take care of people. However, Feeling's decisions can be very cool and unemotional. In everyday speech, feeling and emotion are the same, but in personality modeling, emotion is just one of the tools used by the rational Judging system of Feeling.

Like Thinking, Feeling can draw its primary facts from either the outside world or the inborn world of ideals. Just as everyone must know some numbers and logic in order to make basic decisions, everyone must be at least somewhat aware of basic facts about human relationships. But when Feeling is turned Extroverted, it is pragmatically applied to the real, messy world of relationships. Its effect on personality is very different from when it's rooted in Introverted templates.

EXTROVERTED FEELING LIVES IN GROUPS

Everyone is aware of having an identity, a sense of "I." For people with Feeling turned outward, the sense of "I" feels stronger and more alive when they're in a group of people. They are less sure of who they are when they're alone. Their emotional identity is linked to how they feel in a group, and also to how the group feels about them. It's about finding and knowing their place in the social world.

People who have Extroverted Feeling as part of their personality can't help caring at least a little about people's feelings. They can be making decisions on a Thinking basis, but if they have Extroverted Feeling, they can never completely tune out concerns about how their decisions will change relationships.

The stronger and more dominant this Feeling is in their personality, the more they notice the emotions around them. Their earliest and most important observations about their friends and family members are about emotion. Awareness of other people's emotions seems to pose a question, even a challenge, to the Extroverted Feeler: "what can I do about the emotion that I sense? Can I cheer this person up? Can I share in her happiness? What does his emotion say about who I am?"

Fig. 5-1

The cartoon shows how this person takes his views about relationships from the people he sees around him. The stick figure, as before, represents a human mind. Two people with a heart between them represents all of the ways that people can relate to each other: ideally, with love, but not always. The Extroverted Feeler knows love by watching how people love, but also knows non-love by seeing it, too.

Extroverted functions are pragmatic, exploring, adaptive and open to new facts. That's how Extroverted Feeling looks at human relationships. The way people treat each other is often not even close to an ideal, but an Extroverted function isn't focused on an ideal anyway. It looks for context, cause and effect, and other visible patterns. Because it's oriented to what's possible, not what's ideal, it's usually optimistic. It sees ways to make things happen among people; if one way doesn't work, there's probably another. All ways are equally good, if they work.

Just as Extroverted Thinking was focused on the *numerical* outcome, so is Extroverted Feeling focused on the *social* outcome, how something affects their place in the group. It's about the pragmatic outcomes, reasons and customs. To a certain extent, decisions about people are made in a cost-benefit analysis way. This is especially true when the other person is a stranger or someone who just fills a role (clerk, delivery, or just telephone contact). The relationship (such as it is) is handled in a utilitarian way: whatever works best for me.

Typically, this means politeness, but it doesn't require warmth, a personal touch, or ever remembering that person again. It may be okay to be rude or angry, since the relationship doesn't matter.

Extroverted Feeling doesn't try to justify real cruelty, but much somewhat-bad behavior can be viewed in context, not judged by an ideal. Sometimes people neglect their friends; well it's just the way people are, and you have to take the bad with the good. People have bad days when they blow up unfairly; well, bad days happen and a person can only be so patient. Life is busy, we all forget, we all make mistakes. We also can't expect everyone to tell the complete truth all the time.

Most of all, Extroverted Feelers learn who they are, who "I" is, by how they fit into the group. They can't stop paying attention to what people think of them. If they fit into a group, they feel good about themselves. If they don't fit into a group, they feel lonely, depressed and uncertain.

When they are in a group, they are always paying attention to the group's social order. They can easily identify who in the group has certain kinds of social power. Extroverted Feelers are usually aware of having an agenda of their own, trying to improve their standing in the group. They use their participation carefully, even when they're also just having fun. There are many ways to improve their standing by telling a joke or keeping silent, depending on the social dynamics of the moment, or by appearing loyal to one person or part of the group. People with strong Extroverted Feeling are aware of doing such things on purpose, but they also feel what they're doing sincerely. There is no essential clash between personal expression and social dynamics.

Clearly, peer pressure is a bigger factor, since it is real hardship for them to be different and not fit in. People who shift their habits and attitudes when they're around different people are Extroverted Feelers. If they are in a group of good people, the peer pressure is positive. Kids with Extroverted Feeling can start to get better grades if a group of good students accepts them. On the other side, Extroverted Feelers who are otherwise well-meaning can be drawn into acting badly by negative peer pressure. Acceptance can mean so much that they're willing to do things they normally would not do. This is especially true early in life or during very stressful periods when rejection and going it alone are too hard to face.

Even when an Extroverted Feeler is not trying to fit in with a group, she can have a hard time remaining detached from the feelings of others. If a group's mood shifts, the Extroverted Feeler's mood shifts too, even against her will. There is nothing she can do about it except go away from the people who are influencing her mood so much. It may be that her sense of self is so deeply influenced by emotions around her that she cannot truly remember who she is when bombarded with depression or anger from outside. Even one person's despondency can be enough to invade the Extroverted Feeler's mind.

People with Extroverted Feeling are usually cautious about putting themselves into stressful or depressing situations. On the other hand, they love being in groups with an energetic, positive mood. There are Extroverted Feelers who structure their work and schedule around spending time in positive, optimistic group moods because this helps them remain positive even when they're having personal problems. Working alone is often naturally stressful for dominant Extroverted Feelers. They tolerate it by linking their solitary work to group activities, like working alone to prepare for a team event.

Extroverted Feeling's attentiveness to other people is so natural that people with a strong tendency may not even notice that they've started to walk, dress, talk and think like their friends. They begin to like what their friends like until it's hard to remember a time when they liked something different. It's sincere, too. Perhaps an Extroverted Feeler could try to pretend to like something, but the feeling of "liking" just fits naturally with what other people like. A personal preference, like preferring classical music to pop, could stand up to the group but it would have to be very strong. If it's an average preference, it will take a back seat to whatever the group likes, at least until the Extroverted Feeler finds a group with other interests.

Extroverted Feeling decisions are made primarily based on what will make other people happy. Sometimes there is a self-sacrificing tone, if he has to give up what he wanted. But on the other side, it makes the Extroverted Feeler happy to be liked. Even giving up something he wanted to do, or giving away his favorite things, may ultimately make the Extroverted Feeler happier, since others will be grateful. If there's one thing he cannot stand, though, it's making a sacrifice and then finding that the others aren't grateful; they don't sacrifice back, they don't show how much they like him, or they undercut him in some way. It is very difficult for an Extroverted Feeler to forgive this kind of social ingratitude.

People with strong Extroverted Feeling face a problem when their friends want different things, forcing them to choose between pleasing one friend and another. Whose feelings matter most? The Extroverted Feeler's observations over the years have taught her how to calculate what the possible losses are. How easy would it be to make it up to one of the people later? Is one of them more forgiving? Is there any way to please both people at once, maybe by joking around or making fun of herself? Peacemaking is a very high value, and no expense is spared in lavishing smiles, hugs and attention on someone with whom the Extroverted Feeler wants to make peace.

Even if she can't do what the other person really wants, she will offer some kind of truce or peacemaking comment. Many Extroverted Feelers are reluctant to make direct apologies, since they are concerned that bringing the topic up will only make things worse. "The less said, the better; let sleeping lions lie." They are more likely to create a positive experience with the offended person without any reference to the past trouble.

Newspaper advice columns most often give Extroverted Feeling tips; I once read a column that advised a woman who had done something really wrong to her sister-in-law to just take her out for lunch and never refer to the quarrel. Don't apologize, don't discuss, just act like it never happened.

All Extroverted Feelers would understand that the lunch date was a tacit apology. It doesn't address who was wrong in the quarrel, it just says, "you matter to me, and I don't want to lose you as a friend." The actual quarrel matters much less to an Extroverted Feeler than its message of rejection. If the message of rejection is clearly taken back, then the topic of the argument can be ignored and forgotten. We're still friends; that's the outcome that matters.

Every relationship and every interaction is somehow "about" who the Extroverted Feeler is in the group. Because he does things with such care and deliberation, it can be very hard for the Extroverted Feeler not to take offense at others. The stronger Feeling is in his personality, the more true this is. He knows that if *he* had made that comment, he would have *known* it was hurtful. He would have chosen not to say it unless he had a strategic reason for wanting to put that person in her place. He would only have said it if he really wanted the other person to know how angry he was, maybe in front of other people to create shame. So when his friend makes such a comment and acts like it was an innocent mistake, the Extroverted Feeler can't believe it. The friend must have said it to make him look bad in front of their friends, or for some other strategic reason. Maybe she feels like he's been getting too much attention and wanted to divert attention to herself. Maybe she wanted to let him know that she knew his secret. It can't have been a naive mistake.

The Extroverted Feeler may begin with pragmatic reasoning to form a charitable understanding of a bad interaction. For a very good friend that he doesn't want to lose, he'll start by saying she was just having a bad day. What she said was hostile, but maybe the hostility was not aimed at himself. But if he doesn't get pretty quick confirmation that everything is okay between them, his offending friend will notice a very chilly silence. Invitations and compliments stop happening, increasing the pressure of the hint. He has put his friend on notice that if she doesn't make amends, she will drop off the friends-and-allies list.

This system works well when both friends have Extroverted Feeling. The Extroverted Feeler is demonstrating just how important the relationship was. If the friend didn't matter, the effort would not be worth it. He is hinting for the friend to do something to fix it. Two Extroverted Feelers who speak the same "language" will get it, and the person who said the wrong thing will make a tactful "lunch date" apology to show that the relationship is still important. Depending on how bad the mistake was, how publicly she embarrassed or hurt the other Extroverted Feeler, a brief apology might happen.

But it's important for them to remember that not everyone operates this way. If the friend doesn't have or understand Extroverted Feeling, the relationship may end without them knowing why. An alert and mature Extroverted Feeler can learn to handle the problem more openly at that point and allow his friend a chance to say, "Oh, no, I didn't mean any offense and I've been wondering why you seemed distant."

Extroverted Feelers usually display emotion easily. This is truest when Extroverted Feeling is a strong part of the personality, but even lesser Extroverted Feeling can make open emotion easier to show and receive. Feeling seems meant to be shared. Social hugs are not uncomfortable. Some Extroverted Feelers are very good with words of congratulations or condolences. On the negative side, some seem to blow up with anger when the feeling is not really very deep or serious, as long as there's no social price to pay. Emotion is wired to be on the outside, because what it means is on the outside.

On the other hand, purely personal emotion can be suppressed in a group. An Extroverted Feeler only shows her feelings when she wants to. How she appears in the group right now matters more than some unrelated personal pain or anger, unless she's completely overwhelmed. As long as possible, she will put on a "game face" and cover up what's inconvenient. Again, it can be hard for Extroverted Feelers to understand that not everyone has this ability. They perceive it as a skill that they've learned, and they want to encourage others to learn it. It isn't apparent that although they did learn how to manage their display of emotion, not everyone can learn this skill.

EXTROVERTED FEELING IN LITERATURE

Jane Austen presented many kinds of relationship styles. In *Sense and Sensibility* (1813), her character Mrs. Jennings is a chattering widow with Extroverted Feeling. Here she tries to show sympathy for a broken-hearted girl:

Mrs. Jennings came immediately to their room on her return, and without waiting to have her request of admittance answered, opened the door and walked in with a look of real concern. "How do you do, my dear?" said she in a voice of great compassion to Marianne, who turned away her face without attempting to answer. "How is she, Miss Dashwood? Poor thing! She looks very bad. No wonder. Aye, it is but too true. He is to be married very soon—a good for nothing fellow! I have no patience with him. Mrs. Taylor told me of it half an hour ago, and she was told of it by a particular friend of Miss Grey herself, else I am sure I should not have believed it; and I was almost ready to sink as it was. Well, said I, all I can say is if it is true he has used a young lady of my acquaintance abominably ill, and I wish with all my soul his wife may plague his heart out. And so I shall always say, my dear, you may depend on it..." She then went away, walking on tip-toe out of the room as if she supposed her young friend's affliction could be increased by noise.

Mrs. Jennings discusses what others in their social circles are saying, when she really intends sympathy just for the girl herself. Her strongest expression of disapproval for the man must be couched in terms of what she has said, and will say, to others. When she tries to be very quiet, she is acting out of her sense of shared emotion with the two girls in the room. These are all basic markers of Extroverted Feeling.

In George Eliot's *Middlemarch* (1872), Rosamond, the doctor's wife, advises her husband to think more pragmatically about how his behavior is making him lose patients in their small community.

"Why should you not have a good practice, Tertius? Mr. Peacock had. You should be more careful not to offend people, and you should send out medicines as the others do. I am sure you began well, and you got several good houses. It cannot answer to be eccentric; you should think what will be generally liked," said Rosamond.

The doctor is following his medical principles, probably using Extroverted Thinking. He is pragmatic about germs and fevers, but not about relationships as his wife is.

Extroverted Feeling is especially pragmatic in situations where conversation is about social power, not truth. In Alexander McCall Smith's *The No. 1 Ladies' Detective Agency*, set in Botswana, detective Mma Ramotswe often finds herself in verbal power struggles. In this passage, she is held up at a border crossing by an official who questions how a woman's passport can claim the profession of "detective."

"Many women are detectives," said Mma Ramotswe, with dignity. "Have you not read Agatha Christie?"

The clerk looked up at her and bristled. "Are you saying that I am not an educated man?" he growled. "Is that what you are saying? That I have not read this Mr. Christie?"

"I am not," said Mma Ramotswe. "You people are well educated and efficient. Only yesterday, when I was in your Minister's house, I said to him that I thought his immigration people were very polite and efficient. We had a good talk about it over supper."

The official froze. For a moment he looked uncertain, but then he reached for his rubber stamp and stamped the passport. "Thank you, Mma," he said. "You may go now."

Mma Ramotswe did not like lying, but sometimes it was necessary, particularly when faced with people who were promoted beyond their talents. An embroidering of the truth like that—she knew the Minister, even if only very distantly—sometimes gingered people up a bit, and it was often for their own good. Perhaps that particular official would think twice before he again decided to bully a woman for no good reason.[55]

Mma Ramotswe uses Extroverted Feeling to see that the conversation is not really about information, such as whether a woman can be a detective. Instead, she perceives that it's about the official feeling important in contrast to the dusty traveler in her small truck. She handles the problem not with information, but with a replying show of power.

Eudora Welty describes a Southern funeral in her novel, *The Optimist's Daughter*. Laurel, the dead man's daughter, finds the conversation distressing, while a family friend, Miss Adele, tries to help her see that the people are not really responding to her dead father.

"What's happening isn't real," Laurel said, low.

"The ending of a man's life on earth is very real indeed," Miss Adele said.

"But what people are saying."

"They're trying to say for a man that his life is over. Do you know a good way?"

Here, helpless in his own house among the people he'd known, and who'd known him, since the beginning, her father seemed to Laurel to have reached at this moment the danger point of his life. "Did you listen to their words?" she asked.

"They're being clumsy. Often because they were thinking of you."

"They said he was a humorist. And a crusader. And an angel on the face of the earth," Laurel said.

Miss Adele, looking into the fire, smiled. "It isn't easy for them, either. And they're being egged on a little bit, you know, Laurel, by the rivalry that's going on here in the room," she said. "After all, when the Chisoms walked in on us, they thought they had their side, too."

"Rivalry? With Father where he lies?"

"Yes, but people being what they are, Laurel."

"This is still his house. After all, they're still his guests. They're misrepresenting him—falsifying, that's what Mother would call it." Laurel might have been trying to testify for her father's sake now, as though he were in process of being put on trial instead of being viewed in his casket. "He never would have stood for any lies being told about him. Not at any time. Not ever."

"Yes he would," said Miss Adele. "If the truth might hurt the wrong person."[56]

Miss Adele understands (and probably has) Extroverted Feeling, so she can see how the funeral chatter isn't really about the facts of the dead man's life. It's about the tension and sensitivity between friends and family of the deceased, and also about rivalry between local

---

55: Alexander McCall Smith, *The No. 1 Ladies' Detective Agency* (New York: Anchor Books, 1998), 210.
56: Eudora Welty, *The Optimist's Daughter* (New York: Random House, 1972).

friends and out of town people. Their conversation should not be heard literally, but as symbolic of how they felt about the family.

INTROVERTED FEELING LIVES IN PAIRS

We enter again the zone of inborn knowledge, but this time it's about ideal relationships, not ideal logic and order. And as with Introverted Thinking, which persists in believing that rules "ought" to be followed even against the evidence of messy reality, Introverted Feeling can be very unrealistic. Its outlook does not feel like a personal viewpoint, because it is a template for how the world ought to be. As noted in Chapter 3, "Introverted" probably means that decisions about people are more closely connected with sacred values in the temporo-parietal junction. Making someone feel betrayed, alone or hurt taps into sacred values. Neuroscience can't yet tell us whether some people do have stronger relationship connections to moral decisions, but observation suggests that it's so.

There is a very ancient story that tells about the first humans who lived together in a sheltered garden. In the garden, it was perfectly safe and very beautiful. But after the humans sinned, they were put on the outside. The story says that they never got back into the garden, which was now guarded by an angel with a burning sword. On the outside of the garden, the world was wild and unsheltered. The garden was only a memory. They worked hard, but many things went wrong. Eventually, one son killed another son, and it was not many generations until other men were killing their enemies.

Ever since then, the story goes, people have treated each other badly. Good people and good deeds stand out because so much of what goes on is cruel or careless. We can never know what life would have been like in that perfect, sheltered garden, if those first humans had never sinned. How wonderfully they must have treated each other—how unselfish they were! But when we see or do a very kind, unselfish deed, we catch a glimpse of what might have been.

The story of the Garden of Eden captures the inborn, ideal world of Introverted Feeling. When Feeling is focused on this inner world, it seems to know how people ought to treat each other. It is as though the Introverted Feeler was born with a storybook that tells how relationships ought to be.

The cartoon (Fig. 4-2) shows how the Introverted Feeler doesn't need to look out into the messy real world to know about love. The inner book shows how we should love each other. This knowledge persists even when everyone around him treats each other very badly.

Introverted Feeling does not create the same attachment to a social group that Extroverted Feeling does. Introverted Feeling is also a way of taking care of relationships, because that is the purpose of Feeling. But in another echo of the Garden of Eden, the Introverted Feeler's relationships tend to be based on pairs: you and me. If an Introverted Feeler is in a group of friends, that group feels to her like many friendship pairs, all gathered together in one place.

The group relationship does not feel like it's a collective Us, and an Introverted Feeler rarely, if ever, feels her identity being drawn in or defined by the group. When people with Introverted Feeling must spend time in large groups, they usually lean on some other part of their personality to get by. Each friendship pair is felt deeply, so to draw on that well when the people are swirling around or passing by quickly would be too exhausting. Alternatively, if the Introverted Feeler can create a small space within the group (like off in a corner) and just relate to one person, then Feeling can operate in its comfortable depth.

Fig. 5-2

Although the Introverted Feeler's identity does not get drawn into a group, each relationship pair can be extremely important. Introverted Feelers tend to hold onto friends more tenaciously than Extroverted Feelers. It is a real sacrifice and loss to let a friend go; some of them will go to great lengths to maintain friendship with a person who is drifting away. There's no pragmatism, no sense of cost-benefit analysis. Even if this old friend is dragging him down, the Introverted Feeler wants to hold on.

Introverted Feeling can be a weak, less important part of daily personality, so that the person isn't constantly aware of her feelings. But when it's a strong, central part, her own feelings are very important because they alert the Introverted Feeler when an ideal has been violated. It isn't possible for someone with this system to feel good about something that seems wrong. Breaking a simple rule may not make them feel bad, but if they are mean to someone, or if someone else is mean (to anyone), their early warning system feelings will go off like a burglar alarm even before they have time to think about it.

Imagine that the Introverted Feeler has one video camera looking into the Garden of Eden, and another looking out at what's happening outside Eden. The "Eden Cam" always shows a perfect, untroubled world, but the reality camera usually doesn't match it: someone just did another selfish thing. When the views don't match, it creates uneasiness deep inside. The uneasy feeling might be fear, anger, sadness or some combination of them. It may take time to go find out what happened, but the Introverted Feeler knows that her own emotions are telling her that something is not ideal.

People with strong Introverted Feeling can be very empathetic and driven to help others. In an empathetic response, the Introverted Feeler takes the other person's pain into his own idealistic interior world and adopts the pains as his own, in imagination. This pain is unbearable in the Garden of Eden. If he tries to help, his action is prompted by violation of his inner harmony, not by what other people expect. He cannot bear not to take action, because the pain of suffering violates his ideals. Introverted Feelers are often drawn to charity work, but ironically, they may really struggle with the group dynamics of other helpers. They may expect a non-profit to step outside of its mission or break a by-law in order to meet a human need, and they're generally unsympathetic to leadership issues within the group.

When Introverted Feeling is a central part of personality, it can make the person look like he's preoccupied with his own feelings. In his mind, he is actually scanning and understanding the world, not his feelings. But in using the Introverted Feeling system, he has to pay close attention to how he feels, and he can't brush off those feelings. His feelings tell him about the world; they tell him if people are truthful or if he's living up to his own standards. They're the most important detection system.

If you tell this Introverted Feeler that feelings always lie and you can't trust them, he won't believe you. Worse, if he's young, insecure and impressionable, he will believe you. Then he will make some tragic mistakes because he doesn't have an alternative system for managing relationships. That was his only way: to listen to true feelings. He may have needed help learning to discern the truest of them, but it was a mistake to ignore them.

When the Introverted Feeler's ideals and inner feelings clash with what a group requires, the group nearly always loses. If a wife is in a group of women who all criticize their husbands, and she feels that she can't do this without really letting her husband down, she will just choose not to fit in. She may care a lot about being accepted in the group, but she can't pay the price. If she tries to say something critical about him just to fit in, she will be haunted by guilt. The group relationship is now doomed because it made her violate an ideal. Belonging to a group is never as strong a value as having inner peace with an idealistic nature.

In spite of their idealism about how well they should treat people, Introverted Feelers can become bitter and judgmental if they feel that others aren't living up to those ideals. That's the innate negativity of the Introverted function, which is scanning for danger and problems. The template for safety outlines perfect love, so anomalies like Extroverted Feeling's pragmatism can feel like danger signals. It can be very hard for Introverted Feelers to understand why others are willing to pay a price to fit in. It's even harder for them to understand that they should not always take group behavior seriously.

Introverted Feelers may not be good at editing their inner feelings around other people. They usually put a high value on interpersonal truth. When Introverted Feeling is a weaker part of personality but still operative, it may push someone to tell truths that will hurt the listener. As much as hurt feelings matter, the ideal of pure truth between friends or family matters more.

Ironically, even strong Introverted Feelers can seem emotionally cold. They can be the opposite of Extroverted Feelers in this way; they don't show emotion as easily, and sometimes they are less comfortable with social hugs. It isn't because they don't feel anything, but because group emotion can feel confusing or their personal emotion can feel deeply buried. Emotion is information about truth and the world, according to how inborn knowledge feels, so it's hard to process. Even when they are empathetic, taking someone else's sadness into their hearts, they can appear untouched. At the other extreme, Introverted Feelers can be much worse at not displaying inconvenient emotion. If something shocks or upsets an Introverted Feeler when he's in a group, he may have difficulty acting like nothing is wrong.

In love relationships, Introverted Feeling is usually romantic. Even when it's not a central part of personality, Introverted Feeling still loves a storybook moment. Family relationships can be idealized and romanticized, too. Although people with Introverted Feeling may not seem warm to strangers, they are very warm in the relationships where they can come closest to meeting their ideals, at home with their families.

At the deepest level, a person with strong Introverted Feeling has a sense of injury because real relationships are not ideal. Like the Introverted Thinker who judges the world for not being as orderly and logical as his ideal, the Introverted Feeler is disappointed in the world for not being more like a good story or the Garden of Eden.

Writing stories may be one of the ways that Introverted Feelers try to make the world right again. They know that bad things happen, but they want these bad events to have meaning, so they create narrators who can explain why things happen. Narrators can point out the good motives of people whose deeds are bad, so that it doesn't seem as bleak. And in writing the story, the Introverted Feeler can bring about the kind of rescue and redemption that real life so often fails to deliver. Miracles can happen, and people can find love. You don't need Introverted Feeling to love a happy ending, of course. But when stories end with a touch of the Garden of Eden, they are playing out the Introverted Feeler's deepest wish. Why can't real life be like stories? Why can't people just be kind and loving?

INTROVERTED FEELING IN LITERATURE

Jane Austen's *Pride and Prejudice* (1813) shows us how people with Introverted Feeling can be mistaken for not having feelings at all. Elizabeth's sister Jane did not appear to be in love, although she was, and Elizabeth must accept that others could not recognize Jane's true feelings:

[Mr. Darcy writes:] "Your sister I also watched.—Her look and manners were open, cheerful and engaging as ever, but without any symptom of peculiar regard, and I remained convinced from the evening's scrutiny that though she received his attentions with pleasure, she did not invite them by any participation of sentiment." [Elizabeth reflects:]... He declared himself to have been totally unsuspicious of her sister's attachment; and she could not help remembering what Charlotte's opinion had always been. Neither could she deny the justice of his description of Jane. She felt that Jane's feelings, though fervent, were little displayed, and that there was a constant complacency in her air and manner, not often united with great sensibility.

George Eliot's 1876 novel, *Daniel Deronda*, describes how people without Introverted Feeling can see its effects as eccentric and unpredictable.

Daniel had the stamp of rarity in a subdued fervor of sympathy, an activity of imagination on behalf of others, which did not show itself effusively, but was continually seen in acts of considerateness that struck his companions as moral eccentricity.

Another George Eliot character, Dorothea Brooke of *Middlemarch* (1872), acts out the way deep Introverted Feeling can try to reach out empathetically to another person.

"Trouble is so hard to bear, is it not? How can we live and think that anyone has trouble— piercing trouble—and we could help them, and never try?" Dorothea, completely swayed by the feeling that she was uttering, forgot everything but that she was speaking from out the heart of her

own trial to Rosamond's. The emotion had wrought itself more and more into her utterance, till the tone might have gone to one's very marrow, like a low cry from some suffering creature in the darkness. And she unconsciously laid her hand again on the little hand that she had pressed before. … The waves of her own sorrow, from out of which she was struggling to save another, rushed over Dorothea with conquering force.

Imagine the impossibility of responding in this way to many people at the same time, and you'll see why Introverted Feelers can struggle in groups. Dorothea becomes almost alone in her experience of Rosamond's distress. We can hear also, in the narrator's description, how the inner world of Feeling is almost cut off from the real outside world. Dorothea's emotion and sense of relationship have reality that doesn't derive from the visible world, reality that in some ways overrides the visible world.

In Charles Dickens' famous novel *A Tale of Two Cities* (1859), Sidney Carton explains why he has volunteered to assume someone else's identity in order to die. His Eden-like idealism about relationships carries him through his natural fear of death:

"I see a beautiful city and a brilliant people rising from this abyss, and, in their struggles to be truly free, in their triumphs and defeats, through long years to come, I see the evil of this time and of the previous time of which this is the natural birth, gradually making expiation for itself and wearing out. I see the lives for which I lay down my life, peaceful, useful, prosperous and happy, in that England which I shall see no more. I see Her with a child upon her bosom, who bears my name… and I hear him tell the child my story, with a tender and a faltering voice… It is a far, far better thing that I do, than I have ever done; it is a far, far better rest that I go to than I have ever known."

CHAPTER 6

Judging Functions in Balance

I T'S IMPORTANT TO REMEMBER THAT although the past two chapters talked about Thinking and Feeling as though each person could only exercise one of them, that isn't so. Every personality uses both Thinking and Feeling. We were only talking about them as separate elements, and now we'll start to look at how they work together.

Jung's rules of self-organizing apply to the Judging functions by pointing out two ways in which they could be balanced badly. First, they could have equal strength in one personality. Thinking and Feeling would be co-pilots with equal seniority, with neither one having more practice, efficiency and habit in the mind than the other. This would mean that decision-making dilemmas would often pit money vs. family, competition vs. friends, or strict rules vs. hurt feelings. Second, Thinking and Feeling could be locked in dilemma by being both Introverted or both Extroverted. If so, then the personality would be too focused on ideals and negativity, or too focused on amoral, pragmatic actions.

Both of these cases turn out to be uncommon in real human beings, because the living system really does self-organize toward efficiency. One of the Judging functions is usually stronger in neural connections at birth and by early childhood it has become the default, habitual mode. When this doesn't happen, it's a sign of severe, long-standing stress or even trauma. One of the Judging functions also tends to be more sympathetic to idealistic thinking; it is used less consciously and much less pragmatically.

We'll look first at how it affects personality for either Thinking or Feeling to be strongest, then at how Extroversion and Introversion fall into balance to create a working system of moral conscience.

THINKING OR FEELING AS DOMINANT IN PERSONALITY

As different as the Extroverted and Introverted modes are, both kinds of Thinking agree that logic, order and numbers matter more than human relationships and happiness. Both idealistic and pragmatic Thinkers agree that sometimes the right decision is going to make someone very unhappy. They can both become "hanging judges" who refuse to consider tears when making a judgment.

The two modes of Feeling also agree on elevating human relationships to the highest level of importance. No matter if they are idealistic or pragmatic about people, dominant Feelers pay far more attention to anything about people, compared to whatever they have to do with numbers, things, and stuff on paper. Both kinds of Feelers consider emotion to be an important way of knowing the world, rather than a distraction.

Men are typically thought of as Thinkers, women as Feelers. This is generally true; but the exceptions are large and important. We know the general percentages because for the 3rd edition of the *Myers-Briggs Type Indicator Manual*, they surveyed a national sample of 3000 adults. The people were considered as carefully as possible for racial, sex and age balance (to look just like the larger population). In the MBTI survey, 56.5% of the men's personalities were dominantly Thinking. A fairly large group of men, 43.5%, were a dominantly Feeling type. 57 to 43 isn't equal, but it's not extremely lopsided, either; it turns out that a lot of men are Feelers. On the other hand, the women's personalities registered at 75.5% for Feelers, and only 24.5% for Thinkers.[57] Women who go mostly by Thinking are a clear minority, only one in four. So while it isn't true that the Thinking/Feeling difference is by sex, it's clear why people often think it is, based on how very common it is to meet Thinking men and Feeling women.

Sometimes it's very easy to tell if someone is dominantly Thinking or Feeling, and usually we have strong opinions about identifying our own decision system. Most people can quickly say, "Yes, that's me, I'm a Thinker." Not always; as with anything about human personality, there are people who feel they are a blend that isn't easy to sort out.

It helps if the Thinker or Feeler has gone into a line of work that reinforces the dominant function. In those cases, it's pretty obvious: the Feeling woman who works in Human Resources, the Thinking man who's a licensed electrician; the Feeling man who teaches 5th grade, the Thinking woman who teaches high school science. When outside life has reinforced the dominant function, the Thinker or Feeler may live so much in that mode that it seems to be all they've got: the Thinker is logical, unemotional, and unsympathetic; the Feeler is emotional, sympathetic and relational. But it isn't always so clear, in cases where someone's work is misleading about personality type. The true guide is what the person is really good at, not what they're paid to do.

When someone in a Thinking line of work is unusually good with people, ask yourself: is this a dominant Feeler who is good enough at Thinking work to succeed in it? Similarly, if

57: Isabel Briggs Myers, Mary H. McCaulley, Naomi L. Quenk, and Allen L. Hammer. *MBTI® Manual, A Guide to the Development and Use of the Myers-Briggs Type Indicator*, 3rd edition (Mountain View, CA: CPP, 2003), 156-158.

someone who's working mainly with people seems to make lots of mistakes, ask: what if I'm looking at a Thinker whose work forces him or her to use non-dominant skills?

There's a huge advantage when people can succeed in the "wrong" line of work, so the phenomenon is not rare. Imagine a scientific laboratory, and everyone working there is a dominant Thinker. Now they hire a man or woman who's actually a Feeler, but who was really good at math and chose to go into lab science. The Feeler is out of place, but in a good way. His skills with people benefit everyone. The lab scientists start working together as a team better, though they're not sure why. They annoy each other less. Everyone is smiling a bit more. They sense that the Feeler is different, and they may say things like, "He's too nice to be a chemical engineer." The Feeler often finds himself in line for promotion because nobody else has these skills.

Now imagine a kindergarten where all of the teachers have been Feelers for the last 45 years. They hire a Thinker who wants to get teaching experience for a few years before going back to graduate school. The Thinker has read a lot of studies about brain development in 5 year olds and eventually hopes to become a developmental pediatrician or research psychologist. About halfway through the year at a staff meeting, the Thinker points out a problem in the kindergarten classes that everyone assumed was just "the way things are." It's always been that way. But to the Thinker, it's clear that there's a solution. They talk it over and agree to try. By the time the Thinker leaves for the next stage of career, the kindergarten is using a new approach.

So it's very possible to find dominant Thinkers in predictable lines of Thinking work, but also in Feeling work, and the other way around. The question to ask yourself is not what sort of work he or she does, but how the work is handled. Is your doctor's secretary managing the office on the basis of relationships with others or strict order and rules? Is the doctor himself more interested in the science of what he's doing or in making eye contact with his patients as people? Is the nurse better at efficiently checking off tasks or relating to a nervous patient? Which is carrying the main burden, logic or relationship?

Most people have used their dominant function so much for all of their lives that it's quickly identified as being who they are. They've become particularly good at using it. It's automatic, but it's also highly developed through much practice and experience. Dominant Thinkers are good at their type of Thinking; Feelers are good at their type of Feeling.

Being good at Thinking or Feeling means having it fully integrated with all of life and the rest of personality. There are problems inherent in both ways of being. Thinking is competitive, which can provoke anxiety about success. Feeling can become burned out by caring so much about other people. If your dominant function is fully integrated, you've learned ways to manage and limit these built-in problems. We usually start to meet the problems in childhood situations, and ideally we begin to learn then what helps us cope. How do we know our limits? By occasionally pushing past them, getting hurt, and needing to pull back.

Both functions can cause problems with the outside world, too. Thinkers may be abrasive to other people, which can make it harder for them to "win" at what they're doing. As they go through life, most Thinkers learn to spot danger signs and change their strategies, perhaps drawing from their lesser abilities with Feeling to mend fences. Feeling can make tasks like hiring and firing difficult, and it may also contribute to a low frustration tolerance with competitive tasks. Learning to be good at your type of Feeling means anticipating these problems, forming teams with others who are better at Thinking or training yourself to tap into your lesser Thinking abilities, setting aside relationships concerns.

Children and teenagers are best seen as still learning, but people over 30 usually know how to manage their dominant function well. But there's a darker side of this optimistic truth. Remember that each of us has both Thinking and Feeling. The function that is more favored becomes mature and integrated, while the less used one remains in an almost childish state.

This is especially true when the stronger function is very, very skilled. The more dominant it is, the more it has probably sucked all the air out of the room for the less favored mode. A very strong Thinker (either Extroverted or Introverted) still has a Feeling function to take care of relationships, but too often, Feeling hasn't had much practice. It's the same with Feelers who are very strong in people skills. They use their social smarts to succeed and they gravitate to people work. Thinking's logic and hard decisions about numbers may remain rusty and unpracticed.

The unfavored function is like a left hand (or a right hand, if you're a lefty). You can use it, but it's clumsy. It feels much better to switch back. The neurological pathways have all been laid down by habit and success to favor the other mode. The neural paths for the "wrong" function are literally fewer, weaker and less connected to other parts of the brain.

People with very dominant, strong Feeling skills may not be aware that their Thinking pathways are weak, because they often fall into using a kind of fake Thinking. Their opinions and choices are actually determined by Feeling, so their minds are already made up when they consider the logic. Thinking can be used to create a justification of what Feeling already chose. Just as a lawyer learns to defend any side of a case, a Feeler's logic learns to find ways to make any Feeling decision sound logical. The logic isn't always completely wrong, either. The problem is that it is not as complex as truly skilled logic, and it hasn't usually looked at all the facts, preferring the ones that support the Feeling decision. Since logic isn't a key function, to the Feeler this seems good enough; their Thinking skill set is relatively childish and has low standards.

The difference between true Thinking and the kind of Thinking that is only a cover for Feeling usually only appears in an argument. What happens when someone says, "No, I think you're wrong, and you're missing some facts. You're making a logical mistake, too"? A true Thinker generally responds by listening and asking questions, even if he still thinks he's right. Logic and facts matter, and if there's a mistake, he wants to know about it.

But a Feeler who is using a veneer of Thinking usually gets very upset when challenged. The Feeler doesn't want to have the logical justification stripped away, because the heart isn't going to change its mind. The logical reason isn't actually the basis for the decision at all. The real basis has to do with the much more important values of human importance, emotion and relationship success. Removing the logical cover feels like an attack.

The Feeler whose Thinking gets challenged reacts emotionally, not logically. If he or she tries to maintain the logical argument, it may sound increasingly childish. At the end, the Feeler may be reduced to crying out, "I don't care! You're just confusing things!" That's the last tip off, if it wasn't clear before: the decision was made with Feeling values, and logic isn't really part of it at all.

On the other side, people with very strong Thinking skills usually have much less mature Feeling skills. Since life has rewarded their brains for good problem-solving and fact-gathering, it's rare that they've really had to solve any complicated human relationship issues. Most of the time, they put these issues off, hoping the relationship problems will just go away.

When Thinkers experience their own emotion, it's often felt as disruptive; it clouds logic and makes it impossible to make decisions. By adulthood, most Thinkers have tried to learn ways to suppress emotion so that they aren't impaired very often. They certainly do not trust emotion; they've learned that feelings only lead to blindness and mistakes. They hope that other people will do the same, and they often suggest it. They tell people to calm down, or they suggest that we just sit down and think things out calmly.

In spite of trying to stay calm, emotion may finally overwhelm a Thinker. When this happens, he or she usually loses control for a while. Since Thinking women have hormonal factors that can make them emotional, they may suffer this way more than Thinking men. But for either sex, the process is the same: their Thinking gets blocked by a wave of emotion, and they don't have the skills to manage it. They may have meltdowns, outbursts, or even tantrums. They feel helpless and may act like children, saying things they'll later regret.

Many people believe that it's very hard for a dominant Thinker and a dominant Feeler to make decisions together peacefully. Some books suggest that marriages work better when Thinkers and Feelers only marry others like themselves. That way, they argue, both spouses will prefer logic or relationships, and they are more likely to agree.

There are two problems with this idea. First, if married people see the world in just the same way, they may have the same blind spots too. It may not trouble them personally until their joint blind spot causes a serious life problem. Marriage isn't only about getting along with each other, it's also about being a team to confront problems. Some problems are big enough to sink them both into bankruptcy or tragedy; these are often the very same problems that someone with a different blind spot would have prevented. Survival is worth a few arguments.

Second, the idea that two Thinkers or Feelers are automatically the same overlooks the difference between Extroverted and Introverted modes. An idealistic approach and a pragmatic approach can be as different as Thinking and Feeling themselves. Logic and emotion may sometimes reach the same conclusion, but idealism and pragmatism rarely do. Some Thinkers and Feelers may be better able to cooperate than people who look the same on paper, but who are actually oriented to idealism in a completely different way. It's easier to compare arguments than to get locked into a core-belief division over whether this is, or is not, the moment to be pragmatic or idealistic.

IDEALISM AND PRAGMATISM
BALANCED IN CONSCIENCE

This brings us to the second way that the Judging functions could be caught in a dilemma. Personality works most efficiently when one Judging function is rooted in

Introverted idealism and the other in Extroverted pragmatism. It usually works out this way in real people, since self-organizing is such a basic principle. Of course, as always in real people, it may or may not be clear, consistent or visible. In addition to our original neural organization, we often use patterns and beliefs we learned from others.

Let's look first at why it's not efficient to have two idealistic or two pragmatic Judging functions. In the cartoon below, the stick figures represent these two scenarios. In the figure on the left, there are two inborn books of idealistic morality. One book has ideal logic and order, while the other has ideal love and human relationship. In the figure on the right, all of the Judging functions are placed outside, separate from the inner person. This stick figure has little or no inborn sense of how things ought to be. If people ignore rules, cheat on numbers, or treat each other callously, that's all he knows as reality.

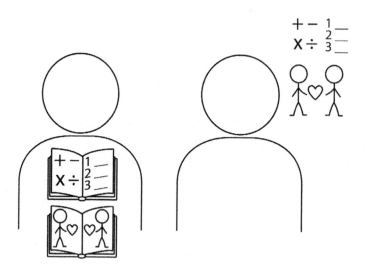

Fig. 6-1

The double-introvert can hardly get through her day because she faces so many dilemmas. She must be on time, but she must not rush or cut off any relationship exchanges in order to be on time; being on time is ideal for Thinking, but giving people as much time as they need is ideal for Feeling. She must be absolutely truthful and unfailingly kind, in order to meet both idealistic standards. There is nothing in her life that can be handled with an "oh well, just move on" attitude, because all decisions must be ideal. The stakes are always high.

The double-extrovert, on the other hand, is not internally focused at all. He's doing whatever works best and gets him ahead. His dilemmas are of a different nature: sometimes it's not possible to be first in a social group and also first in a logical, number-oriented task. One attempt takes time and energy away from the other; it's not easy to become the best at something and *also* make your friends happy. Worse, without an internal moral sense of danger, he chooses the wrong moment to be careless about rules and finds himself arrested. Or he chooses the wrong relationship to sacrifice for popularity and suddenly nobody trusts him. He didn't notice that the stakes were higher than they appeared.

There are definitely real people who have these imbalanced priorities, and we usually notice that they're struggling. Someone without any pragmatic "just get it done" mode becomes neurotic and gradually stops taking risks or even leaving the house. Someone without any idealistic root of "I must because I should" behavior comes off as psychopathic; he will eventually be excluded from society, because his unpredictable patterns of offending and cheating make him a dangerous friend.

The brain's principles of efficiency ensure that in most people, the Judging functions settle into a pattern of complementary action. In the cartoon below, either Thinking or Feeling is Introverted, while the other is Extroverted.

Fig. 6-2

To the left, the figure has an inner book of logic that reminds him of how the world ought to be ordered and run; his inner world says, "I must do this; I could never do that." His identity is based in knowing these rules of moral order. But when he wants to know how to treat other people, he looks outside himself. As long as he doesn't really violate a rule, he can treat people whatever way works best, focusing on outcomes.

To the right, the figure has an inner book about love; it tells her how people really ought to treat each other and insists that her identity depends on treating people that way. But by contrast, she looks to the outside world to understand rules and logic. As long as she doesn't hurt people in a way her inner book would condemn, she can do whatever works, including breaking some rules.

Conscience needs both a red light and a green light, a way to say "yes" and another to say "no." The Introverted functions both emphasize sacred values, personal responsibility, identity and danger. They are the half of conscience that says "no" most strongly. The Extroverted functions, on the other hand, both emphasize outcomes, flexibility, and circumstances. We tend to think of conscience as only the "no" side, but we shouldn't overlook the "yes" voice of conscience. What we do not permit is balanced by what we do; what we feel guilty about is balanced by what we don't.

Guilt is a deterrent among the emotions; its purpose is to penalize actions that might lead to trouble later. It's a warning flag. Introverted Thinking and Feeling are both templates of danger. They tell us what the world should be like, so that we can recognize when something has gone wrong. Guilt signals that we're on the wrong side of archetypal safety lines.

Introverted Thinking and Introverted Feeling are connected to very different sorts of archetypal ideals. Even in its idealistic moral form, Thinking never strays far from numbers. There are definitely problems and dangers that can be defined by numbers: you're late. You're under age. You don't have enough money. You have too many items. Your army is outnumbered. Your portion is unfair. Formal rules are related to numbers, as they come in lists and are often numbered. Logic and numbers go together, and rules are part of logic. Every rule is an if-then statement: if you do this, you will be arrested and charged. If you don't register in advance, you won't get in. There are also transcendent moral rules: do not lie; do not steal; do not cheat. (Moral rules are even summarized in the famous Ten Commandments, another number.) If you break these rules, you will be outside the safe bounds of moral order. Introverted Thinking seeks safety by making sure that numbers and moral logic are satisfied.

Introverted Feeling's archetypal ideas are completely the opposite; they can't be quantified at all. They are more like paradigms of behavior, like little dioramas showing how things ought to be. Here is a mother who never stops loving her child, no matter what happens. Here is a pair of lovers who tell each other only the truth. Here are friends who never let each other down. Here is warm love that forgives all. Here is love that never does any harm. These paradigms represent complete safety in perfect love.

Introverted Feeling's template of safety and danger suggests that straying from the paradigm will bring harm. A mother allows her child's problem to block love for even a short time, which brings harm to the family. One of the lovers tells a lie, which breaks the relationship and casts both into loneliness and possible harm. A friend lets the other down, and not only does this cause harm, but the loss of relationship permits further harm that they can't even see yet. To Introverted Feeling, it even feels dangerous not to forgive. Maintaining anger against someone is a low-level state of war. That's the opposite of perfect love, wherein lies safety.

When Introverted Thinking is the root of conscience, facts are clear and unheated by emotion. This thing is wrong because it violates order, logic, law or numbers. I call this type of conscience "cool," to refer to the level-headed, unemotional quality of its judgments. When Introverted Feeling is the root of conscience, everything can be reduced to some kind of fear about falling short of perfect love. It's "warm," because it wants to avoid the loss of the warm, safe, good feeling of mutual love.

Cool conscience uses Thinking for its idealistic, danger-scanning half, so Feeling is the Extroverted, pragmatic, risk-taking half. Relationships may be very important to someone with cool conscience, but they don't trigger the really deep sense of danger that rule-breaking does. Cool conscience is less likely to feel actively guilty about letting down a friend, if letting the friend down was a necessary part of upholding logic, numbers and rules. If keeping the friend meant breaking logic or rules, the guilt caused by Introverted Thinking would spoil any joy in the friendship. Maintaining rules at the expense of a relationship would cause regret, but not real guilt. Lasting guilt goes with violating the template of safety and danger.

Warm conscience, on the other hand, uses Feeling for its idealistic, danger-scanning half. Thinking is the Extroverted, pragmatic half that evaluates outcome, not moral danger. Warm conscience is focused on sometimes small, brief violations of love, friendship, family and loyalty. Guilt over letting a friend down would usually outweigh considerations of logic, numbers or rules. The stronger Introverted Feeling is in the personality, the more it would cause a stab of pain at every memory of that look in the friend's eyes, that look that said "you didn't stand by me."

Both kinds of conscience have in common an important factor: the template of safety and danger becomes part of identity. There are many times when either cool or warm conscience says "no" because we feel internally that "I'm not the sort of person who does such a thing." Cool consciences include rules about behavior, not just numbers; they may frame it as a "code of conduct." Warm consciences do care about following most rules, although they care less about the number ones; following rules can be part of identity, thus part of relationships.

We start with the theoretical to make things plain, but in human beings, they aren't neatly divided. Conscience of both kinds imposes the rules we all agree on, simply because we all agree, and says, "I'm not the sort of person" who would be mean, abandon the sick, keep a lost wallet, and so on. The offense of doing something felt as wrong is against myself. We agree on what's wrong more often than not, so we all hew to the same general sense of morality, with either type of conscience.

That's one reason that it can be hard to identify clearly which kind of conscience is working in a personality. Most situations don't ask us to balance a friend against, say, a sum of stolen money. These things do happen, but not to most of us, not most of the time. In a normal, peaceful society, relationships and rules don't usually conflict. We can determine what's right without having to choose. Cool conscience and warm conscience agree that you should tell the truth, pay your bills, and be kind. In daily situations, we do sometimes have to choose which to put first, a relationship or a number, but it's usually a small matter of spending a little more or less, or being on time. We can irritate each other by choosing differently, but not much more. There are times when cool and warm split off sharply, and there are times when the stakes are high, but they should be infrequent.

Second, our working consciences are usually not simply the neural balance that's been struck between brain regions. We're the product of family, experiences and belief systems, too. In many daily situations, we don't even stop to consult our true conscience, because we don't need to. There's a social expectation of what we're going to do, and we know it. Not living up to expected behavior may make us feel guilty, but it's usually a bit different. We may feel guilty because of internalizing the conscience of one of our parents, for example.

Third, it's often hard to see what the true conscience orientation is, partly because of family influence, but also because there are some equally strong, separate, forces in personality. In Chapters 7 through 9, we'll look at how Perceiving can also provide a template of safety and danger. Since routine daily life doesn't force many new situations or dilemmas on us, we can handle most decisions without actually consulting right and wrong. If society doesn't tell us what to do, the Perceiving part of personality may guide us. In some personality balances, Introverted Thinking or Feeling has a prominent role and we're quickly made aware of just how the personality handles questions of guilt. But in others, it may take an unusually hard or public decision for us to see moral conscience in action.

Cool conscience is not the same as using Thinking for a dominant part of personality, nor is warm conscience the same as having dominant Feeling. Personality can have cool conscience rooted in Thinking, but at the same time, its use of Extroverted Feeling may be much more active and observable. We shouldn't identify a Thinking conscience with being unsociable or shy; in fact, Extroverted Feeling might be the largest slice of a cool conscience personality type. Cool conscience operates in the background, setting limits on Feeling's optimistic social risk-taking. Where Feeling, on its own, just wants to do what gets the best social outcome, Introverted Thinking is saying "no" to some things. No, you can't lie. No, you can't move ahead in line. No, you can't make that cruel remark. Those things "would just be wrong," it concludes.

Of course, the opposite is true also: personality with warm conscience may be visibly, noticeably active in its use of amoral, pragmatic, optimistic Thinking. We may not feel any emotional "warmth," or rarely, in this personality where warm conscience is setting the limits. But it's operating in the background, by setting limits. Extroverted Thinking on its own just wants to win, and it's willing to break some rules if there won't be a heavy penalty. Feeling imposes the limits by saying "no." No, you can't be unfair to an old friend. No, you can't give your sister the smaller piece. No, you can't lie to someone who has been truthful to you.

Warm and cool conscience may be most visible when people have to make decisions about enforcing rules on other people. Rule enforcement comes along in family situations, as well as in wider society. In family situations, warm conscience has a tendency to look at how punishment will affect the emotional tenor of relationships. Cool conscience is concerned mainly, or only, with the actual rule broken and its stated punishment.

A parent with warm conscience is more likely to ease back on punishment if he or she feels that the child has come to some real understanding of right and wrong, probably through conversation. A parent with cool conscience is more likely to believe that the child will only learn from cause and effect, so the cause (wrong) must be followed by effect (punishment) regardless of conversation. Cool conscience parents are much less likely to feel sorry for a child who's been grounded or stripped of electronic toys, because cool moral decisions are less tied to emotion. Warm conscience parents may follow through with a punishment but find some way to soften the impact on relationship, such as keeping the child from being isolated during the punishment. (I once kept my child company at a school detention; he served the detention and filled out math worksheets as the teacher directed, but he was not alone.)

People aren't so simple that we can say that enforcing punishment is always a marker for conscience rooted in Thinking, because there are always other reasons. But at base, it's a good sign to watch for, if you're trying to understand someone's personality balance. It may also be one of the ways their personality comes out in public, when they're commenting on whether someone ought to be punished by a court. Introverted Thinking says that if a rule is broken, the punishment should be levied precisely as according to law, without looking at circumstances. Introverted Feeling feels that the purpose of law is to make people's lives better, so if a punishment makes someone's life worse, perhaps it's better not to enforce it strictly.

Juries may sometimes be visibly split by warm and cool conscience patterns. When a jury considers how to judge and sentence a crime, the crime is usually long past. If it's a murder, the victim has been dead for a few years, while the defendant is still very much alive. If the defendant expresses remorse, warm consciences are likely to listen and care, while cool consciences are more likely to think "that's nice, but the fact of the crime does not change." If it's a lesser charge, such as burglary, assault or drunk driving, warm consciences on a jury are probably even more open to considering how hard life has been for the defendant and his family. Jurymen with warm conscience may find it difficult to convict someone of non-violent crime like fraud, when years spent in a dangerous prison seem harsher than the original crime.

It would again be too simplistic to say that warm conscience, rooted in Introverted Feeling, is always more lax or forgiving. Rather, what Introverted Feeling considers dangerous and unforgivable is not the same as what Introverted Thinking does. Consider a boyfriend-girlfriend relationship. Cool conscience is most attentive to things that can have numbers attached to them: birthdays, cost of gifts, being late, number of hours spent, number of events attended, fairness of time spent with extended family, and outcomes achieved. In a quarrel, cool conscience usually defends itself with quantifiable things: "After all I've spent on you!" or "You don't even care that I stayed up all night working on this!" "All those times you were late and I didn't say a word!" "How many holidays do we spend with your family, compared to mine?" as well as the classic, "Haven't we been through this before?"

Warm conscience is most attentive to things that can't be quantified. A warm conscience person may forget and overlook numerical issues like special dates, costs, and number of hours, but even small violations to its paradigm of real love can have the impact of a meteor. Warm conscience argues about things like, "Why did you just stand there when your brother made fun of me?" or "I don't believe you really understand why this bothers me." It asks, "Don't you see what this could lead to, if we don't fix it?" and "Couldn't you see how hurt I was?" To cool conscience, a one-time event may seem small because it only happened once, but to warm conscience, it is a worrisome wrong paradigm that could lead to serious relationship damage.

Warm and cool conscience may be very visible during any period when a relationship must be saved or ended. Of course, divorce is the most serious relationship break, since it has an impact on children, extended family, property and the future, in addition to the feelings of the husband and wife. Divorce is such a complicated issue, since it also brings in family history, belief systems and mental states like depression. But as a general rule, cool conscience sees marriage as a promise that must be kept and resists divorce across the board. Warm conscience tends to look at the value of the relationship and the others attached to it, such as with children. Warm conscience takes stock of how far from the perfect paradigm of love the couple has strayed and how much damage can be expected if this same hurtful paradigm continues into the future. Cool conscience looks for a quantifiable event as a reason to divorce, so that its weight can be set against the original vow, in the balance scales of justice.

Divorce is made more complicated by its network of beliefs and values inherited from parents and grandparents. Most people don't feel like free, independent agents when choosing whether to stay or leave. There are often strong conscience statements handed down in the family. They're usually cool conscience ones about not breaking a vow, but occasionally there's a family that goes the other way, handing down a warm conscience dictum that nobody should be trapped in misery.

Divorce is often the event that triggers final emotional separation from parents, even among older adults who literally moved away many years ago. It takes a crisis with profound long-term consequences to lay bare the difference between learned rules of conscience and innate ones. A parent's conscience style influences his or her children deeply, perhaps even more deeply when it's the opposite of the child's innate conscience orientation. It's good for a child to hear a moral argument that isn't innate in her own mind. At the same time, dilemmas in adult life may be harder to solve if the parent's "voice" goes against the grown child's natural personality balance. Sometimes the parental "voice" is intrusive and causes shame and conflict. Especially for people under 30, the "parental voice" sounds like their own inner voice. They may have deeply conflicting views of what's right to do. It can feel like both Feeling and Thinking are Introverted, but except in rare cases, the real problem is a conflict between inborn and learned conscience, between the parental voice and your own.

Typically, it takes time and some especially painful dilemmas to begin to resolve which voice is really your own. The key is that inborn conscience is integrated into your personality in many ways, not just in terms of the dilemma at hand. When you follow a conscience dictum that isn't really integrated into the way you function, the results may be uncomfortable because they force you to do things you're not very good at. It just won't work out well, even if "everyone" thought it was the best (or obviously "right") decision. If you decide against your inborn nature, you may also feel angry about the decision you felt you had to make, because the rest of your personality is pushing back.

CONSCIENCE IN COMMUNITIES

Parental voices are not the only outside influences on conscience. As children and also as adults, we're surrounded by community beliefs shaped by conscience. Usually, the prevailing conscience of a community follows the warm or cool pattern. It's possible that these patterns are even clearer in groups than in individuals. Individual people are often inconsistent, sometimes in merciful ways. Groups often push consistency to its limits; if they exclude a class of people, they make no exceptions. People hear each other speaking about right and wrong, reinforcing shared beliefs until some tenet seems universal and unchallenged.

We arrive in young adulthood with a blend of personal, inborn conscience and the conscience style that prevailed in our families. As we leave home, work, and vote, we are influenced by community conscience as well. When life is easy and there are no dilemmas, there's probably no conflict between inborn and learned conscience. As with the parental voice of conscience, we only pull away from community ideas of right and wrong when a dilemma or crisis forces us. But there's often a gentle, chronic fraying inside when some persistent inner voice questions social judgments of right and wrong.

We can see community conscience patterns in organized religion, civil society, and political culture. Religion may be the clearest example, since moral teaching is a major purpose. I can speak about Christian churches from personal observation, and I believe that since conscience styles come less from specific doctrine than from human nature, the same tendencies are true of other religious groups.

Traditional churches strongly emphasize and instill the principles of cool conscience, for two reasons. First, church teaching is based in the Ten Commandments and usually pushes back against the secular world. Churches emphasize that when life seems chaotic, that's when it's most important to remember objective right and wrong. Most Sunday School lessons and sermons stress the values of Introverted Thinking, reminding people that while doing what's right they may lose friends. They are usually very concerned about peer pressure and modern tolerance of sin. The message is very clear that moral rules matter more than relationships.

At the same time, churches are social groups. As the other half of cool conscience, Extroverted Feeling is best at handling the needs of a group of people, not as individuals perhaps, but as a group. There is a lot of organized sociability, with many opportunities for people to smile, hug and share dinners. Adults make friends by helping run programs for children and special occasions, as well as by attending events for men or women. Extroverted Feeling naturally organizes people by age, sex, leadership rank, and talents. Pretty much any large group falls into these patterns, so the people who are interested in leadership usually have Extroverted Feeling. So cool consciences nearly always form the leadership of most traditional churches.

As an alternative, there are two patterns of warm conscience that churches can be organized around. Warm conscience values personal relationships, and these are hard to maintain in a large group. So one pattern keeps the church structured around smaller groups, while the other emphasizes charitable works. In the small-group pattern, there's usually doctrinal focus on relationships, self-development, and emotionally fervent belief. While traditional moral teaching is believed and taught, it's not emphasized as much as one's "personal walk with God." In the charitable-works pattern, the church's role in the world is to develop small ministries to the poor. They collect clothing for shelters or run a food pantry, usually maintaining a face to face presence with the poor instead of just donating to the United Way (though they may do this too). In these churches, traditional moral teaching may be explicitly downgraded in importance, by comparison with being helpful and accepting to your fellow man.

Some readers may feel strongly that one or the other of these models, warm or cool, is the right one, either because of natural conscience agreement or because it's what they are culturally part of. I just want to point out the benefits and disadvantages of each one. The cool conscience model is good at providing a firm moral structure for many people who benefit by belonging to a community where some disorderly or harmful behavior is truly not tolerated. Alcoholics who want to stay away from drinking may flourish in such churches, and these churches are also good at supporting people in a resolution to stay married even when they're somewhat unhappy. Maintaining such standards is very good for individuals and for the community; these churches are a big part of rural and small town communities.

As a drawback, people with warm consciences may find themselves in personal dilemmas that they can't share, since their emotional distress is unlikely to be understood by cool conscience culture and leadership. People who break rules often lose relationships in the church very fast, because the culture makes it so clear that moral rules are more important than individual relationships. Members are discouraged from friendships with rule-breakers. Fundamentalist churches, which are always on the cool conscience model, can leave misfits feeling terribly lonely and unhappy.

In the warm conscience church model, clearly much charitable and emotional benefit can be found. These groups tend to be warmly inclusive, which can also be very helpful to people struggling with problems like alcoholism or an unhappy marriage. There is a lot of emphasis on emotional healing. Both the charitable model and the small group/relationship model churches often have support groups specifically to give emotional help to people in difficult situations. These groups are usually open to non-members and sometimes the groups include ministries to marginalized people like immigrants, transgendered people or the mentally ill.

As a drawback, of course these groups may be uncomfortable to people with natural cool conscience, who feel that their innate values don't matter. And when the leadership tends to draw people with warm consciences, several things can go wrong. Without some leaders who have Extroverted Feeling, there may be nobody who can detect and solve a serious group-dynamics problem that's brewing. Since Extroverted Thinking, which is pragmatic about both morals and numbers, is the other half of warm conscience, there may be risk for financial mismanagement. De-emphasizing traditional moral teaching for emotional support can also permit moral slips that finally cross lines even for these nonjudgmental groups. So while cool conscience churches run the risk of alienating and chilling people who don't fit in, warm conscience ones may run the risk of sudden scandal.

Secular, civic culture is another influence on conscience. It, too, can take on the general tone of either warm or cool conscience. In a pluralistic society, we usually hear arguments from both sides, but in smaller parts of society, not so much. The cultures of small nations, states, cities and regions may carry a basic bias. People are usually quite aware whether they are at odds with cultural conscience or not.

As an example of conscience on a national scale, Japanese culture, which puts such emphasis on personal honor and shame, seems to be passing on Introverted Thinking values. Failure to achieve a goal is shameful; there isn't another way that would have been equally right, as Extroverted Thinking might have suggested. As in traditional religion, the precepts of cool conscience are institutionalized and just presumed to be correct. It might be very uncomfortable to be born into Japanese culture with a natural tendency to warm conscience. As they say, "the nail that sticks out will get hammered down." People who choose to break social rules in favor of friendship may pay a high price.

By contrast, the culture of Nepal seems to lean toward Introverted Feeling values. The people are known for gentleness, good will, and tolerance.[58] We know that not everyone in Nepal is truly kind, because it's not possible that any group of human beings are all gentle and kind. The majority culture, though, seems to put pressure on people to behave as though they have warm consciences. It could be a difficult experience to have a cool conscience that sometimes balks at tolerance or feels that compassion isn't merited.

The examples of Japan and Nepal involve generalizing in a way that perhaps can't be done with any accuracy. Please read them as illustrations of an idea, not as statements of fact about these countries. The idea is that culture can reinforce some conscience principles more than others, and that being out of sync is always going to be uncomfortable or worse.

American culture is very hard to see in a unified way, because it is so large, sprawling, and decentralized. At this time it is probably, on balance, more oriented to warm conscience. That may not have been true at times in the past. It's likely that during times of rapid change and immigration, we lean toward warm conscience so that we can accept and tolerate as much as possible. American business culture may also encourage Extroverted Thinking, which is the pragmatic, get-it-done side of warm conscience.

Small communities where relationships and businesses are all within the same network may be able to uphold strict social order and honor-based rules. So while the general American culture is mostly biased to warm conscience, smaller ethnic cultures may be biased in the opposite way. It would be possible to be a person with cool conscience, in a family with more warm conscience habits, in an ethnic community or church biased toward cool conscience, in a nation oriented toward warm values. It's not only possible but common for us to live within so many layers of conscience norms.

Warm and cool conscience influence how we evaluate political agendas. It's very tempting to exaggerate the role of conscience because identifying our conscience precisely with a political party allows us to declare the other party to be morally wrong. I need hardly point out how strong a temptation this is. But instead, I want to suggest that our own conscience orientation frames an issue in warm or cool terms, almost regardless of what the political opinion is.

Political plans are not about right and wrong, because they are about processes and strategies. We may believe that a process or strategy will lead to a moral result, but this is usually due to our life experiences, education or community beliefs. Attitudes to political plans, though, are always based in moral thinking. We see some issues as not moral because we're using an Extroverted mental process to evaluate them. Other issues we see as highly moral because we evaluate them with an Introverted process. We're rarely aware of which way we're evaluating, unless we know that some profound personal experience or trauma is active.

You can be for or against the death penalty, for either relationship reasons or number/ logic reasons. For example, you don't believe that taking a life now can restore the life lost in a murder, so it only harms human relationships—or you may believe that the relationship harm done in a murder is so great that calloused killers simply cannot be allowed to live. On the other side of the fence, you can be against the death penalty based on numbers: you don't

---

58: Brent Massey, *Where In The World Do I Belong?* (Jetlag Press, 2006), 90. Massey's short book presents the results of a survey of foreign students about the cultural values of their home country.

believe statistics support its deterrent effect, or you see racial disparity that must represent injustice. Or you can be for it based on numbers: each death saves the state many years of costly incarceration. Either conclusion might be supported by either type of motivation. Even the basic statement, "it's wrong to kill another human being," can be a reason to support the death penalty (for a murderer) or oppose the death penalty (because it kills the convicted human being).

Political parties definitely appeal to conscience styles in bidding for votes. It's generally visible and relatively easy to see. "Candidate A cares about people," says one ad. "Candidate B spends responsibly," says another. We get appeals to approve or disapprove of a candidate's moral decisions, for example, "Tell Candidate C that it's just wrong," or "Tell Candidate D to stop imposing his morals on others." At different times, or in different regions, the same party may appeal to warm conscience voters or to cool conscience ones. The appeal is generally not so much to individual moral conscience as to social attitudes about morality. Is supporting an expansion of welfare a question of fairness, of caring for vulnerable people, or of spending money we don't have? Objectively, it's about all of these matters and more, but each community (region, city, church or family) probably reduces the question to just one of them. That way, it's possible to create a coherent, simple position we can live with: I'm for it, or I'm against it, because that's morally right.

Perhaps the clearest way that warm and cool conscience line up with social and political attitudes comes when some question pits individual happiness against social order. Warm conscience is usually in favor of individual happiness, while cool conscience is usually fighting for social order. To take an older issue that's mostly fading from controversy: how do we respond to unmarried mothers? Most people in the past saw this as a question of social order, using cool conscience reasoning: "She did something wrong, and we need to discourage it, even if she's a nice person." An unmarried mother could expect to be excluded socially; even and perhaps especially her family carried out at least some small penalty to make it clear that her life decisions should not be imitated. Making her and her child feel bad, they reasoned, was to prevent many other people from falling into wrong behavior. It seemed like a small price to pay for maintaining a social order that benefited many.

Even in the past, on the other hand, some people with warm conscience reasoned, "The unmarried mother's actions and decisions happened years ago, and her child is innocent. Excluding her teaches people to be unkind." Further, they reasoned, when young people make their decisions based on fear of the social order, the results are rarely good. In a time when social order still mattered most, some people with warm conscience made a point of acting in the opposite way.

Gradually, the argument made by warm conscience changed the way people typically behave in the United States, and unmarried mothers are not treated in a prejudicial way now. We see the same process going on with many other issues where rule-based social order is giving way to relationship-based flexibility. How you feel about the changes may have a lot to do with your inborn orientation of conscience. Do you feel that society is becoming more inclusive and kind, or that the social order is breaking down and will lead to danger? Introverted Thinking and Feeling are by nature based in templates of safety and danger, so it's inevitable that each side of this social-order balance makes half of us very uncomfortable.

Each reader probably feels strongly tempted to believe that his own orientation of conscience is the safest and most likely to turn out right in the long run. Inborn knowledge is like that; it feels like information about the world, not like an opinion. Breaking out of its constraints seems dangerous. We may take note of times when warm or cool conscience decisions led to disaster, as reinforcement for our beliefs. Shored up with our own experiences and others', we may believe that our type of conscience is not only morally right but practically safest and best.

However, the fact that both kinds of conscience keep on occurring, in about equal numbers, suggests that neither of them has an edge in long-term consequences. When we make a decision based on the morality of either Thinking or Feeling, the decision will mean keeping or losing a job, a friend, a community or a family. Sometimes, cool conscience decisions work out to preserve us from loss. Other times, warm conscience ones work out. There may not be any way to know in advance which type of decision will "work."

The really important thing to understand about inborn conscience is that your innate, natural orientation to Thinking or Feeling is integrated with your entire personality. This means if you make a decision that works with, not against, your deepest feeling, you're more likely to be able to carry it out. If you are unhappily married and your cool conscience tells you that divorce would be wrong because you made a promise, you probably have other Thinking and Feeling skills to help you work out this decision for the best. By the same token, the unhappily married person with warm conscience, who sees relationship and emotional damage and chooses to divorce, probably has other Thinking and Feeling skills to help work out the least harmful way through the divorce. When you make a moral choice that's integrated with your other motivations and skills, you usually feel you did the right thing.

As difficult as it may be to understand the opposite orientation of conscience, it can be very illuminating to see that another person really is operating by a different, separate, but integrated and complete system. You may never feel comfortable with that other person's moral choices, but you can understand why he or she does. It may be easier to forgive when you understand, and it is probably easier to keep peace when you can predict accurately what sort of moral choice another person is likely to make. Many terrible family rifts could be greatly helped by this kind of understanding.

We'll now turn to the Perceiving functions, Sensing and Intuition, with the same level of detail. How do our minds shape attitudes even before Judging can take place? How does what we see become who we are?

CHAPTER 7

Sensing

Perceiving begins when we wake up, open our eyes and ears, and start paying attention. Our senses tell us everything we know about the world, and they convey a stream of information that's way more than the brain can handle. The ear hears everything, the eye sees everything, the skin feels every temperature change and movement of wind, and so on. The mind needs filters or it will be overwhelmed.

Sensing and Intuition, the two kinds of Perceiving, together cover all of the information we take in. Sensing perceives things, events and facts, while Intuition perceives connections between them. They can both be Extroverted or Introverted, which makes little sense if we use the everyday definitions of those words. Sensing must be turned outward, not inward, since we're looking and listening to the world. But Sensing can be Introverted, if we mean that it's guided by an inborn template of how things ought to look. Introverted Sensing is idealistic, archetypal and resistant to change. Extroverted Sensing is pragmatically open to facts and things exactly as they are, in the moment. It's realistic and flexible.

As the five senses, Sensing is critically important to survival, but as a function of personality, it's not about staying away from fires or cliff edges. In the mental economy, it's about how much attention we pay to how things ought to be or how things really are. All of us use Sensing, but it's a dominant part of some personalities.

EXTROVERTED SENSING LIVES IN THE MOMENT

When Sensing is tied to pragmatism and observation, it's most closely tied to the direct physical senses. Of course, Sensing is always tied to the physical senses: but because it's a mental process, not exactly the senses themselves, it can have stronger or weaker connections. When the connections are many and strong, Sensing is able to keep track of many sensory details.

Fig. 7-1

The cartoon shows us a personality whose Sensing mind is focused on the real world of nature outside of his own mind. He sees the sun as it moves, and he sees the tree as it really is. He sees much more, but in the cartoon, the sun and the tree stand for all of the visible real world that we perceive.

Of course, in a neuroscience sense, we can't ever directly perceive the world, but instead our brains assemble an impression from the many sensory facts we take in. We already know that some people can't tell the difference between certain colors or tones; the physical eyes or ears may not perceive all of the sensory information, or the brain may not assemble it properly. Color-blindness makes us stop and think about what the world literally looks like to another person's eyes. Is it the same to everyone? Not really. We live in the same world, but in another way, we each live in our own world, the theater put on by our senses and mind. We depend on our "worlds" being nearly identical, for safety and so that we're all talking about the same things.

It's useful to remember the existence of our personal "worlds" when we think about Sensing as Extroverted or Introverted. The Extroverted Sensing function is the best at assembling a rapidly changing, highly colored, realistic mock-up of the outside world. The "movie" it shows on the "screen" of consciousness is very accurate. Extroverted Sensing means being consciously present in the world, in the moment. It processes quickly, with many channels open, without being too dragged down by memories. It takes in now—and now—and now—endlessly.

When someone's mind mostly uses Sensing to process the outside world, his personality tends to accept the chaotic, constantly-changing disorder of it all. First, people with Extroverted Sensing have good neurological ability to take in the view quickly. They don't usually have difficulty processing speed, like driving fast or playing fast video games. They usually have a high tolerance for a lot of sensory stimulation; many of them like roller-coasters and sports. If Sensing is a very strong part of their mental structure, they may crave and seek out sensory stimulation like this. They like adventure vacations and brightly-lit stadiums. Anyone who loves the noise and crowd of a nightclub dance floor must have Extroverted Sensing. It isn't only about noise and chaos, though. Extroverted Sensing is also keenly tuned to the grandeur of nature: walking on the beach, starry nights in the desert, and the awesome height of mountains.

With easy acceptance of sensory bombardment, Extroverted Sensing personalities can be pragmatic and easy-going about the imperfection of the outside world. It's a necessary trade-off for being very alert to detail, because nothing in the real world is even close to perfect. Every tree has a broken branch, and every leaf has a spot or hole. No human face is symmetrical, and no song is perfectly in tune. Every film has mistakes. If you brought a perfectionist attitude to close examination of the real world, you might get tied up in worrying over all of the little slips and mismatches. Instead, Extroverted Sensers are usually able to shrug off small imperfections and take in the big picture. They're typically able to get things done without worrying endlessly over tiny mistakes.

A strong brain orientation to observation of detail helps a mind see patterns in the world. Memories may have a lot of sensory detail woven in, and even if these memories are not conscious and labeled, they still contribute to recognizing trends and norms. In fact, this type of Sensing doesn't generally lead to strong conscious memories, since it's focused on each moment as it comes. There are far too many moments to remember them all consciously. But overall, unconscious automatic memories build up and create an uncanny ability to spot patterns in the outside world. Extroverted Sensers tend to be best at noticing a change in the weather, and after years of observation, they usually have a good idea of what it means when the wind shifts a little or a new cloud pattern appears. They are also good at patterns of automobile traffic and movements of the human body.

Nobody is better at reading body language than a strong Extroverted Senser. Details that may be invisible to others are, to her, starkly obvious and beyond possibility of ignoring. She can't help noticing slight changes in face color, or in the way a muscle is outlined along a bare arm. When fingernails change color or legs cross, she responds as if the other person wore a sign saying, "I am tired" or "you are putting too much pressure on me." She's almost afraid to spend time with a married couple she hasn't seen for a while, because she will know instantly, without a word, whether they are considering divorce. Their bodies will tell the story, and the Extroverted Senser sometimes can't explain what it was she saw. At other times, she is conscious of what she saw and can explain it in words. Crowd situations are equally telling; the Extroverted Sensers will pick up signs of an impending riot or problem an hour before anything happens.

Extroverted Sensers are good salesmen, for the same reason. This is true even when that kind of Sensing is not the strongest part of a personality. And when Extroverted Sensing skill is very strong in a personality, you're looking at the world's best salesman. He can spot which of two people is most likely to buy his product, and he can usually detect the unspoken objection of the naysayer. He can tell when he's made a good point and when to back off because it's hopeless. He's also good at addressing groups. As he reads the crowd's faces, he feels more alive. His manner becomes connected to their mood, and does it without much conscious thought. It's all part of an Extroverted Senser's feeling that he's part of the world.

This kind of people reading isn't about truly understanding their feelings. Some kinds of face reading require the observer to feel the same emotions; looking on, he recreates in his own feelings something like what the other person is feeling, and this helps him to understand empathetically. It can be a good way to understand people, but it's energy-depleting to feel what others are going through, and it depends on having many emotional memories.

But the external body reading of Extroverted Sensing doesn't require this inner experience. It doesn't force someone to step outside of himself and "feel" someone else's life; it lets the Extroverted Sensing observer stay in his own shoes. It's a matter of recognizing detailed patterns and changes in people, like shifts of the weather in the natural world. In general, it is more pragmatic than inner empathy. It doesn't ask, "what would it feel like to be the other person?" but instead asks, "what effect should the other person's emotional state have on me? What should I do about it?" Observing the other's emotional state means knowing more about the world and how to act in it, including the other person's "weather."

With greater attentiveness to the outside physical world, there is usually improved ability to control the Extroverted Senser's own body, including the face. Film acting means knowing how to convey emotion through physical movements and be able to repeat the same nuances in many different takes. Stage actors need to know how to make large visible motions that will seem plausible and realistic, and they need to keep track of where they are on the stage, and where they're supposed to come to a stop so that the spotlight will shine correctly when the stage goes dark. Actors of both kinds need to have a good ability to live in the moment, so that they seem as convincing on the tenth take, or in the fourth week, as in the first. Extroverted Sensing is good for all of these things.

Like all Extroverted functions, Sensing has an optimistic, can-do attitude. It sees the physical world as full of potential that just needs to be explored and confirmed. For every problem, there's a solution. When someone with Extroverted Sensing is operating in the physical world, she tends to be energetic and optimistic. On the other hand, being shut out of using Extroverted Sensing can cause her to become depressed. It isn't just hard for them to sit still; it blocks them from using their most forward-looking, confident functions. Extroverted Sensers are likely to become depressed and pessimistic when they're restricted by illness or imprisonment. As long as they can move, they can stay positive.

Pragmatism can make the Extroverted Senser comfortable with ignoring rules or customs that seem to be unimportant. Extroverted Sensers make great first responders and are often found in roles as firemen and policemen, but they don't like to do things "by the book." They react in the moment as it makes sense to them. If it's not in their official role to do something extra, Extroverted Sensers do it anyway. These extras are often very positive and creative. But in a negative sense, they can also be careless about written regulations. If they're working hard, they don't see the sense in being held accountable for missing some small checkmark detail.

Extroverted Sensing almost always goes with good physical coordination. Driven to live in the external world, they're usually good athletes. When they aren't gifted with conventional team sports skills, they're good at solitary challenges like car racing, rock climbing or distance running. People with Extroverted Sensing are happier when exercising, so they usually stay involved in some kind of training throughout life. Of course, they also love to watch sports, and in middle age, watching can substitute for doing so that even Extroverted Sensers get out of shape and overweight.

Extroverted Sensing usually helps with all kinds of physical courage, too. An Extroverted Senser is most likely to be the brave individual who rushes into danger or faces a bully. He feels he can calculate the risks accurately minute to minute, and he's optimistic about his chances of prevailing. And if not, if his life is put in danger, he's less troubled than some other people. Living fully in each moment, he doesn't have time to worry about the future. He feels it's better to have lived fully and die young, than to live out a long, cautious, depressed but safe life. The Extroverted Senser isn't trying to "be" anyone, he or she is just living each hour as it comes.

EXTROVERTED SENSING IN LITERATURE

Mark Twain, best known for writing about Tom Sawyer and Huckleberry Finn, trained as a steamboat pilot on the Mississippi River before he was a writer. His book *Life on the Mississippi* (1883) told a generation of train passengers what the earlier days of the steamboat had been like. He describes Mr. Bixby, the pilot who trained him, as a man with extraordinary powers of Extroverted Sensing. Mr. Bixby could read the river "as if it were a book," and here he tries to explain to the young writer how it's done:

Now I had often seen pilots gazing at the water and pretending to read it as if it were a book; but it was a book that told me nothing. A time came at last, however, when Mr. Bixby seemed to think me far enough advanced to bear a lesson on water-reading. So he began—"Do you see that long slanting line on the face of the water? Now, that's a reef. Moreover, it's a bluff reef. There is a solid sand-bar under it that is nearly as straight up and down as the side of a house. There is plenty of water close up to it, but mighty little on top of it. If you were to hit it you would knock the boat's brains out. Do you see where the line fringes out at the upper end and begins to fade away?"

"Yes, sir."

"Well, that is a low place; that is the head of the reef. You can climb over there, and not hurt anything. Cross over, now, and follow along close under the reef—easy water there—not much current. … You are well up on the bar, now; there is a bar under every point, because the water that comes down around it forms an eddy and allows the sediment to sink. Do you see those fine lines on the face of the water that branch out like the ribs of a fan. Well, those are little reefs; you want to just miss the ends of them, but run them pretty close."

The young pilot found it extremely hard to learn this level of observation. While practice and experience helped, we know that the future writer did not remain long as a steamboat pilot, perhaps because he just lacked the ability to sustain this much Sensing in the moment.

Annie Dillard writes about her family in 1950s Pittsburgh, in her memoir *An American Childhood* (1987). Her father probably had Extroverted Sensing, as shown in his love of dancing and loud music:

We did a lot of dancing at our house, fast dancing; everyone in the family was a dancing fool. I always came down from my room to dance. When the music was going, who could resist? I bounced down the stairs to the rhythm and began to whistle a bit, helpless as a marionette whose strings jerk her head and feet. We danced by the record player in the dining room...'Turn that record player down!' Mother suggested from the living room...

Father opened the cabinet and turned the volume down a bit. I opened my eyes. 'Remember that line in On the Road?... Kerouac's in a little bar in Mexico. He says that was the only time he ever got to hear the music loud enough. I always remember that.' He laughed, shaking his head; he turned the record player down another notch. If it had ever been at all, it had been a long time since Father had heard the music played loud enough. Maybe he was still imagining it, fondly, some little bar back away somewhere, so small he and the other regulars sat in the middle of the blaring band, or stood snapping their fingers, drinking bourbon, telling jokes between sets.[59]

The next writer demonstrates Extroverted Sensing not by describing it in a character, but by using it directly. John Berendt, writing about Savannah, Georgia in *Midnight in the Garden of Good and Evil* (1994), doesn't seem to miss a single detail of the outside world, moment to moment. Notice how many sensory details he includes in this night-time scene:

Minerva picked up her shopping bag and headed out the back door. We followed close behind as she made her way down the lane with a slow and ponderous stride. As she approached the next house, an old man got up from a chair on the porch and went inside. A window in another house closed. A door shut somewhere. Two men standing beside an oleander bush parted when they caught sight of Minerva and withdrew into the darkness. In a few moments, we reached the end of the lane. The sliver of a new moon hung like a slender cradle over a grove of tall, dark trees. We were at the edge of a graveyard. On the far side, a hundred yards beyond the trees, a floodlit basketball court cast a pale gray light into the graveyard. A boy was bouncing a ball and taking shots at the basketball hoop. Thunk, thunk, thunk.....proinnng. Otherwise, the graveyard was deserted.[60]

Another famous writer who used Extroverted Sensing in his writing was George Orwell. Best known for 1984, he also wrote works of journalism in 1930s England. In *The Road to Wigan Pier* (1937), Orwell described his stay in a cheap boarding-house in the grimy industrial town of Wigan. Like Berendt, Orwell could follow many sensory details, minute to minute:

The first sound in the morning was the clumping of the mill-girls' clogs down the cobbled street. Earlier than that, I suppose, there were factory whistles which I was never awake to hear. There were generally four of us in the bedroom.

...All the windows were kept tight shut, with a red sandbag jammed in the bottom, and in the morning the room stank like a ferret's cage. You did not notice it when you got up, but if you went out of the room and came back, the smell hit you in the face with a smack.

...Downstairs there was the usual kitchen-dining room with its huge open range burning day and night. It was lighted only by a skylight, for on one side of it was the shop and on the other side the larder... in the middle of the room was the big kitchen table at which the family and all the lodgers ate. I never saw this table completely uncovered, but I saw its wrappings at various times. At the bottom there was a layer of old newspapers stained with Worcester Sauce; above

59: Annie Dillard, *An American Childhood* (New York: Harper and Row, 1987).
60: John Berendt, *Midnight in the Garden of Good and Evil* (New York: Random House, 1994).

that a sheet of sticky white oilcloth; above that a green serge cloth; above that a coarse linen cloth, never changed and seldom taken off. Generally the crumbs from breakfast were still on the table at supper. I used to get to know individual crumbs by sight and watch their progress up and down the table from day to day.

The dean of Extroverted Sensing writers was Ernest Hemingway. He didn't just have Extroverted Sensing, he built his entire writing style on it, intently focusing less on ideas and more on every action and detail. He aimed to write only what was "true" and "real," and by that he meant the most direct sampling of Extroverted Sensing. Here's a typical passage from his first successful novel, *The Sun Also Rises* (1926):

It was a warm spring night and I sat at a table on the terrace of the Napolitain after Robert had gone, watching it get dark and the electric signs come on, and the red and green stop-and-go traffic-signal, and the crowd going by, and the horse-cabs clippety-clopping along the edge of the solid taxi traffic, and the poules going by, singly and in pairs, looking for the evening meal. I watched a good-looking girl walk past the table and watched her go up the street and lost sight of her, and watched another, then saw the first one coming back again. She went by once more and I caught her eye, and she came over and sat at the table. The waiter came up. "Well, what will you drink?" I asked.

Each detail is important in its turn. Someone else might focus on the writer's interior thoughts, but Hemingway tells instead what he saw and heard, what happened and in what order. The girl walked by, came back, and walked by again, not because some meaning was involved but because that's what she did. It was real.

INTROVERTED SENSING SEES AN IDEAL WORLD

Introverted Sensing is very, very different from Extroverted Sensing. In processing the Sensing world, it maintains an inner vision that has its own reality. It's about knowing the world, but not about knowing it in a pragmatic, moment to moment way. Introverted Sensing knows what the world *should* be like, so that it can compare what it sees and hears with the inner ideal. Its archetypes are visual, for both things and people.

Just as the Introverted Feeler seemed to know instinctively how wonderful ideal love was in the Garden of Eden, the Introverted Senser seems to have seen Eden's perfect beauty. There were no dead trees in Eden. The plants were healthy, the animals were in harmony and balance with the environment, and the people acted and looked just right. Reality is monitored by the standard of Eden, though not consciously. Things are always in need of being straightened up, trimmed, retouched, decorated and framed.

In the cartoon below, the personality knows the world most strongly through an inner book of photos. While physical eyes and ears must process actual sensory detail, the mind processes sensory detail mainly by filtering it through a pre-existing picture book. The inner book already knows what things should look like: nature, people, and the way we behave in roles to each other.

Fig. 7-2

The inner photo album is filled not with actual photos, but with possible images. The images seem to comprise most of the scenery and events of the person's possible life: birthdays, graduations, weddings, births, parties, reunions. The images show what these and other possible events should look like: what people should be wearing and how they should behave. There are possible images for "home," "family," "husband," "wife," "church," and many other stock figures in life. Each possible image could be considered an archetype.

When someone with this inner photo album goes through life, events and people show up to match the possible images. They are recognized, in a way; they fill in the actual detail of the possible image, as actual crystals grow from a theoretical lattice. "My home" goes from a general notion to an actual Cape Cod house with a little side garden. "My wife" goes from possible image to an actual woman with a certain color hair. Not just any real image will do, though; only some real things fulfill the outlines of the archetypal images.

Perhaps the most important thing to notice about Introverted Sensing's photo album is that it is not infinite or expanding. For every possible image that it provides, there are many impossible images that can't ever be accepted. If the image of "my home" could be a Cape Cod house, a brick split-level, a white Colonial, or several other kinds of homes, it is emphatically not various other homes: a trailer, an apartment, a rundown or messy place, or any place that might fulfill an archetypal image of a Bad Home. The details depend on the individual's life: a trailer or apartment might fit neatly if it's typical of the image of a settled, good home. What will never fit is something that fits a negative archetype (like a "haunted house") or is completely outside the limits of possible ideas, like a yurt or a cave.

Introverted Sensing can be seen as an aesthetic conscience, telling what's "right" or "wrong" about appearances. Whatever is most ideal is right. Whatever is most disorganized, accidental, damaged or otherwise far from ideal is simply wrong. Aesthetic conscience is applied directly to the appearance of things. Everything around Introverted Sensing needs to be clean, organized and beautiful. Although Introverted Sensing would probably not claim that the opposite of "clean, organized and beautiful" is "morally wicked," permitting dirt and disorder would cause uneasiness, fear and guilt.

People with Introverted Sensing have the strongest affinity for role archetypes among personalities. They have a clear sense of what it means to be masculine or feminine, usually living out clear, well-defined images of men and women. Introverted Sensing is not in the lead on our time's "gender bending." They are not likely to be atheists, having also a clear sense of the archetype of God. They're also keenly aware of other roles, both in real life and in fairy tales. Introverted Sensing knows what these roles look and act like: teacher, priest, mother, father, coach, cop, soldier, president; king, queen, prince, princess, wizard, witch, knight, woodcutter. The images don't have physical detail, but they restrict acceptance of details that don't fit the possibility, the archetype.

If you want to know what Introverted Sensing thinks a king looks like, sort through a stack of pictures of real men, and see which ones Introverted Sensing rejects. What you're left with could be ten men with very different features or skin color, but there will be something they have in common. This is the archetypal image of a king: it probably includes height, old-fashioned style of dress, good eye contact and facial symmetry. In countries with traditional monarchies, Introverted Sensers are usually firm supporters of keeping up the tradition. As long as the king or queen fills the role without serious crime or scandal, Introverted Sensing accepts monarchy as proper and right.

People with Introverted Sensing are careful to look like any role they're expected to fill. Hired as a teacher, the Introverted Senser will not show up to work dressed like a coach, a dancer or a hairdresser. The role of "teacher" implies some self-effacement and certainly downplaying sexual traits; it also implies projecting optimism and discipline. We can't say what a teacher must look like in terms of colors or style, but we can say that the archetype of a teacher must reject sexuality, darkness, and carelessness. It must be proper, above all.

People with Introverted Sensing are almost incapable of making mistakes about what role appearance should be; it's a deep instinct to get it right because the inner image feels both real and imperative. The converse is also true: the wrong image feels profoundly wrong. When someone in a role doesn't look right for the role, Introverted Sensing refuses to believe in it. When a role requires such a careful image that it includes a uniform, lack of that uniform may entirely undermine credibility for someone with Introverted Sensing. A uniform may also be enough, on its own, to uphold authority in otherwise shaky situations.

Introverted Sensing loves ideal beauty more than anything else. Beauty is safety. Idealistic Sensing spends a lot of time being disappointed, because the real world fails to look like its archetype most of the time. There's a whole art industry devoted to creating pleasing ideal images of nature. They're restful to the eyes of an Introverted Senser because they live up to the ideal and don't disappoint.

We can see it first by looking at photos and paintings that are featured on greeting cards. Greeting cards are highly archetypal because they are intended to be symbolic. They aren't the spontaneous thoughts we express on any old day, they are carefully arranged thoughts and images to go with the sort of occasion that has "possible image" outlines in the Introverted Sensing photo album: graduation, wedding, birth or funeral. Even if the real event fails to meet ideal standards, the greeting card chosen for it can present the ideal bride, baby, bouquet, butterfly, bird, swan or covered bridge.

Craft stores have large sections devoted to scrapbooking, which is the art of presenting imperfect real events as if they matched the ideal archetype. Stores sell pre-cut letters, stickers, stamps, and stylized images like seashells, hats, flowers, cats, and a wide array of other objects. The scrapbooker takes photographs of a real person, event or trip and organizes them into stylized, idealized layouts. A beach vacation might have been the worst trip you ever took, on which everyone got sick and the children cried most of the time. But after its photos have been scrapbooked, it looks like the ideal beach trip. There are no photos of the bad times, and the photos showing smiles and sand are now framed with idealized images of sand pails, shells, sunshine and happiness.

Introverted Sensing also seeks personal meaning in the world. Not only are there possible images of future things and events, there are also strong image memories of past ones. Good memories have created images with real detail: the favorite teddy bear, your grandmother's house, a baby's shoes. As archetypal images become engraved with real detail, they become sacred. It's possible that Introverted Sensing is closely connected with long-term memory storage, but if these Sensers don't actually have more vivid memories, at least they are among those whose memories feel most meaningful.

Antiques are often part of Introverted Sensing's decorating taste. Antiques are either filled with personal meaning (if they have been in the family) or good at meeting the outlines of an archetypal idea. Because their image has been around for a long time, they are more likely to have left a stamp on early ideas of images. Nothing looks as much like ideal Christmas as an antique sled or lantern, because so many engravings from the past century included such details. Tradition is usually felt as a sacred value.

Introverted Sensing can be very strong and dominant, or it can be a lesser part of personality. When it's dominant, it forms a worldview, shaping every aspect of life with a heavy hand. The way I look, the way you look, the way the house looks, the way the holiday looks, all of these need to be the best literal match for the archetypal images. It exerts a strong influence on lifestyle and career decisions, because it tends to steer people into image-based roles. They are actually living out archetypes, though usually unconsciously.

When it's a lesser part of personality, Introverted Sensing becomes more of an artistic style. It is not as practical and powerful as a worldview, and for this reason, it can be much less realistic. The artistic side of Introverted Sensing is somewhat like its dominant worldview in valuing the past, loving beauty, and pressing for ideal images. But instead of using realistic everyday images, aesthetic Introverted Sensing can use historical, romantic images as decoration. It's often focused on fine detail like lace, filigree, iron scrollwork, Persian-carpet flowers, folk embroidery, dollhouse furniture, or calligraphy. Introverted Sensing (including the worldview kind) always loves a walled garden filled with roses, a sort of archetypal image of paradise with destructive things walled out.

In its aesthetic form, Introverted Sensing ties in with imagination and memory. Things become invested with personal meaning by matching some image in the photo album, so that familiar objects feel like "mine" even if they are public property, like a particular park bench where I experienced strong feelings and events. These familiar things, connected to deeper archetypes, feel more significant than their simple reality; when aesthetic Introverted Sensing is operating strongly, the things may seem somewhat alive.

Role-playing games, which allow someone to take on the persona of a folk-tale figure, probably originated among people with aesthetic Introverted Sensing. Computer games and Renaissance Fairs have grown to cross personality type lines but probably still have a large identifiable group to whom the archetypal identity is central and important. They may already feel as though they were born in the wrong time and should have been wizards or knights.

Introverted Sensing also has a strong influence on how people use words, both as a worldview and as an artistic sense. Each has a slightly different influence. As a worldview, Introverted Sensing provides a strong template for correct, ideal use of words. Correct spelling, good grammar and neat presentation all matter. Introverted Sensers can be very good editors and proofreaders. They know how the world ought to look, including a page of writing.

On the other side, artistic Introverted Sensing ties word use into archetypal images. The result is using language as symbols, because words feel invested with meaning that's larger or higher. This is also true of worldview Introverted Sensing: looking at a flag, the Introverted Senser "sees" patriotism, safety and home. It's much more complicated, and with a less literal connection, for aesthetic Introverted Sensing. Looking at a rose, the Introverted Senser may "see" love, the fleeting nature of beauty in life, or other personal meanings we can't guess at. As an artistic sense, Introverted Sensing is a large part of writing poetry. Imagistic poems that use descriptions of things as a way to talk about ideas or feelings are tapping into aesthetic Introverted Sensing. People with the stronger, more literal worldview Introverted Sensing may not find its artistic, less literal, poetic style easy to understand.

Like every inborn instinct, Introverted Sensing often comes across as somewhat or very negative and pessimistic. The pragmatic optimism of Extroverted Sensing is usually notably missing. While it has unbounded enthusiasm for ideal images, the disappointing real world often sees a tentative frown. An Introverted Senser has strong likes and dislikes. These likes and dislikes may be for clear, culturally shared reasons, or they can just be private ways in which archetypal images accept or reject the visible world.

Introverted Sensing usually sees the past as better meeting the ideal, too. Today's world is the most disappointing of all, except for the world as it will be next year, if things keep going downhill. Old movies are always considered better than new ones, and old music is very clearly better than new. New books can't match the standards of the books we already have; intellectuals with Introverted Sensing often believe that the novel is a dying art whose peak is past. While people with Introverted Sensing can work in technology fields, they are not usually first adopters of new technology. Whatever we already had was probably good enough or better, and learning new skills in the physical world is not a joy.

Introverted Sensing may be the greatest force in the world for maintaining property, keeping up tradition and passing on good habits to the next generation. As much as the term first sounds like a contradiction in terms, Introverted Sensing is present (as either worldview or artistic sense) in an easy majority of personalities, about 66%.[61] It's not only common, it's actually very familiar, once we understand what it is.

61: *MBTI® Manual, A Guide to the Development and Use of the Myers-Briggs Type Indicator*, 3rd edition (Mountain View, CA: CPP, 2003), 156-158.

INTROVERTED SENSING IN LITERATURE

In the Extroverted Sensing passages, I could show characters who had detailed, fast-paced, realistic observational powers, and also passages of writing that used that same observational power to describe what was happening. It's harder to find clear examples of Introverted Sensing in books. This is partly because writing is supposed to describe sensory details for the reader; in a way, it's artificially nudged in the Extroverted direction. Introverted Sensing does show up, in both characters and written passages, but we have to look more closely.

Introverted Sensing sees, hears and feels, but it connects the Sensing world with an inner vision. First, let's look at a character with this trait. In Mary E. Wilkins Freeman's short story, "A New England Nun" (1891), Louisa lives in a house where everything is precisely where her mother had kept them. Her fiancé, Joe Dagget, returns after many years' absence but finds he cannot fit into the prim, orderly house:

Presently Dagget began fingering the books on the table. There was a square red autograph album, and a Young Lady's Gift-Book which had belonged to Louisa's mother. He took them up one after the other and opened them; then laid them down again, the album on the Gift-Book.

Louisa kept eying them with mild uneasiness. Finally she rose and changed the position of the books, putting the album underneath. That was the way they had been arranged in the first place.

Dagget gave an awkward little laugh. "Now what difference did it make which book was on top?" said he.

Louisa looked at him with a deprecating smile. "I always keep them that way," she murmured.[62]

Louisa's Sensing abilities are Introverted, acting almost as a conscience for how things should look. Instead of observing how things look, sound and feel, she observes only how they fit or don't fit with her inner vision. The books' placement is not about the books; it is linked to her mother, perhaps the deepest archetypal role.

Marcel Proust's multi-volume novel *In Search of Time Past* is filled with the ruminations of artistic Introverted Sensing. In *Swann's Way* (1913), the narrator explains that as a teen he had mostly forgotten his childhood. Then, one day in Paris, the taste of tea brought back what it had felt like to be a child. His writing dwells on the moment in exhaustive detail, but with very little sensory description of the actual cookie and tea. (Imagine how differently the Extroverted Sensing writers, such as Hemingway or Orwell, would have described the event.)

For many years already, everything about Combray that was not the theatre and drama of my bedtime had ceased to exist for me, when one day in winter, as I came home, my mother, seeing that I was cold, suggested that, contrary to my habit, I have a little tea. She sent for one of those squat, plump cakes called petites madeleines that look as though they have been moulded in the grooved valve of a scallop-shell. And soon, mechanically, oppressed by the gloomy day and the prospect of a sad future, I carried to my lips a spoonful of the tea in which I had let soften a piece of madeleine. But at the very instant when the mouthful of tea mixed with cake-crumbs touched my palate, I quivered, attentive to the extraordinary thing that was happening in me. A delicious pleasure had invaded me... I had ceased to feel that I was mediocre, contingent, mortal. Where could it have come to me from—this powerful joy? I sensed that it was connected to the taste of the

---

62: Mary E. Wilkins Freeman, "A New England Nun," *Great Short Stories by American Women*, ed. Candace Ward (New York: Dover, 1996).

tea and the cake, but that it went infinitely far beyond it... And suddenly the memory appeared. That taste was the taste of the little piece of madeleine which on Sunday mornings at Combray... when I went to say good morning to her in her bedroom, my Aunt Léonie would give me after dipping it in her infusion of tea or lime blossom... After the death of people, after the destruction of things, alone, frailer but more enduring, more immaterial, more persistent, more faithful, smell and taste still remain for a long time, like souls, remembering, waiting, hoping, on the ruin of all the rest, bearing without giving way... the immense edifice of memory.[63]

The smell and taste reopen his connection to past archetypal identity, innocent childhood. He does not move past it to new sights, sounds or smells, but instead holds the evoked memory close as something with its own reality. The interior world is more important than the exterior; the outside Sensing world is important only as a path inward to ideals.

Proust's second novel *In a Budding Grove* (1919) gives us an example of a young adult who cannot stop focusing on the unfamiliarity of his hotel room.

[My room] was full of things which did not know me, which flung back at me the distrustful look that I cast at them, and, by taking no heed of my existence, showed that I was interrupting the course of theirs. The clock... continued without a moment's interruption to utter, in an unknown tongue, a series of observations which must have been most uncomplimentary to myself, for the violet curtains listened to them without replying... I was tormented by... a large mirror with feet which stood across the corner, for I felt that until it had left the room, there would be no possibility of rest for me there.[64]

His observation of color and detail cannot detach itself from his inner world. Instead of using Extroverted Sensing to notice and describe details of the curtains, clock, and mirror, he fits them into images of curtains, clocks and mirrors that he has already known. Forced into templates of what he already knows, they don't fit. His imagination suggests that the unfamiliar things are as uneasy about him as he is about them.

We can see Introverted Sensing at work in two characters from George Eliot's *Middlemarch* (1872). Rosamond, the doctor's future wife, modeled her identity on an archetypal notion of what "ladies" were like, although her family was wealthy from hard work, not from inherited land or social class. Rosamond imitated not her own mother (who was friendly and unpretentious) but an ideal:

For Rosamond, though she would never do anything that was disagreeable, was industrious; and now more than ever she was active in sketching her landscapes and market carts and portraits of her friends, in practising her music, and in being from morning till night her own standard of a perfect lady, having always an audience in her own consciousness, with sometimes the not unwelcome addition of a more variable external audience in the numerous visitors of the house. She found time also to read the best novels, and even the second best, and she knew much poetry by heart.

The vicar's elderly mother is just as rigidly devoted to an ideal social role and its beliefs, but her eyes are not on modeling the aristocracy. She is upholding all beliefs and traditions of the past, believing first that over-eating must be the sole cause of sickness. The doctor whimsically points out that perhaps some people are sick because their parents, not themselves, over-ate,

...but Mrs. Farebrother held that view of things dangerous: Nature was more just than that;

63: Marcel Proust, *The Way by Swann's*, translated by Lydia Davis (New York: Penguin, 2002).
64: Marcel Proust, *In a Budding Grove*, trans. C. K. Scott Moncrieff (New York: Modern Library, 1998)

it would be easy for any felon to say that his ancestors ought to have been hanged instead of him. If those who had bad fathers and mothers were bad themselves, they were hanged for that. There was no need to go back on what you couldn't see.

"My mother is like old George the Third," said the Vicar, "she objects to metaphysics."

"I object to what is wrong, Camden. I say, keep hold of a few plain truths, and make everything square with them. When I was young, Mr. Lydgate, there was never any question of right and wrong. We knew our catechism, and that was enough; we learned our creed and our duty. Every respectable Church person had the same opinions... I shall never show that disrespect to my parents, to give up what they taught me. Anyone can see what comes of turning. If you change once, why not twenty times? ...I am not likely to follow new lights, though there are plenty of them here as elsewhere. I say, they came in with the mixed stuffs [cloth] that will neither wash nor wear. It was not so in my youth: a Churchman was a Churchman, and a clergyman, you might be pretty sure, was a gentleman, if nothing else."

To old Mrs. Farebrother, moral questions, religious doctrine, and social roles are equally important and nearly always overlap. A clergyman must be from the land-owning class, and his beliefs about God could then be taken for granted. Introverted Sensing includes all of these layers in one archetypal image without trying to break it down to ask, well what about a gentleman with wrong beliefs, or what about a worker's son with good faith? It's all unified.

In fantasy and science fiction stories, archetypal roles are often conveyed directly by fairy-tale images. Roles like "lady" and "clergyman" don't need to be suggested by tradition and social context if they can be openly stated as "princess" or "wizard." The Victorian children's classic *A Little Princess* (1905) by Frances Hodgson Burnett shows a character using fantasy to model her own daily behavior. Twelve-year-old Sara has gone from riches to rags at a London boarding school, where she is now underfed, overworked and treated with contempt. But Sara has stocked her imagination with archetypal roles from fairy tales and history. She decides to identify with an inner vision of who she is, not with the outer reality.

"Whatever comes," she thought, "cannot alter one thing. If I am a princess in rags and tatters, I can be a princess inside. It would be easy to be a princess if I were dressed in cloth of gold, but it is a great deal more of a triumph to be one all the time when no one knows it. There was Marie Antoinette when she was in prison and her throne was gone and she had only a black gown on, and her hair was white, and they insulted her and called her Widow Capet. She was a great deal more like a queen than when she was so gay and everything was grand. I like her best then. Those howling mobs of people did not frighten her. She was stronger than they were, even when they cut her head off."

When Sara behaves according to the princess archetype, even while doing a servant's chores, there is a strange gap between her visible and invisible circumstances:

...it seemed as if the child were mentally living a life which held her above the rest of the world. It was as if she scarcely heard the rude and acid things said to her; or, if she heard them, did not care for them at all... While the thought held possession of her, she could not be made rude and malicious by the rudeness and malice of those around her: "A princess must be polite," she said to herself.

Finally, sometimes literature directly tells us the worldview of Introverted Sensing. Around 900 A.D., an Old English poem called "Maxims II" described the world's order. Its verses don't distinguish visual order, natural order, and social situations. They are all just part of how the world should look—how it should be. In 900, "fairy tale roles" were actual ones: king, queen, earl and dragon.

The King shall hold the realm. Fortress be seen afar,
made with the skill of giants on earth,
built of ashlar blocks. Wind in sky is swiftest,
thunder oft loudest. Among all Christ be greatest,
but fate is strongest. Winter is coldest,
spring frostiest (so long cold!),
summer sunniest (sky sweltering!),
autumn is triumphant, health bringing
year's fruit, all good things sent…
…Hawk be on glove,
ever untamed; wolf be in den,
miserable loner; boar be in thicket,
tusked strongly. In homeland be
good laws at work. Arrow be in hand,
spear shining gold. Gem be in arm-ring,
high and lofty. River be in waves
mixing with sea-tide. Mast be at mid-ship,
sail-yard at rest. Sword be on breast,
lordly iron. Dragon be in mound,
proud of ancient treasure. Fish be in water,
schools ever spawning… Troth be in Earl,
wisdom in man. Wood be in land,
branches blowing. Bright be on earth
green still abiding. God be in heaven
deeds ever Judging.

Clearly, in the poet's view, anything out of its place is a problem. Seasons need the right weather; what use is a warm winter or a cool summer? Untamed animals don't belong indoors, while ships and weapons must never be allowed to fall into disrepair. Laws must be good, just as the tower must be tall enough to see from far off. What is a tower if it isn't tall? So what are laws if they are unjust?

The poem mentions two archetypal Christian images of God: "Christ be greatest" and God as a Judge. At the same time, it mentions one of the pre-Christian archetypal images of God as impersonal Fate (which is strongest, says the poet). This poem is not a doctrinal statement, it is a collection of all traditional concepts. God and Fate are both archetypal notions in the culture, so they must both be right. It's not about logic or even faith, it's about inherited worldview.

CHAPTER 8

Intuition

I'VE SAVED INTUITION FOR LAST for several reasons. It's the most difficult mental function to understand and talk about; we needed the foundation of understanding the other three in order to attempt grappling with Intuition. We're consciously aware of Thinking, Feeling and Sensing; Intuition, on the other hand, can be completely invisible even when we're using it.

Its operation is invisible; further, its work is to "see" what's invisible. It sees connections, both real and imagined—or both actual and potential. If what we perceive with our senses has to be qualified with a reminder that we assemble a movie in our minds, one that could be colorblind or otherwise distorted, then what can we say about Perceiving connections with Intuition? What sort of reality is this, which is invisible, impossible to verify, and also detected by an invisible system?

And yet Intuition is probably the central key to the human experience. It plays a larger or smaller role in personality, but its role is always important even when it's in the background. It shapes or creates aspects of the human experience that are as diverse as faith, imagination, invention, revolution, prejudice, superstition, and luck.

Like the other mental functions, Intuition can be Extroverted or Introverted. In other words, it can be pragmatic, exploring, and questioning; or it can be instinctual, idealistic, and pessimistic. It can be dominant in a personality or non-dominant. It's the chameleon of the mind: it may be hard to see against some backgrounds, easier to see against others, but it's always there.

As if we needed one more reason for Intuition to be difficult, in later chapters it will be symbolized by the letter N. When we start to blend and balance the elements on personality in self-organizing systems, we'll need shorthands for all of them. Some are easy, like T for

Thinking or F for Feeling. S works for Sensing, but using I for Intuition runs into a problem. We'll also need E for Extroverted and I for Introverted. One of the words beginning with "i" has to give up rights to the first letter. Traditionally, it's been Intuition that has undergone yet one more chameleon change, being called by its second letter N. For now, this isn't an issue, but it's worth noting in advance.

INTUITION: BOTH CONSCIOUS AND UNCONSCIOUS

Thinking seems to line up mostly with left-hemisphere frontal lobe logic, and Feeling with right-hemisphere frontal lobe emotion-processing. Sensing could probably be seen as a network of the many areas of the brain that monitor physical senses, motion and where we are in space. Intuition, however, seems to be "invisible" partly because it's a network of connections between conscious thought and nonverbal, unconscious processing.

Neuroscience defines the unconscious in terms of speed: whatever is done faster than 250 milliseconds (give or take a few) is unconscious. Conscious thought is the remembering, comparing function that deliberately lags behind by split seconds or even longer. The conscious mind may not be a particular organ of the brain; in fact, it's probably not. A best guess at this time is that consciousness is created by a network of neurons: it's not an organ or lobe, it's a layer.[65] Intuition seems to be a kind of layer like this, perhaps one connecting non-sensory awareness regions. When an idea from Intuition arrives in our consciousness, we feel that we saw it in a flash or in no time at all. We may be aware, briefly, of just how fast unconscious thought really is.

When Intuition is operating weakly in the background of our minds, it gives us hunches. A lot of people use these hunches to buy lottery tickets. They are aware that there is no logical process telling them to choose 37 or 73, and there's no relationship value in it either. Sensing can't tell them which number will win. But they feel that they can divine a meaning from events around them, perhaps from having seen a lucky number or a lucky color.

This kind of weak Intuition senses that events aren't entirely random, though it can't explain why the shirt color of the person in front of you at the Lotto line should determine how you pick your numbers. The connections it sees may be imaginary, but sometimes they're right in a way that we can't define. Perhaps the connection was glimpsed so fast and unconsciously that the conscious mind really can't explain it, and therefore reaches for a word like "luck."

A higher form of hunch helps us choose other non-logical options in daily life, like which store to try first to find a scarce item. People have hunches like this about many things. "I just had a hunch that I should call my mother, and it turned out she had just fallen down the stairs." "I had a hunch that if I went back to that same field later in the day, I'd find my lost dog, and there he was!" Sometimes they describe it as a "nudge" to do something. "I felt a nudge to cross the room and talk to that man, and it turned out he was very depressed and needed help."

65: Jeffrey Gray, *Consciousness: Creeping up on the Hard Problem* (New York: Oxford University Press, 2004), 173.

Intuition often sees patterns. It alerts us when some detail or event doesn't fit the pattern. Since it's an unconscious process at work, it takes a little while for the conscious mind to work it out in words. Detective stories demonstrate this use of Intuition. The stories always lay out many facts and alibis, then the detective works his way through them with logic. But logic usually brings him to a dead end, because he is missing some critical piece of information. He usually saves the day by having a hunch about one of the witnesses, and when he follows it up, he finds the clue that returns his logic to a solid footing.

What is this kind of hunch? It's usually something in the witness's story or appearance that the detective can't at first explain, but he feels that it raises questions about how much he can trust the witness. After the case is solved by bringing out the missing facts, he can explain what his hunch was, in logical terms like, "The witness claimed to be from London, but he said some words that only Americans use," or, "For a man who claimed he had been walking all night, his shoes were too clean." But at first, he just feels troubled about the witness. There was an emotional, logical, sensory or other kind of pattern that his Intuition was watching, and it rang an alarm. The alarm had no words, but it demanded that he look again.

Intuition can also provide seemingly impossible leaps of knowledge, especially when someone's mind is already trained in a special area of knowledge. One of the most famous intuitive leaps in science came when a research chemist was trying to understand how the atoms of a gas, benzene, fitted together. Logic wasn't giving him an answer. As August Kekulé told the story later, he solved the problem by falling asleep, and this allowed his unconscious Intuition to work on the problem.

I turned my chair to the fire and dozed. Again the atoms were gamboling before my eyes . . . long rows sometimes closely fitting together, all twining and twisting in snakelike motion. But look! What was that? One of the snakes had seized its own tail and the form whirled mockingly before my eyes. As if by a flash of lightning I awoke. Let us learn to dream, gentlemen.[66]

Kekulé worked out the technical details once he was awake, and in 1865 he published a paper showing that benzene was formed in a ring, with alternating single and double bonds. Intuition as an unconscious process had shown him the concept of a ring, which allowed him to solve the rest of the problem with logic.

There are amazing cases of people who can look at a math problem and solve it instantly, without any figuring. This, too, would be a function of Intuition, though none of us can claim that it's a common daily use. It may be more common than we know, but we think of it as rare. Often, but not always, extraordinary Intuition like this is paired with the disability of autism. Someone with a speech disability might be able to write the answer to "5623 x 3487" as fast as you could recognize a friend's photograph. Neuroscience doesn't know how this gifted sort of Intuition happens. It's possible that many brains can instantly compute numbers, but only a few brains have an Intuition connection that flashes the answer into conscious thought. The rest of us have to work it out longhand or use a calculator.

Intuition has a middle range of complexity, where it isn't producing simple hunches or "seeing" a scientific theory or an answer in math. In this middle range, it sees connections between ideas. All books are based in this kind of Intuition. Authors usually plan non-fiction

66: O. Theodore Benfey, "August Kekulé and the birth of the structural theory of organic chemistry in 1858," *Journal of Chemical Education* 1958 35 (1), 21.

books as a way to answer a question about how things are connected. Each book makes clear, first, the question that it hopes to answer. What caused the war? Did this candidate lose the election because of his campaign's mistakes or his personality? How do today's trends connect with the future to suggest what will happen next? Why did the stock market crash, and will it recover soon? Why are prices rising? What is personality? The book provides facts, but its main work is connecting them to find the answer to the question.

Many novels can be seen as posing Intuition questions about people. What would it be like if you were born in another country? What would it feel like to find out you were adopted? What is it like to be rich? What would happen if sworn enemies were trapped on a sinking ship and had to cooperate in order to survive? What do people feel after they've committed murder? How can anyone forgive a murderer?

Stories don't pose these questions in the same up-front way that non-fiction works do, but the questions underlie the plot. They expand the reader's personal store of experience by showing far more kinds of connections between people than the reader can find in daily life. People learn from fiction by adding to their store of Intuitive knowledge, so that they can draw on it as if from their own memories. In a sudden flash of Intuition, they can see connections between a real-life situation and what happened in the book.

Some recent books have been devoted to understanding the use of Intuition. Gavin de Becker's *The Gift of Fear* explains how our unconscious minds may observe danger signs before our conscious minds are aware of them. De Becker emphasizes the importance of paying attention to unconscious thinking so that we don't screen out these clues simply because they can't yet be consciously explained. Malcolm Gladwell's book *Blink* explores the mental gift of knowing something at a glance, for example, looking at a well-done art forgery and just having a feeling that something is wrong with it. Readers who want to know more about the subject of Intuition in general will appreciate the insights of these books.

EXTROVERTED INTUITION MAKES MAPS

Extroverted Intuition is primarily about exploring what the world means. Like other Extroverted functions, it's optimistic about asking questions and finding answers. It expects to find answers outside in the world through observation and comparison.

The personality in the cartoon (Fig. 8-1) is looking out at the world to see how roads and bridges connect places. He's asking the question, "What does this bridge connect to on the other side?" That's how it is with all connections in the outside world: questions lead to exploration, which leads to answers.

Extroverted Intuition is about possibilities in the world. When Intuition is primarily focused on the outside world, it is keenly aware of not knowing yet which things are connected. It believes that until there's been time and attention to see things close up, anything could be connected.

The world is full of possibilities. Extroverted Intuition sees potential among people: new relationships, possibilities for growth, ways that people could get together to solve problems, new faces waiting to be discovered. It sees potential among numbers and facts: new methods, new machines, ways that problems could be solved differently. One explanation is not enough, since it might not be the right one. Extroverted Intuition can see many more possible connections and solutions. None of them can be excluded until it's been proven not to be possible.

Fig. 8-1

Above all, Extroverted Intuition questions what may lie beyond the surface of things. In this way, it's the opposite and sometimes the antagonist of Sensing. Sensing is a specialist at surfaces and appearances: what exists, and what it looks like. Extroverted Intuition asks whether the surface may be concealing something hidden. As an Extroverted function, this Intuition tends to expect that good things are hidden behind the surfaces: we are missing out on opportunities when we don't see them. As an Extroverted function, it's also optimistic that the unknown can become known, even if takes some persistent questioning. It's important to turn over every rock, because a cure for cancer is hiding under one of them.

Extroverted Intuition tends to organize the other functions into helping, like assistants to a detective. This seems to be true whether it's an important, dominant function or a lesser background one. Intuition asks the questions but needs facts, logic and relationships to find answers. The other parts of personality are already operating, so Intuition just steers the investigation via questions. We may see Thinking and Sensing doing most of the work, unaware that they are reporting to Intuition in the background.

Extroverted Intuition can form a very useful partnership with Thinking to understand mathematics. When those two mental functions are most dominant, there can be extraordinary math ability. Advanced mathematics, and most especially in research stages, is entirely the product of Extroverted Intuition's questions. It may also help with visualizing spatial relationships. Intuition sees connections, which can be literally geometric connections. Connections between other things may be seen as if they were shapes made of connecting lines. This is a big part of advanced mathematics; without it, there would be no ongoing research in geometry.

It's also a big part of seeing analogies between things. Cause-and-effect connections, like a foot kicking a ball, are easy to see. But there are many other kinds of connections, such as parallels, overlap, opposite, or similarity in shape but not scale. When we make analogies, we're seeing these kinds of relationships and connections. Extroverted Intuition seems to be especially drawn to making analogies as well as learning from them. When it's dominant, the personality can come up with unusual but very pointed analogies.

During the time of writing this book, I've sometimes told friends that all conversations and events are, "like the Sioux using a buffalo: nothing is wasted." That's not a common analogy, but it sprang from a quick mental search for "things shaped like the way I am using human interactions." Extroverted Intuition found the image in less than half a second, and immediately I could put it into words. My Extroverted Intuition, which is pretty dominant, maintains a very thick file of "things with similar shapes" or "with similar motions." It's as if every fact, event or emotion gets cross-filed under not just itself, but also every possible angle that it could be viewed in. A quick "connections search" turns up several of them in less than half a second, so that I can select the one that best suits the friend I'm talking to—or the one that I think is funniest. Much of this book is built from Extroverted Intuition's analogies, as I try to convey the ideas I've seen by showing you what they're like.

Inventors almost always have Extroverted Intuition. An inventor has to look at an existing method or tool and notice something about it that could be improved. Most of us just keep using the tool without asking "could this be better, faster, or easier?" The inventor's mind asks questions, then using Extroverted Intuition it generates possible solutions. A good inventor can visualize his new idea, spotting problems in a design that still exists only in his mind. Most of the work goes on in the inventor's mind, but his hands will soon be busy too, making drawings or molding materials.

Extroverted Intuition is also drawn to ways to make the imagined possibilities real, even if they don't work quite as perfectly as imagined. They're driven to finish the "map" of meaning in whatever they're working on. Extroverted functions are oriented to the outside world, so are motivated not only to see outside connections but to make them better understood or known by others. What's seen in the mind needs to be painted, built, written, or staged.

When it's a dominant part of personality, Extroverted Intuition is an enemy of routine. Routine makes you do the same thing every day at the same time, instead of something different. Therefore, routine excludes possibilities, and Extroverted Intuition doesn't want them excluded. In a nondominant role, Extroverted Intuition doesn't seem to interfere with necessary routine, but when it's strong, it may actively disrupt it. Our stereotype of an inventor includes her (or his) absent-minded lack of routine: working all hours, eating breakfast at any time of day, not changing clothes for several days, and inventing gadgets that will take over routines by operating on timers. That's what it looks like when Extroverted Intuition simply takes over.

When it's not a dominant part of personality, Extroverted Intuition doesn't interfere with routine. In fact, when it's a lesser part of personality, it's balanced by strong Introverted Sensing, which is a great keeper of routine. When it's in this lesser role, rather than disrupting routine it just suggests questions to research, pushing the personality to read books and learn more about things. It acts as a manager or coach to Thinking and Sensing as they learn about planting gardens, fixing machines, managing a company, or implementing new strategies or technologies. Operating this way, it doesn't create any sort of eccentric behavior, instead only enhances and drives learning.

Another very big part of Extroverted Intuition is its effect on imagination. Much of what we mean by "imagination" is probably just a division of Intuition. It means seeing possibilities that aren't real at this time. Some possibilities that aren't real at this time can be made real, if we plan and work. Others are just not real, and perhaps never will be. Extroverted Intuition can see both, but it is especially fond of the kind that is completely unreal.

Extroverted Intuition is responsible for fantasy literature, especially science fiction. When Intuition is dominant, it may invent science fiction and other fantasy. (It's a safe bet that a majority of science fiction writers have Extroverted Intuition.) Even when it's operating as a lesser part of personality, it is fond of unpredictable plot twists and surprise endings. Extroverted Intuition likes to pose "what if?" questions, so it loves stories and movies that also do this.

One drawback for Extroverted Intuition is that seeing so many possibilities can make it hard to choose just one. At an extreme, strong Extroverted Intuition can waste an entire day by constantly suggesting that there's something else you could be doing; you are missing out on possibilities by staying on task. If you listen to this voice, you'll never finish anything. Extroverted Intuition points out that you could read this book, but look, there's another book over there that's just as important. You could become a doctor, but you could also become a teacher; you could go to college, but you could also spend a few years in a band or a Buddhist monastery.

Every choice presents a door that, when closed, will change your life and limit your options, and Extroverted Intuition can resist making such choices. It needs to be kept in check by Judging functions so that it's not left insisting that all options are equally important. Given free rein, Extroverted Intuition knows no limits on finding new ideas. As a background function, it is generally well-governed: directing research but not running off into the wild. When dominant, though, Extroverted Intuition is always revving, like a horse that wants to pull the carriage off into a field at breakneck speed.

EXTROVERTED INTUITION IN LITERATURE

One of America's greatest inventors was George Washington Carver. He used his training as a botany professor to invent many products out of Alabama's poor soil and scanty plants. He called his use of Extroverted Intuition "creative and applied science:"

Creative and applied science is coming to our relief as never before, and showing us the fabulous wealth we have in our own varied deposits of clay ranging in color from the snow white kaolins and China clays, to the choicest of ochres, rare ambers, vandyke browns, choice Indian reds, beautiful siennas and rare deposits of Fuller's earth. Nearly one hundred valuable medicinal plants which would yield readily to cultivation, loom up here and there all over the South, making pharmaceutical drug manufacturing plants a paying possibility... The cow pea, with its many uses; the soybean with its thirty-five or more products; the velvet bean furnishing an equal number of products; the pecan with its eighty-five products; the sweet potato yielding its 118 products; and the humble peanut, which some regard as the marvel of all marvels, with its 199 products.[67]

67: Gary R. Kremer, ed., *George Washington Carver: In His Own Words* (Columbia, MO: University of Missouri

Carver assumed that clay, sweet potatoes and peanuts could produce a wide array of products, using even peanut shells to make a hard, polished surface for cabinets. Others assumed that little or nothing could be made from these materials, but to strong Extroverted Intuition, every molecule had some kind of use waiting to be discovered. Tuskeegee Institute, where Carver taught and researched, was founded by another man with strong Extroverted Intuition. Before founding his new college, Booker T. Washington did a survey of everything that poor black people in post-slavery Alabama needed to know. In his autobiography, *Up From Slavery* (1901), Washington laid out the many questions and problems he hoped his school could solve.

Of one thing I felt more strongly convinced than ever… that something must be done more than merely to imitate New England education as it then existed… We wanted to teach the students how to bathe; how to care for their teeth and clothing. We wanted to teach them what to eat, and how to eat it, and how to care for their rooms. Aside from this, we wanted to give them such a practical knowledge of some one industry, together with the spirit of industry, thrift and economy, that they could be sure of knowing how to make a living after they had left us… We wanted to give them such an education as would fit a large proportion of them to be teachers, and at the same time cause them to return to the plantation districts and show the people there how to put new energy and new ideas into farming, as well as into the intellectual and moral and religious life of the people. All these ideas and needs crowded themselves upon us with a seriousness that seemed well-nigh overwhelming. What were we to do?

Using Extroverted Intuition, he rejected the traditional school model that had been used for centuries. Instead, he first made a list of needs, then designed a school program to fit them. Washington used Intuition with Feeling to ask questions about people, while Carver paired Extroverted Intuition with Thinking to solve science problems. The action of Intuition is the same: posing an open-ended string of questions, making no assumptions, and trying every possibility.

Not all inventors become famous, and some people with Extroverted Intuition feel restricted in their daily lives. Annie Dillard's memoir *An American Childhood* (1987) describes the restlessness her mother felt when her role in life did not permit her to become a real inventor:

Mother's energy and intelligence suited her for a greater role in a larger arena—mayor of New York, say—than the one she had… She saw how things should be run, but she had nothing to run but our household. Even there, small minds troubled her; she was smarter than the people who designed the things she had to use all day.

"Look," she said. "Whoever designed this corkscrew never used one. Why would anyone sell it without trying it out?" So she invented a better one. She showed me a drawing of it. The spirit of American enterprise never faded in Mother. If capitalizing and tooling up had been as interesting as theorizing and thinking up, she would have fired up a new factory every week, and chaired several hundred corporations.

She didn't like the taste of stamps, so she didn't lick stamps; she licked the corner of the envelope instead. She glued sandpaper to the sides of the kitchen drawers, and under kitchen cabinets, so she always had a handy place to strike a match. She designed, and hounded workmen to

Press, 1987), 116.

build against all norms, doubly wide kitchen counters and elevated sinks. To splint a finger, she stuck it in a lightweight cigar tube. Conversely, to protect a pack of cigarettes, she carried it in a Band-Aid box.[68]

Extroverted Intuition is a dominant influence in fiction, especially in fantasy and science fiction. Both genres allow us to ask questions and imagine things that are completely impossible in the world we live in. In *The Magician's Nephew*, C. S. Lewis imagined not only an alternative world, but also a "world" that is not even a world. Two children, Digory and Polly, find themselves in a park-like place filled with little ponds. They arrived there apparently through one of the pools, so they realize they can go home by jumping back into it. But instead of just doing this, Digory uses Extroverted Intuition to make a leap of comprehension about what this place really means.

"I've just had a really wonderful idea," said Digory. "What are all the other pools?"

"How do you mean?"

"Why, if we can get back to our own world by jumping into this pool, mightn't we get somewhere else by jumping into one of the others? Supposing there was a world at the bottom of the pool?"

"But I thought we were already in your Uncle Andrew's Other World or Other Place or whatever he called it. Didn't you say—"

"Oh bother Uncle Andrew," interrupted Digory. "I don't believe he knows anything about it. He never had the pluck to come here himself. He only talked of one Other World. But suppose there were dozens?"

"You mean, this wood might be only one of them?"

"No, I don't believe this wood is a world at all. I think it's just a sort of in-between place."

Polly looked puzzled. "Don't you see?" said Digory. "No, do listen. Think of our tunnel under the slates at home. It isn't a room in any of the houses. In a way, it isn't really part of any of the houses. But once you're in the tunnel you can go along it and come out into any of the houses in the row. Mightn't this wood be the same?—a place that isn't in any of the worlds, but once you've found that place you can get into them all."

"Well, even if you can—" began Polly, but Digory went on as if he hadn't heard her.

"And of course that explains everything," he said. "That's why it is so quiet and sleepy here. Nothing ever happens here. Like at home. It's in the houses that people talk, and do things, and have meals. Nothing goes on in the in-between places, behind the walls and above the ceilings and under the floor, or in our own tunnel. But when you come out of the tunnel you may find yourself in any house. I think we can get out of this place into jolly well Anywhere! We don't need to jump back into the same pool we came up by. Or not just yet."

"The Wood between the Worlds," said Polly dreamily. "It sounds rather nice."[69]

Fantasy fiction imagines alternative places, people and ways of life, while its subset, science fiction, re-invents physics. Douglas Adams' story *The Hitchhiker's Guide to the Galaxy* often uses the narrative tone of historical writing to "explain" imaginary concepts of time, place, movement and being. The passage below explains that improbability itself can be used as a form of locomotion (and I'll refer to this again in Chapter 9).

68: Annie Dillard, *An American Childhood* (NY: Harper and Row, 1987), 115-116.
69: C. S. Lewis, *The Magician's Nephew* (London: Bodley Head, 1955).

The Infinite Improbability Drive is a wonderful new method of crossing vast interstellar distances in a mere nothingth of a second, without all that tedious mucking about in hyperspace. It was discovered by a lucky chance, and then developed into a governable form of propulsion by the Galactic Government's research team on Damogran.

This, briefly, is the story of its discovery.

The principle of generating small amounts of finite *improbability by simply hooking the logic circuits of a Bambleweeny 57 Sub-Meson Brain to an atomic vector plotter suspended in a strong Browning Motion producer (say a nice hot cup of tea) were of course well understood—and such generators were often used to break the ice at parties by making all the molecules in the hostess's undergarments leap simultaneously one foot to the left, in accordance with the Theory of Indeterminacy.*

Many respectable physicists said that they weren't going to stand for this, partly because it was a debasement of science, but mostly because they didn't get invited to those sorts of parties.

Another thing they couldn't stand was the perpetual failure they encountered in trying to construct a machine which could generate the infinite *improbability field needed to flip a spaceship across the mind-paralyzing-distances between the farthest stars, and in the end they grumpily announced that such a machine was virtually impossible.*

Then, one day, a student who had been left to sweep up the lab after a particularly unsuccessful party found himself reasoning this way:

If, he thought to himself, such a machine is a virtual *impossibility, then it must logically be a* finite *improbability. So all I have to do in order to make one is to work out exactly how improbable it is, feed that figure into the finite improbability generator, give it a fresh cup of really hot tea... and turn it on!*

He did this, and was rather startled to discover that he had managed to create the long-sought-after golden Infinite Improbability generator out of thin air.

It startled him even more when just after he was awarded the Galactic Institute's Prize for Extreme Cleverness he got lynched by a rampaging mob of respectable physicists who had finally realized that the one thing they really couldn't stand was a smart-ass.[70]

Adams does not expect us to take the idea seriously, as the satirical tone makes clear. But he does want us to keep our ideas very, very loose and ready to accept pretty much anything. That's the spirit of Extroverted Intuition: clear your mind of expectations, explore, and be ready to adapt.

INTROVERTED INTUITION READS AN INNER MAP

When Intuition is focused on inborn, archetypal knowledge, it is still about connections, but it asks questions in a different way. In some ways, that's because it doesn't ask questions; Introverted Intuition already knows archetypes of truth and connection. Its key question is why the world doesn't make sense, as it should, as the archetypes make sense. Like other Introverted functions, Intuition can be confident, stubborn, idealistic and always scanning for danger.

70: Douglas Adams, *The Hitchhiker's Guide to the Galaxy* (London: Pan Books, 1979).

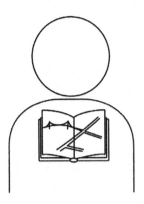

Fig. 8-2

The cartoon shows a personality that has a book inside: it's an atlas of meaning. There are maps of both familiar and unknown places. As odd as this sounds, people with Introverted Intuition have an innate sense that they already know what the world means: they just have to find out what the places look like. Their question isn't "where does this bridge lead?" it's "what does that place look like, when I get there?" Introverted Intuition explores the world not to find connections, but to prove them. It doesn't make maps, it takes photographs to pin on maps. The places were already there, they just needed to be experienced. Archetypes of meaning and connection need to be filled out, not discovered.

Introverted Intuition is the tightest link between consciousness and the unconscious, nonverbal, lightspeed parts of the brain. Like Introverted Sensing, it shows a different character when it's dominant in a personality from when it isn't. When it's dominant, it feels strongly that it knows more about the world than other people do, and it leads to personalities of a cynical or even revolutionary flavor. When it's not dominant, it leads to strong prejudices and superstitions.

As an Introverted function, this kind of Intuition is both idealistic and critical. Knowing true meaning seems like the most important thing for survival, and true meaning is felt as wonderful and beautiful. By contrast, false meaning, when passed off as true, seems disgusting beyond words, and also extremely dangerous. Propaganda and hypocrisy make people with Introverted Intuition very angry—not that anyone likes these things, but the critical skepticism of Introverted Intuition feels them as mortal danger.

Knowing truth means safety, in this template of safety and danger. If someone deliberately blocks an Introverted Intuiter from knowing the truth, it's felt as reckless or criminal endangerment, not merely as an inconvenience. People with this type of Intuition are drawn toward anyone who has experience and information that can enlighten them beyond whatever is officially and publicly known. They like to find books that explain parts of life or the world that are not usually discussed. Sometimes it's part of a directed research project, but just as often, it's simply a strategy for safety, because there's no way to know when this off-beat knowledge will come in handy.

Just as Introverted Sensing can be a sort of aesthetic conscience that wants things to look right, Introverted Intuition can act as a conscience about meaning. It tends to be antagonistic to how things look; it sees past appearances. It's aware that appearances can be used to support hypocrisy or cover up falsity. Appearances become suspect, in fact. People or situations that look too perfect make Introverted Intuition uneasy, an anxiety that does not abate until it's certain that all relevant truth is visible.

People with strong, dominant Introverted Intuition are almost always intellectuals of some kind, depending on their circumstances. They may be laboratory scientists, clinical researchers, therapists, literary critics, musicians, priests or ministers, lawyers or even professors working in rare fields like archeology. They're most likely to end up in work like this if they were born or easily found their way into academic circles. When they're born with economic limitations or in a social world that isn't intellectual, they have the same nature but they are less able to apply it directly. Music, religious ministry and journalism are still likely to draw them, if not in a way that supports them financially, at least as a passionate side interest.

Journalism is a good example of how Introverted Intuition works. Journalists watch events and people, then they become interested in doing extra interviews, travel and other research to expose what's really going on. How do they know what to investigate? Much of the time, it's Introverted Intuition directing their attention. Feeling like they already know meaning, they recognize that there's a hole in the outside narrative. They sense that something is being covered up. Guided by Intuition, they begin to explore the facts with Sensing, Thinking and Feeling. When they discover the true story, they recognize it as what, in some sense, they knew all along.

Like Extroverted Intuition, the Introverted form produces imagination. However, it's somewhat less likely to encourage an anything-goes kind of imagination. When it's involved in writing fiction, it tends to be more purpose-directed. Instead of open-ended what-if questions, it poses scenarios that can test and explore ideas, often developing worlds with consistent networks of meaning. If they write fantasy or science fiction, the stories may have a message or moral, in contrast to how open-ended Extroverted Intuition stories may be. Writers with Introverted Intuition are also strongly drawn to inspirational writing. They imagine stories that will show an ideal meaning in life, inspiring people to try harder to reach it.

Paired with strong Thinking, Introverted Intuition is good with science, engineering and machines. Although few people can make a career in pure science research, those with strong Introverted Intuition are most likely to rise into those rare niches. The scientific method is basically just Introverted Intuition's way of going about business. It was written down so that others could learn it, but Thinkers with Introverted Intuition naturally test hypotheses and design experiments.

Introverted Intuition is often drawn to seeing connections between numbers with graphs and figures. As strange as it sounds to people who don't use Introverted Intuition much, some people seem born understanding graphs. Graphs show a visual system of lines or bars to tell us how different numbers are related to each other. They are a natural tool for people who already have a sense of how things are connected. Of course, graphs can be used by people with other abilities, and they can be used to explore connections in the outside world. But it's only Introverted Intuition that seems to cast its own thoughts in terms of graphs.

Introverted Intuition can give someone an edge in working with all kinds of machinery, from workshop tools, to engineering principles, to quantum mechanics. Especially when the same person has strong Thinking skills, the engineering approach to life just makes sense. Introverted Intuition will be helpful in complicated "hunches" about science, too. August Kekulé's sudden insight about a molecule forming into a ring may have been Introverted Intuition at work.

When Introverted Intuition is working with good Feeling skills, it is often critical of the way society is organized. The leaders of "social justice" movements are nearly always in this zone of personality. They don't buy official explanations of why things have to be the way they are; they don't believe government reports. If personal experience has led them to understand why some parts of society are broken, they can accept the problem but try to change it. If they don't have personal experience, they often reject all explanations and insist that the problem could be solved if people would just look at it honestly. Poverty, crime, and sickness may seem to them like temporary issues if only people would stop believing what they're told.

Introverted Intuition is often pessimistic and negative. It can't stop noticing all of the mismanagement in the world. Businesses are making stupid decisions, and government even stupider ones. Political parties are corrupt and weak, in their eyes; they are often Independent voters even if they support one party's agenda. They just can't believe in parties, since party images and slogans are another form of false appearance. They are probably a majority of staffers at non-profit organizations whose mission is to criticize officials, parties and platforms.

The pessimism of Introverted Intuitives can be really striking. While working for change and often doing much good themselves, they usually expect some part of "the system" to break down within their lifetimes, if not sooner. The real estate bubble will burst, or some part of the economy will go bust, or we'll have a revolution. They regret the disorder and harm these things will cause, but their regret is overshadowed by their absolute conviction that it's inevitable. The downfall will be awful, but at least it will reveal truth for once. Where Extroverted Intuition optimistically believes in rapidly turning over as many rocks as possible, looking for that cure for cancer, Introverted Intuition believes in turning over rocks, but carefully and from two feet away if possible. Some rocks have rattlesnakes under them!

While dominant Introverted Intuition often creates intellectuals, its non-dominant form is most often found in people of action. They usually have a bent toward rebellion and revolution, coming from their skepticism and love of action. If there's a local push to elect some new candidates to the school board and "take over" the schools for reform, people with strong Introverted Intuition are usually leading and staffing the effort, and others with weaker Intuition but stronger Sensing ability to act are often the foot soldiers. On the large scale, when people conspire to overthrow a dictatorship or lead a guerilla movement, those with Introverted Intuition will be at the center, both as intellectuals and as fighters. There's a wide range of medium rebellions and revolutions between those two extremes: ideological rebellion, artistic revolution, political reform, and critical commentary. Introverted Intuition nearly always wants to battle "the man" in some form, with ideas or action.

When Introverted Intuition is not dominant in a personality, it's not as integrated, as it is in scientists and journalists. Most of the personality's heavy lifting is carried out by more dominant Sensing, Feeling or Thinking. But even when Introverted Intuition is weak, it's still present and active.

Two forms that less dominant Introverted Intuition can take are prejudice and superstition. Forget for a moment the "official" prejudices that we've all been taught not to harbor. We can have these prejudices, of course, but we can also create our own. These start by just having a vague but clear Intuition that someone is up to no good or is has something to hide. Strong Introverted Intuition would seek proof, in science or fact-finding. Weaker Intuition isn't usually in control of things like that, but it keeps its eyes open. Even without proof, the suspect person seems dangerous. Then the Intuition hunch can become generalized: everyone who even looks like this person is trouble. That's where it becomes prejudice. It could be prejudice against church people or against non-church people, against some immigrant group or against people who make more money than we do. Weak Introverted Intuition sees connections and gives them reality.

Superstition is another way of seeing connections, but in a simpler way. It amounts to observing that certain things happen at the same time, and seeing a connection between them. Some superstitions are learned from other people and may not be innate. Innate superstition always comes from Introverted Intuition, so it feels real and compelling even when there are logical arguments against it. The connection between winning at gambling or sports, and this action or item, feels real. It feels so real that ignoring it seems truly dangerous. That's the nature of an Introverted function: to keep us from danger. So people may develop strong opinions about what's lucky or unlucky, and if pressed to do something unlucky, they feel very real fear.

Skilled, integrated, well-developed Introverted Intuition may take years to learn properly. Too much early discouragement can stunt its development so that the person who leans on it doesn't ever achieve a full potential. Children with strong Introverted Intuition are often stubbornly sure that they're right, and in order to learn how to use and manage this function, they need many experiments in which they test their convictions. If the consequences are too severe to bear, they may pull back and become afraid to try again. Similarly, if parents add to the natural consequences by making fun of the child's wrong decision, the same thing can happen. Introverted Intuition is extremely sensitive to criticism and leans toward perfectionism already. On the converse, being protected from consequences means reinforcing the stubborn, negative side of Introverted Intuition, rather than the experimental, testing side. Introverted Intuition is not an easy personality function to manage.

INTRODUCED INTUITION IN LITERATURE

Perhaps because detective stories are so popular, it's not hard to find Introverted Intuition at work in stories. Let's start with a weaker form, the hunch. Shakespeare's character of

Hamlet appears to work by Introverted Intuition. In Act II Scene II, he has a hunch that his old college friends did not come to visit on their own volition, but are part of some kind of plot. "What make you at Elsinore?" he asks:

> ROSENCRANTZ: *To visit you, my lord; no other occasion.*
> HAMLET: *Beggar that I am, I am even poor in thanks; but I thank you: and sure, dear friends, my thanks are too dear a halfpenny. Were you not sent for? Is it your own inclining? Is it a free visitation? Come, deal justly with me: come, come; nay, speak.*
> GUILDENSTERN: *What should we say, my lord?*
> HAMLET: *Why, any thing, but to the purpose. You were sent for; and there is a kind of confession in your looks which your modesties have not craft enough to colour: I know the good king and queen have sent for you.*
> ROSENCRANTZ: *To what end, my lord?*
> HAMLET: *That you must teach me. But let me conjure you, by the rights of our fellowship, by the consonancy of our youth, by the obligation of our ever-preserved love, and by what more dear a better proposer could charge you withal, be even and direct with me, whether you were sent for, or no?*
> ROSENCRANTZ: *[Aside to GUILDENSTERN] What say you?*
> HAMLET: *[Aside] Nay, then, I have an eye of you.—If you*
> *love me, hold not off.*
> GUILDENSTERN: *My lord, we were sent for.*

The most famous literary detective, Sherlock Holmes, used Introverted Intuition in addition to the Extroverted Thinking that an earlier passage displayed. In *A Study in Scarlet* (1887), he explains to Watson, the narrator, how he may not even need to see a crime scene to solve the case:

> *"I'm a consulting detective, if you can understand what that is. Here in London we have lots of Government detectives and lots of private ones. When these fellows are at fault they come to me, and I manage to put them on the right scent. They lay all the evidence before me, and I am generally able, by the help of my knowledge of the history of crime, to set them straight. There is a strong family resemblance about misdeeds, and if you have all the details of a thousand at your finger ends, it is odd if you can't unravel the thousand and first. Lestrade is a well-known detective. He got himself into a fog recently over a forgery case, and that was what brought him here."*
> *"And these other people?"*
> *"They are mostly sent on by private inquiry agencies. They are all people who are in trouble about something, and want a little enlightening. I listen to their story, they listen to my comments, and then I pocket my fee."*
> *"But do you mean to say,"* I said, *"that without leaving your room you can unravel some knot which other men can make nothing of, although they have seen every detail for themselves?"*
> *"Quite so. I have a kind of Intuition that way. Now and again a case turns up which is a little more complex. Then I have to bustle about and see things with my own eyes."*

In other words, when Holmes's Introverted Intuition finds that it doesn't have an adequate map already, he has to take "photos" with Sensing, and pin them onto the "map" of meaning. Then, with the addition of a few Thinking deductions, his Intuition is ready to work again. Holmes is a good example of someone with Introverted Intuition who had much freedom in early life to test his maps, so that as an adult, he is extremely confident.

Aleksandr Solzhenitsyn described a similarly strong Intuition system which was less about facts and logic, and more about people and relationships. In *The Gulag Archipelago* (1974), he describes the many details of political arrests and imprisonment. Among them, an inmate must learn not to trust prisoners who look the same as everyone else, but who are in fact informers only pretending to be prisoners. His personality appears to have very strong Introverted Intuition, so he was able to detect these false prisoners immediately and without mistakes. It began the first time he shared a cell with other men and had to set up a cot:

I was helped by a young fellow my own age, also a military man. His tunic and aviator's cap hung on his cot. He had asked me, even before the old man spoke, not for news of the war but for tobacco. But although I felt openhearted toward my new friends, and although not many words had been exchanged in the few minutes since I joined them, I sensed something alien in this front-line soldier who was my contemporary, and, as far as he was concerned, I clammed up immediately and forever.

I had not yet even heard the word "nasyedka"—stool pigeon—nor learned that there had to be one such "stool pigeon" in each cell. And I had not yet had time to think things over and conclude that I did not like this fellow, Georgi Kramarenko. But a spiritual relay, a sensor relay, had clicked inside me, and it had closed him off from me for good and all. I would not bother to recall this event if it had been the only one of its kind. But soon, with astonishment, and alarm, I became aware of the work of this internal sensor relay as a constant, inborn trait.

The years passed and I lay on the same bunks, marched in the same formations, and worked in the same work brigades with hundreds of others. And always that secret sensor relay, for whose creation I deserved not the least bit of credit, worked even before I remembered it was there, worked at the first sight of a human face and eyes, at the first sound of a voice—so that I opened my heart to that person either fully or just the width of a crack, or else shut myself off from him completely. This was so consistently unfailing that all the efforts of the State Security officers to employ stool pigeons began to seem to me as insignificant as being pestered by gnats: after all, a person who has undertaken to be a traitor always betrays the fact in his face and in his voice, and even though some were more skilled in pretense, there was always something fishy about them.

On the other hand, the sensor relay helped me distinguish those to whom I could from the very beginning of our acquaintance completely disclose my most precious depths and secrets—secrets for which heads roll. Thus it was that I got through eight years of imprisonment, three years of exile, and another six years of underground authorship, which were in no wise less dangerous. During all those seventeen years I recklessly revealed myself to dozens of people—and didn't make a misstep even once. (I have never read about this trait anywhere, and I mention it here for those interested in psychology. It seems to me that such spiritual sensors exist in many of us, but because we live in too technological and rational an age, we neglect this miracle and don't allow it to develop.)[71]

Introverted Intuition also assists people to understand the philosophical (therefore invisible and hidden) meaning of events. Long before he was a famous writer, George Orwell served as a British policeman in colonial Burma. The natives were not allowed to have guns, which placed Orwell and other white men in a position of separation and power. So, for example, if an elephant killed someone, only a British officer had a gun to shoot it. Having

---

71: Aleksandr Solzhenitsyn, *The Gulag Archipelago*, trans. Thomas P. Whitney (NY: Harper and Row, 1974), Book I, Part 1, Chapter 5.

the gun appeared to make a British officer powerful, but Orwell describes a moment when his Introverted Intuition told him that his colonial rank actually made him powerless:

And suddenly I realized that I should have to shoot the elephant after all. The people expected it of me and I had got to do it; I could feel their two thousand wills pressing me forward, irresistibly. And it was at this moment, as I stood there with the rifle in my hands, that I first grasped the hollowness, the futility, of the white man's dominion in the East. Here was I, the white man with his gun, standing in front of the unarmed native crowd—seemingly the leading actor of the piece; but in reality I was only an absurd puppet pushed to and fro by the will of those yellow faces behind. I perceived in this moment that when the white man turns tyrant it is his own freedom that he destroys.[72]

The importance of the incident, to Orwell, is not whether or not the elephant died. He is telling the story because *Intuition* recalls it as a turning-point, when he suddenly saw that the appearances of colonial government were a false mask. He could see the truth that the appearances had been covering. Orwell's career as a journalist brought him many more such moments of sudden insight.

Martin Luther King Jr. is one of the most famous moral crusaders, working for social justice. In his famous "Letter from Birmingham Jail" (1963), he explains how his Introverted Intuition told him the difference between laws that should be kept and laws that must be challenged.

An unjust law is a human law that is not rooted in eternal law and natural law. Any law that uplifts human personality is just. Any law that degrades human personality is unjust. All segregation statutes are unjust because segregation distorts the soul and damages the personality. It gives the segregator a false sense of superiority and the segregated a false sense of inferiority. Segregation... ends up relegating persons to the status of things. Hence segregation is not only politically, economically and sociologically unsound, it is morally wrong and awful... Thus it is that I can urge men to obey the 1954 decision of the Supreme Court, for it is morally right; and I can urge them to disobey segregation ordinances, for they are morally wrong.[73]

The difference, he says, lies in the ideal, archetypal meaning of justice and of being human. If you can see the archetypal truth, you won't be fooled by the visible appearance of a contrary law. Sensing helps you discover what the laws are, but Intuition shows you what they should be.

John Lennon's lyrics often demonstrate Introverted Intuition's idealistic certainty that it knows the real meaning of the world, in spite of appearances. His song "Imagine" suggests that Intuition can envision a perfect world that has never existed:

Imagine no possessions
I wonder if you can
No need for greed or hunger
A brotherhood of man
Imagine all the people
Sharing all the world...[74]

72: George Orwell, "Shooting an Elephant," *A Collection of Essays* (San Diego: HBJ, 1981).

73: Martin Luther King, Jr. "Letter from Birmingham Jail," *The Christian Century* (June 12, 1963).

74: John Lennon, "Imagine," *Imagine* album (Capitol: 1971).

CHAPTER 9

Perceiving Functions in Balance

IN CHAPTER 6, WE NOTED that Thinking and Feeling could be at loggerheads if they were equally strong and both oriented to idealism or pragmatism. The Perceiving functions have the same problem; Sensing and Intuition are both for processing information, but they do it so differently that they could compete, not cooperate.

Sensing is about knowing facts and, as Jung called it, the world that is "in flux." Sensing tracks what is, as it changes (flux). The key word is "is." What is: that's the entire, absorbing focus of Sensing. Intuition, by contrast, focuses on the invisible and on what, in a sense, *does not really exist* in Sensing's terms. Intuition looks past the appearance—what is—to see what is hidden. In its simplest form, it looks for what is hidden, but in more advanced forms, Intuition is interested in what truly does not exist: potentials that have no concrete reality yet, if they ever will.

Sensing needs mental resources for directly sampling and tracking the factual world. It really has to come first, since it is critical to survival. Intuition should always function as an add-on, using only the processing space that's left when Sensing has finished its important role of seeing and hearing. And yet there are times when Intuition is critically important for survival too. It is especially important in times when a lot of facts are changing rapidly and we don't know why.

The solution we see at work in personality is that for a large majority of people, some kind of Sensing is clearly a top priority, a dominant function. Intuition still plays an important role, but it operates in the background and often handles tasks that are less important. On the other hand, in a minority of personalities, the priorities are reversed. For them, some kind of Intuition is more dominant than any kind of Sensing. Sensing is still used to avoid walking off cliffs, but it's often relegated to a sort of hobby or artistic role, while Intuition directs most of the person's attention.

Sensing and Intuition can also play a role in conscience. We'll look first at the way personality is shaped by Sensing or Intuition being dominant. After that, we'll see how the Perceiving functions can filter the decisions of conscience.

SENSING AND INTUITION AS DOMINANT IN PERSONALITY

Most of the mental functions we discuss are pretty evenly distributed among people, but there are three exceptions. One of the best-known is how more women have dominant Feeling, while more men have dominant Thinking. The ratio between Feeling and Thinking among women is pretty high, about 3 to 1, as mentioned in Chapter 6. When a personality trait isn't evenly distributed, we're probably looking at something that environment had a hand in shaping.

Human behavior in communities seems to supply a reason for the prevalence of Feeling among women. Because women have always been very involved in relationship work among their children, well-integrated and developed Feeling is a good trait. Mothers and wives can have dominant Thinking and it's often a very good thing when they do, but it's undeniable that if your society wants you to do nothing but child and baby care, Feeling makes this role much easier to bear. Until the last few centuries, families chose brides. They looked at family stability, which may itself be a marker for the older women having strong Feeling, and when they evaluated the girl, they probably looked for signs of relationship ability in her character. Over time, as traits are passed along genetically and shaped in other ways we don't yet understand, Feeling became the majority trait among women.

We see a parallel situation with Sensing and Intuition and a similarly lopsided set of ratios. Among both men and women, around 73% have dominant Sensing. The reason may be similar to the way Feeling is favored among women, that as past families evaluated marriage choices, they saw greater value in people who were good at dealing with the real world, not ideas. It also may be that Sensing is the default state of most brains, while having dominant Intuition may be a recessive genetic trait.

But there's another interesting disparity among people who have dominant Sensing (this is the third lopsided ratio). When I say "dominant Sensing," I am grouping both kinds of sensing, Extroverted and Introverted, together. If we separate the two kinds, we find that Introverted Sensing is much more common. Among people with strong, dominant Sensing, about 2/3 of them have idealistic Introverted Sensing.[75] Extroverted Sensing has so many strengths; why should it become the 1/3 minority among Sensing personalities?

As before, we can only speculate about how human behavior in groups may have favored some traits over others. Extroverted functions are always more optimistic, as well as more pragmatic. That is, they are less alert to danger and more alert to opportunities. While

---

75: *MBTI® Manual, A Guide to the Development and Use of the Myers-Briggs Type Indicator*, 3rd edition (Mountain View, CA: CPP, 2003), 156-158.

Extroverted Sensing must be best at picking up the sensory details that signal danger, it may be slow to recognize them as dangerous, not merely challenging. Pragmatic, opportunistic and optimistic, Extroverted Sensing may too often assume that the situation at hand is manageable. This works out wonderfully when it's true. However, there are many times when Extroverted Sensing's bold optimism about physical challenges leads to disaster and death. We often see people like this conquer many adventures, only to die at last in some kind of accident.

On the other side, all Introverted functions are not only idealistic but also cautious, critical and poised to reject options. Introverted Sensing is more likely to interpret a situation as dangerous, sometimes wrongly. On average, across time, this has probably been an advantage more often than not. We could not survive wars without Extroverted Sensing's courage and recklessness; but as individuals, those people with Extroverted Sensing who charge ahead may help win the battle—but die before it ends. The survivors are the more cautious people who took more precautions.

It's also likely that as civilization turned more people away from hunting, toward both agriculture and trade, Introverted Sensing did well. Hunting requires fast sensory processing and instant decisions, traits of Extroverted Sensing. But farming and trade require a lot of foresight, envisioning dangers well before they happen. Guarding against danger in farming isn't like warding off spears in battle. Farming caution has to do with saving the right amount of grain for spring seed, developing wise routines for when to plant, weed and harvest, and understanding the value of one harvest as compared to another. Caution in trade has the same requirements: choosing what to buy and when, where to carry it for sale, and how much to charge. Introverted Sensing was probably best at tasks like this.

So there are two key reasons why Introverted Sensing has an advantage in a civilized place: caution and better ability to plan. If the advantage was greater, no doubt we'd see an even lower number of Extroverted Sensers. But it isn't. Extroverted Sensing is still extremely important, and if anything, we over-value it. Look at the energy we put into playing and watching sports. Perhaps dimly recalling how valuable athletic skill would be if our civilization was directly put into danger, we praise and esteem fierce competition. No matter how important caution and planning are, we tend to fall in love with bold, brave people who take risks.

What we see most often is teamwork between two people with dominant Sensing, one Introverted and one Extroverted. Most successful farms and businesses have a pair like this at the core. It may be a husband and wife, father and son, mother and daughter, siblings, or unrelated co-workers who rose to the top and formed a management team. If either of them leaves the team (in a family, probably through death or divorce), the business starts to fail.

We all recognize these teams; they have a certain standard appearance and division of labor. Let's suppose such a team, and we'll call the Introverted Senser "Ivan," and the Extroverted Senser "Ed." Even if you didn't know personality terminology, you'd know these men at sight. Ivan dresses neatly and prefers to handle the office work. He keeps the books, fills out ordering forms, and meets customers. Ivan is good at small talk; he is often good with words—he's educated or he likes to read, or he's a good storyteller. Ed, on the other hand, hates to dress up and would rather be outside or in a warehouse. He manages large equipment and animals; he works long hours without saying much. Ed may be very smart, but he's less likely to strike people as bookish or educated, partly because he just doesn't say much on the job. He may tell good stories, but he's usually too busy moving about.

Typically, Ivan runs the office, while Ed does the hands-on work. A team of Extroverted Sensers goes out in a van, installing wiring or furnaces in houses. They climb telephone poles or move boxcars. They're good at estimating size and speed, and they're always optimistic that the job can be done. If the wiring is messed up or it looks like something won't fit, they try to improvise, and they often succeed. They don't give up easily on tasks that involve movement, space and size because that's where their optimistic pragmatism is most at home.

The Introverted Senser can do the same kind of work, but he's better at the office work and probably prefers it. Physical space and things seem to present a lot of barriers. Introverted Sensing isn't as good at sizing up physical tasks and just winging them. It's critical, pessimistic and perfectionist. When Ivan has to do the physical work—moving boxcars or installing furnaces—he relies on routine ways to do it. He also uses logic and measurements. If something goes wrong, he gives up faster. When things don't look right, he quickly assumes they just won't work.

Extroverted Sensers hate the office work, so they're happy to manage field work. However, no business can run without communication and keeping records. Ed would rather face the task of building a doghouse out of yellow and pink forms than writing numbers into exactly the correct places. He hates that work and quickly gives up. Here, Introverted Sensing's critical perfectionism is helpful because Ivan can see at a glance when the form isn't completed. He feels a sense of satisfaction at getting it done right; to put it another way, Introverted Sensing is rigged to make him feel downright uneasy when the form doesn't look right. Detail work is part of his template of safety and danger. He has no difficulty with the tasks that make Ed nuts.

The hands-on work was being done centuries before office work mattered. Physical work is a matter of building and maintaining our dwellings on earth, while office work is important only in keeping track of money. In times when taxes were simpler and there were fewer middlemen, there wasn't much office work. Introverted Sensing may have had a less important role compared to bold, quick Extroverted Sensing. But in our time, Ivan can always find work. If anything, the need is greater with computers taking over for paper. If you made a mistake on an old-fashioned paper form, it was just a mistake; if you make that mistake in a computer field, it could cause bigger problems. It's no wonder that Introverted Sensers are so necessary and successful in modern businesses.

Let's return to the other Perceiving minority, those with dominant Intuition. Dominant Intuition tends to be about as much of a minority as dominant Extroverted Sensing. Rounding off the numbers (to the closest "whole people"), out of four people, two are like Ivan, one is like Ed, and the fourth has some form of dominant Intuition. The two kinds of Intuition discussed in Chapter 8 are all divided up among this last 1/4 of people, so when we start to look at people with each kind of Intuition, the percentages drop into small numbers very fast.

When Intuition is a dominant part of personality, it directs the largest share of mental energy to perceiving invisible connections. Having dominant Intuition probably begins with a richer network of neural links to nonverbal areas that question and compare. Whenever the brain has a stronger neural network for something, it reaches greatest efficiency by using it. So when the Intuition network is particularly strong, the mind becomes organized around connections, meaning and ideas.

Facts are still gathered by Sensing in a literal way, but a relatively small number of facts and observations get used to milk as many connections as possible out of them. The mind can be unprepared or reluctant to observe and perceive more Sensing facts until the connections are all sorted out. When Intuition is the chief focus of the mind through a lifetime, it has time to create a vast invisible structure. As a major part of personality, the invisible structure of meaning is tightly woven into decisions and memories. It steers all other mental activity and often feels more real than the facts themselves.

A personality that has Intuition as a consuming interest is generally not as good at processing the factual world. Intuition competes for mental energy (and typically wins) against Sensing. Most people with dominant Intuition can still get by in the factual world, but they are generally a bit detached and absent-minded. During the time that their minds are taken up with pondering connections and ideas, they're usually relying on automatic learned actions to carry out daily life. They see, hear, walk and drive, but only partially. Their minds are only completely engaged when actively working on how things are connected. This absent-minded, automatic handling of Sensing is good enough most of the time, but it's never as efficient in the factual real world as direct, dominant Sensing (of either kind).

There's really only one time when strong, dominant Intuition suddenly comes into a leading role: a time of rapid change or uncertainty. Sensing's greater talent with factual and concrete things may be much less helpful when life is suddenly changing. That's why, in a community of busy Sensing people, that minority of Intuition-obsessed personalities is necessary for survival.

There are major times of change as well as minor, daily or hourly changes. There are changes of technology, and of population and politics; there can also be times when the ways people relate to each other are shifting rapidly. For every kind of change, there is someone with strong Intuition who has been "absent-mindedly" preparing for it. The early signs of change were visible through a shifting pattern of connections, and they seemed even obvious to this one person who's been watching. Between the earliest signs of change and the immediate, urgent crisis, there may have been years, months, or days passing. Intuition used the time as efficiently as possible to have a framework of understanding ready, even if it looked to others like mere daydreaming or obsessing.

Some people with strong Intuition are positioned where they can "save the day" frequently, in big ways. They're wealthy and in leadership roles, or they're highly educated and can invent machines or methods to solve new problems. Others may have only a few chances to influence changes. Some may spend a lifetime daydreaming about new ideas but never have a chance to put them to use. When the moment of change comes, they're in the wrong place or lived in the wrong century.

For this reason, dominant Intuition is a high-stakes gamble. It's completely necessary in every human community; but for individuals, it is sometimes a losing bet. Dominant Intuition comes in slightly different forms and is usually highly selective about what kinds of problems it wants to solve. Some people are prepared to help with changes that only truly occur after their deaths. Others have insights that are beyond what anyone is prepared to accept at this time. These individuals may never really find a role in life that makes good use of their abilities. They may become eccentric, bitter, or just resigned to not achieving something great. Some people with strong Intuition succeed in material ways, while others don't. The ones who succeed may be able to compete successfully with people who are good at Sensing skills, even if their own minds are often distracted. Civilization helps others by creating special niches for daydreaming, inventing, and writing.

Books are the lifeline for Intuition. Intuition is somewhat involved in all book-writing, and writers often have dominant Intuition. More importantly, Intuition's ideas can reach across time through preservation in writing. Whenever books are collected, it's more likely that the brilliant ideas of a past time can be put to use now. Then it doesn't matter if the person who thought of the ideas was born in the wrong time or place. (At least, it doesn't matter to us now. It was still a shame at the time.)

Children who have dominant Intuition are usually very interested in books. Books present an alternative world; even if they tell completely factual information, they tell of things outside of the child's personal experience. They provide facts that Sensing could not have observed personally, maybe about other parts of the world or past times. Also, books often explain and suggest some connections of meaning.

In our time, books appear to be displaced in childhood by video games and movies. Some children with Intuition find these good enough replacements, but others cling to books. There's a simple reason. While movies and computer games also depict alternative worlds, books traditionally require readers to fill in their own visuals. Reading is less of a Sensing experience; readers have to draw from their memories and create their own connections. That's what Intuition pulls the mind toward; it's an invisible, abstract experience.

In children, dominant Intuition usually has a lot of imagination mixed in. These children read fantasy, historical fiction, science fiction and fairy tales. As stories suggest new connections and ideas, their minds dwell on them, sometimes at the cost of remembering to do chores or homework. Dominant Intuition can also be specifically a pursuit of meaning, usually turned toward science and engineering. These children like non-fiction best, as long as it explains new ideas. They tend to learn everything possible about some subject, to the point where greater knowledge would require skills they don't have yet, like advanced math or laboratory work. Seeing some new field of learning, their attention is drawn in another direction, and they do the same thing.

In later school years, those with dominant Intuition gravitate toward working with abstract ideas. An abstract idea is a type of invisible connection; we create words for the connections themselves, then for connections between the connections, then for categories of connections, and categories of categories and connections between categories. That's the realm of abstract thought.

As a field of study drifts away from real things and events, it is probably going to interest only people with dominant Intuition. In any academic field, it's possible to work more with things or more with abstract ideas. In physics, you can work with high tech machines doing experiments, or you can analyze what others have done and write papers comparing the numbers and ideas. In anthropology, you can spend a lot of time in the field living with a group of people, or you can spend minimal time in field work and mostly write theoretical papers about others' field work. At its more concrete levels, the work may interest many kinds of people, but at the most abstract level, it offers interest only to strong Intuition.

For this reason, you find more dominant Intuitives in academic work. My personal estimate is that the general-population ratio of 3 dominant Sensing personalities for every one Intuitive personality is exactly the opposite in college faculties. These are civilization's protective niches for daydreaming, inventing and writing. In big universities where many kinds of work go on, the ratio may not be as high as 3 dominant Intuitives for every one Senser, but in small liberal arts schools, it's probably that high. In departments like mathematics, the faculty may be 100% dominant Intuitives.

The culture of an institution changes with a dominant Intuitive majority. Intuition asks questions, above all. It's difficult to be an administrator in a place with a lot of people questioning every decision. When people use the expression "it's like herding cats," they may be talking about trying to force a group of dominant Intuitives to band together against what they feel are their personal principles and interests. Intuitive identity is often shaped around being different from the outside world, so whatever is mainstream cannot be popular here. Personal appearance is either downplayed or used for individual statement; looking like a role is just not an important value. When professors look like what we expect, it's mostly because our expectations have already been set by the absent-minded, often quirky academics of our past. It's the culture of people who are more interested in meaning and connections than in getting things done.

PERCEIVING AS A CAMERA LENS

When we need to make decisions, we use a Judging function; however, it's important to remember that the options presented to Thinking or Feeling have already been screened by Perceiving. Sensing and Intuition could be thought of as the lens of a movie camera, that is, our eyes looking out on the world. Moral decisions can be made only about what the camera lens has already "seen." When the camera lens has a narrower, Introverted field, it has already screened out many ideas and actions.

Remember how Thinking and Feeling worked together to create conscience. In each conscience team, one Judging function is idealistic, stubborn, negative, and feels like it's reality rather than an opinion. The other is pragmatic, flexible, optimistic, and very aware of observing (rather than being) reality. The introverted one is full of prohibitions; the extroverted one is permissive. The balance of both allows each person to keep a range of flexible options, while at the same time maintaining clear lines that cannot be crossed, so that other people can trust him.

We're going to look at not just two, but four ways that Sensing and Intuition work together. First, of course they have the same attributes of introversion and extroversion: one Perceiving function is idealistic, stubborn, negative and feels like reality, while the other is pragmatic, flexible, optimistic and observant. However, with Perceiving we need to look at the relative importance of Sensing or Intuition in each personality, while with Judging it wasn't as important. We talked about how Thinking or Feeling may be more dominant, but we didn't need to distinguish how this changed the operation of moral conscience. With Perceiving, we need to do this; we need to break it down according to which is primary and dominant because when Perceiving is in a minor role, its effect is dramatically different from when it's in a major one. In a top, dominant position, Perceiving is as powerful as a camera's lens: it shapes the entire world view. In a minor position, it can't be described as shaping world view; it's more like aesthetic taste or interpretive tendency.

Because Perceiving is like a camera lens, I'm going to explain the four ways it works by talking about movies. The analogy to movies makes the rest of the chapter much easier and more fun to read, but it may present a false scent. When I talk about an aspect of personality being like a film genre, it may sound as though people with this mental function love these movies. It's very possible that they do. But movies are also entertainment, and people may love some movies that have no connection to their personality framework.

When a Perceiving function is very strong in personality, I'll refer to it as the director. It's the director's vision that governs everything in the film. Each Perceiving team has a less important function, too, and in this analogy, it's like a script writer. It gives ideas, writes lines, creates characters, and makes jokes, but it doesn't control the final product. Each of the four ways that Introverted and Extroverted Perceiving can be paired creates a different director-writer team.

Let's start with movies that are most like the worldviews of Introverted Sensing and Intuition. The two Introverted Perceiving modes are both narrow in some ways, both quickly spotting the negatives in life. Both uphold archetypal ideals, but just as Sensing and Intuition could work against each other if they were not balanced in personality, so too Perceiving ideals attempt to cancel and deny each other. One values archetypes of formal roles and appearance, while the other tears those things aside in the search for archetypal hidden meaning. In typical personality balances, Perceiving functions can't both be Introverted, so this conflict doesn't usually happen inside one mind. It does, however, show up frequently between different personalities.

Introverted Sensing is most closely tied into visible human archetypal images: mother, father, child, king, thief, wizard, old wise woman, and so on. Classic old Hollywood movies, too, are based around these images. In classic Westerns, the audience could tell who was good or bad by hat color. In films set in the fashionable city world, literal colors didn't identify, but the actors could usually be recognized easily by type: mother, father, child, hero, heroine, authority figure, wise counselor, or villain. Old Hollywood movies closely imitate the way Introverted Sensing shapes worldview.

Let's suggest that the main Perceiving function acts as a movie director, the person who controls the creative process and most story and editing decisions. To illustrate how old Hollywood films were like Introverted Sensing, take Frank Capra as an example. His *Mr. Smith Goes to Washington* (1939) is a pitch-perfect example of how Introverted Sensing sees the world through social role archetypes.

Jefferson Smith (Jimmy Stewart), is a young Scout leader appointed to fill out a Senate term. Early in the film, Mr. Smith takes a sight-seeing tour of Washington, D.C. In a democracy, there are no iconic royal symbols of archetypal "king" authority like crowns, thrones or castles. Instead, we have monuments, statues, buildings and (most importantly) significant words carved into stone. Mr. Smith's awe-struck reverence for these symbols emphasizes archetypal authority: America's "king" is an abstract idea based in shared history and words. So that's one key archetypal image that shapes the film.

More than once, the camera lingers over portions of Lincoln's Gettysburg Address; once, a young child reads its last lines out loud. Because Senator Smith was a youth leader, the movie features a large number of children, mostly boys. Together, the boys fill in an archetypal image of an innocent child who hasn't yet faced the ugly reality that ideals get violated. It's important to adults in the movie that the children must be kept unaware of corruption for as long as possible: "How could I go home and tell the children?" they ask.

The new senator is a frontiersman who is sometimes called "Daniel Boone" behind his back. In America, the frontiersman is another key archetypal figure. Daniel Boone's name stands for a time when the country was innocent, like a child. A man cast in this role has primitive manly virtues, but none of the sophistication of the city. The city stands for temptation, corruption, compromise and loss of courage.

As an archetypal contrast to Daniel Boone, the senior senator has been nicknamed "The Silver Knight." A knight's archetypal role is to defend the king, the rightful authority. But this "knight" has been corrupted by the city. He is secretly defending an unelected man whose wealth has taken power away from elected officials, and therefore from the people—and very explicitly, also from the innocent children. It's a fourth explicitly archetypal image of traditional social roles. The same image is evoked again when young Mr. Smith's attempts at reform earn him the nickname of "Don Quixote," the knight who tried to find worthy causes and sometimes made mistakes. He "tilted at windmills," mistaking them for giants waving their arms. Quixote's name brings to the idea of the knight a special strain of idealism. So the movie presents combat not only between the two senators as knights, but between the archetypes of city sophistication and noble innocence (of children and Daniel Boone).

The really key point is that in this type of film, as in Introverted Sensing's worldview, the true archetypal ideals must win. City sophistication and the false knight can look like they're winning, but eyes must be opened to the true ideals and roles, even in defeat. And in the end, the true archetypes must win. As Capra's movie plays out, innocent children rally around the true knight until the false knight has a crisis of conscience. The moment of victory isn't through actual defeat of the forces of corruption, rather it comes when the "Silver Knight" returns to his true king, the ideals of legitimate authority.

When Hollywood classics use the structure of social role archetypes, the plot often hinges on a direct threat to the archetypes themselves. The characters in the story have individual traits and problems, but most importantly they fill archetypal roles well. In the plot, circumstances challenge their ability to stay true to ideal roles, but a happy ending means that the archetypes win. We see the pattern clearly in "Mr. Smith Goes to Washington," but it's also true of the classic romantic comedies produced in that period.

In *An Affair to Remember* (1957), Cary Grant and Deborah Kerr are both engaged to be married when they meet on a boat. They aren't exactly married, but being engaged places them into archetypal roles of husband and wife. As archetypes, husband and wife who are a pair must be loyal to each other and blind to other possibilities. They are the most ideal pairing of the male/female opposites. To Introverted Sensing, the ideal of marriage is extremely important. However, in this movie, the value of the characters' existing engagements is not very great, and they feel strongly drawn to each other. Now what?

Circumstances have put both man and woman into conflict with their archetypal roles. In some movies, they might throw away the roles for love, or at least for momentary passion. But in a movie with an Introverted Sensing worldview, the archetypal ideals must win. The story must end happily, because it's that kind of movie, but a happy ending must preserve the individuals fulfillment of ideal roles.

In this case, they agree to return to their formal roles and try to disengage from engagements. Both were marrying for money, so they need time to earn money on their own. They plan to meet exactly six months later, if both are now free of old roles and still want to create a new archetypal attachment. Eventually, through various trials, the characters find each other again now without obstacles, ready to form a new pair as ideal husband and wife. The happy ending of this type of classic Hollywood comedy is that, in the end, the individuals have resolved all conflict with their archetypal roles. Reality and appearance again match.

It would have been possible to tell the story by allowing the man and woman to become a couple without resolving their role conflicts. But if the screenwriter had given them a happy ending this way, the movie would not have fulfilled its purpose. The man and woman might have been happy, and some viewers would have been satisfied. But the genre's worldview demands that nobody can be happy when a social role archetype has been violated. A happy ending can only be happy for the archetypal roles.

The end of *Casablanca* (1942) is a perfect example of this rule: husband and wife stay together even when the wife is in love with another man. Viewers who wanted her to go with her old flame, not her current husband, are disappointed. But the husband fills two archetypes, not just husband but also knight, as an anti-Fascist freedom fighter. A happy ending can't mean happiness for individuals, it must mean upholding true archetypes. The old flame hasn't been living up to ideals, so his act of redemption is giving up the girl while saving the knight. If he hadn't done this, he'd fall into the archetypal role of villain, and villains can't have happy endings. For a director who cares a lot about ideal social roles, this was the only possible right ending.

We can see in these movies the first rule of how Introverted Sensing shapes a worldview: social role archetypes form a higher reality that cannot be violated. In one sense, violating archetypes is not a plot option. The possibility exists and even tempts the characters, but if they could violate archetypes and still be happy, it would be a different kind of movie. In the world of Introverted Sensing, you are always playing an archetypal role. If you aren't a hero who upholds ideals, then you're a villain.

If the most dominant kind of Perceiving can be described as a director, we can view the less dominant one as a script writer. The rules of balance in personality tell us that if Introverted Sensing is the director, then the script writer must be its complete opposite, that is, Extroverted Intuition. We'll see later what happens when Extroverted Intuition gets to be the director, but in this current studio, it is only writing scripts at the director's request. The director has an inviolably orderly worldview, but he doesn't want his movie to be a bore. As script writer, Extroverted Intuition can scan for possibilities as much as it wants to. It writes in surprising events and plot twists. The director remains in control; the plot twists are just the circumstances through which ideal archetypes will be resolved.

We actually see this pairing in old Hollywood comedies. No coincidence is too improbable; events can get chaotic and downright crazy. Characters get hit by cars, lose their memory, exchange identities, travel at a moment's notice, follow whims, and buy strange things. Women pretend to be men, and men pretend to be women, and the disguises actually fool everyone. Shakespeare's comedies and Bollywood movies have the same traits: the characters are kings, princesses, knights, clowns, or villains, but they can do anything. They die and come back to life, they join in large dance scenes, they pull off impossible feats. In fact, it becomes clear that the more stable the social roles are, the more the movie can afford to entertain outlandish plot twists.

In human personality, Extroverted Intuition has a similar role when it's the lesser one balancing Introverted Sensing. It can generate ideas, but it can't ever overturn the importance of living up to the ideal of archetypal roles like king, knight, mother, father, child. Life can be changed, but all changes must work within archetypal social events on the small scale, like Christmas, Thanksgiving, and birthdays, and on the large scale, like school, work and retirement. People meet new other people, but all relationships must be structured by the archetypal roles: marriage, parenthood, and citizenship loyalty. You can move to a foreign country and eat crazy foods, but you're still Robert's wife or Margaret's husband no matter who else you meet; you're still loyal to your family roots even when unusual events push you into dilemmas of action.

That's the worldview of Introverted Sensing when it's in a leading role in personality, acting as the film director. People with this "director" usually conduct their lives in very traditional ways because it's just unthinkable not to. The nature of an Introverted function is to feel that it knows not only truth but reality; to step outside what Introverted Sensing is comfortable with would be like walking off a cliff. The mind can't even take in what it would be like to walk off a cliff on purpose, nor can this type of personality take in what it would be like to turn against archetypal social order.

On the other extreme, Introverted Intuition can also act as a film director in personality, shaping worldview so much that certain things become unthinkable. However, Introverted Intuition is so different from Introverted Sensing that the world it creates is like a separate, parallel universe. What each world considers "unthinkable" is almost completely opposite. We can begin to understand Introverted Intuition's worldview by looking at a very different film genre that was produced during the same time, beginning in the 1940s.

While Capra's movies were living up to social role archetypes, directors like Fritz Lang, Billy Wilder and John Huston were creating a dark world of anti-archetypes. Some of these directors had come from Germany, fleeing Hitler's rise to power. In Germany, they had already been making experimental, pessimistic films, but now they had a personal experience of exile and fear to convey. Their outlook on life was translated into American stories that we know as Film Noir.

Most of these movies were created during the time of black and white production, so they are literally black (noir). But the darkness is not only about scenes at night or lack of color. In these movies, the world itself is pessimistic and far from ideal. Social role archetypes exist, but they act as false fronts; they cover more important identities. That's the really key difference between Film Noir and the Hollywood classics that were produced at the same time: in one, the social role archetypes must win, while in the other, social roles without exception are false fronts that must be ripped away. Introverted Intuition has its own set of archetypal ideals, but they are not about social roles. Instead, they're about hidden truth.

In *Double Indemnity* (1944), a beautiful blonde woman first appears in the role of wife and mother. In a classic Hollywood film by Capra, her role would give her virtues of compassion, loyalty and nurturing. But in Film Noir, her role is a mask that hides hidden truth. In this case, truth slowly comes out: she is not loyal or nurturing and although she can protest against murder, she has already killed someone.

Double Indemnity also presents a man who looks like a Hollywood knight. He even sells protection (insurance) which ought to make him a true knight. However, we soon find out that his appearance is another deceptive mask. With barely any moral consideration, he decides to help the wife murder her husband. Because of his knight-like social role, he can devise ways to hide clues to their crime from the authorities. He is an anti-knight.

In a movie directed by Capra, the anti-knight would feel a crisis in his identity, prompting him to turn back to his correct archetypal role. But with Billy Wilder (one of the German refugees) directing Film Noir, there are more important archetypes at work. Here, Introverted Intuition is exploring how appearances should be torn away to expose truth. Finding truth is the goal: truth itself is the archetypal ideal pursued in a Noir world. It's not that Introverted Intuition is against archetypes, because by its Introverted nature it values archetypal ideals above everything else. The difference is that its inborn ideas are not about social roles and appearances. Intuition's archetypal ideals are about truth, which may be the literal enemy of roles and appearances.

And here we come to the really important figure in every Film Noir: the truth-seeker. He's often a detective; in *Double Indemnity*, he's the claims investigator for the insurance company. He talks openly about how central Introverted Intuition is to him: he calls it "the little man inside" who knows truth before the facts have come to light. The truth-seeker's appearance is usually against him; he is the opposite of the beautiful but wicked people. He may be short or unhandsome, and he's often an alcoholic with many problems of his own. He may have spent some time in the outskirts of the criminal world. If people were asked to sort out photo cards for men who might play the role of a "knight," this character would never be selected. But in the Noir world, he is the one who upholds the true protective role: he finds The Truth. He pulls off the masks.

In Hollywood classic films and Introverted Sensing, the social role archetypes for government are good, pure, and trustworthy. But in the dark world of Introverted Intuition and Film Noir, authority figures like politicians and cops are morally ambiguous. While some policemen or prosecutors are interested in truth, many Film Noir courts and cops compromise with truth in really unacceptable ways. In *The Postman Always Rings Twice*, attorneys make deals so that murderers get off without penalty. In *The Maltese Falcon*, the criminals and private eye cut a deal on who's going to be blamed, since the cops are assumed to not really care. In *The Long Good-bye,* the police are foul-mouthed, harsh, deceptive, and perhaps unwilling to dig for the truth. Sometimes the police are openly taking bribes from organized crime, so that the truth-seeker runs into danger from both government and villains. It's clear that the police and courts ought to seek truth and follow ideals, but the genre's bitter presentation is that no idealism in officials can be expected, and those who naively expect it usually come out badly hurt. Government is another false appearance to strip away.

Introverted Intuition believes in ideal love, integrity and loyalty, but it looks for them in unexpected places. In Film Noir, villains may turn out to be merciful or honest, or they may turn out not to be villains at all. Discredited characters may keep their word or make sacrifices for each other. Lovers are truest when the plot has led you to expect nothing of them. The leading couple, on the other hand, can be in love in a big, obvious way, but their love is a mask that needs to be pulled away so that ugly truth can be seen. If they colluded in a crime, their love can't last, because evil can't be part of ideal love.

The happy ending for Film Noir, as for Introverted Intuition, is full disclosure of truth. Truth is the most important archetypal concept; its trueness matters more than the content. Truth can be ugly or comforting, and in a way it doesn't matter. Archetypes must win, but that just means that truth must come out.

When Introverted Intuition is the director, Extroverted Sensing is a script writer and also operates a camera. Extroverted Sensing doesn't believe in prettying up reality: there are broken windows, trash in the streets, and stark outlines. In fact, the camera style forms a real contrast with the classic Hollywood of Introverted Sensing. In that first genre, everything looks like it's on a set in a studio. Everything looks just as it should, ideally. So do people; romantic scenes may have a soft focus to blur outlines and create a sense of hazy unreality. But the style of Extroverted Sensing rejects all of that idealization of image.

There's another, somewhat related, film genre that shows us Extroverted Sensing's camera style even more clearly. The fiction of Film Noir was created on sound stages like any other art of its time, so the amount of gritty realism was limited. But in contemporary documentaries, we get truth-seeking ideals and harshly realistic images. Documentaries are always looking for hidden meaning. When they aren't investigating deception, they are just showing us things too far away for us to see, such as slum life in Manila. But most of them are based on the pessimistic premise that someone is using false fronts to keep us from seeing truth. As in Film Noir, a social role or appearance is being used as a cover. It has to be torn away so that we can see the truth.

There is almost no limit to their visual realism. Cameras can be hand-held like a smart phone, hidden in clothing, carried on a gyroscope to eliminate the up and down motion of walking or—just for realism—not carried on a gyroscope so that every up and down jog is felt visually. Documentaries seek out ugliness because that's often where they find truth. The moments of film gold are when they find a hidden toxic dump, a newly-found mass grave, or starving refugees that the world has been overlooking. It's ugly all right, but that's the point. Truth is beautiful even if we see it in something ugly; realism and truth-seeking go together.

People with strong Introverted Intuition and secondary Extroverted Sensing see the world very much as if they're in a documentary or even a Noir mystery. Introverted Intuition, as a worldview, means that the inborn ideal archetypes are not about roles or looks, rather they are about the truest truth. In a way, truest truth is defined by whatever is the opposite to the appearances. Extroverted Sensing in a secondary role works as an assistant to notice sensory details so that truest truth can be seen with all its wrinkled, patchy, shadowy, or brilliantly glowing visuals.

Let's turn now to personalities in which the most important Perceiving function is not Introverted. Instead of being idealistic, archetypal, and innate, it's Extroverted: pragmatic, exploring and open to all possibilities. Its camera lens is generously wide-angle, restricting nothing.

Extroverted Sensing is like the director of an action movie, a "thriller." Let's start with a big budget, because this movie may need to be filmed on location around the country or world. We're going to need cranes to lift cameras up for shots looking down, and we're also going to need two helicopters. The movie will blow up one building and burn down another. The actors and actresses in the action thriller need a lot of skills. They're going to be scaling walls, dancing on a rooftop, scuba diving, and juggling. Of course, we'll need some stuntmen too. In the Extroverted Sensing cast, we want some very beautiful women and handsome men, but we also want some average and even strange looking men and women, too. They can expect to change costumes often: we've got ballroom glamor, some prison interiors, and one great scene in the snowy Alps. We want to see and feel it all.

In this action thriller, there's nothing possible that is ruled out. The movie doesn't need to look any certain way, as long as we capture all of the realistic sights and sounds. We'd like to make the audience dizzy when the camera shows an inside view of a helicopter crashing. No scene is too shocking to be excluded. The leading lady doesn't need to look pretty all the time, either. Nobody needs to look like anything as long as they can get the job done.

That's how Extroverted Sensing works when it's a major driver of personality. Of course, all of these things can't happen at once, and for most people in real life, the scene in the Alps won't ever be possible due to budget restrictions. However, even if real life is dull or we can't afford helicopters, Extroverted Sensing doesn't consider much to be "unthinkable." It would be weird for a school teacher to fight a forest fire or a nurse to discover Inca treasure? So what, do what you want; do what comes to hand. Formal roles don't matter, and it matters even less to do the same thing today that was done yesterday.

Remember that Introverted Sensing as director favored iconic buildings, such as the monuments in Washington, D. C. Introverted Sensing's favorites list includes the Golden Gate Bridge, the Eiffel Tower and bridges over the Seine River, scenes of London, and more. They show up in both old and new Hollywood. Extroverted Sensing uses the same list, but there's a twist. Extroverted Sensing, as director, plans to blow them up.

Action movies have destroyed the White House, Los Angeles, and downtown New York hundreds of times. *Independence Day* (1996) shows most major cities being destroyed, but it also singles out some iconic images: the White House and Capitol Dome, New York's Empire State building, and the Eiffel Tower in Paris. Many other action movies target the Statue of Liberty: lopped off, buried in sand, blown up, flooded, or used as a staging base for some bizarre attack. Extroverted Sensing may not be searching for truth by destroying archetypal images; it's just exploring "what if?" What would it look like?

Extroverted Sensing does not give archetypal appearances much reverence. Its directing taste destroys fine clothing, expensive cars, and four-tier wedding cakes. It's also very fond of watching things turn into other things. Ever since digital film techniques permitted faces to turn into other faces, action movies have loved making spies peel off the "face" you thought was real. Their fingers dig into the jawbone and pull upward, and suddenly the plot has completely changed. One of its highest values is literally unmasking archetypes.

As a director, Extroverted Sensing makes sensory realism the highest value, instead of putting it to the service of an ideal the way documentaries do. But as we've seen before, whenever one of the Perceiving functions has a major role in personality, its complete opposite has a minor role. When Extroverted Sensing is the director, Introverted Intuition acts as consultant and script writer. It's the same team that made Film Noir and gritty documentaries, but the director and script writer have traded jobs.

In fact, action movies are like documentaries (or even Noir) turned inside out. The top priority is to deliver action details and motion, but in the background, the plot is often about unmasking deceptive appearances. Sometimes they are literally masks, as in the CGI technique of peeling off a face. Sometimes, iconic buildings conceal things like alien bases, so that blowing them up reveals truth. If the hero works for the CIA, he will eventually discover a double agent (another false appearance). If the hero is a journalist checking out some sleepy small town, he'll uncover corporate wrongdoing that ends up burning down the town.

Introverted Intuition is a script writer on this set, but it knows that exposing truth is now just a plot device, not the main focus. When it was the director, the whole film was about finding truth, but now they've swapped jobs. Here, a hunch is better than a long explanation; investigative research is good, but not on screen time. When we compare action movies to documentaries, we can see how differently Perceiving functions act when they're in control, as opposed to when they're not. In a documentary, the point is to convey the full truth, using realism to make it clear and interesting. In an action film, it's the other way, the point is to convey the realism, using the truth-seeking angle to understand the action.

In personality, Extroverted Sensing has few biases about how things must be. It's more likely to get nervous when life is presented as narrow and already determined, because this means that a lot of options aren't even being presented. Extroverted Sensing wants to see those options, too; why should anything be ruled out of hand? Furthermore, secondary Introverted Intuition takes a pessimistic view of what it considers "Greeting-card" appearances and roles. It's great to look good, but roles may give a false impression. What good are they, then?

Extroverted Sensing and Introverted Intuition are completely opposite, but they agree on these few things: that getting things done matters more than looking right, and that finding options that work matters more than sticking to roles. Sensing thinks it's about getting things done, while Intuition sees it as a question of truth, but it comes out enough the same that they can work together well. When Extroverted Sensing has a larger role (the movie director), personality tends to be more optimistic, focused on what can be done in the real world. When Introverted Intuition has the director's role, the personality tends to be pessimistic, focused on just how many false fronts have to be ripped away.

The fourth team has a very different set of biases and missions, as it features Extroverted Intuition as the director. It's optimistic and exploring like Extroverted Sensing, and sometimes it features action and even explosions. But it's not really about gritty reality at all. Extroverted Intuition is exploring alternative realities, not possible actions in this reality. When Extroverted Intuition is the director, we head straight for science fiction. Blowing up the White House could happen, but why not suspend gravity or break the space-time continuum instead?

Science fiction always poses "what if?" questions. Animation is great for Extroverted Intuition movies because anything is possible in a drawing. Disney animations first began to play with the possibilities: what if a flower bed began to sing and talk? What if people became very small? What if machines were alive? What if an invention could make anything fly? Digital animation makes it even easier to imagine these impossibilities.

Extroverted Intuition can't stop asking questions. What if three-dimensional space suddenly became two-dimensional? What if all color went to black and white? What if animals kept people as pets? What if water flowed upward? What if Venus fly-traps grew really big and took over New York? What if house flies turned out to know God? What if speaking some random word meant instant death? What if -1 had a square root? There's really no end to the list of possible realities. And here we can see the difference between possible events (Sensing) and possible realities (Intuition). They overlap some, but exploring options in alternative reality means changing such fundamental things that the usual connections and meaning can't be counted on. Cause and effect may be changed, whereas an action movie depends on cause and effect.

The Matrix (1999) presents a world in which apparent reality turns out to be a computer program. Actual reality is very different; each human being is really a barely-developed body used as a battery unit while the brain dreams of "life" in the computer program. So, what if apparent reality was a computer program? What if? Well, then it could be changed at will—and we see this in the film, where a déjà vu moment means that the change was briefly visible. If doors are only pixels, they can suddenly be bricked up. And if death itself is only a trick, then it isn't real unless the real human mind agrees to play along. If apparent reality is only a program, it can be altered by abstracting one's mind from belief.

Dr. Who (1963 to present) is a series of British television shows about time travel and aliens. It presents some basic what-if questions in its premise: what if aliens were attacking and only a specialist could see through their disguises and guess their strategies? What if that specialist had to move through time, following the aliens? What if the struggle against the aliens lasted more than one lifetime, so that the same specialist mind must be reborn in other bodies? Each episode then presents its own what-if questions. What would happen if a time traveling alien-fighter showed up in a certain historical period? What would happen if the time traveler interfered with history? What if aliens could detect changes in history and use them as cracks in which to enter reality? What if the moon was really an egg waiting to hatch? What if trains could go through space? What if vampires are actually alien fish in disguise?

Another British book, *The Hitchhiker's Guide to the Galaxy* (1979), challenges some key archetypal concepts of reality. When Earth is destroyed to make way for an intergalactic highway, an ordinary British man is saved by his friend, who turns out to be an alien. In this bright, optimistic alternative world, their spaceship is powered by a computer that calculates how improbable some wild coincidence or impossible event would be. Once it has calculated a probability number, then the thing happens. Drawn by wildly improbable coincidences, the ship finds itself in different locations and times.

What does it mean to have an engine that creates reality merely by calculating how improbable something is? This idea changes the meaning of an engine, but it also challenges the meanings of movement and location. What can be more archetypally fundamental than the meaning of "location"? It's one of the innate ideas we're born with: I am here, you are there. But in science fiction, Extroverted Intuition can blow up even archetypal concepts like place, time or being.

The mood difference between the Introverted and Extroverted forms of Intuition is very clear in this movie-genre analogy. Film Noir's director, Introverted Intuition, was also exploring possible meanings, but it was pessimistic. Poking around for truth can expose ugly and dangerous things like corpses and cobras. Film Noir characters are doomed because their options are limited to hiding or discovering truth. In personality, Introverted Intuition is wise and canny, but it focuses on avoiding dangers and dead ends, looking for the one true path. By contrast, Extroverted Intuition is optimistic and even a bit reckless. When it sees new possibilities, it assumes they will work out well: under every rock is a new treasure, not a dead body. Its tone is bright, not dark, and its characters have few limits, only ones imposed by the story's premise. Just calculate how improbable something is, and you'll have it.

That's how Extroverted Intuition operates when it's a major driver of personality. It is optimistic about solving problems as long as unusual or new solutions may be tried. In real life, Extroverted Intuition can't suspend gravity or travel in time. But it may suggest radical solutions that stand conventional behavior on its head: drop out; move away; walk into public and start shouting; refuse to attend; do things in reverse order; see if the rules can be suspended just by asking. Presented with a big problem, Extroverted Intuition begins to think of every possible option. Using logic or experience, it screens the options to select two or three that are most likely to succeed. It may not act on the crazy options, but it certainly generates and considers them. Why not? While other parts of the personality may feel discouraged, strong Extroverted Intuition never loses optimism because it believes that there are always more doors to try opening. What if the most improbable door was the one leading to a solution?

This extreme optimism and openness requires some balancing limits, otherwise it's just too wide open. Of course, there's a second Perceiving function at work, as in the previous pairs. When Extroverted Intuition is the movie director, its opposite Introverted Sensing is one of the script writers. Introverted Sensing has a much smaller range of authority when it's a lowly team member, but it has a definite limiting effect.

As a director, Introverted Sensing could limit possible realities to ones in which archetypal images and roles were always primary. As a script writer, Introverted Sensing still has a mandate to keep social roles close to archetypes. It's an important balance to Extroverted Intuition. When so much else floats in science fiction, characters are often kept simple and unified. For example, *Dr. Who* may be re-born in different bodies over time, but his personality never changes. His words and actions are the most predictable elements of the story. His assistant may look like anything, but he or she is reliably loyal in the role of helper.

No episode plays with the what-ifs that Film Noir majors in: what if this trusted friend is actually lying? None of that here. Everything else floats, but characters are reliable.

Further, Introverted Sensing often draws science fiction toward clear archetypal social roles in the fairy-tale sense. *Star Wars* (1977) consciously uses folk story roles: princess, knight, old wise man, thief, villain. *The Matrix* has similar roles: Neo is the hero who must become a knight, Trinity is the princess he's supposed to fall in love with, Morpheus is a king, while Cypher is the classic villain. The Oracle doesn't even have a personal name; instead, the archetypal role of future-teller, "oracle," is enough.

Science fiction has such a strong tendency to fall into fairy-tale roles that one subgenre is nicknamed "space opera." *Star Wars* is space opera; it was inspired by the comic book *Flash Gordon* (1934), which was also space opera. Space opera has strong, stable archetypal roles and presents its action as a battle of good against evil. There's no subtlety about the characters. Good is good, and evil is evil. A happy ending means that good finds the weapons, wisdom and clues to physically win against evil. It could include repentance on the part of someone evil, but it will have to be repentance in defeat and probably just before expiring. The victory of good has to be absolute.

The contrast of Extroverted Intuition's extreme flexibility with Introverted Sensing's rigid adherence to ideal roles shows us just how important balance is in personality, just as in movies. Of course, there are science fiction movies that don't present such balance. Their free-wheeling universe may be dark and pessimistic, or their characters may present not only flexible, but even fluid and deceptive personalities. The tether on both reality and characters may be quite elastic and even confusing. But most such movies don't achieve widespread or lasting popularity because the human mind is overwhelmed by either too much fluidity or too much rigid pessimism. Art can create it, but human personality finds it uncomfortable.

For example, *Memento* (2000) mimicked and reproduced the confusion of lost memory by presenting the story of its memory-loss character in backwards time order. Leonard cannot remember beyond about five minutes, so the story moves in five minute sets. The final scene is told first, without any preparation, and then the scene just before it, so that the viewer is continually disoriented by not knowing what happened just before. It's a brilliant technique, but the story's extreme disorientation is compounded by a pessimistic narrative. When the movie closes by explaining the beginning, the story's meaning turns into complete darkness; any hope that Leonard achieved his goal gets crushed. The technique is like Extroverted Intuition which can explore alternative ways of being conscious, but the story is like Introverted Intuition in which hidden possibilities are bad and dangerous. The movie is admired for its achievement but not often watched.

By contrast, *Groundhog Day* (1993) may be the most-watched film of our time. It takes an Extroverted Intuition premise, that the rules of time can be suspended such that the same day repeats as an endless loop. The story plays with all possibilities suggested by the premise: what if the hero drives off a cliff, doubtless killing himself? Of course, it turns out that even so he can't turn off the endless looping, but wakes up yet again to the same day. But the human story is optimistic. Given the same day over and over, he learns to become a hero knight who can win the princess. When his lesson is finally learned, time stops looping.

It's perfectly balanced between Extroverted Intuition (unreal rules for time) and Introverted Sensing (hero archetype).

So completely opposite Perceiving functions can agree on a few things, enough to work together. Extroverted Intuition never stops asking questions, but it isn't interested in unmasking social roles. It wants to open doors and turn over stones, but it just isn't interested in roles. Introverted Sensing, when it's most dominant, makes those traditional roles into the greatest guide in life, but it doesn't mind research questions about other things in life. As opposite as they are, the two partner up so as to leave archetypal images and roles untouched but question and re-invent everything else.

PERCEIVING ACTS AS A FILTER FOR CHOICES

So what, exactly, does all of the movie discussion mean for human personality? Technically, only Judging makes decisions about priorities like right and wrong. Conscience is rooted in idealistic, Introverted Thinking and Feeling. But just by shaping what sort of story we think we're living in, Perceiving can become part of conscience. This is particularly true of Introverted Perceiving, since it is idealistic and stubborn. It can have a profound influence on what we choose to do, to the point that the lines between Perceiving and Judging are blurred in some consciences. Extroverted Perceiving, by contrast, tends to stay separate from moral conscience because it's about opening up, not closing, options.

In both the Hollywood classic and the Film Noir worldviews, representing the Introverted Perceiving personalities, characters have limited options. The whole point of each film genre is to fulfill its archetypal goals—correct roles or hidden truth—and actions outside of those goals are not possible. The director's control is very tight. In a Hollywood classic film, the leading lady won't murder someone; in Film Noir, almost invariably she will. You could make a movie that stepped outside of their rules, but it would no longer be in that genre.

An Introverted function is inborn in the same way that animal instinct is. It is very difficult to train an animal to disbelieve its template about safety and danger. Circuses can be rightly proud of training dogs or lions to jump through flames. If you've ever had to run toward something that terrifies you, not away from it, you know how nearly impossible it was, and how much had to be at stake for you to do it. Your brain's fear circuits are intended to rescue you by simply not permitting you to do it, and usually only the self-sacrificing desire to save another person is enough to overcome the physical paralysis.

I believe that our inborn templates for how the world ought to be are just as strong. We have logic and other reasoning powers to overcome them, but by far most of the time, the templates shape our reality itself. They operate from the non-verbal part of the brain that we're not often conscious of, which makes them even stronger.

The Introverted Perceiving functions, both Sensing and Intuition, exercise such tight control because they are trying to keep us safe. They can generate the same sense of fear that a rabbit feels when it sees a hawk circling in the sky. The sky isn't supposed to look like that; the template for "sky" has clouds, wind, and small flocks of birds, but it does not include something big enough to cast a shadow, so the rabbit reacts by freezing or hiding. The "hawk" might turn out to be something perfectly harmless (like a radio-controlled toy next door), but the rabbit isn't going to risk finding out.

Introverted Sensing's templates for human social role archetypes are also set up to detect danger. Safety, to Introverted Sensing, means that everything looks right: mothers, fathers, babies, kings and knights are all in place, doing what they do. When Introverted Sensing is operating as a major part of personality, it blocks choices and options outside of traditional social roles because those options are like a circling hawk. They're not in the ideal template, which is like the rabbit's template of the sky. As long as traditional social roles are clearly operating, it's safe. Foreign, unfamiliar roles and options might be okay, but it's not safe to stick around and find out. The possibility of acting outside of the safety template is linked to emotional danger signals that include fear, shame, and guilt.

It's the same with Introverted Intuition, although it operates in the opposite way. To Intuition, the safety template is about knowing the truth that's behind masks and appearances. Safety is a clear sky; it means complete transparency and access to information. It's also about keeping the self within the network of known, understood meaning. The network of meaning isn't visible the way Introverted Sensing's uniforms and roles are, but its perception is very strong in non-visible ways. Acting outside of the network of meaning would be dangerous. The possibility of stepping outside of the meaning that Intuition senses then creates a sense of emotional danger. Being prevented from knowing the truth, or even being required to trust blindly in appearances, causes the same kind of uneasiness.

Moral conscience is the work of Introverted Thinking and Feeling; it applies its templates, provoking feelings of fear, shame and guilt for stepping outside of safe boundaries. The Perceiving templates aren't about moral right and wrong, but they provoke the same set of feelings. For that reason, when Introverted Perceiving is very strong in a personality, its danger signals operate as a kind of conscience. Doing or choosing outside of its template creates shame and fear that feels moral, even if it isn't.

That's how Perceiving can create a stand-in for conscience that operates so strongly as to control day to day actions. A true moral conscience, based in Thinking or Feeling, is also present, and it can be strong and active. But it just isn't needed for day to day decisions, since the Perceiving filter handles so many of them.

Two interesting things emerge from the way these functions are balanced. One is that in personalities controlled by an Introverted Perceiving filter, the nature of moral Judging conscience—whether it's warm or cool—is masked by the Perceiving filter. The other is that while it's hard to really fool Introverted Judging about right and wrong, it's possible for Introverted Perceiving to slip into some moral mistakes without intending to, without even realizing it until the situation becomes very plain.

Introverted Sensing uses social roles as a primary way of deciding who to be and what to do. It's heavily influenced by society, usually for good. Society has an archetype of the sort of bad person who steals, curses, brawls in public, fails in school, abandons his family and squanders his money. To Introverted Sensing, taking even one half-step toward becoming this person is unthinkable. It's unthinkable because it would trigger feelings of fear, shame and guilt. Many people with strong Introverted Sensing get these feelings just from tiny things like being late, saying a slightly bad word, losing their temper with more than one person present, and so on. Just dressing like the archetype of a bad person would feel awful. As a behavior-modification program, the inborn archetypal template works really well.

Either warm or cool conscience can be paired with Introverted Sensing, but if Sensing is primary, then the Judging conscience is auxiliary. You might know someone like this pretty well but go months without seeing true moral Judging conscience called into action. When you do finally see it, it may surprise you by being more feeling-oriented, or conversely more rule-oriented, than the person's daily behavior led you to expect. That's because it's drawing on a completely different inborn template, one that has nothing to do with social roles or how things look.

Introverted Intuition does the same thing, but it's harder to understand first because it's an uncommon feature of personality, and second because it's so profoundly invisible. As a guide to daily behavior, it may steer down most of the same paths as Introverted Sensing, because Intuition recognizes that being predictable and meeting society's expectations is safer than the alternative. On the other hand, it has an innate fear of trusting appearances; to listen to authority blindly would be dangerous. The type of authority may be a moral authority, like traditional church, or a political authority, like a politician or even (for a child) a teacher. Introverted Intuition thinks it's imperative to question these authorities, regardless of what sort of moral question is in play.

So in the same way, warm or cool conscience, which is rooted in a completely different inborn template, may be masked behind Intuition's daily behavior choices. People with Introverted Intuition are often bold about challenging and questioning authority on moral questions, but in a dilemma, they're likely to make a moral choice that's very different from their line of argument. People with Introverted Intuition who seem to delight in creating logical arguments against authority may turn out to draw from warm Feeling conscience in an actual dilemma. In the opposite way, those who challenge authority in a highly emotional, people-oriented way may actual determine their own moral dilemmas with firm Introverted Thinking rules.

Introverted Sensing and Intuition create very strong attitudes toward society. Sensing tends to assume that society's structure is good, until proven otherwise. Intuition, of course, suspects that society's structure is a mask covering some important truth. Safety and danger are perceived in directly opposite places: for Sensing, danger is in overturning society's structure, while for Intuition, danger is in blindly accepting it without questions.

Introverted Perceiving's idealistic worldview is put under special stress during times when society somehow turns negative. Both Sensing and Intuition have biases for or against cooperating with society and both of them are heavily dependent on context. If society is good, it's good to be for it. But what if society turns negative? Sensing can make it very difficult to step out of supporting roles, leading people to participate in morally bad things. And when something in society is bad, Intuition wants to question and fight it, but in rebelling, it may also lead to morally bad actions. In both cases, the moral severity has to become very obvious and clear before the idealistic supporter or rebel can see it.

The 20th century saw many examples of totalitarian societies that turned negative, forcing people to choose between managing daily life and jettisoning their entire worldview. Worldview that's deeply rooted in unconscious personality is so much part of us that rejecting it, reframing the world, is traumatic. Most people avoid trauma at all costs. Because Introverted Sensing and Intuition are so opposite in where they seek safety, they often have opposite reactions to society's turning negative.

The rise of Hitler's Third Reich provides us with some clear examples of how negativity pressures idealistic Perceiving. The Nazi Party took care to use many visual archetypal signs of kingship. Although we can look back and see that it was a dangerous, fringe movement that seized power, its use of archetypal signs for legitimate government hid this fact from many people, particularly those who feel emotional connection to archetypal social roles. They used symbols from the Roman Empire, such as the "fasces," a bundle of sticks that symbolized the authority to punish. They also used symbols from pagan Germanic times, such as lightning bolts and Wagner's opera cycle about the pagan hero Siegfried. Mass rallies with thousands of people shouting and saluting reinforced the idea that all of society had accepted the Nazi Party as the legitimate government. People with strong Introverted Sensing usually run as high as 50% of the population, so the Reich's use of visual, emotional, traditional appearances helped at least half the population feel comfortable with trusting their authority.

Using the cover image of a "king" archetype, the Third Reich could take unusual actions without immediately raising suspicions that something strange was going on. After all, part of being the king—or a modern government—is being allowed to do things that would be wrong for citizens. We the people can't declare war or put people in prison; these are privileges of the legitimate government (archetypally, the king).

For people whose personalities were directed by Introverted Sensing, the imagery of power successfully served as justification for a string of drastic changes. When the Nazi government nationalized industries, detained persons, annexed territory or declared war, it seemed reasonably appropriate. Seen through the filter of Introverted Sensing, these issues didn't seem to present any moral choices to individuals. Those employed in the civil government or military could understand correct behavior by staying in their own archetypal social role and filling it properly.

Of course, we see now that many such people were drawn into domestic and war crimes by "obeying orders." Even in the early Nazi years, there were doctors and nurses ordered to withhold food from disabled people until they died. Policemen were told to overlook some riots or arrest innocent people. The military found itself going on senselessly aggressive invasions. But as long as the orders seemed more or less within what a government could order, nearly all of them accepted orders as justification for what they did. Eventually, the orders became more extreme, more obviously wrong. In hindsight, it's obvious that many of those receiving orders should have refused them. We know that many individuals were definitely troubled about their work and some secretly made exceptions based on moral conscience. But as long as life flowed along normally with the right appearances, many people did not feel that any moral choices were being posed.

By contrast, the small minority with Introverted Intuition must have been alarmed as soon as the Nazi Party began drawing on traditional imagery. For the Film Noir director, every image is a mask, a false front. When the Third Reich piled on so many appearances and symbols, they were increasingly nervous, not increasingly reassured. The earliest dissidents, student activists and secret rescuers would have been drawn from the ranks of these Introverted Intuition personalities. Enough is known of Dietrich Bonhoeffer, the Lutheran pastor who died in Hitler's prison, that we can say with confidence he was one of them. It's likely that people with a Film Noir worldview found it difficult even to pretend to say "Heil Hitler."

During the same period, the Bolshevik Revolution in Russia was going through an opposite process. In 1917, revolutionaries began to tear down all of the old symbols of kingly power. Their founding philosophers probably had the truth-seeking, anti-appearance worldview of Introverted Intuition, and so did many early adherents. The king and his family were quite literally imprisoned, humiliated, and then shot. Palaces were opened for public use. Titles of honor like "my lord" and "baron" were forbidden, to make everyone into socially equal comrades. Government would be through workers' councils, called soviets. The national rulers of the new Soviet Union didn't use any symbols of kingship. Eventually, the Soviet Union's government began to use some archetypal heroic art, but on the surface, the posters were raising up lowly workers, not kings, for honor.

To people with a strong sense of archetypal social roles, that is to Introverted Sensers, the Bolsheviks were obviously dangerous and evil. When they could, they fled as refugees, and some fought back in a civil war. Those who could not flee or fight had to watch helplessly as revolutionaries destroyed churches, as well as palaces.

What's really interesting is that a vocal minority in Europe and America felt strongly the opposite way, that is, in support of the Soviet Union. Destruction of archetypal symbols seemed okay, as long as the destruction revealed truer truth. Introverted Intuition has a weakness for utopian ideals, with a tendency to focus on the ideal goal and overlook the problems of how to get there. The West was dependent on journalists in Moscow and Leningrad to report on events and people. As it happens, Introverted Intuition is also drawn strongly to journalism as a way to dig behind masks and false fronts.

The result was that journalists reporting back to New York and London were often fairly positive about what was going on. The Soviet Union did the same things that Hitler did a few years later: nationalized industries, uprooted populations, arrested individuals, annexed territory and declared war. But where Hitler was building up archetypal social symbols, the Soviet Union was tearing them down. Journalists with Introverted Intuition may have felt good about Soviet iconoclasm in the same reflexive way that Introverted Sensing Germans felt good about Hitler's regal image.

In both situations, people became blind to moral choices as long as the social context seemed to confirm their Sensing or Intuition ideals. If the system seemed right, it must be doing right things, and then being part of it, following orders, must be right too. But when they had the opposing Perceiving worldview (iconoclastic under the Nazis, or monarchist under the Soviets), they felt and saw a sweeping indictment of the system. In both cases, the social structure provided a moral context that provoked Introverted Perceiving either to accept and adapt, or to rebel and fight.

When the social structure turns negative, those with Introverted Perceiving may be drawn not just into supporting it in a general way, but into taking personal actions that would have seemed morally wrong in another context. On the one extreme, a German civil servant signs off on a cattle car full of human beings who are headed for death. Personally, he is a kind, compassionate neighbor and friend. He may feel some discomfort about what he has to do at work, but his social role feels more compelling than mere personal choices. On the other extreme, Bonhoeffer, a gentle Lutheran pastor, joins a plot to assassinate Hitler. In no way would he normally plan to kill a human being, but his personal sense of meaning drives him to define murder, in this case, as a good and moral act. In the Soviet Union, some revolutionaries were so caught up in the new ideology that they could betray their friends and even mothers.

In our century, we see similar situations in which a normally kind, caring person gets swept into terrorism or cults. Perhaps some of the explanations can be found in this personality framework. Certainly, actions that normally would have horrified this man or woman are now carried out with moral blindness. Perhaps Introverted Sensing was drawn into following an archetypal "king" or "prophet" figure and accepted "following orders" as a higher good than normal kindness. Conversely, perhaps Introverted Intuition was intent on establishing a utopia, one that requires sweeping away the dross of old, tainted society with all its masks and false fronts. Feeling like they're part of a structure (visible or invisible) becomes its own layer of reality, masking the simple meanings of good and bad.

Last, there are much smaller, more personal situations that can mislead Introverted Perceiving; it doesn't always require a war or revolution. Any time the social context seems chaotic, it causes someone with Introverted Sensing a lot of stress, making it hard to focus and relax. Living with disorder or chaos triggers the safety/danger alarm system so much that it can produce feelings of uneasiness that are akin to guilt. If it looks like there's some action that could be taken to restore order even for a short time, but it might hurt someone or even involve breaking a rule, the person with Introverted Sensing may feel strong temptation to just do it. Moral clarity gets blurred by being in a context that feels wrong already.

The same thing can happen to someone with Introverted Intuition, but the chaos and distress may be much more internal and invisible to others. It's extremely stressful for them to be forced into situations where the visible, official relationships don't match their inner sense of meaning, like having a teacher who seems to know less than the student, or having to be around (or in) a hostile marriage. Again, the inner stress feels similar to the distress of guilt, so if breaking a rule or hurting someone looks like it will put meaning back into place, it may be pretty tempting.

The person (victim) who gets hurt in such situations can't see what is driving the person with Introverted Perceiving. The stressful context may be obvious, or it may not, but either way, it didn't seem like sufficient reason for this hurtful thing to happen. Objectively it may not be; in this case, an explanation is not an excuse. What happened may have been just wrong. But it may help to understand that Introverted Perceiving has a special susceptibility to shifting context.

Extroverted Perceiving, whether Sensing or Intuition, does not exercise this kind of filtering control over choices and actions. The moral patterns are in some ways easier to understand. Extroverted Perceiving is about keeping all options open, generating questions and alternatives. People with Extroverted Perceiving in a strong directorial role don't like to be defined by situations and roles. They often defy traditional roles and conventional thinking.

If they relied on Perceiving to make moral choices, as the Introverted perceivers often can, the Extroverted Sensing or Intuiting ones could live as wild rebels. Sometimes they do, especially early in life. They are more likely to go into hard drinking or recreational drugs, and they are more likely to break the law in small ways like speeding and trespassing. They're more likely to get into sex at earlier ages or stay too late at parties.

But for the most part, they outgrow the rebel stage and may even bypass it. This is because moral conscience has a more important role in personality when the "film director" is permissive. If anything is possible and nothing is unthinkable, then every decision must be referred to the Judging court of right and wrong. People with Introverted Sensing or Intuition may not easily verbalize why some action is unsafe or dangerous, instead saying vaguely that, "it's just not done." Extroverted Perceivers, on the other hand, hear their Thinking or Feeling conscience speaking clearly, even in times when they do wrong. They know that what they did was a lie, a spiteful action, or theft. They had reasons for choosing the wrong option, but usually they saw all options.

A personality with Extroverted Sensing does not feel so much constrained by social roles to act the way people expect. Many people with Extroverted Sensing privately admit that even in their responsible daily lives, there's a wild thought in the back of the mind that if things get too bad, it's possible to walk away from it all and disappear into the wild. They really are more likely to quit jobs, move far away, suddenly marry or suddenly divorce, or even abandon children during difficult times. When they don't, we can thank their Judging function for saying "no" to those options. Generating options is one thing, accepting them morally is another. With cool conscience, they may say to themselves that "it would just be wrong," while with warm conscience, they imagine the pain of someone they love.

Extroverted Intuition is less about actions and more about thoughts and beliefs. Customary, traditional ideas don't feel like laws, and certainly they don't feel like the law of gravity. If science fiction can suspend gravity, Extroverted Intuition can defy custom. But unlike Introverted Intuition's pessimistic worldview, Extroverted Intuition rebels against convention optimistically. It suggests inventions, start-ups, years abroad, and unconventional careers. In extreme times, Extroverted Intuition can invent new philosophies that might justify all kinds of unusual actions and lifestyles. As with Extroverted Sensing's potential to just run away, when nothing is unthinkable, the only guide is the Judging conscience. Beliefs are sampled but may eventually be rejected because they create a moral collision, in ideals of rules or of love. Taking action always comes down to a Judging decision. Warm or cool conscience rejects alternatives and ideas for explicitly moral reasons.

Sometimes it isn't easy to spot a warm or cool conscience at work, since human beings present mixed reasons for anything they do. But the nature of Extroverted Perceiving may make it easier to tell cool from warm in personalities where it's strong. Introverted Sensing and Intuition exercised such a strong filter that warm or cool Judging could be hidden, but Extroverted Perceiving can't hide the nature of its Introverted Judging.

In fact, there's an odd phenomenon with these personalities. Because Extroverted Perceiving is all about generating options, they tend to be fairly non-judgmental and easy-going. They're more interested in what they're doing or reading than in making choices. They can even appear indecisive in some contexts. But when they're pushed into a moral choice, these easy-going natures can suddenly speak up loudly, even ferociously. Judging does not have difficulty verbalizing why a wrong action is so very, very wrong. As a result, people who don't understand this aspect of personality may find it surprising that someone who appeared to accept anything is suddenly putting down his or her foot, saying, "No, that's just wrong, I won't do it."

Personalities with Extroverted Perceiving are most at risk for problems when conscience matures later. During the teenage transition years, the conscience network that will make this person a reliable, moral adult may not be neurologically available yet. Although rules and memories are present, during times of instant decision-making they may not be present. We see this especially with Extroverted Sensing, and especially with an undeveloped cool conscience. Depending on peer pressure and opportunity for rule-breaking, these young people cause their families a lot of worry and often do short terms in jail or even prison. They're lucky to arrive at age 25 with neither criminal records, head injuries, nor surprise babies.

Even when no major rebellion or acting-out occurs, such personalities may seem self-centered. Extroverted Perceiving may be the strongest driving piece of personality, such that during this time period, their sense of identity truly does lie in exploring options. Asked to stop and look inside for moral direction, they may feel disconnected. Asked to do routine chores for other people, they may fume and often forget. Past age 25, their own sense of honor toward rules or people will handle it. Until then, immaturity keeps the personality imbalanced, with a tendency in favor of risk and exploration.

PART THREE:
BALANCING PERSONALITY

CHAPTER 10

Organizing the Mind

WE COME NOW TO THE main task of understanding dynamic personality: assembling all of the parts. First let's review both the parts and the fundamental rules of how living systems organize. Assembling the parts of personality into working models means careful, logical application of the rules to the parts.

The first rule of self-organizing systems is that they move away from states that require a lot of energy to maintain, toward low-energy states. On a snowy mountain slope, this means snow piled on a steep incline shifts toward an avalanche, the sudden movement of snow down to its angle of repose. In a rabbit's olfactory system, it means moving from unpatterned neural signaling to well-used patterns of remembered smells. In personality, it means moving away from uncertainty and dilemma toward a settled pattern of habits. In these settled patterns, the stronger, better-practiced systems handle most of our actions and decisions. This way, we get tied up in dilemmas only in unusual situations. Most of the time, habits have already settled how we'll process and move in the world.

The mind processes the world first by Perceiving its information, then by Judging how to organize its importance. Perceiving includes directly Sensing the world outside, but also using Intuition to perceive how facts are connected. Judging uses logic and numbers in Thinking, but also relationship values in Feeling. The four basic processes of Sensing, Intuition, Thinking and Feeling can be rooted in idealistic, inborn knowledge (Introverted). They can also be pragmatic and oriented to scanning the outside world (Extroverted). These are the parts that self-organize into habitual, easily-maintained systems.

We've already discussed how the Perceiving and Judging functions organize themselves. It would be very inefficient for all Perceiving or all Judging to be idealistic. We really can't get along in the world without pragmatic exploration that's willing to learn from what it sees and make compromises. On the other hand, if all Perceiving or all Judging was so pragmatic that it cared only about what works, not what's right, this too would be inefficient. Not only would such unlimited behavior annoy other people, it would also keep the brain in an exhausting state of openness. Thinking and Feeling can balance each other, with one of them idealistic and the other pragmatic, to create conscience. Sensing and Intuition also balance each other to create a personal worldview. Each personality has both of these pairs operating, so all four parts need to fit into an overall balance.

In Chapter 2, I discussed the three organizing rules suggested in Jung's *Psychological Types*. First, it's most efficient for personality to use one of these mental functions as its habitual driver. This one can be called the most dominant part of personality. Up to this chapter, I've described how a mental function can be dominant only in a theoretical way, saying that if it's dominant, this is what it will do. I've also described relative kinds of importance, such as what it's like when one kind of Perceiving is more important than another. We'll now begin to consider them seriously as first, second, third and fourth in importance.

Jung suggested two rules to accompany the basic principle of efficiency, in order to govern how the second most important part can work efficiently with the most important part of personality. Just as we don't want dilemmas between Perceiving and Judging, we also don't want such clashes between the two strongest parts. So when the most important role is held by a Judging function, the second one must be a form of Perceiving; conversely, when the most important is a kind of Perceiving, the second must be a type of Judging. As another consideration, when the most important role is introverted, the second one must be extroverted. The reasons are the same as given in past chapters: if the mind's function isn't well divided between Perceiving and deciding, and between pragmatic optimism and idealistic pessimism, then there will be too many high-energy states of dilemma and uncertainty.

The simplest way to show how personality balances is to use a mobile as both analogy and model. We've all made simple hanging mobiles in art class, when we were children. At its very simplest, the mobile needs two crossed arms and some objects hanging from them. Here is a simple sketch of this really basic mobile.

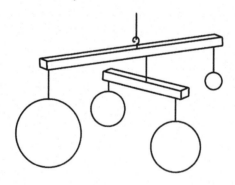

Fig. 10-1

If we looked down on the mobile, from above, we'd see something not unlike the first diagram in Chapter 2. In this simpler, static model, the point was only to show that Perceiving and Judging are categories of thought, while the other four are the types of Perceiving and Judging. So Perceiving and Judging were crossed arms, like the crossbars of the mobile.

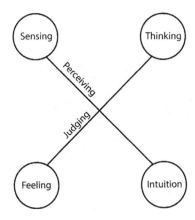

Fig. 10-2

So let's start by imagining that we can pick up the simple X-and-balls diagram above, and make it three-dimensional, complete with strings. There's a central string, which we'll use to hang it up; this central string is attached near the center cross. If you remember how mobiles worked in art class, you'll know that it isn't important to make sure that everything is centered and symmetrical. What matters, instead, is that it balances. Look again at my mobile sketch; I've deliberately shown the crossbars not centered, nor the balls equal sizes. We know from physics that a smaller object on a longer arm can balance a larger one on a short arm. The mobile can play with many relationships like this, so that many mobiles built on the same general plan are all somewhat unique.

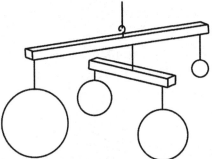

Fig. 10-3

I've also drawn my mobile sketch so that one ball is visibly largest, on the left. On the right, balancing the largest, is a ball that's clearly the smallest. In between, there are two balls that appear to be different sizes. One is a little smaller than the biggest, while the third is a little larger than the smallest. When we use this mobile as both analogy and model for balancing personality, we want to consider the balls as neatly ordered in size and importance: first, second, third, fourth.

As in the picture, the largest and smallest balls are on the same crossbar. In the analogy, this means that the largest and smallest parts of personality will also be on the same "crossbar," that is, they are both Perceiving or both Judging. The two parts in the middle, one relatively larger than the other, are also on the same crossbar. They, too, have to be the same category of thought. So in the mobile, one crossbar is for Sensing and Intuition, the other for Thinking and Feeling.

For example, the balls could be arranged like this:

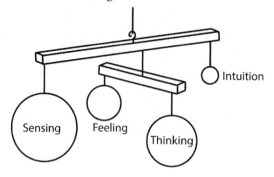

Fig. 10-4

Equally, they could be balanced with Judging functions on the other crossbar, making up the largest and smallest balls:

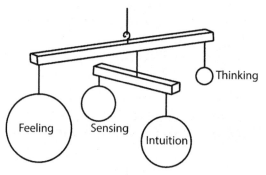

Fig. 10-5

In Chapter 6, we discussed how either Thinking or Feeling must be Introverted, leaving the other to be Extroverted, and in Chapter 9, the same about Sensing and Intuition. So we can also put notes on the mobile's balls this way:

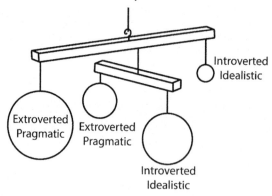

Fig. 10-6

You can see how there are multiple ways the balls could be labeled. Each one is a possible personality. There is only one more important rule to remember: Jung's rule that the first and second most important parts must also be the opposite of each other.

As you can see, the long words we've been using are going to become clumsier and harder to impose on little mobiles. In this chapter and the next, we'll begin to use letter abbreviations. Here, I'll start using E for Extroverted and I for Introverted. "E-Thinking" is short for Extroverted Thinking. To sketch out a first possible personality, I'm choosing to put Extroverted Thinking into the first, largest ball. It is the most important part of this personality.

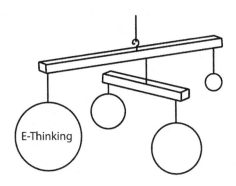

Fig. 10-7

Because I placed E-Thinking on the largest ball, I already know what the smallest one will be. By the rules, it has to be the other Judging function, Feeling, and it has to be Introverted.

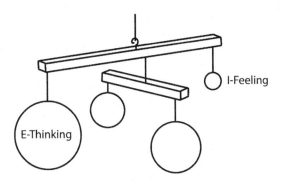

Fig. 10-8

Once I've placed E-Thinking in the largest ball, I have limited choices for the second ball. It must be Introverted, so that it's the opposite of the largest ball. And since the largest ball is Thinking, which is a type of Judging, the second ball has to be a type of Perceiving. It must be Introverted, but I can choose either Sensing or Intuition. Mentally flipping a coin, I chose Intuition.

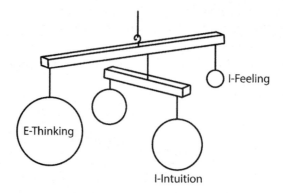

Fig. 10-9

Clearly, the unlabeled ball, which is the third largest in size, can only be one thing. It must be the other Perceiving function, and it must be the opposite of Introverted.

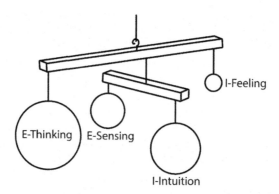

Fig. 10-10

This personality mobile follows the rules for being a balanced, efficient mind. In Chapter 11, we'll look at how a personality like this would act, based on how the top two "balls" balance each other. But for now, let's generate another personality. I'm going to choose something completely different for the largest ball, and of course, once I've done that, the smallest ball has to be filled in, too. Notice that I can choose any of the mental functions for the largest ball. There's no rule that it has to be Extroverted, it can truly be any of the things described in Chapters 4, 5, 7 and 8. Here, I've chosen Introverted Sensing.

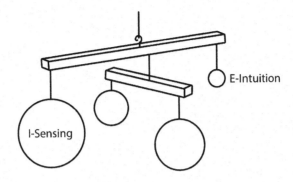

Fig. 10-11

I get another free choice now. I know that the inner crossbar has to be the two Judging functions, because I already filled in the first crossbar with Perceiving, but I can choose which goes in the bigger ball. Flipping an imaginary coin, I choose Feeling. Now my choices are gone; whether it's Introverted or Extroverted is already determined. When I put Introverted Sensing in the largest ball, I forced my choice for the second: Extroverted. The rules control the rest, so here is the second possible personality.

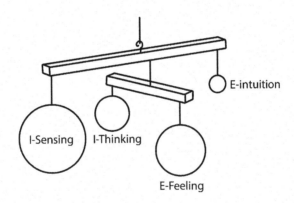

Fig. 10-12

So as you create possible balanced personalities, you have three choices, one for each of Jung's three rules. First, which is biggest? I'm going to pick Feeling this time. Second, am I going to make that biggest ball Introverted or Extroverted? There's not yet enough information to bring in the rules, so I get to pick: Introverted. Already, before I make my third choice, the rules force me to put Extroverted Thinking into the smallest ball.

167

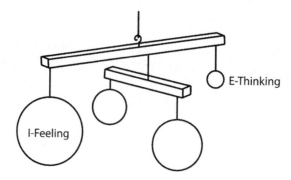

Fig. 10-13

My last free choice is for the second ball. The rules force it to be Extroverted, to balance the biggest ball. But I can choose: Sensing or Intuition? Another coin toss, my last free choice is Sensing. Now the rules fill in the third ball, and there's another complete possible personality.

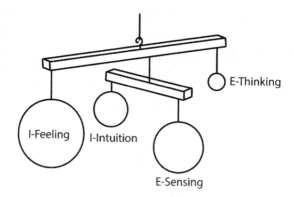

Fig. 10-14

There are sixteen logical possibilities, sixteen ways that you can label the balls without repeating the exact same pattern. If you like, try to generate a few more. In the next chapter, all sixteen will be discussed.

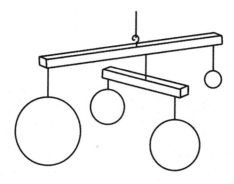

Fig. 10-15

CHAPTER 11

The Top Two

THE TWO MOST IMPORTANT DRIVERS of personality need to form a close working partnership. At best, they work together so well that we don't notice them as distinctly separate parts when we think about someone's personality. They're like some flavors that combine into blends that we recognize as new tastes. Chocolate, for example, strikes us very differently when it's blended with coffee as mocha, or when it's combined with peppermint or peanut butter. Garlic has its own taste, but it's also part of both curry and chili powder, where we perceive it as part of a new flavor. We'll see the same synergy when something like Sensing blends with either Feeling or Thinking, creating a new flavor of personality. Although the parts can be separated, we often don't feel them as separate when we think about personalities we know well.

In this chapter, we'll look at all sixteen possible combinations suggested in the last chapter, but we'll only focus on those top two functions. Full personality descriptions require more, and they're presented in Chapter 12. But here, we just want to get a sense of the unique flavor of each top-two set.

I'll continue to use the mobile as analogy and model, but the images will be much smaller. With smaller mobiles, I need shorter abbreviations. Instead of writing out either "Extroverted Thinking" or even "E-Thinking," I'll write "E-T." T is an easy abbreviation for Thinking, F for Feeling, and S for Sensing. However, the word "Intuition" presents a problem. Its first letter, I, is already in use to stand for "Introverted." That's the convention in writing about personality, and even without such a custom, I wouldn't want to take the letter I away from Introverted, since it also suggests words like *innate*, *inborn*, and *idealistic*. So conventionally, Intuition's second letter N is used. "I-N" here will mean "Introverted Intuition."

WHEN THE KING IS EXTROVERTED

Up to this point, if I refer to "you," the reader, we're talking about, and often looking into, your own mind. But to understand the general effect of Extroversion and Introversion, we need to step into an observer's role. So in this section, when I talk to "you," we are both standing outside, observing how a third person is processing the world. "You" and I are part of the outside world, to this third person that we're talking about. We're interested in how this person's mind works, but we're mainly looking at how that mind comes across to you. How does that person look, not from his or her point of view, but from the outside?

In general, when you meet and talk to someone, you are interacting with that person's most important personality function. It's the part that habitually, routinely handles the world for this mind. This is especially true when the most important, highest priority mental process is Extroverted. When the "King of the Mind" is pragmatic and intent on picking up cues from the outside world, you will feel its attention not only because it's habitually in control, but because you are part of the outside world. The part of this person's mind that is King is designed to learn things about the world, which right now means you.

Below are four possibilities in which the #1 priority of a personality is a pragmatic, outgoing, extroverted process. In each of these personalities, an Extroverted mental process is the King (the most important function). When you talk to each personality, the Extroverted process is eagerly reaching out; but as you can imagine, they all do it in a little different way.

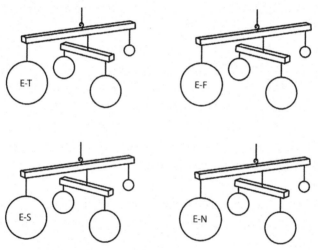

Fig. 11-1

Extroverted Thinking, the first King, may engage you in a discussion of politics or some kind of fact-based topic. Want to impress King Thinking? Know facts and numbers; know the kind of facts that an influential, logical person likes to know. Thinking tends to be competitive, since it's also interested in who's got more power and authority. If it knows more facts, you lose; this, of course, could make Thinking very happy. But if you can keep Thinking company in comparing numbers, you've made a friend.

When Extroverted Feeling is King, you're all about relationship, emotion, and your role in the group. King Feeling is interested in who you know and how they feel about you. It's scanning your small talk for clues about your attitudes to people in the room and their attitudes toward you. It's listening to your stories and taking notes. If King Feeling likes you, you may get a big hug or an invitation.

When pragmatic Extroverted Sensing is King, you're a target for observation. The ways you move and talk get noticed and perhaps mirrored back to you. You're drawn into an event that King Sensing is enjoying; the other person expects you to find the noise, speed or excitement of the event just as thrilling as he or she does. The person in whom outgoing Sensing is King may tell exciting stories with gestures and laughter, and it may be time for action too: practical jokes or a game of volleyball.

When exploratory Extroverted Intuition is King, the person you're talking to sees you as an unexplored potential. He'll ask a lot of questions about what you know and where you've been. You aren't being sized up the way Thinking and even Feeling were doing; rather, Intuition is picking your brain, looking for news. What new things do you know? How can your comments be connected to other things in the world? Can you see connections the way Intuition does, and can you add new ideas?

In common speech, we'd call all of these personalities "extroverted" or "outgoing." But it's clear that each is outgoing in a different way. It's more accurate to say not that the person or even the personality is outgoing, but that their top mental priority is an outgoing, pragmatic, exploratory one. They're using an Extroverted function to talk to you. As you stand and talk, you experience this person as extroverted and engaging. "Nice person," you'll say. "Very outgoing." But you are really experiencing only one part of who this person is.

Of course, you know from past chapters that each of these personalities also has some idealistic, Introverted parts. When you talk to these personalities, you aren't as immediately struck by the presence of the second, Introverted function. If you know what to look for, you can pick it up, but it's not out there chatting with you in the same way. However, in each of the types of people represented here, the two biggest functions are working together like right and left hands. While calling the most important one the King, we'll call the auxiliary helper the Prime Minister.

In the next image, I've assigned an Introverted function as the #2. I followed the rule: when the largest ball is a Judging function, the second largest must be a Perceiving function, and vice versa. Let's look at four possibilities.

The first one has pragmatic Thinking as King, but idealistic Sensing is the King's top adviser. When Thinking and its Prime Minister, Introverted Sensing, are working together well, you can't easily separate them. Sensing is shaping what seems important in the world, and Thinking is making decisions about it. Introverted Sensing complements logical Thinking with a strong sense of propriety and attention to detail. This personality has a sense of how things and people ought to look. He or she dresses neatly in a conservative, traditional way. With this neat, conservative sense of how the world ought to look, the personality is also interested in traditional problems of logic. Thinking does its calculations in ways that put life in better order. Although the Thinker is probably not an artist, Introverted Sensing puts a value on fine art. This personality might collect paintings, visit historic mansions, or appreciate national parks. It's probably competitive about having a nicer house, applying Thinking competition to archetypal and artistic appearances.

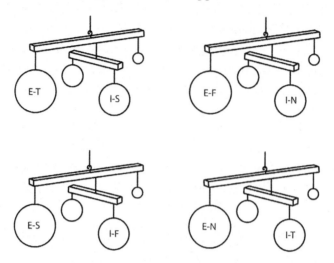

Fig. 11-2

The second personality has Extroverted Feeling as the King, but the Prime Minister is idealistic, Introverted Intuition. When they work together, the chemistry creates a strong focus on what people and relationships mean. This person isn't just observing, engaging with people, or trying to score points socially. He or she is also trying to understand you with an idealistic sense of meaning and connections. Choosing how to make small talk may be a pragmatic decision (Feeling), but there's always an undercurrent that is idealistic and inventive. Don't try to impose traditional choices on this person; he or she may go along with them but might also surprise you with a tactful denial. This personality likes to read (or may write) books about people, psychology, and theology.

In our third example personality, Sensing is top priority, but there's idealistic Feeling near at hand. While Extroverted Sensing is reveling in a world of touch, smell, color and sound, Feeling is always pushing to turn that riot of sensation into a way to bring people closer. If it's summer and everyone goes out to play volleyball, it's this personality who notices that one of the players is shy and unconfident. He or she smiles and encourages, standing close to help a bit. While loving the motion of the game through Sensing, idealistic Feeling will only be truly happy at the end of the day if relationships got better, too. This personality loves to be in a big crowd of people, making them laugh and smile, creating harmony. Cooking for all of those people may just be even better.

In the fourth personality, outgoing, pragmatic Intuition is exploring the world for meaning, but at its side, idealistic Thinking is suggesting mechanical and moral principles to harness meaning. Left to itself, Extroverted Intuition would come up with a new idea every day. But when it's closely partnered with a strong rule-oriented conscience, Intuition disciplines itself to complete projects on time. Since Thinking, even as a conscience, is also oriented to machines and numbers, as Prime Minister it nudges King Intuition toward interest in mechanical principles. Personalities with this combination are usually very interested in how machines work and fascinated with new scientific ideas. They are drawn to events like science fairs, where a new idea might help them win (Thinking is always competing!).

That's only four of the logical combinations that can be made with the two largest balls in the mobile. What would it be like if we left Thinking, Feeling, Sensing and Intuition where they are now, but swapped around the #2 labels to create another four possibilities? At the moment, we have someone wearing a suit and talking about facts, another listening intently to someone's feelings and seeking moral meaning, another playing volleyball while bringing people closer, and the fourth seeking new ideas in science and math. Watch the difference it will make when we change Prime Ministers.

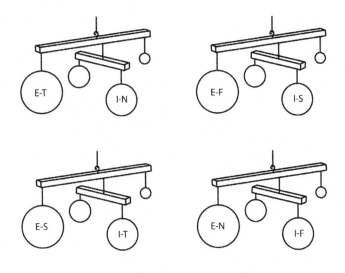

Fig. 11-3

The Thinking personality now has a different type of meaning drawing its attention. King Thinking still processes facts and logic, and it's still interested in figuring out how much power and authority you have. But it's no longer organized around an ideal of propriety. Instead, Thinking's attention is directed to hidden meanings. Intuition was born feeling that it just knows what the world means, and it also believes that most people miss the point and waste their time. When this personality talks to you, it's sizing up your wisdom. You may be asked to suggest some connections between facts, and if you have some experiences that are new, you will be quizzed in a friendly way until the Thinking mind has absorbed what you have to say, so that Intuition can chew it over. Intuition likes to make internal sarcastic comments to Thinking, as a way of competing with the world behind its back.

The Feeling personality is organized around idealistic Sensing now. While Feeling's chief interest is still in group dynamics and being liked, its attention is pulled toward beautiful, neat, clean objects. Beautiful objects and a clean environment make people happy, so they improve the Feeling personality's relationships and raise status in the group. On the other hand, the Feeling/Sensing combination here can have very strong feelings about what's ugly or out of place. Talking to you, perhaps at a formal banquet in someone's honor, this personality evaluates you for how well you fit standards of both traditional rightness and group cohesion. When things look just right and people are happy, this personality has little more to wish for.

The Sensing personality in this set is still primarily driven to experience the world of sound, touch and sight, but now it is organized around idealistic Thinking. Here, too, Introverted Thinking draws the attention toward machines, which are paragons of logic. The sensory world plus machines often means motorcycles and power tools. Introverted Thinking is idealistic about keeping rules and being on time, but at the same time it's still interested in who comes in first or has more authority. One way to combine those traits with pragmatic Sensing: competitive sports! This personality relates to you mostly through competing against you, often in a friendly way, or forming a team with you to take on some kind of project or challenge.

The fourth personality, with strong Extroverted Intuition, is now assisted by idealistic Feeling. When a personality is driven to recreate the Garden of Eden and, at the same time, explore the world for meaning, it is always drawn to making new human relationships. Each person (including you) that Intuition chats with is someone who could, even for a moment, help create perfect friendship or love. Instead of mainly competing with people, this personality sees new friends or falls in love. People also become material for discovering new ideas; they can be combined in new ways or brought together to do newer and greater things. This personality cares little for rules, because a rule says that there is only one way; Intuition knows that there are many ways to do everything. All new ways to do things are equally good, unless they might hurt someone, which idealistic Feeling will not allow.

WHEN THE KING IS INTROVERTED

We can create another set of possible personalities by moving the Introverted mind processes into first place, not second place. On the mobile, the Introverted versions of Sensing, Intuition, Thinking and Feeling will now appear on the largest ball.

What difference will this make in the personalities? Chiefly, for all of these new possibilities, if you were standing there talking to someone with this set, the mental part that's talking to you would no longer be really the most important part. People refer to these personalities as "introverts" in general, because they feel that something is being held back from conversation. When you stood and talked to the eight personalities above, the idealistic, inborn part was there, and it was shaping how things went, but it wasn't really in charge. Instead, an outgoing, pragmatic part was in charge, and that part was chatting you up, exploring your possibilities. Now, it's the other way. The Extroverted part is still talking to you, but it is the second most important part. You are no longer talking to the King. The King is sitting off to the side, exchanging looks with the Prime Minister, and he's really in control. But the outgoing, Extroverted Prime Minister is delegated to talk to you under normal circumstances.

This automatic delegation of energy may be why people identified as introverts find it tiring to be around people for long periods of time; they are running a more costly mental function at full speed. Only when they have time to let their more efficient King function run alone for a while will their energy reserves build back up.

I'm going to present these personalities in a bit different order. Now that we've looked at the difference the Prime Minister (the second function) makes, I'll present both options that could balance the first function. In this way, we'll go through Introverted Thinking, Feeling, Sensing and Intuition, in pairs. This will conclude all sixteen logical possibilities for balanced personalities.

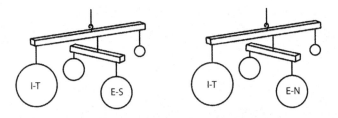

Fig. 11-4

Above, we see how Introverted Thinking is now most important, first paired with pragmatic Sensing and then with exploring Intuition. In the Sensing personality shown first, the Prime Minister for Outreach (the Extroverted function) is focused on the chaotic real world of sound, touch and sight. This personality may still be interested in talking to you about sports or other real-world adventures. Playing volleyball or going hiking together still seems like a great idea. But a large train of thought, the real King, is tucked away; it can be logical, mechanical, or even competitive. Thinking, whether Extroverted or Introverted, is always interested in who came in first, second, third and last. This private, reclusive side of the personality is not driven to dive into Sensing experiences, as its Extroverted Prime Minister is. It may feel drawn to one-on-one competitive sports, and it is probably happy spending long hours alone, immersed in logical tasks like figuring out why a machine doesn't work or finding a math error. This personality balance is more focused on moral decisions than in the type where Sensing was King. When idealistic Thinking was the Prime Minister, King Sensing could forget about morality when really drawn into excitement. But when orderly, idealistic Thinking is the monarch, it's much harder for excitement to drown out the voice of the idealistic, inborn Rule.

In the second variation, idealistic Thinking is again the chief focus of the personality's energy (the King), but exploring Extroverted Intuition is Prime Minister. When you talk to this personality, Intuition is likely to draw you into a speculative conversation about possibilities. No field of possibilities is likely to bore Intuition, whether it's politics, sports, history, science, pop culture, theology, or family relationships. The topic only has to be exploring and speculative. However, the guiding interest for this personality's exploration is not relationships, it's idealistic logic. When speculating on ideas about people, this personality isn't as likely to want to go out and explore them for real. Instead, it quickly moves to the question of what kind of logical process could help out. In theology and relationships, it may be a principle of logical morality. In science or politics, it could be mathematics. Even if the owner of this personality doesn't have the math skills to carry it out, he or she thinks, "If we could get a number for such and such, we could figure out the answer." Exploring is good, but this personality is fundamentally driven to calculate answers, often silently ruminating on the best route to the most accurate answer.

Now let's look at two personalities in which the #2, the Prime Minister, is again either pragmatic Sensing or exploring Intuition. But the King sitting quietly nearby is now idealistic Introverted Feeling, not Thinking. In the earlier section, we looked at personalities that combined Feeling and Sensing, or Feeling and Intuition. Here, they are similar to what we've talked about before, but there's a subtle difference of priority that comes with an Introverted function being the private King.

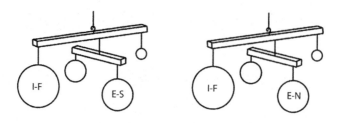

Fig. 11-5

We talked about how the Feeling personality with Extroverted Sensing as King would be an enthusiastic picnic volleyball player while paying attention to relationships. Here, we see the roles are switched; Extroverted Sensing could still be great at volleyball, but Feeling is really in control. At a picnic, this personality is more likely to sit with someone who appears lonely or help with young children, making the game a lower priority than one-to-one relationships. Outgoing, exploratory Sensing makes it easy to connect with other people in activities; but left alone, this personality is usually drawn to experiencing the Sensing world in more personal ways, often by making things with his or her hands. Wilder kinds of Sensing fun are reserved for when it's clear that all individual relationships are sidelined.

The second personality (shown above) is also controlled by idealistic Feeling. When you sit and talk with this personality, there's an intense bond formed in a one-on-one conversation. Outgoing, exploring Intuition is chatting with you about life, but idealistic Feeling is using the conversation as a lasso to catch an answer to the question, "what would it feel like to be You?" The inner thought process is about how relationships should be, but the outside connection with the world focuses on "what if?" There are long inner conversations between Intuition and Feeling, as Intuition notices things in the world and Feeling ponders what they mean for human relationships. This personality is comfortable with silence and isolation for hours at a time, because the inner conversation is rich enough to keep isolation from feeling truly alone.

In the next set, the top function is Introverted Sensing. As discussed in Chapter 9, it acts as a movie director, restricting the mind to attitudes and behavior that uphold ideal archetypes of social roles. In these two personalities, the Hollywood Classic effect is very strong, since Introverted Sensing is actually the private King, not just the Prime Minister.

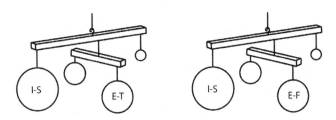

Fig. 11-6

In the personality on the left, with Thinking as Prime Minister, there's a general focus on logic and order, so Sensing's ideal is most often about neatness and visual perfection. The world this personality wants to inhabit is beautiful, symmetrical, and clean. Outdoors, it should be like a well-tended garden; indoors, it should be like a clean, traditional apartment. Extroverted Thinking pragmatically takes care of the day's schedule in life outside the mind; most people with this kind of personality go into law, engineering, or administration, where the day's tasks involve numbers and logic. But Sensing keeps track of the many things that don't look right; it forbids chaotic, senseless actions. It resents disorderly behavior as much as it dislikes a messy room or an unraked lawn.

When idealistic Sensing is working with Feeling as Prime Minister, the world's disorder is noticed most of all in the realm of human behavior. The personality shown here is most likely to choose work among people, since pragmatic Feeling is always helping direct attention and skills toward them. But as pragmatic Feeling navigates through the home, school or work world, idealistic Sensing notices many things that are just wrong. The ugliness may be dirty or messy places, but it's often disorder in social relationships. Leaving children or homeless people out in the cold is "just wrong," so Sensing prompts Feeling to find a way to help. Correcting bad grammar and spelling seems to be another specialty of this blend.

Now, at last, we come to the two strongest "Film Noir" personalities. In these personalities, there's a primary filter of Perceiving at work, searching for ideal meaning. It's the King, whether it's assisted by Thinking or Feeling as Prime Minister.

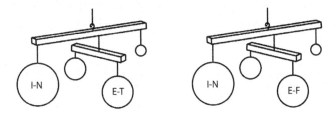

Fig. 11-7

These two personalities are similar in many ways. They both leave people with an impression that they're not saying everything they're thinking, which is true. Both have a tendency to be sarcastic when they think someone else is in the wrong. The sarcasm comes from the sense of knowing how things are connected, and feeling like others surely must know it, too; it also comes from a strong sense of alienation and being different. Even in childhood, people like this know they see things in a different, minority way, and they often find that other people think they're wrong. They feel—in fact they know with stubborn certainty—that they aren't wrong. Most people with this personality balance can tell stories about being proved right over time. They learn to expect this cycle of being rejected and proving right; sarcastic comments anticipate "here we go again." (It isn't actually true that they are always right, but they prove right just often enough to confirm the feeling.)

The Thinking version of the personality can become somewhat distanced from people. Relating to the outside world mainly through logic and numbers, this personality focuses on learning skills to get better and better at being right. When Introverted Intuition and pragmatic Thinking work together, the result is the Scientific Method. In this method, you make an educated guess about what's going to happen or what's really true, and then you design an experiment to test if you're right. Really good experiments use rigorous logic to consider all possible options, and the most brilliant experiments use some creative thinking to come up with an outlandish way to actually test these things. And that's basically how this personality thinks, by nature. They tend to become very hurt if people question their accuracy or abilities. If the hurt happens in early years, they can lose confidence profoundly and may always maintain a little distance with other people.

The Feeling version of this personality, by contrast, draws close to people naturally and easily. However, the constant sense of inborn meaning makes it hard for them not to take their personal relationships very, very seriously. As children, they pick up on the emotional problems of adults around them; it can be overwhelming to sense meaning so strongly without any real experience to balance it. In some cases, their inborn knowledge can verge on extra-sensory perception. Because it's so intense, they tend to go through periods when they isolate themselves even from their best friends. Extroverted Feeling directs their attention to so much information about people that at times, they have to close their "eyes." The only way to do this is to be alone. They are usually strongly drawn to whatever helps them make sense of what they're perceiving; a really high number of them go into some form of psychology or religious ministry work. Many (if not all) of them appreciate meditation and yoga.

NAMING THE PERSONALITY TYPES

When Carl Jung wrote *Psychological Types*, he created terms for the mind's functions, but he did not create names for "personality types" as such. Naming and defining personalities came later, with the work of Isabel Myers. Myers and her mother, Katherine Briggs, devised a letter code system to name personalities so that Myers could write a personality-sorting test. This test became the well-known Myers-Briggs Type Indicator® assessment. Others may have tried to find better names for personality types, since the letter code isn't easy to remember.

But over time, it's the letter code that stuck, so in this book, I'm going to use the standard letter codes, with many thanks and much credit to Myers and Briggs.[76]

It isn't completely straightforward to go between the standard names and my explanations. The letters in each type name are usually explained as menu choices, as I discussed briefly in the first chapter. Because I explain personality using a dynamic, balanced model, the letter codes don't directly match my presentation. Myers and Briggs were looking at the same personality balances, but they took note of different things to name the types.

In this chapter, we've looked at the top two mental functions and how they work together. The Myers-Briggs system is mainly focused on these two, which form the middle letters. However, it was not important to Myers to note which was the top function. So in the letter code, they are not arranged in order of first and second. Instead, the Perceiving letter is always first, while the Judging letter is second. So the first two personalities I described would have middle letters ST and SF, while the last two, just above, would have middle letters NT and NF.

The dynamic, self-organizing model depends a lot on understanding whether S, N, T and F are Extroverted and pragmatic, or Introverted and idealistic. But in type names, the letters E and I don't mean this; instead, they tell you only whether the top function, the "King," is Extroverted or Introverted. As discussed earlier in the chapter, we often get a general sense of a personality being "outgoing" or not based on this fact. That's what the first letter, E or I, captures.

The last letter in the code, P or J, signals whether a Perceiving or a Judging function is the Extroverted one. As we know, in the top two, one has to be Extroverted, and it can be either Perceiving or Judging. Myers' idea was that when a Judging function is managing contact with the outside world, the personality is more judgmental and decisive. These personalities end in J. On the other hand, when a Perceiving function is exploring the world, the personality may seem more interested in processing and doing; these personalities end in P. The Myers-Briggs types that end in J are also the ones that I would say have an Introverted Perceiving "film director," either Hollywood Classic or Film Noir. The types that end in P are the types with pragmatic, exploring "film directors," either action movies or science fiction.

Translating between my system and the Myers-Briggs one may feel a bit like going from Fahrenheit to Celsius. In math classes, we always have to convert some temperatures from one to the other, but it's clumsy. Similarly, I will demonstrate two mechanical conversions from my system to the Myers-Briggs. But just as with temperature, it's much easier to remember them in a general way. We know that water freezes at 32 in one system, at 0 in the other; it boils at 212 in one system, and 100 in the other. It's easier to become familiar with the names than to calculate and derive them.

Here is one personality as defined by a self-organized mobile. Its top function is pragmatic Extroverted Thinking, assisted by Introverted Sensing.

76: Myers-Briggs Type Indicator, Myers-Briggs, MBTI and MBTI Logo are trademarks or registered trademarks of the MBTI® Trust, Inc., in the United States and other countries.

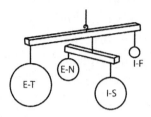

Fig. 11-8

To capture this in the Myers-Briggs letter code, we write the letters for Thinking and Sensing, but they must go in this order: ST. Then we ask, is the biggest ball Extroverted or Introverted? Here it's Extroverted, so the first letter will be E. When it's managing the outside world in a pragmatic way, which function is it using? In this case, it's using a Judging function which also happens to be the biggest ball—the same one already used to answer the "E or I" question. So the last letter will be for Judging, that is J. This personality type is ESTJ.

Here is another demonstration for a balanced personality mobile:

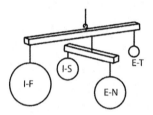

Fig. 11-9

The two top functions here are Feeling and Intuition, and Intuition's N has to be written first, so the middle letters will be NF. Now we ask, is the biggest ball Extroverted or Introverted? It's Introverted; the first letter will be I. But which of those top two is Extroverted? In the first mobile, both questions were answered by the biggest ball, but here, the Extroverted one is second, and it's a Perceiving function so the name ends in P. This personality type is INFP.

Notice that while the letter codes, ESTJ and INFP, look like complete opposites, there's actually some similarity between the two in my terms. Both of them have Introverted Sensing, that is, a fondness for archetypal visuals and social roles. Both of them have Feeling as the idealistic Judging function, so I'd say that both have warm conscience. If we looked only at the mobile, we might see them as much the same. However, the letter code is also correct in suggesting how very different they are, when they're balanced in such opposite ways.

To the extent that the conventional Myers-Briggs letter codes are easy for you to remember, they can serve as yet another layer of meaning and interpretation. There are some interesting parallels and contrasts when you translate between my models and the letter types. However, most readers are not going to remember the conversion meaning, nor do they need to. The explanation is here, so you can refer back if it's ever needed.

But now we'll simply use the letter names to indicate each of the sixteen balanced personality models. They may already be quite familiar. If you don't find them familiar or memorable, it's okay. You still understand the ways personality is balanced.

CHAPTER 12

Personality Profiles

THIS CHAPTER IS A REFERENCE section that lays out the sixteen logical possibilities for balanced personalities. They're named by their conventional Myers-Briggs labels, followed by a quick summary of the top two functions. Then, there is a simple cartoon drawing to help summarize the way Thinking, Feeling, Sensing and Intuition are organized for each type. More important functions are shown as larger images, and drawn above less important ones. Each drawing is accompanied by a mobile showing the dynamic balance of the type.

Biographical examples are embedded in the personality descriptions. I have tried to be very careful, using someone's name only when a wide range of personality traits supports their inclusion in a type description. Biographical examples are only footnoted when they use direct quotations. For further information about someone's personality, you can check a list of the biographies I found helpful, which is provided in the Appendix.

For each type, I can tell you an approximate percentage of its occurrence. These numbers are provided by the *Myers-Briggs Type Indicator® Manual*, 3rd Edition, where they report the results of a careful survey of personality types.[77]

I've organized the types by the four Perceiving groups discussed in Chapter 9. There are many other ways to group them, of course. This way just connects the profiles with past chapters.

77: Myers-Briggs Type Indicator, Myers-Briggs, MBTI and MBTI Logo are trademarks or registered trademarks of the MBTI® Trust, Inc., in the United States and other countries.

FIRST GROUP: INTROVERTED SENSING

There are four personality types that feature Introverted Sensing as one of the top functions. It's the Perceiving structure that can be compared to Hollywood classic films in which the Introverted Sensing director exercises tight control over style and content, with Intuition acting only as a scriptwriter, helping do research or solve problems. Most decisions are made according to what's appropriate and expected, so the actual Judging conscience takes a back seat. When the personality type name indicates T or F as a top function, the root of conscience is actually opposite, so its cool or warm nature is masked by more visible Introverted Sensing.

ESTJ

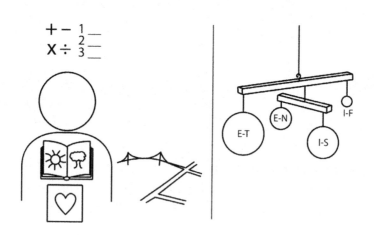

Fig. 12-1

#1: Extroverted Thinking
#2: Introverted Sensing
11.2% of men, 6.3% of women

In this type, Extroverted Thinking is King, but it operates only within a strict worldview of Introverted Sensing. Pragmatic, competitive logic is willing to do anything that would help with success, but "anything" is neatly circumscribed by tradition and custom. ESTJs compete within and govern the culture and society they live in, so their personal goals, options and values exactly match whatever this culture is. They can be found all over the world, many of them would vehemently disagree with each other as their cultural values clash. There are ESTJs upholding and defending every political party, religion, and social class; at the same time, they are realistic and pragmatic about the limitations and imperfections of each one. Idealism resides in the system itself, and the solution to problems is to make the system work better, to push the people in its roles closer to their archetypal images, not to tear down the system.

ESTJs may be the most dominant personality type in America, being both relatively common and very decisive. Their abilities have always served them well in a nation with self-government at many levels. In early colonial times, ESTJs were always ready to serve on town councils and juries. Self government, like self discipline, appeals to the ESTJ's vision of an orderly world in which each person has a role in maintaining the social order. Rising to the top in representative governments, writing laws that made sense to them, they laid the foundation for future ESTJs to succeed. Most institutions (government, school, business and church) are comfortable and rewarding places for ESTJs.

ESTJs are naturally drawn into the many roles in society that require objective order-keeping without much emotion involved. They administer justice with cool confidence and emotional detachment. Judges, presidents, principals: all of their job titles tend to mean either "decider" or "leader." Young ESTJs seek careers that have clear upward tracks so that they can eventually reach positions of power. George Washington was America's first famous ESTJ; many top generals, cabinet secretaries and company Chief Executive Officers are ESTJs, so their names dominate headlines. First Lady, Senator, Presidential candidate and Secretary of State Hillary Clinton seems to be a very good example of an ESTJ woman. Many or even most elected officials share this type.

ESTJs can have fun, but they don't tend to be spontaneous or think first of entertainment. Work comes first, even in childhood; it's doubly motivated by competitive Thinking logic and by Introverted Sensing's instinct about how things should be. ESTJ children usually have clean rooms and it comes naturally to them to do their homework. They take on after school jobs and save money. As adults, they rarely let things slip through negligence. While money and success motivate them, ESTJs are equally motivated by helping maintain the order that they inherited. Work is there to be done, and whether the ESTJ likes the work or not, he or she feels compelled to make sure it is kept up so that things don't fall apart.

An ESTJ is comfortable with the responsibility that comes with power and typically does not hesitate to impose punishments. Keenly aware of what everyone ought to be doing, she is just as keenly aware of failure. Since the ESTJ operates consciously on a principle of duty, she generally assumes that other people failed consciously and need a sharp correction to stop them from doing it again. ESTJs don't usually feel sorry for the people they punish, and it can be very difficult for an ESTJ to see that her judgment might not have been right. In the best circumstances, ESTJ discipline can save the day, as when young Major Eisenhower's very strict imposition of quarantine rules at Camp Colt, his first command post, saved many lives in the 1918 Spanish Flu epidemic.

In a darker vein, ESTJs can misuse power if they feel that the social rules permit it. We see it in political scandals; if ESTJs were angels, we wouldn't need checks and balances on political power. For another pattern of power abuse, movies often portray older men with ESTJ personalities when they want to show, for example, an FBI director with a vendetta or a businessman who seeks to murder a rival.

Another movie, *Mean Girls* may show us a less-noticed dark side of the ESTJ personality. Based on Rosalind Wiseman's book *Queen Bees and Wannabes*, the story portrays high school girls who use their good looks and money for strategic social power. As Wiseman describes the "Queen Bee" in her book, "Through a combination of charisma, money, force, looks, will and social intelligence, this girl reigns supreme over the other girls and weakens their friendships with others, thereby strengthening her own power and influence."[78] The "Queen Bee" is a social role that girls step into when they are more confident and strategic than the girls around them. The meanest "Queen Bees" are probably ESTJ personalities, to whom it comes naturally to exercise power and deal out pain. We can observe other examples on reality shows where models compete; some beautiful faces cover highly strategic, competitive personalities.

Extroverted Intuition, the third function, helps ESTJs understand possibilities and new ideas in the world. Intuition usually acts as a research assistant to Thinking, so it's not usually very good at understanding relationships. ESTJs are not empathetic and don't easily see other points of view. On the other hand, Extroverted Intuition allows them to find new, intuitive solutions to practical problems.

For example, Eisenhower, when he was a West Point cadet, found that he was better at coaching football than playing it. In his early years as an Army officer in Texas, he coached local prep school football teams to victory as an off-hours job. It's very clear that his later ability to plan a strategic war campaign began with the intuitive ability to see opportunity while coaching sports; he had a knack for sizing up which players or soldiers to put in the right positions. Eisenhower was among America's first stateside officers to see a European tank, and he became a champion for developing its possibilities; his exploring Intuition could see new ways to plan war strategies with the new technology.

Introverted Feeling, the fourth and weakest function, is the root of conscience. It's not actively in use much of the time, since Introverted Sensing's strong worldview already provides a daily guide for right and wrong. Warm conscience mostly handles unusual cases and private family life. As an example of an unusual situation, suppose the ESTJ has authority to impose a punishment on someone who has broken rules, but Feeling suggests that a higher good is served by showing mercy. Empathy is brief and limited, but an ESTJ may recall a time when she was also in need of mercy for the same kind of flaw. We sometimes see ESTJ judges develop unexpected compassion for someone who has transgressed the law; the judge still hands down conviction and sentencing, but he may add a gruff (but heartfelt) speech of inspiration and affection. Introverted Feeling is also responsible for how former President Jimmy Carter chose to spend his time in charitable work for the poor, which at the time was not typical work for former Presidents.

Idealistic Feeling also gives ESTJs an underlying warmth that their families appreciate most of all. They are capable of great sacrifice for the people they care about, and they typically say little as they make these sacrifices. Love is a very private matter for an ESTJ, and the people who are most aware of their feelings may be those who are farthest removed from the ESTJ's power structure. An oldest son of an ESTJ who follows his father into business is less likely to experience his father's warm side than the younger children or, even more, the grandchildren particularly when they are babies. The sternest "hanging judge" may be the

---

78: Rosalind Wiseman, *Queen Bees and Wannabes: Helping Your Daughter Survive Cliques, Gossip, Boyfriends and the New Realities of Girl World* (New York: Three Rivers Press, 2009), 87.

most indulgent grandparent. In this role, he has no need to focus on competition or power, so Introverted Feeling can have its freest expression.

As spouses, ESTJs tend to be loyal. Some are comfortable with low-key affection in public, but most reserve warmth for strictly private times. They manage relationships in a structured way; each person should have his or her due. Even when spontaneous love has faded, an ESTJ spouse tries to make sure that birthdays and formal events are honored as they should be. In return, they expect to receive structured dues. As long as their expectations are clear and can be met, ESTJs can be easy to please, since they rarely keep people guessing.

ISTJ

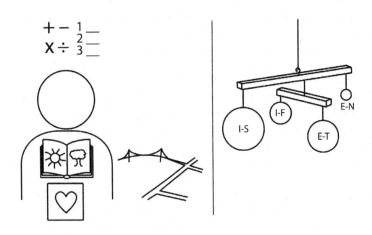

Fig. 12-2

#1: Introverted Sensing
#2: Extroverted Thinking
16.4% of men, 6.9% of women

For ISTJs, Introverted idealism is a primary attitude to life; it provides methodical habits to navigate the world. These personalities are usually notably careful, precise and neat, as they try to adhere to Introverted Sensing's vision of perfect form. They are deeply aware of archetypal social roles, knowing exactly how people should look and behave. Extroverted Thinking gives them a realistic grasp of the world's facts, but at some level ISTJs never accept chaos and disorder as just the way things are. They use logic and hard work to make chaos conform to order.

ISTJs are drawn to many professions, but always to a logical, orderly line of work within each field. Engineering, law, police work, and teaching all strongly attract ISTJs (when they are teachers, ISTJs are most likely to teach older students, not elementary school where kids need a lot of spontaneity and play). These four fields of work all help to maintain society's infrastructure, whether reinforcing buildings and roads, enforcing law in mediation, courtrooms and highways, or passing on behavior norms and useful information to the next generation. ISTJs seem uniquely aware of the dangers of entropy; they know that without maintenance, things will fall apart. Other kinds of people can notice decay and help fix things, but only ISTJs make it a primary interest to be sure society doesn't forget the details that maintain the predictability of life.

ISTJs focus mostly on their own role in maintaining the world, but they are happy to direct and admonish a few people around them. They are rarely driven to exert a wider influence, but they are aware of the power of setting a good personal example. Being tolerant and friendly to everyone is a high value, so they maintain a forgiving attitude to other people's slips as long as possible. Within their family, though, they feel a greater responsibility to correct and speak out. ISTJ parents and spouses are not tolerant of laziness, carelessness and being late.

Institutions that help maintain society are extremely important to ISTJs. Whatever religion they are part of, they are both faithful and keenly interested in the Thinking logic of its theological and canonical structure. If they are not part of any formal religion, ISTJs will find other institutions to fill that place. Because maintaining order in society is such a high personal value, just filling their role in events and services gives ISTJs an important emotional reward. They are most likely to show up for humble, dirty volunteer work like cleaning roadsides or planting flowers. An ISTJ who's under stress in other areas of life will become more faithful than ever about volunteer help like this, since it feels so directly rewarding.

The motivation patterns of an ISTJ make him unlikely to become famous. The few ISTJs who are well-known seem uncomfortable with the attention and clearly did not seek it. Two Presidents seem to have been ISTJs, and both came into the highest office only when the sitting President died. Although Calvin Coolidge rose in Massachusetts politics due to his excellent skill as an orator, he was very reluctant to put himself forward and became known as "Silent Cal" when he was Vice-President. Both Coolidge and Harry Truman, the other ISTJ, are better described as hard-working men of strong party loyalty than as ambitious competitors. Truman said that he had never wanted any of the political offices he held; each time, he ran because it was his turn to be on the Democratic ticket, and then he always worked as hard as possible.

Their third function, Introverted Feeling, is the root of conscience for unusual situations and private matters. It doesn't operate with truly "warm" freedom as in some other personalities, since Introverted Sensing imposes such a strong framework. It's most likely felt in unshakable loyalties and personal warmth. It's important for them to know that their friends feel loved; they are good at remembering gift occasions and speaking a few words of appreciation. When congratulations are in order, ISTJs will be first in line to shake your hand and try to put a smile on your face.

Queen Elizabeth II, perhaps the most famous ISTJ in the world, was trained to use her Introverted Feeling to create a personal moment with each person she must speak with. She seeks to relate her own life or interests in some way, even with the many protocol restrictions on what subjects she may talk about. The Beatles played at a Royal Variety Show in 1963, and when the Queen asked where they were playing next, she responded to the town's name by saying in a neighborly manner, "Oh, that's near us!" (meaning Windsor Castle).[79] Her smile remains warm, one to one, even after she has spent many hours smiling at strangers in crowds.

Extroverted Intuition is the last and weakest function, experienced mostly by hunches, associations, and of course academic research. ISTJs aren't likely to use Intuition to explore for new answers about connections and causes, because most such questions are already answered through traditional understandings of science and history. An ISTJ raised in a non-religious or liberal home will be a staunch believer in evolution, while his twin raised by religious fundamentalists will defend creation just as firmly. ISTJs who are oriented to reading and research may well study more about these things on their own, but it's rare that they will take personal study in a direction that challenges society's accepted answers.

On the other hand, Extroverted Intuition works with Extroverted Thinking for good verbal abilities and interest in learning about the world. Many ISTJs are avid readers with strong interest in history. They also appreciate verbal cleverness, especially if it's quiet and understated. President Calvin Coolidge, an ISTJ, was known as a silent man, but he came to his success in politics by being a riveting orator. When he did speak, his words were careful and precise; he was rarely wrong about facts.

Most ISTJs place a low value on psychology, because to them it seems that psychology is making up complicated explanations for things that are really not that hard. People ought to try harder and care more about doing things the right way, and to most ISTJs, that is a sufficient answer; anything more seems like making excuses for inadequacy. It can be very hard for an ISTJ to accept that some people really do have a mission in life that doesn't contribute to maintaining society, and equally hard to accept that some people are already doing their best when they are clearly not working up to an acceptable level. Warm conscience, however, insists on personal kindness to all.

ISTJs often marry someone who is very different from them. Perhaps because their personal vision for life is so strong and unified, ISTJs are drawn to people who are happy amid more chaotic Sensing. They may also like the role of helping rescue someone who gets into minor scrapes. These marriages work out as long as the outgoing, fun-loving spouse is also dedicated to keeping up society and does his or her part while valuing the ISTJ's faithfulness. An outgoing spouse can help the ISTJ find more ways to relate to people, developing a range of family and couple activities. This isn't always easy for someone who may prefer to spend hours alone, recuperating from the stress of work. But once an ISTJ spouse or parent sees social activity as part of the mission, it's almost certain to happen.

79: Sally Bedell Smith, *Elizabeth the Queen: Life of a Modern Monarch.* (New York: Random House, 2012), 195.

ESFJ

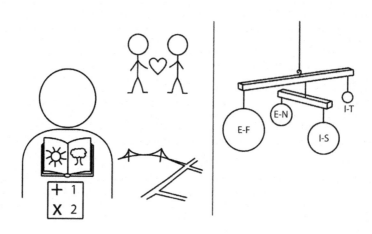

Fig. 12-3

#1: Extroverted Feeling
#2: Introverted Sensing
7.5% of men, 16.9% of women

ESFJs are a well-known type in women, but they are surprisingly common in men, too. They are all about making other people happy while fulfilling traditional social roles. Everything they touch has value to them primarily in how it relates to the people they love. They love intensely, and they buy, cook and give with care, lavishly if they can afford it. Introverted Sensing gives them a firm idea of how the world ought to be, often in a visual sense. ESFJs want their environments to be neat and attractive; disorder and chaos bother them a lot. Disorder violates their inner ideal of an orderly, good world.

Extroverted Feeling draws such personalities to roles where they teach and guide younger or weaker people. ESJFs account for a very high number of preschool and elementary school teachers, but can also be found caring for the elderly. These roles are emotionally rewarding to them as they perceive, day to day, that they are doing their duty and also making people happy. These twin goals define nearly everything an ESFJ wants to do. They may also account for a high number of pediatric nurses and doctors.

Hollywood's on-screen mothers have usually been portraits of ESFJs. Donna Reed, who played the wife in the classic movie *It's a Wonderful Life* was a real-life ESFJ who found herself typecast. In that movie, her character Mary Bailey has unswerving moral decisiveness. While her husband worries and feels discouragement, she is always shown fixing the house, taking care of the children, and saying the right thing at the right moment. The famous last scene around their Christmas tree is a tableau of ESFJ values: her clean, polite children around a lavish, traditional tree in the parlor that she thriftily restored.

Hollywood has always done a very good job presenting stereotypical ESFJs, probably because the personality conforms so closely to the archetypal ideal of parents, especially mothers. The personality type is comforting and stable, often used as a moral anchor in stories. Ironically, most actors and actresses who portray them are, in reality, much wilder, more competitive, or less traditional. But true ESFJ personality types do well in talk show formats; Regis Philbin is a good example of a man with this gentle, traditional personality type.

Extroverted Feeling and Introverted Sensing blend to elevate family traditions above most other values. ESFJs are the type most likely to hang out seasonal decorations and remember everyone's birthday with a card. Decorations for a holiday are usually the same every year, and some traditional decorations may be very old. New ornaments are only added if they have personal meaning, usually as gifts or a child's handmade project. History must feel continuous; ESFJs serve the same Christmas dinner every year because in doing so, they feel united with older relatives who have passed away and younger ones who will, in their turn, remember the ESFJ when he is gone. They also love to maintain photo and video collections to remember the past. Many craft stores have huge sections devoted to decorative materials to make very neat, orderly, appealing scrapbooks. Scrapbooking is an art activity that particularly appeals to ESFJs.

Extroverted Intuition, as a third function, gives ESFJs a sense of humor that comes out most in group situations. They like to think of funny songs, jokes or skits, somewhat along the lines of the farcical plots of old Hollywood comedies. Extroverted Intuition's other role is nonverbal, providing hunches and sixth senses about people. It can be very strong and useful, working out solutions to people problems. As a literary example, in the Botswana-based "No. 1 Ladies' Detective Agency" book series, ESFJ detective Mma Ramotswe uses her Intuition to solve cases of deception and offenses against traditional morality. Extroverted Intuition can also create active prejudices and dislikes. Working with cool conscience, the prejudices usually identify people who are not conforming to society's structures. ESFJs can be tremendously kind and generous to outcasts, but only if they're apparently innocent; ESFJs do not want to reward rejection and rebellion. Saying, "where there's smoke, there's fire," they avoid these people, sometimes ready to believe the worst of them.

Introverted Thinking is the fourth function, but it has a strong role in rule-based conscience, making it very difficult for an ESFJ to let people down by calling in sick or changing her mind. Cool conscience insists that promises must be kept, rules must be followed, and calls to duty must be answered. The ESFJ cool conscience focuses a lot on right behavior in groups, since its pragmatic half (Feeling) is about people. ESFJs can be wonderfully kind and yet extremely strict, not hesitating to punish someone socially. If someone has let them down, they make sure there's a price to pay. Forgiveness is given gladly, but only when the offender has admitted the wrong and made up for it, perhaps indirectly. Without any penance, the offender falls from grace as a friend and is never regarded quite the same. Many ESFJs are aware of having this punitive trait, but they see it as positive, because it allows them to be good administrators for important traditions and services.

ESFJs are often social leaders in traditional institutions like churches and schools. As girls, they may fill the role of "Queen Bee," organizing their friends to behave in ways they approve of. Compared to strategic Thinking Queen Bees, they are warmer and kinder toward followers, but they may feel much stronger personal anger when a friend disappoints. Their own identity often blends with their strong sense of tradition and institutions, so that it's hard for them to see the difference between their personal goals and objective goodness.

ESFJs are usually social leaders, less often administrative ones. They do not tend to run for President or lead corporations. They want to lead to an extent, and in values-related ways. For example, Dr. James Dobson of Focus on the Family seems to be an ESFJ who used his doctorate in child psychology to become an advocate for traditional discipline methods. His first best-seller was called *Dare to Discipline*; its cool-conscience outlook recommended firm, at times unempathetic correction for children's immature weaknesses. He became a political activist when he perceived that new divorce laws were changing the landscape of the traditional American family. As a leader, he promotes many charitable and good causes, but at the same time, his ESFJ orientation toward traditional institutions has prompted him to take political positions against social change.

ESFJs have great respect for marriage and other family institutions. They may be the personality type most likely to marry and least likely to divorce. Once married, they are very conscious of being bound by their vows, and they consider duty and keeping promises a higher calling than happiness. An ESFJ divorces only under great duress, and usually after a lot of betrayal and cruel treatment. Until the point when he or she is abandoned, the sense of doing what's right can sustain an ESFJ through many sorrows.

ESFJ parents are warm, organized, and authoritarian. A chore chart pinned on the refrigerator symbolizes the ESFJ's approach to raising children: everyone has a duty, and to every duty there is attached a reward and a punishment. ESFJ parents do not feel sorry for a child who is crying over a punishment that they feel the child deserved. Two children fighting over a toy will find the toy gone, regardless of who had it first and who feels that this isn't fair. If an ESFJ feels that a child was only half guilty of the mistake, she will still punish him, because that seems to be the safer side to err. But after the child's tears are dried, he may find the ESFJ parent offering a treat, not to apologize for the punishment, but to show affection and restore harmony.

ISFJ

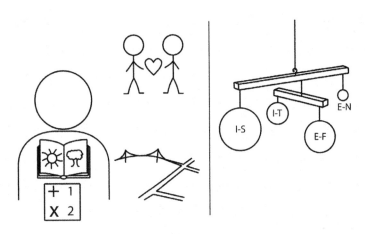

Fig. 12-4

#1: Introverted Sensing
#2: Extroverted Feeling
8.1% of men, 19.4% of women

ISFJs are very similar to ESFJs, but because they are primarily cued to their Introverted Sensing's vision, they are not only less group-oriented but also more likely to be a little bit unconventional. They care a great deal about relationships with Extroverted Feeling, but their relationships come in smaller, more ideal, less pragmatic packages. ISFJs are less willing to accept routine neglect and mistakes between people as "just the way life goes." They care a lot about people's happiness, and they're interested in meeting emotional needs even if a conventional structure isn't already in place.

ISFJs are keenly aware of the physical needs of people around them, having a strong archetypal sense of what someone's life ought to look like. They care a great deal about the poor, the sick, the lonely and anyone with other needs. ISFJs light up with purpose and caring when they are in contact with someone that society might reject: a retarded child, a sick baby, a lonely old man, a homeless family, a recovering alcoholic. They don't need an audience or society's approval. Just being there, feeling that they've nudged life a bit closer to the ideal, is enough. Of course, ISFJs aren't limited to helping humans, either; they are champions of hurt and homeless animals. They even give extra water and an encouraging smile to a sad-looking potted plant. ISFJs don't set out to be unconventional, but by caring so much about the needy, they may find themselves in that position. If it's conventional to ignore the homeless, that's one convention the ISFJ is ready to break.

Like ISTJs, quiet ISFJs are focused on others and do not go into professions that will lead to personal fame. When they do become known, it's almost in spite of themselves. Clara Barton, the Civil War nurse, had an ISFJ personality. She had worked as a teacher and at the US Patent Office for many years when she brought some donated supplies to a war field hospital. The shock of seeing so many sick and suffering men drew her in personally, so that she devoted the rest of her life to nursing. Although she never tried to become famous, in later years she used her name recognition toward other charitable projects, including establishing the American Red Cross. Mother Teresa, who died in 1997, was another ISFJ who achieved striking fame by setting out to do the least fame-seeking work. A teaching nun by training, she founded a one-woman poverty care service in Calcutta. Eventually she became the head of an order dedicated to hospice care.

Extroverted Feeling in most ISFJs makes them so acutely aware of other people's feelings that they can have a hard time knowing their own feelings. Their own reactions to rejection or failure can be harder for them to process, because such feelings seem selfish. Most ISFJs deny hurt feelings and sadness, but those closest to them can tell that they actually do feel these things. Sometimes there is a fleeting moment when the emotion is visible, before the ISFJ has time to push it away. But then it's gone, and it won't be long until it's been buried in positive activity toward family, home or helping.

For this reason, ISFJs can fall into the trap of neglecting truly important emotional signals. They can't always tell the difference between good self-sacrifice for the needy and unhealthy self-sacrifice. They are perhaps the type most likely to end up in long-term unhealthy relationships; they are particularly prone to marrying alcoholics. The role of perpetually rescuing and serving an abusive-but-needy person suits the emotional needs of many ISFJs; but that doesn't mean the role is any healthier for them than for anyone else. It only means they are less likely to be aware of the pain, since the role is so similar to the helping role they're cut out for. When ISFJs are drained by being in a co-dependent sort of relationship, they are less likely to have as many active helping roles in the world, and they are less likely to feel free to be involved in non-helping, fun activities.

Introverted Thinking, the 3rd function, provides a very strong sense of morality, supporting Introverted Sensing's vision that things ought to be a certain way. "Do the right thing" sums up an ISFJ's approach to life. Cool conscience supplies them with certainty about what's most important in each situation; they know what should be sacrificed and what must be saved. Inconvenience and fun rank low, while religion, duty, and alleviating suffering are the top priorities. ISFJs don't tend to tell other people what to do very often, but when they do, they always expect that others "just know" the same things they know. What's right to do is self-evident to them, so an ISFJ just urges you to do what's right, confident that you know it too.

Extroverted Intuition is their fourth, weakest, function. Like ISTJs, they rarely seek answers beyond what people generally hold to be true. However, they are more open to psychology, since it's about relationships. They tend to be very interested in new discoveries about health and disabilities, for the same reason. They may ask difficult questions about why people's needs are going unmet, but they do not want to challenge society's foundations by probing too deeply. Under stress, they may find that weak Extroverted Intuition leads them astray with apparent but coincidental connections. Like some other types, they may believe things that others would call superstitious. If they have been too much disappointed

194

in society, they can also be prone to accepting conspiracy theories that would seem to provide an explanation for the failure.

ISFJs often have very strong verbal skills and are good students (probably another use of Extroverted Intuition). Many are avid readers, especially enjoying books that explore human potential while rewarding characters whose intentions are good. Laura Ingalls Wilder may have had an ISFJ personality; she began with practical but well-written farm articles, then began her famous series of books about her pioneer childhood. ISJFs are good at professions that keep words in order, such as editing and secretarial work. ISFJs may go into teaching, perhaps equally drawn to the emotional needs of young children and the writing skills required in higher education. Clara Barton and Mother Teresa both taught schools for the poor before going into nursing. Barton had been an outstanding student with strong spelling and language skills, and before her foray into nursing, she became the first woman clerk in the US Patent Office.

ISFJ spouses are practical and dedicated. Their marriage is the center of life, and usually not even volunteer work is permitted to subtract from this centrality. People who value fashion and appearances should not marry ISFJs, since they are universally practical and goal-oriented. An ISFJ would dress up for a charity event, and he or she will always dress appropriately for traditional events like church. But solid goodness and comfort will always take precedence over detail, glamor and decoration.

The wives of US Presidents are often ISFJs. Rosalynn Carter and Laura Bush both seem to fit the model. Both ladies only became known due to their much more ambitious, outgoing husbands' achievements. Rosalynn's White House style was noted for its informal practicality. As First Lady of both Georgia and the United States, she used her status to promote care for the mentally ill. Laura Bush, a shy librarian, also maintained a traditional but non-glamorous personal style while promoting libraries and reading to children. Bush also made a point of being involved in Special Olympics ceremonies. With some notable exceptions, the role of First Lady has been shaped around ISFJ tendencies: tradition, modesty, and good works.

As parents, ISFJs are both giving and demanding. They will sacrifice any pleasure of their own for their children, but at the same time, they expect the children to follow this example. An ISFJ's children are usually drawn into volunteer roles at church or school; they can also expect family holidays to include lonely guests. If a child is unwilling to accept needy people or wants to hold onto self-centered privileges, the ISFJ parent will let him know gently but firmly that it's time to do the right thing.

SECOND GROUP: EXTROVERTED SENSING

This group of four personality types follows the Perceiving pattern of action-thriller movies. Pragmatic, exploring Sensing has a prominent role, with cynical Introverted Intuition acting as a critic in the background. Because their Perceiving pattern allows so much openness, Judging conscience is placed in a key role. In this group, the personalities with strong Thinking are also using it for cool conscience, while those with strong Feeling have warm conscience. The nature of this moral conscience is usually clearly visible, since it is not masked by a stronger Introverted function.

ESTP

Fig. 12-5

#1: Extroverted Sensing
#2: Introverted Thinking
5.6% of men, 3% of women

The ESTP personality type is, of all types, the most present in the present. With Extroverted Sensing as their primary function, they live in sync with the motion and noise of the world's every moment. ESTPs feel this presentness in the present to such an extent that it can become overwhelming. They are not able to screen out the motion, sound and detail bombarding their senses. Introverted Thinking has a full-time job sorting out the stream of sensory data, deciding what should be in focus and what, if possible, ignored. In a potentially free-floating sea of impressions, Introverted Thinking's rules for ideal logic and order are necessary.

ESTPs are best known to other types for moving fast and seeking thrills. It may be that ESTPs rush into sports like sailing, racing, climbing, skydiving, and football to organize their Sensing function by channeling it into rule-based speed, danger or even pain. Linking strong cool conscience to this effort is extremely important. Jackie Robinson, the baseball player, used sports to focus his strong ESTP personality twice. When he was young, he was leader of a small street gang until a church baseball league drew him into the rule-oriented, civilized aggression of sports. Later, when he was asked to become the first black player in the white leagues, he had to control his temper in the service of a higher purpose. To help other black athletes, Robinson steeled his will to endure insults without even turning his head. The high energy that used to be free to get into fistfights was channeled into changing national customs and attitudes.

ESTPs naturally go into fields of work that use ESTP skills like coordination, risk tolerance, face-reading and multi-tasking. Sports, the military, and all facets of building and road construction are natural ESTP magnets. Commission sales and start-up businesses attract them more than hourly or established work. ESTPs make good small business owners, particularly when they can work alongside their employees at the restaurant, store or truck. If they have artistic or theatrical talent, they become stage performers. Ernest Hemingway, an ESTP writer, wrote best-selling novels with short, colorful sentences about safaris, sailing and bullfighting, all of which he had to do and watch in order to write about them (poor man!). When ESTPs find a field where they can succeed, they climb easily. They become team captains and military officers, and they're among the types most likely to run for political office.

In the modern age—since television performance became part of the role—ESTPs are frequent candidates for President. In office, ESTP style is to delegate, not micromanage. They are comfortable with the hectic pace of the White House, since they transition easily and need minimal down time. Caution may not be their strong suit. Even before the television age, ESTP President Theodore Roosevelt created the image of a big presidency. In addition to his role modeling for Presidents who hunt big game and practice strenuous sports, he began traditions for parades and military bands. He was also characteristically quick to intervene in the affairs of other nations. His saying, "speak softly but carry a big stick" suggests how freely he used threats of military force. (Of course, most ESTPs never have the opportunity or even the wish to become national leaders.)

Although they tend to focus on physical training, ESTPs can be very smart with both book knowledge (based in Thinking) and observational, practical knowledge. Roosevelt, as a child, was remarkable for his encyclopedic knowledge of nature and bird-watching. Hemingway was also known for his vast factual knowledge of the world. In fact, Hemingway was also part of a long ESTP tradition: war correspondents. Many photographers and journalists who travel to dangerous places share Hemingway's personality type. Like the river pilot who taught the young Mark Twain how to navigate the Mississippi River even at night, they're highly attentive to everything they see and hear and very tolerant of risk. They often write and produce award-winning news copy and documentaries.

Their third function is Extroverted Feeling; ESTPs show emotion easily and are attentive to the emotions of other people. However, Feeling is also the pragmatic half of cool conscience. ESTPs are not known for empathy and compassion to other people. They read faces, bodies and emotions, and they care about relationships, but they don't feel what other people are feeling, nor are they driven to comfort and soothe. At best, Extroverted Feeling makes them great salesmen and political campaigners. ESTP salesmen can read body language and discern in an instant how best to persuade a customer. At worst, pragmatic Feeling makes ESTPs callous to suffering, especially if Introverted Thinking believes the suffering was deserved. An ESTP parent who grounds his teenager won't waste a second feeling sorry. When compassion doesn't require empathy, ESTPs are more comfortable. They're famously generous and heroic toward innocent victims of fires and accidents.

Dr. Phil McGraw, an ESTP psychologist, is most comfortable using his training in show business. When he was in private practice counseling, Dr. Phil found it very difficult to be patient because of his low empathy: "I got so tired of listening to people whine, I could scream."[80] It's easy for Dr. Phil to point out to his guests which rules and principles they've broken or ignored. To Introverted Thinking, it's all very obvious.

Introverted Intuition, the fourth function, may lie mostly dormant in an ESTP's daily functioning. It's least active when the ESTP individual has devoted most of his or her energy to developing a high ability in Sensing. Athletes spend most of their waking hours since childhood practicing and exercising, developing their bodies, coordination and reflexes. By midlife, the main sign of Introverted Intuition is a wide range of superstitions; these are routine and customary among professional athletes. Professional athletes have lucky charms of all kinds, and they may do elaborate or odd rituals to ensure success in a game. "It's bad luck not to believe in superstition," they may believe.

On the other hand, when ESTPs are involved in more cerebral, strategic work, or when they're working a lot with people, Introverted Intuition is part of understanding how the world works and guessing very quickly what to do next. It's clearly also teamed with Feeling and Sensing in nonverbal recognition of what's going on with other people.

In later life, ESTPs do well to take up some serious religious or philosophical study. This comes naturally, because ESTPs tend to feel at home in religion, as long as it isn't too rigid. The well-known singer Madonna shows us this ESTP pattern. For many years, her high-energy stage shows involved parody or even mockery of the Catholicism she'd grown up in. When she became interested in the most esoteric, mystical branch of Judaism, Kabbalah alone became her religious practice, without further conversion to mainstream Judaism. In an interview, she said, "I'm a big believer in ritualistic behavior as long as it doesn't hurt anybody, but I'm not a big fan of rules."[81]

ESTPs may have the richest lives when they are able to marry people who are much more inwardly-centered and compassionate. Although they gravitate to other exciting, fun people in friendships and dating, many ESTPs seem to have an instinct that they need to marry quiet, kind people who won't compete with them, but who can balance and advise them instead. The tendency of ESTPs to run for President may be why more than one First Lady has been a shy, practical ISFJ who balanced a less cautious, more outgoing partner.

The ESTP personality's strengths and weaknesses do not make a strong partner in solving relationship problems. After a few attempts at fixing things, an ESTP spouse may feel inclined to walk away. It isn't from lack of love, but that they are quickly frustrated. Their problem-solving approach emphasizes trying something different when the usual method doesn't work, which can make them incredible firefighters and other types of first responders. But relationship problems are usually solved patiently, by slow stages, over a long time, and ESTPs are not wired that way. Conscience makes them stay engaged, but they often feel an overwhelming discomfort, longing to get away and be free. Married to a similar action-oriented personality, ESTPs can have a lot of fun but may break up fast as soon as trouble comes. Married to someone who is patient and good at understanding people, they can get the right assistance to make it over the long haul.

80: Sophia Dembling and Lisa Gutierrez, *The Making of Dr. Phil* (Hoboken: Wiley, 2004), 82.
81: Madonna interview, "Truth or Dare," *Harper's Bazaar*, November 2013, 254.

ISTP

Fig. 12-6

#1: Introverted Thinking
#2: Extroverted Sensing
8.5% of men, 2.4% of women

ISTPs are the world's natural mechanics, though many are also very successful at sports and the military. Introverted Thinking provides an often non-verbal way of understanding the world in mechanical terms. Extroverted Sensing in the #2 role keeps ISTPs motivated to put their hands on things to understand them, applying logic directly to sensing.

Introverted Thinking's cool conscience tends to be practical and direct in the ISTP personality. As the top function, Thinking sees rule-following as self-evident and non-optional, as long as the rules in question are truly drawn from the natural world. If formal rules seem frivolous and a distraction from how things really work, ISTPs resent having to follow them. In the same way, they readily follow orders in a hierarchy, unless they're being asked to do things that don't make sense in the real world. An ISTP follows his captain into the fiercest battle, but he'll quietly rebel against unnatural rules that make practical life harder.

Drawn to work with the things they're best at, ISTPs are always found in close contact with machinery. Academically gifted ISTPs gravitate to physics and engineering; they are more interested in applied work in labs than in the theoretical math of higher physics, even if they're able to understand and work with the abstract material. ISTPs can be found at all machine levers from nuclear power to forklifts and cranes; they make up much of the world's tool-oriented workforce in electrical wiring, carpentry and plumbing. ISTPs also have a natural affinity for computers and computer programming. They can be good at accounting, bookkeeping, and tech support.

ISTPs are usually very good with issues of body control and training, too. Physical therapy and chiropractic manipulation both make innate sense to ISTPs; many women with ISTP personalities find their way into these professions. ISTPs are also found in the more analytical, skill-oriented roles in sports, particularly in baseball. Athletic talent can be found among many personality types, but ISTPs are perhaps foremost among those whose mental traits will support repetitive, intense physical training until the body responds as close to a machine as possible.

Famous ISTPs are usually athletes, often in sports where there are so many ISTPs that their personality traits color the sport's culture. Major league baseball pitchers like Nolan Ryan are usually ISTPs, and so are most race car drivers. Both Dale Earnhardt and his father, Ralph, seem to have been ISTP personalities who used few words, concentrated deeply, and lived for sensory thrills. They were also known for doing much of their own mechanical work; the drive to combine types of physical control makes most ISTPs unwilling to divide using machines from fixing them. They know that most people aren't as good with their hands as they are.

Roberto Clemente, the Pirates' legendary 1960s outfielder, was an ISTP personality whose interest in physical control extended beyond the ball field. After getting chiropractic treatment for arthritis in his neck, he built up a library of books on chiropractic techniques. Chiropractic work is solitary, quiet, and precise; it views the body somewhat as a machine in need of mechanical work. Clemente often helped friends and other players with both massage and chiropractic adjustment; one of his post-career goals was to set up a luxury chiropractic spa in his native Puerto Rico.

With increased understanding of machines comes some loss in both verbal fluency and understanding people. Introverted Intuition, their third function, generally supports their logic and work skills, not their people skills. They have good hunches and a sense of just knowing how things work. ISTPs wish that everything made as much sense as the rules of physics and engineering, and they may choose to devote most of their time to the things they understand. They are classically slow to speak, with both Introverted Intuition and Thinking needing time to think first.

ISTPs may generally strike people as serious and a bit detached; they participate in social activities with a slight reluctance. King George VI is depicted in the movie *The King's Speech* as a shy, stuttering man who became king when his brother suddenly abdicated in 1936. He probably had an ISTP personality, and he suffered under the constant demands to speak and greet publicly. The only part of his career as Duke and King that was known to give him real pleasure was his role in touring industrial plants after the first World War; he also loved guns and airplanes.

Intuition can be very strong and useful, when it's given sufficient time and use. Scientific training, in particular, pulls Introverted Intuition into a large role at work. Jacques Cousteau, a quiet, practical ISTP, used it to co-invent the first Aqua-Lung and a number of innovations in underwater photography.

Commitment to traditional religion may help the ISTP's Intuition to see connections in events, since religions offer explanations of how things are connected. Seeking meaning in religious texts and services can also help to balance their huge devotion to the sensory world.

When Intuition is neglected in favor of hard training in the ISTP's Sensing strengths, it can fall into simple superstition. Intuition always creates a sense that things are connected, but the ISTPs who are most dedicated to Sensing leave their minds little time or energy to figure out how these connections work. Especially when they're under stress, they may feel that things are connected in non-logical ways. Many baseball players believe that they have to wear a lucky shirt in order to win games, or they have actions that must be done in just the same order each time. Since they can't actually control whether they win games, their Intuition just guesses that there may be a connection between coincidental events and success. So on the day of a game, they must repeat whatever they did (or didn't do) when the last game was won. You can see this demonstrated in the movie *Moneyball*, when Oakland's General Manager refuses to be present for any game, believing that he'll bring bad luck. In some cases, superstitions pile up to extremes of weirdness and complexity.

Extroverted Feeling is the fourth and weakest function, but the primary one for managing relationships and emotional expression. Even if they seem detached, ISTPs may care very much what people think, and then they try to conform and please. If their strengths in logic and observation aren't enough to manage a relationship problem, ISTPs may not have much finesse to fall back on. Under stress, they may react with emotional outbursts of frustration and feeling that they don't understand very well themselves. These emotions are unwelcome interruptions, and most ISTPs manage them as interruptions without gaining deeper understanding. They are eager to get back to working on what they're good at, since it calms them from these disruptive feelings.

ISTPs do not generally enjoy leadership positions. They may be promoted into leadership due to their technical skill, but they aren't comfortable and will leave the role as soon as possible. They do, however, like to be autonomous. ISTPs can be very happy small business owners. The more their chosen business keeps them directly involved with the nuts and bolts, the happier they are. They accept direction reluctantly. Their awareness of the gap between authority and accuracy can make them grumbling rebels, but it's never because they want to take over. They just don't want their skills made irrelevant by rules and directives that don't make sense.

In marriage, ISTPs do well when times are good, but can struggle when there is chronic conflict that isn't easily solved. They are happiest in physical support roles, like keeping things fixed. Broken and decaying parts in a house tend to bother ISTPs very much, so they are motivated to show caring by tending these visible things. Talking about love or conflict isn't easy and may be almost impossible for some. ISTPs probably experience the greatest stability in marriage when they are paired with someone who easily provides structure and predictability. Plain, clear rules and expectations keep conflict to a minimum; the best spouse for an ISTP is good at smoothing over conflict without requiring verbal confrontations.

ISTP parents have the same strengths and weaknesses with their children as in the marriage. Tasks that require them to do something are the most welcome. ISTP men whose children want to learn sports are like fish in their native water, but they can also happily do other things. When a relationship with a child needs to be healed, an ISTP parent is likely to suggest a special outing. Doing something together brings a feeling of togetherness.

ESFP

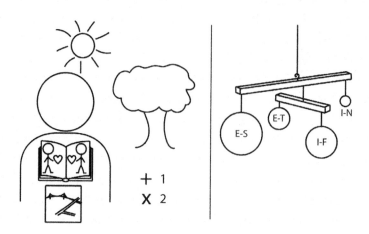

Fig. 12-7

#1: Extroverted Sensing
#2: Introverted Feeling
6.9% of men, 10.1% of women

ESFPs start with strong pragmatic, exploring sense about the real world. Their world of action is as open as the ESTP's, and they often go into the same kinds of adventures and sports. Everything that might be done in the physical world seems possible. However, the ESFP's second function is warm idealism about human relationships. Warm conscience based in Feeling is strong and usually easily visible.

ESFPs care as much about home life as do ESFJs, but their priorities are in different places. Although they care about beauty, they aren't wired with an idealistic notion of the Sensing world, preferring instead a riot of color, motion, and variety. ESFPs at home are most often found up to their elbows in activities that will lead to big meals and laughter. They value spontaneity over tradition, so they are less devoted to creating perfect holidays.

Planning ahead is a practical tool, not a life goal. Most ESFPs are proud to show how their pragmatic Sensing smarts can improvise with what's on hand. On Julia Child's television cooking shows, her staff learned that she never showed irritation when planning failed. She was happy to cut meat with a wooden spoon if they forgot a knife, or ad-lib lines when something turned out wrong. She became known for theatrically throwing food onto the floor and starting over, but most of the time, things worked out perfectly because in the process of cooking and filming, she knew how to nudge the final product away from its mistakes by improvising.

Instead of using rules and logic to organize all of this energy, ESFPs structure life around relationships. They tend to be romantic and enthusiastic, but they are also as non-judgmental as possible. Introverted Feeling is the root of warm conscience, which values most of all how people feel and how relationships can be encouraged, not cooled. When friends disregard rules, ESFPs turn a blind eye unless someone is getting hurt. Criticizing and confronting a friend over a mere rule is not likely to happen. They're also very slow to act in a punitive way toward a friend who wronged them; if possible, they'll move on and forget.

For their own actions, their consciences can also be easy-going about rules. Warm conscience pairs idealistic Feeling with pragmatic Thinking, which looks skeptically at rules to see if they truly matter. When rules can be brushed past without relationships consequences, you can count on most ESFPs to do it. They may be late to meetings or events as long as they feel the group can overlook or forgive. They may bow out of volunteer commitments at the last minute, if they don't feel any personal bonds with others in the group.

With optimistic Sensing and warm conscience, ESFPs can find it very hard to be realistic about what they're able to get done. Everything seems possible, and they want very much to say "yes" to it all—and get it all done, too. It's difficult to forgive themselves for not being supermen who must limit their promises and time to just a few things.

Extroverted Thinking, the third function, can be very strong in some ESFPs. It gives them a flexible way of looking at the world, so that they can innovate and improvise easily. ESFPs who are good at math can do well in science. Those who aren't as academic still remain alert to practical numbers and logic. Thinking is also interested in understanding and analyzing the world. As an Extroverted function, it isn't focused on right and wrong. It encourages a competitive spirit, and it looks for practical solutions to real-world problems. What works is what needs to be done, unless (and only unless) it will hurt someone, in which case Feeling's alarm goes off.

Introverted Intuition is the ESFP's weakest function, but in different individuals it may be strong and important or relatively weak. When it's strong, it teams with Thinking to create almost a second, alternative persona, the scientist. ESFPs who use Intuition and Thinking this way can work well as engineers. When they're in the engineering mode, they're serious and thoughtful, focused on logic and connections. Given any excuse, though, humor and warmth flash out; ESFP scientists can give funny presentations on academic subjects. ESFP comedians are using the same cynical Intuition and amoral Thinking when they come up with hilarious stand-up routines. In any case, Introverted Intuition contributes to a sense of irreverence about society's traditions and institutions. Few things are off-limits for humor, just as anything can be blown up in an action movie.

Like other personality types with Extroverted Sensing, ESFPs may also leave Introverted Intuition to a dormant role, where it works mostly in hunches, prejudices and even superstition. Even in this weaker role, it helps with understanding people and situations. ESFPs who are conscious of using hunches would probably not consider Intuition's role "weak," but instead see it as a nonverbal, rapid way of knowing what to do and who to trust. Introverted Intuition may also influence how they express religious belief. ESFPs may find visible and tactile signs of faith comforting, since they create links of meaning within the Sensing world. They may gravitate toward expressions of faith that use special foods, incense or body motions like making the sign of the cross.

It isn't easy to pin down a few lines of work that ESFPs might go into, because they can be found nearly everywhere. They are least likely to do work that requires a lot of judging and correcting others; they are most likely to do things that let them move around. ESFP teachers are most likely to work in kindergarten or gym, but whatever they teach, they are likely to create hands-on experiences for their students—since this is how they'd prefer to learn. They are very likely to want to go into some kind of performance, such as acting or singing, but they usually find ways to perform in or outside of work. An ESFP engineer cracks jokes at work and volunteers for the children's story time at church; an ESFP nurse finds ways to put children at ease with a joke or funny face. The ESFP car salesman goes by a genial nickname like "Uncle Leo" and always asks about your grandchildren.

ESFPs on television are often cooks, comediennes or reality TV stars. Lucille Ball's character on "I Love Lucy" portrayed a stereotyped ESFP personality: warm, outgoing, funny, and active. Carol Burnett, an ESFP comedienne of the 1970s, also exuded spontaneity and general non-judgmental love for people. Reality television is perfect for people with low privacy boundaries and high sociability; those who really thrive in that setting are mostly ESFPs.

ESFPs are typically fun dates. ESFP men can plan a fun time like nobody else, and ESFP women are usually charming and full of smiles. They usually love family life; ESFP women and men both love to cook and are very affectionate to children. They are happiest in marriage when no problems need to be addressed, but they would prefer to address problems as briefly as possible and then "move on" and not speak of them again. If a marriage goes into a time of protracted conflict and change, an ESFP is not well-equipped to deal with the constant stress. Never meaning to hurt anyone, they may cope in ways that end up hurting or abandoning people. When this happens, ESFPs typically feel very bad, but they really want people to just forget what happened and move on. If they are drawn into a vicious cycle of trying to cope and unintentionally causing conflict, ESFPs may just walk away. Larry King's many marriages and divorces may be an extreme example of this ESFP tendency.

As parents, ESFPs are full of fun. They are not typically strong disciplinarians, but they care a lot about teaching children to cook, play games, and develop sports skills. They are inclusive, tactfully looking for a child or adult who seems to be left out, and finding a role for them. They tend to show love mostly through gifts, touch, and spending time.

ISFP

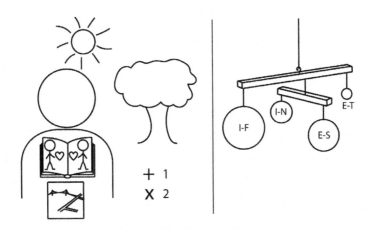

Fig. 12-8

#1: Introverted Feeling
#2: Extroverted Sensing
7.6% of men, 9.9% of women

It's rare for ISFPs not to have a prevailing artistic touch in their lives, regardless of professional art training and income. Visual art is one of their highest values, stemming from the dominant Introverted Feeling that emphasizes love and harmony, and the Extroverted Sensing that keeps them present in the world, unable to overlook sensory detail. Needing beauty and harmony, unable to abstract themselves from their environments, ISFPs create visible projections of harmony all around them.

Introverted Feeling is the strongest part of the ISFP personality, and of course, it's also the root of warm conscience. ISFPs don't need to put much thought into morality or how they treat people, but instead, they just act out of their inner need for harmony. They find it difficult to act in a punitive, forbidding, or off-putting way even to people they don't like. With people they like, they find it nearly impossible to say "no."

If special circumstances require them to act harsh or unfeeling, they react to this dilemma by panicking and doing anything to get out of it. Conflict can be very difficult for ISFPs, and they often have difficulty putting their sense of right into words. It's easy for them to feel disarmed and overwhelmed by someone who's more verbally aggressive. Also, they can be very shy; Fred Astaire, one of history's famous ISFPs, was described as almost impossible to interview. While he was comfortable performing in front of audiences, he hit inner barriers and conflicts when it came to explaining himself in words.

Because the draw toward beauty in the Sensing environment is so strong, ISFPs often find some kind of work that allows them to make some piece of the world prettier. Visual art, of course, is open for those with drawing talent. ISFPs with acting ability are irresistibly drawn to theater and everything connected with it; they may become costume and lighting designers, puppeteers and animators, or stage and film actors. Music talent draws them toward performance, while athletic ability draws many of them to take up ballet or gymnastics. ISFPs can be found in working with hair and clothing styling, jewelry design, tailoring, cosmetics and skin care, interior decorating and landscaping. Of course, ISFPs can go into fields of work that aren't related to appearance, depending on their opportunities and other abilities.

Wherever they are, they are sure to add touches of visual interest and beauty to their workplace and home. Their sense of beauty may be unconventional, since their Extroverted Sensing keeps them constantly aware of nature's chaos and variety. Instead of using traditional Christmas ornaments, an ISFP may use things collected from nature. Dried orange slices, local dried flowers and berries, and popcorn: the decorations cost almost nothing, but the arrangement leaves a lingering impression of beauty in every visitor's mind. A bird's nest on a table, arranged with the right linens and a few shells, can be more striking than an expensive Chinese vase. It's this ability to see beauty that already exists and bring it forward that is the unique ISFP touch.

The other side of the balance between Introverted Feeling and Extroverted Sensing is an intermittent wild streak that occasionally breaks out. In the middle of putting people first and being artistic, an ISFP may suddenly do something very uncharacteristic. As long as they feel it's not hurting anyone, or perhaps in an act of frustration, they may dance all night, start a bicycle trip across the country, or take a lover. These wild streaks can steer their lives in new directions or remain interruptions in a quiet life. When "wild streak" behavior gets rewarded financially, ISFPs can turn into pop superstars like Elton John, whose eye-catching stage antics covered a quiet personality.

Introverted Intuition, the third function, helps the personality make sense of the world in the background; it lends a sense of already knowing how things operate and what they mean. When ISFPs know something intuitively, they may still have trouble putting it into words. Their Intuition tends not to be analytical; they take things as they are, as a whole. The ISFP's pairing of dominant Extroverted Sensing and Introverted Intuition can result in deep absorption in non-verbal pursuits. One of the leading French Impressionist painters, Edgar Degas, kept a notebook in which he used words only to describe visual impressions and plans to paint: "Graduated blue sky... the ground at the front a grey-violet shadow... Look for some turquoise in the blue."[82] Many of his friends and fellow painters in Paris were also ISFPs.

Extroverted Thinking, often the best function for verbal self-defense, is their weakest function. Especially early in life, it may not be well integrated with the rest of personality. When an ISFP has already tried ignoring conflict or internalizing it as his own fault, Extroverted Thinking has to rise to the occasion. It may work out well, but sometimes the ISFP lets loose a shower of somewhat logical accusations and then retreats, feeling deeply wounded by the loss of harmony. Princess Diana, who probably had an ISFP personality, may have been an extreme example of this pattern (though with added heights of mood instability).

82: Sue Roe, *Private Lives of the Impressionists* (New York: Harper, 2006), 114. Many of the original French Impressionist painters had personalities very similar to Edgar Dégas; Monet, Pisarro, Cézanne and others may have also been ISFPs.

In maturity, Extroverted Thinking becomes a valued partner in figuring out better ways to resolve conflicts. Designer Tim Gunn, who co-hosts the American fashion design competition show "Project Runway," is known for a signature phrase of encouragement: "Make it work." He has explained that "make it work" stands for a lifelong maturation strategy to stop literally hiding from conflicts and learn to solve them. As a child, Gunn responded to conflict by hiding in the house or yard, at first working harder to make sure he could not be found even by the family's bloodhound. When he learned that he felt less anxious overall if he made the best of the bad situation, he began to use Extroverted Thinking to see new solutions. In design classes, he taught students that if they gave up and started over on projects, they would lose the most valuable lesson of finding a way to fix the problem. "Make it work" stands for pushing logic and creativity to farther limits instead of giving in to emotional pressure to quit. ISFPs who don't learn this skill remain limited by dominant Feeling's need for harmony.

ISFPs are one of the personality types most prone to continue in abusive relationships, feeling helpless to create change or break things off. When an ISFP decides to make a change, typically the change is sweeping and permanent. Change is too hard to do by small steps, each of which creates another conflict; better to throw it all out or move away. In spite of the difficulty with conflict, ISFPs generally like the state of marriage and find it easy to live with another person. As long as their personal environment isn't disturbed or overruled, they can be flexible, living and letting live. Sidestepping most conflict, they are warm and friendly on a daily basis. It's important for an ISFP to marry someone with better conflict skills. Paired with another conflict-averse type, the ISFP is really left open to the world's slings and arrows, unable to defend except by throwing it all away or hiding.

ISFP parents are gentle, cooperative, and very patient in teaching. Their greatest strength is in doing activities with their children, teaching them to do many things in daily life. They are delighted to bring arts activities into a child's life, from violin lessons to planting flowers, or from ballet to historical re-enactment. Discipline can be difficult when the ISFP parent is trying to raise a stronger-willed, resistant child.

THIRD GROUP: INTROVERTED INTUITION

The third group of personalities has the idealistic, narrowly-focused "Film Noir" worldview. While they tend to be critical perfectionists about their own place in the network of meaning, they take a negative view of "the blind leading the blind" in the world around them. Paired with Introverted Perceiving, their top Judging function is always Extroverted and pragmatic; this means that their Introverted root of conscience is somewhat masked. The personalities with prominent Thinking actually have a warm Feeling conscience in reserve, while those with strong Feeling use cool Thinking conscience to measure morality.

ENTJ

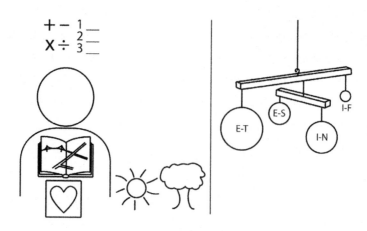

Fig. 12-9

#1: Extroverted Thinking
#2: Introverted Intuition
2.7% of men, 0.9% of women

ENTJs are the most pragmatic and concrete of the dominantly Intuitive personalities. Because Extroverted Thinking has the top role, they are focused on long-term competition and success. Like all Intuitive types, they are interested in abstract ideas, but they are mostly interested in ones that will help them succeed. Ideas that are highly imaginative, unrealistic or wholly theoretical can only hold their attention for a short time. Intuition is mainly targeted at strategy: the ability to see goals and opportunities that are invisible to others.

Law, business and finance are the top ENTJ magnets. All of these fields have to do with long-horizon Thinking to position oneself to reap later benefits. They're also good places to exercise Introverted Intuition's critical eye. ENTJs always maintain some distance between their personal point of view and the institutions they belong to, or even lead. They're usually critical of the current power structure. For that reason, they're less likely to be found in positions of power where patient climbing was necessary. A large concentration of ENTJs can be found in venture capital and start-up companies. However, any line that an ENTJ goes into, he or she will bend it into a strategic direction. Musical, artistic, literary or mathematical talent can all be directed toward mastery of skills, and then toward control of whatever enterprise the ENTJ is involved in.

When ENTJs work their way up through an existing power structure, it's usually as a disruptive force. They are the "Young Turks," the ones who challenge the older leadership before their own turn comes around. Jack Welch became the Chief Executive Officer at General Electric when he hadn't been with the company as long as some other candidates, and he campaigned for the position so that he could make deep, long-lasting changes in corporate structure. ENTJ challengers usually want to mold company or school structure after their own values: competition, autonomy, responsibility and skill excellence. Welch's changes at GE included a rating system of A, B and C for employees, with C's getting no raises and A's getting double-sized ones. He wanted managers to re-rate employees each year, so that as the group improved, employees who didn't constantly strive would find themselves falling behind. It's debatable if this was really a positive idea for employees, but it certainly models the ENTJ value of never-ending competition.

One of the ENTJ's highest values is autonomy. He doesn't want anyone to tell him what to do, and this rule runs deep and wide. Autonomy is key to understanding why ENTJs want to be in powerful positions without first climbing the ladder of dutiful subordinate positions. Many of them are not really thirsting for power over other people, but they seriously resent being responsible for other people's mistakes. Ideally, they want autonomy for everyone, but when someone else's choices may ruin and limit the ENTJ's autonomy, his attitude is, "Okay then, just hand me the keys. I'll take over to make sure it's done right."

ENTJ children experience frustration on a daily basis, because as powerless dependents, they have little control over any aspect of life. They argue fearlessly and deeply resent punishment. If they are shown logically that they are incorrect, they may be able to accept this, but without logic, they will never accept a power play. Some ENTJs are angry, oppositional children, while others find ways to win autonomy by earning money or seeking leadership. Some ENTJs are struggling students during childhood. Their kind of intelligence is not well measured by the hourly tasks of school, which may strike them as pointless. Their ability to think in long spans of time, years ahead, usually doesn't do much good until they enter their teens. Some ENTJs find that they don't do well in school until they reach a level of specialty studies, such as law or business, that is a natural fit with their strategic thinking.

An ENTJ's third function is Extroverted Sensing, so they are often avid travelers who enjoy the colors, food and adventures of seeing the world. ENTJs have a hard time not caring about winning, so they are also drawn to sports hobbies that permit them to win, like tennis or karate. They also like to take on athletic challenges such as running marathons, even if the challenge is just personal. They may also be drawn to visual design or music, which allow them to make Thinking decisions about Sensing issues. Their ability to block out any Thinking purpose at all and merely enjoy Extroverted Sensing may be limited. Having fun with no strategic purpose will only do for a short time.

Introverted Feeling is the fourth function and the root of conscience. Many ENTJs can go long periods of time, especially early in life, without noticing that they have a relationship-oriented warm conscience. Strategy and competition settle most questions of behavior, and they may only notice Feeling in music appreciation or books (some ENTJs even like poetry). But eventually, dating, marriage and children frame a set of decisions and values that aren't competitive. Warm conscience in family life prompts them to give up advantages to help those who are younger, weaker or just emotionally dependent. Most ENTJs are happiest when they can maintain private family zones of close, warm relationships with no strategic or power struggles. Happy family life may even bring out Introverted Feeling's romantic tone.

Abraham Lincoln may have had an ENTJ personality in which warm conscience pushed him to seek political power only through the ideal of abolition. He was keenly aware of the legal and constitutional arguments posed by Southern states, and his Thinking recognized their logical and legal validity. On the other hand, he had a strong personal feeling that no one can have a natural right to rule over anyone else without their consent. A personality balance that gave idealistic Feeling a greater role might have rushed into emotional activism, but Lincoln focused on strategy and nuance. When he finally ended slavery, it was a logical response to external power struggles, not an emotional reaction.

The ENTJ is rarely confident about matters of the heart. Falling in love is frightening because it entails the loss of control, perhaps even of autonomy. If he's at a stage of life when he is highly focused on mastery of skills, his Intuition and Thinking may be taking up so much brain space that he can mainly evaluate people as potential rivals or allies. An ENTJ is likely to choose a life partner in terms of being an asset to the master plan, without enough regard to whether the person is a truly good fit in emotional terms. If unwisely married, an ENTJ is likely to stick it out to the bitter end, always downplaying emotions against the higher good of the family—or even just the challenge of making it work.

It's even harder for an ENTJ woman to find love, since the personality fits better in a male archetype. ENTJ women may come across as too dominant and competitive for the men they date. They may be most likely to find lasting love with a philosophical, literary man whose self-imposed goals aren't threatened by the ENTJ's career goals. England's Queen Elizabeth I was probably an ENTJ; she knew she would lose some political power to a husband, even if she was still Queen in name, so she chose to remain single. Prime Minister Margaret Thatcher, on the other hand, found a quiet, unassuming man who didn't mind his comparatively low profile as she climbed in politics.

It's important for an ENTJ to pay some attention to non-competitive sides of life, especially as he grows older. ENTJs aren't likely to go to talk therapy, but they can at least deliberately stop and think about mistakes they have made in the past and consider the emotional reasons. Spending time with children is a natural way to exercise Introverted Feeling (and Extroverted Sensing). Reading romantic fiction may help them connect with their latent romantic feelings, too. Of course, to most ENTJs, any romantic fiction that they read will have to be impressive and strategic in its own way. That's okay, there's always Jane Austen.

INTJ

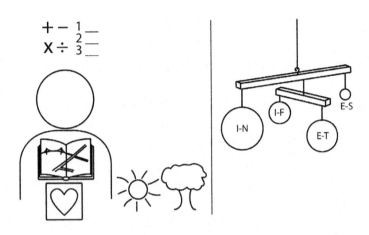

Fig. 12-10

#1: Introverted Intuition
#2: Extroverted Thinking
3.3% of men, 0.8% of women

INTJs have primary Introverted Intuition, one of the two types to have this mysterious "inner map" as a primary function. Because it is paired with Extroverted Thinking, their Intuition tends to explore the realms of what can be known, rather than what can be felt. Like any personality type, they can be found in a wide variety of professions, but science is the natural field of INTJs. The rules of laboratory procedure and scientific inquiry are based on the ways of thinking that come naturally to INTJs. Extroverted Thinking keeps all options open, ready for new evidence from facts and logic. Introverted Intuition remains confident that there are ways to test for connections while remaining properly skeptical about certainty.

In everyday affairs, INTJs usually have a sharp sense of what is the correct decision or method, especially concerning themselves. They tend to make career plans early and can follow a long preparatory program without feeling a need to reassess their original plans. In addition to natural and laboratory sciences, they are drawn to law, economics and history.

A hallmark of the INTJ's Film Noir response to the world is sarcasm. With one eye always focused on Introverted Intuition, they see what's wrong with the world quickly and in detail, but they know from experience that it isn't likely that anyone will fix the problem or even listen to them. Sarcastic comments that take note of anomalies allow INTJs to vent their frustration without losing their sense of balance.

Florence Nightingale, who pioneered modern nursing in the Crimean War, is a surprisingly clear pattern of these INTJ traits. She went into nursing out of frustration at being denied a career in mathematics, literally running away from her family's life of social calls and leisure. She spent only a few years in active war nursing, but during that time, she used her scientific and mathematical talent to study the relationship between nursing care methods and death rates. She documented that the simple physical acts of boiling sheets could reduce mortality; she developed the use of medical statistics more than anyone in her generation. She remained involved in the scientific study of nursing long after her active duty ended. In her 1858 book about hospital administration, she presented a new kind of circular graph, which she had invented. Her INTJ sarcasm came out frequently, as when she commented that one hostile doctor's royal award of "KCB" stood for "Knight of the Crimean Burying Grounds."[83]

INTJ perfectionism can be a strength, but it can also turn against them. This is particularly true if the INTJ becomes focused on him or herself as the "lab experiment," not on an outside object. Every human being discovers, over the years, that self-perfection is impossible, but INTJs are among the personality types slowest to give up. It is even worse for the INTJ if he or she was raised in an environment that did not build confidence. INTJs whose parents shared their values are most likely to have confidence that their efforts are good enough. INTJs who are raised in difficult families, or by parents who dislike the values of the INTJ type, may suffer from anxiety. They can see the intuitive ideal, but they can't reach it. Their anxiety will be worse if they have learning disabilities to get in the way of academic perfection. It is always a challenge for them to relax and accept life as it is, not as it should be.

INTJs want to exercise strong dominance over their immediate surroundings and responsibilities. They are not usually comfortable with managing other people, and they rarely like to manage a large department. For one thing, a larger zone of dominance waters down how much the INTJ can enforce the same high standards that he has for his own work. It's much easier to maintain precision and accuracy when the INTJ can control only what he does with his own hands and in his immediate area. They can be quite argumentative if their zone of control is challenged.

An INTJ pushed into a long-term executive role may be uncomfortable. INTJs, who rely so wholly on themselves in a pinch, are not always good leaders even in a field where natural brilliance led to promotion. One striking example seems to be Richard Nixon, an INTJ lawyer whose witty sarcasm, early in life, made him popular with political party leaders who promoted him to the Senate and eventually the Presidency. Although he was extremely logical and intelligent, he struggled with the demands of practical leadership. His discomfort was visible at times, and especially as his Presidency fell into a grimly negative spirit. Nixon's focus on protecting himself from enemies was probably the natural Film Noir response of Introverted Intuition.

The INTJ's third function is Introverted Feeling. Warm conscience makes them, first, strongly loyal to friends and family. Their own actions are governed by the rule of not hurting people who love them. They're also reluctant to judge others, preferring to give another person's conscience scope for autonomy. While they believe there are objective rights and wrongs, they're very aware of context, and also of how false appearances can be. Moral judgments of others are penciled in, ready to be erased or changed if more information alters

83: Elspeth Huxley, *Florence Nightingale* (New York: Putnam, 1975), 143.

the picture. Warm conscience within a Film Noir worldview can find itself in a pinfold occasionally. The first response is harsh and critical because it's directed at someone in authority, but then the real person (not just the role) becomes more visible, which requires mercy. INTJs are much less comfortable criticizing fallible human beings than institutions and appearances.

Introverted Feeling manages family relationships, to some extent friendships as well. INTJs are not likely to tell a white lie to smooth things over, because warm conscience suggests that pragmatic logic is consistent with real kindness in telling the truth, harsh as it might be at first. Sometimes this works out well, but it may also cause very hard feelings. INTJs aren't well equipped to figure out how to reconcile in this situation, so they may lose some relationships. On the other hand, their own inner critic won't let them be anything less than perfect (in their own eyes, and in context) in their own decisions. They find it hard to apologize, but also feel uncomfortable with lack of personal harmony. Self-criticism is their most likely conclusion, perhaps coupled with an experimental approach to finding a different way to handle things next time.

Weak Extroverted Sensing, the fourth function, allows an INTJ to interact realistically with nature and the outside world, but not as a first choice. INTJs tend to live in their heads and need some prodding to get out and exercise Sensing. Stephen Hawking's neurological illness so restricted his ability to interact with the world that he learned to turn off Sensing for the most part. Even in fairly early stages of his disease, he had days when he pulled inside his mind and lost awareness of anything outside it. He seems to have been absorbed in his Introverted Intuition and these periods of abstraction usually produced new ideas in physics, when he finally emerged from them and could try to speak again. While his disease process made all of this necessary, his personality structure allowed him to apply his energy inwardly; many personality types would not be able to make such an adaptation.

INTJs tackle marriage and parenting as they take on other projects: with an intention to do it very well. They are likely to read books on family matters so that they won't be caught off guard. On the other hand, they often have emotional blind spots that leave them helplessly open to mistakes. INTJs are dependent on spouses with good emotional instincts who can help them see and remedy their blind spots. Lacking this balance, an INTJ can have a very difficult time navigating life outside of work, so it is particularly important for this type to find a mate who not only can see the blind spots but can also present them in a way that doesn't discourage the often-brittle INTJ perfectionist soul.

ENFJ

Fig. 12-11

#1: Extroverted Feeling
#2: Introverted Intuition
1.6% of men, 3.3% of women

ENFJs are tuned first to Extroverted Feeling, and at times, they may seem entirely devoted to the feelings of others. They have a very large capacity for relating to the feelings of many people and reading the mood of each group of people they encounter. Introverted Intuition serves as the teammate of Feeling, always steering the ENFJ to see meaning and connections in human relationships. The most notable result is a desire to teach, especially to do moral and emotional teaching. Keenly aware of meaning, ENFJs can't rest until they have imparted wisdom to the people around them.

As children, they are usually leaders who want to tell other children what to do and think. When they do it well, they are genuine social leaders; when they still lack social tact, they can come across as bossy or even bullying. ENFJs have a lifetime project to learn how to balance their need to instruct with the needs of others to listen. By later life, ENFJs know when to keep silent and when to speak, and they have usually developed some area of expertise that allows them to take a turn at a podium of some kind. They blog, syndicate, lecture or go on speaking tours; many ENFJs become famous.

Martin Luther King, Jr. is one of the most famous ENFJs. By the age of 26, his natural skills drew him to leadership of the Montgomery bus boycott. He was a good, confident public speaker, but he also had tact and could judge when it would be better to keep demands low, and when it was right to press for more. When he had returned to the South after seminary, he didn't know he would end up as the leader of a civil rights revolution, but he had already felt very strongly that he needed to be there as a leader in waiting.

ENFJs are most often drawn to areas of work that permit them to train teachers, as a way to multiply their teaching impact. They can be found in universities teaching education, psychology, religion and philosophy. An ENFJ who enters a field of work like business, science or law gravitates to any training roles available. Although they are drawn to non-profit work, ENFJs can be comfortable working in a corporate environment as long as they have a role in promoting emotional well-being. They may train managers, write ethical codes for organizations or teach advanced classes. ENFJs are also happy in management roles, since they can focus on the people they are managing more than on the direct content of the work. In non-profit work, they like fundraising and setting long-term goals.

ENFJs are strongly drawn to writing inspirational books, and they are comfortable with speaking tours and marketing campaigns. A typical ENFJ title is something like "Ten Steps to Happiness," and the book explains how the common perception of a good life is mistaken, since their Introverted Intuition can see past appearances. The book shares the intuitive emotional principles that have worked for the ENFJ author, on the assumption that they are universal, not personal, truths. The authors of titles like *The Secret* and *Knowing God* are probably ENFJs.

Oprah Winfrey, one of the most famous contemporary ENFJs, promotes books more than she writes them. She refers to her book club as a "mission" with the twin goals of urging people to read "great books" and helping them have better lives. That's the ENFJ touch: they aren't just selling books, they're changing lives by sharing their personal feelings about what they love.

The ENFJ's third function is Extroverted Sensing, which helps keep their goals pragmatic and real-world. Some ENFJs may be very good at organizing their households, offices and daily life, but others may need to work at it. Sensing and Intuition often connect to create a strong sense of Mind-Body connection in the ENFJ. There are many positive aspects to this connection; many ENFJs go into the medical profession with the goal of reforming medicine or making the whole world, not just a few people, healthier. On the negative side, ENFJs may be especially prone to physical ailments caused by emotional distress. They often gravitate to eating only organic foods or following careful regimens for maintaining an optimistic mindset, since these things are very necessary to their own wellbeing.

A lot of the "holistic health" movement comes from ENFJs who have learned some method or rule that helps them feel stronger. As natural moral leaders, they feel driven to share their tips with as large an audience as possible. They may start new companies or write books to promote new "wellness" methods, and many doctors who have regular speaking slots on regional or national television, like Dr. Mehmet Oz, are ENFJs.

In those with a specific artistic gift in art or music, Extroverted Sensing can become a very strong function that blends with Feeling and Intuition. ENFJs are drawn to the world of classical music if they are blessed with such talent; one survey found that about 16% of professional musicians are ENFJs.[84] Yo-Yo Ma seems to fit this model, being outgoing, kind, and always interested in creating a new sort of project to lead. For example, although he is known as a cello master, he also created the "Silk Road Ensemble," a recording collective that blends ancient, primitive, folk music with the music of other regions and times. Instead of being content with his own personal recording career, he formed a way to network and

---

84: Anthony E. Kemp, *The Musical Temperament* (New York: Oxford University Press, 1996), 78.

expand the recording careers of unknown musicians in remote places. Many ENFJ musicians are drawn into teaching at high levels of skill and influence.

Their fourth and weakest function is Introverted Thinking, but ENFJ decisions tend to lean on relationship choices, not logic. Introverted Thinking has its greatest influence as the root of conscience, and as such it can be a fierce enemy of the pragmatic, amoral logic of Extroverted Thinking (when they encounter it in others). Part of their moral leadership stems from their cool conscience certainty that they know what's right, in an objective and absolute way. Extroverted Feeling leads them to be involved in groups that take moral stands. They become preachers and crusade leaders, usually at the forefront of every "die in," march or other justice movement.

When Introverted Thinking does not provide enough actual logic as balance to Feeling, ENFJs can lose perspective. If they're in politics or activism, they may lose the ability to see where self ends and the moral cause begins. Pragmatic toward people who appear to be enemies of justice, they can use corrupt or harsh means to achieve what they see as a justified goal. Their speeches will continue to be as idealistic and inspiring as ever, since they are not perceiving any clash between the end goal and the means they are using to achieve it.

ENFJs are the personality type most likely to report that they believe in God,[85] and it's usually a personal, mystical sense stemming from Introverted Intuition, not just acceptance of traditional theology. They may become megachurch preachers or begin teaching their personal views as theology for a group. Here, too, they can lose perspective in a prophetic voice or belief about destiny. At best, their influence stays positive; at worst, they can become cult leaders to whom their followers devote everything.

ENFJs have a strong need to exercise a lot of control in family relationships. They are attentive to people's emotional needs, and they use tact, rather than force. Still, it does not sit well with them to see relationships going in ways they do not approve, and they will take steps to change things. If necessary, cool conscience allows them to act punitively or withdraw in disapproval even from those they love. In marriage, ENFJ partners set the tone and make key family decisions. They are happiest if they have chosen to marry someone who can be flexible in adapting to the ENFJ's dictates while still keeping an independent spirit that can challenge and balance.

85: *MBTI® Manual, A Guide to the Development and Use of the Myers-Briggs Type Indicator*, 3rd edition (Mountain View, CA: CPP, 2003), 238. For belief in God, ENFJs score 91% in the MBTI national sample, with ESFJs, ISFJs and ENFPs tied for second at 90%.

INFJ

Fig. 12-12

#1: Introverted Intuition
#2: Extroverted Feeling
1.3% of men, 1.6% of women

The search for hidden meaning in human relations characterizes the INFJ's life. The primary function, Introverted Intuition, gives the INFJ a sense of knowing that there are hidden meanings which must be understood as deeply as possible. Introverted Intuition working with Extroverted Feeling turns the search for meaning toward the human soul in all of its presentations. INFJs may feel that they "just know" things about the meaning of life. Most of them are not driven to share their sense of meaning with a large number of people; they tend to work in small groups or write profound books without broad appeal.

Much of the INFJ's wisdom, especially early in life, comes from good ability to read nonverbal messages in people's faces and behavior. It's a natural ability for them, since it applies Introverted Intuition to Extroverted Feeling. They can understand not just what people say, but also what they don't say, what they say about what they don't say, and even what they don't say about what they say. Much of their mental processing during childhood is taken up with gathering these clues and organizing them into a general theory of people.

As Extroverted Feelers, INFJs are drawn to be around people a lot, but because they are most deeply oriented to the Introverted function of Intuition, they often need to withdraw and spend time alone. This allows their unconscious mind enough time to understand what Feeling has been managing. In a balanced lifestyle, an INFJ can work this out easily, but usually there are periods when an INFJ has too much of either society or isolation, and either state can push him into distress. Nelson Mandela seems to be a good example of an INFJ who felt himself to be primarily introverted, but was often surrounded by people and felt no difficulty speaking to large groups. His prison years gave him enough solitary time to know himself without getting lost in others.

INFJs are the type most likely to report extra-sensory perceptions of various kinds. Their focus on nonverbal communication is already bordering on extra-sensory. Some INFJs describe "catching" moods, such as suddenly feeling suicidal or elated, and they sense that these moods were involuntarily projected by passing strangers. At a more developed stage, an INFJ may sense good or evil strongly, as though a physical apparition were present. INFJs may be drawn to New Age fields like energy therapy or spirit healing, because their own personal perceptions fit the theories. At the most extreme, INFJs may be psychics who assist the police in solving mysterious cases, or who feel that they can sense the future or communicate without words.

INFJs go into any field that captures their attention and talents with a promise of making a difference in society. There are INFJ lawyers, journalists, writers, social workers, doctors, and even politicians. Most INFJs would be uncomfortable working in a high-profit field like banking, so they gravitate toward non-profits that aim to benefit the environment, animals or children. They are also likely to enter fields of ministry and theological study. Dietrich Bonhoeffer, who is now most famous for his execution by Nazis for being in a plot to kill Hitler, knew from the age of 14 that he wanted to be a theologian. Although his family favored careers in science, Dietrich always had an innate sense that God was alive and mattered to people. When his brothers criticized his decision, saying that the church was irrelevant and God didn't exist, the young teenager replied that, "God still exists even if you knock my head off."[86]

INFJs often go into some form of counseling as a career, but they also do personal counseling with friends. They are wise and quiet listeners who prefer not rushing to speak, since they are processing nonverbal impressions at the same time as listening to words. They prefer to have profound influence over a few people than to reach thousands a little bit, so that when they become talk therapists or pastors, they are content with this personal scope.

Their third function, Introverted Thinking, strengthens their sense of logic and rightness. Cool conscience is not often used to criticize friends and family, but it is readily directed at authorities. Private persons have contexts for their failings, and INFJs understand this without needing to judge. But systems, laws and customs are another matter. INFJ protest style does not usually seek the spotlight, but focuses on civil disobedience and personal choice. INFJs may act alone to do something for justice, and they may even have difficulty working with groups that only partially share their values.

They are the personality type most likely to accept a jail term for political or activist reasons; their cool conscience blends with the Film Noir worldview to point out that a court's conviction may be a false appearance, and really only truth matters. The search for truth can lead them into investigation and activism, even up to taking up arms. INFJ George Orwell, for example, volunteered to fight in the Spanish Civil War and was nearly killed there, long before his writing became famous. Nelson Mandela and Mahatma Gandhi both began as INFJ lawyers and then became leaders by accepting imprisonment. Early modern

86: Eric Metaxas, *Bonhoeffer: Pastor, Martyr, Prophet, Spy* (Nashville: Thomas Nelson, 2010), 38.

muckrakers and reformers, as well as contemporary prisoners of conscience under repressive governments like Cuba and Burma, probably were and are INFJs.

Introverted Thinking's tendency to assert the importance of rules-based morality can create tension with Introverted Intuition, which often challenges traditional rules. INFJs try to create the right balance by using Intuition to discern which values are most authentic for each situation. It can also be very difficult for them to learn how to balance their strong Feeling for people with rigid Thinking about rules. The classic novel *Jane Eyre* is about a young INFJ who slowly learns how much she can listen to each of these functions; when she listens to only one of them, she always falls into error and confusion. The novel's happy ending shows her finally in balance, able to defy tradition in some respects while listening to it in others, following her feelings in some ways and logic in others.

Their weakest function, Extroverted Sensing, tends to be very important to most INFJs. While some personality types easily neglect the weakest function, INFJs tend to use and cherish their Sensing abilities. Many are drawn to art of many kinds. They seem strongly drawn to yoga and ballet, and INFJs can be found in visual arts as well. Music, though, is the INFJ's special kingdom. In a 1981 survey of professional classical musicians, an astonishing 21% were INFJs. This is an even more remarkable number when compared to the same survey's figures for student musicians, only 9% of whom were INFJs.[87] Among people with equally good musical talents, INFJs seem more willing to become "starving artists" instead of finding another career path.

It is clear that the INFJ's Extroverted Sensing, though technically in the weakest position, connects to the dominant functions through art, and INFJs end up feeling very strongly about their pursuit of art, perhaps especially in songwriting, a strong INFJ pursuit. Any pop song with an overt values message, especially a message that challenges society, is probably an INFJ product. John Lennon had been an art student and in later years returned to creating visual art; but during his most famously productive years, he was focused on lyrics of idealism. His song "Imagine" may be considered the INFJ's anthem.

In friendships, love and families, INFJs are loyal and kind, but they can also be difficult to be around. Their needs for sociability and isolation may fluctuate unpredictably so that those closest to them must observe carefully or be caught by surprise when the INFJ suddenly needs to be alone. Conflict with friends and family is always hard for INFJs. Some avoid conflict because they cannot bear the interpersonal pain, while others are driven to frequent conflict in order to argue their strong opinions. Hobbies like music, art and yoga may help by giving regular periods for quiet, introspection and calm, so INFJs are likely to withdraw to such activities during times of conflict.

FOURTH GROUP: EXTROVERTED INTUITION

The last four personalities are like science fiction movies; they all have strong Extroverted Intuition with expansive, optimistic imagination. Operating in the background, weaker Introverted Sensing colors images with tradition and romance. As with the Extroverted

---

87: Anthony E. Kemp, *The Musical Temperament* (New York: Oxford University Press, 1996), 78.

Sensing group of personalities, Judging is necessary to provide moral direction amid the openness. In each type's name, the T or F for Thinking and Feeling also corresponds to its root of moral conscience. Warm or cool conscience is not masked by another strong Introverted function, since it's in one of the top two slots.

ENTP

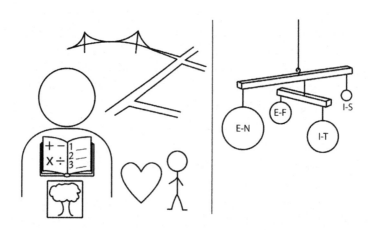

Fig. 12-13

#1: Extroverted Intuition
#2: Introverted Thinking
4% of men, 2.4% of women

ENTPs balance an almost self-contradictory pair of strengths. Led by exploring, pragmatic Intuition that never stops questioning authority, they also lean on idealistic, introverted Thinking. When Thinking is working with scientific and mathematical facts, it's focused on logical order. ENTPs are naturally drawn to research and development in computer programming, mathematics, architecture, engineering and all branches of science. At the same time, idealistic Thinking insists on high standards of moral logic, which ultimately come from human experience and tradition. Human tradition is the very thing pragmatic Intuition is challenging, and yet rules are the ENTP's source of moral vision.

Under stress, ENTPs can find themselves driving their personality's car with one foot on the accelerator and one foot on the brake. They want to dethrone all conventional thinking and received wisdom, but cool conscience judges the world in terms of absolute right and wrong. By the one measure, rebellion and revolution are good, but by the other standard, they're evil. Perhaps in order to resolve or set aside their internal contradiction, ENTPs rarely focus on moral issues. They are much more comfortable in the world of mechanical and scientific endeavors. They drive revolutions in technology and avoid other controversy.

Extroverted Intuition has a cognitive style based in creative analogies. If one thing is like another, then perhaps what's true of one could be true of the other. Thomas A. Edison, the leading inventor of the late 19th century, was certainly an ENTP. Many of his ideas came through analogies to existing things in the machine or animal world. Edison was also able to generate an unlimited number of changes in design, as logic sorted out experimentally which designs worked. In an interesting link, one of Edison's machinist friends also made escape-act gadgets for Harry Houdini, another ENTP inventor.

ENTPs like to be dominant in creating new things of all kinds. They define some unexplored zone in technology, science, philosophy, art, or music, and begin a race to the top. The young Paul McCartney, probably an ENTP, was drawn to the cutting edge of the newest music, teaching himself and learning new guitar chords anywhere he could. After he had mastered rock music, he was always seeking out new projects on the side: avant-garde art, Beat poetry, an underground newspaper, an indie bookshop, experimental music with John Cage's disciples, and any other new idea that came along (including recording two completely different pieces of music on one album so that a listener could try using different sides of his brain to separate them).

ENTPs are as competitive in the world of ideas as their S counterparts, the ESTPs, are in the world of sports. They love team challenges in which they can take the lead in a highly-motivated group. Since they are focused largely on Thinking tasks, they are most likely to be found in intellectual team challenges: quiz teams, math teams, and invention or robotic challenges. Young ENTPs are drawn to computer games in droves and their values shape the culture of online gaming. Randy Pausch, the computer science professor at Carnegie Mellon University who responded to his terminal cancer diagnosis by giving a famous "Last Lecture," described his lifelong dedication to winning every game that came his way. During the lecture, students carried onstage a series of giant stuffed animals that he'd won at carnivals. Pausch's entire lecture serves as an outline of the ENTP personality's values.[88]

But ENTPs don't need a formal game to compete. They like to one-up anyone who's nearby, including siblings, friends, strangers and parents, if they can. They'll try to figure out a way to do something faster, better, or just differently. Whatever they can do, they want to be one point up. ENTP women may find this aspect of the personality type socially difficult, since most other women compete subtly on social terms, not openly on intellectual ones. They may find themselves making friends mostly with men who don't perceive them as feminine, which can be another layer of difficulty.

ENTPs are happiest and most productive in work environments that allow them to bounce between working in teams and being alone. Whatever they are doing, there will always be some middle-length horizon of completion or competition, such as a project or grant term. They're not likely to be found in people-care work, middle management and anything requiring repetition; an ENTP caught in such a job will be planning an exit as soon as possible. Otherwise, they might go into any field that captures their attention and uses their talents: music, art, architecture, mathematics, sciences, law, or education. Within that field, they will manage their time and options in an ENTP way.

88: Randy Pausch, "The Last Lecture: Really Achieving Your Childhood Dreams," Carnegie Mellon University, September 18, 2007, posted at https://www.youtube.com/watch?v=ji5_MqicxSo. Also, Randy Pausch and Jeffrey Zaslow, *The Last Lecture* (New York: Hyperion, 2008).

The emotional range of an ENTP is easily seen, because passing emotions are worn openly. Extroverted Feeling is their third function, and coupled with their dominant Extroverted Intuition, it usually presents in a cheerful, enthusiastic way. Feeling is sympathetic by its nature, and it helps them be more attentive team members when they're in the midst of a competitive project. They care about what people think of them, and they don't generally like to alienate everyone around them. They want to look appropriate and fit in; they appreciate approval and aren't perfectly comfortable taking a lone stand on an issue. Paul McCartney's widespread reputation as the "nicest" Beatle was very much a function of Extroverted Feeling guiding him to be genial and outgoing.

But Extroverted Feeling can also cause sandstorms of emotion, as they are easily angered, irritated and outraged. If you live at close quarters with an ENTP, expect to hear yelling now and then. Sadness in other people distresses ENTPs. They want to be around happy people, because it allows them to do their best thinking when they don't need to exercise compassion or make moral judgments. Sadness in other people is likely to motivate them to suggest solutions, since invention is the ENTP's go-to mode for most problems. If that won't work, the shared emotion may feel overwhelming.

The difficulty of pleasing people and integrating emotion presents a danger over time. By adult years, everyone needs to be good at assessing friends and lovers, and our emotional reactions to other people are important indicators of where we stand with them. ENTPs who have learned to brush aside their "inconvenient" feelings may not be good at breaking off with friends or lovers who are bad for them. Their enthusiastic response to life and basic sympathy can also set them up for falling in love easily, whether it's with the right person or not.

The fourth, weakest function in the ENTP personality is Introverted Sensing. Any connection that ENTPs have to the real, sensory world should be encouraged. If they are doing hands-on inventing, they will probably remain integrated with their Sensing abilities. If they do only theoretical or programming work, they need to be involved in music, art, cooking or sports to stay grounded.

Especially in young ENTPs who grew up with computer games slaking their appetite for competition, the real Sensing world may grow a bit dim. An ENTP child's room is probably a mess, and he doesn't like to keep a schedule. He may lose things frequently. Older ENTPs can be classic absent-minded professors who run late to everything, lose their keys, and walk into walls. This is probably going to be an increasing problem for ENTPs, with more and more innovation taking place within a computer's non-sensory world.

Introverted Sensing is a smaller but contributing part of the tension in this personality framework. Its effect on understanding people can be to emphasize traditional, archetypal roles, but the ENTP's innovative streak may already have carried him or her into a lifestyle that doesn't fit archetypes. Extreme love of innovation exists uneasily with archetypes of mothers, children, kings and other social roles. Under stress, the effect may be to work with Introverted Thinking's cool conscience framework to see the world in terms of villains and heroes. Nuance for concepts may not extend to nuance for people. ENTPs share with their related type, the INTPs, a love for comic books and space opera; in those worlds, moral nuance is not needed.

Family life can be a challenge for ENTPs. By nature, family relationships are not competitive, and family problems are usually solved with routine and repetition, not with new ideas. Cool conscience strictly directs them to do well at family life, but empathy may not come easily, so they may be frustrated and feel that it's a task requiring things they can't do. They do best when paired with someone who can soothe frustration and help them understand interpersonal relationships. Then they can use fun ideas and warm Extroverted Feeling to include everyone, and that's when they're at their best.

INTP

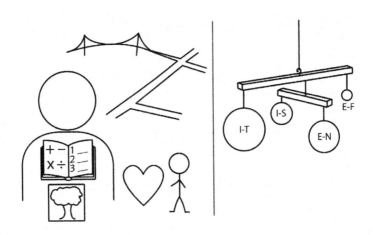

Fig. 12-14

#1: Introverted Thinking
#2: Extroverted Intuition
4.8% of men, 1.8% of women

INTPs are the quietest, most intense of the Thinking types. Their primary focus is on inner idealistic logic, giving them frequently a distracted, absent-minded attitude to the outside world. Grounded in Introverted Thinking, INTPs are rarely law-breakers, but Extroverted Intuition's drive for pragmatic exploration and questioning gives them a flexible, sometimes unconventional view on life.

INTPs are drawn to work that allows them time to take things apart and lay out the parts in order. This can mean literally taking apart machines, but it has abstract applications too. There are many things that other people perceive as "black boxes" or as unified wholes, which INTPs are sure could be de-mystified if someone could just take them apart well enough. These include the economy, government, the educational system, the human mind, literature, history, music, art and really everything. When an explanation is presented to an INTP, he wants to peel back another layer and find answers to questions others have not yet asked. Anything that can have the word "theory" attached to it will draw INTPs: music theory, economic theory, linguistic theory, psychological theory.

If there is one particular field in which INTPs have led the way, it's mathematics, where most of the leaders have been quiet, focused, intense men and women. Isaac Newton is arguably the most influential INTP in world history, since he changed the way we see the world. The science and mathematics taught at Cambridge in 1661 was mostly medieval. On his own, Newton discovered the works of Descartes and Galileo and worked from their ideas toward defining and measuring things like velocity, gravity, time, light and infinity. Most of his discoveries were made while working alone, in notebooks, posing mathematical questions to himself and answering them.

Charles Dodgson, who wrote fiction as "Lewis Carroll," was another INTP whose primary line of work was in developing and teaching mathematics. But he also had a lifelong interest in writing nonsense literature, most famously *Alice in Wonderland.* There's a strong connection between INTPs and fantasy literature, especially science fiction. INTPs love to read science fiction, but they are the personality type most responsible for writing it, too. Their logical minds' love of math and science combines with Extroverted Intuition's interest in asking what would it be like if impossible things could happen.

Like ENTPs, INTPs can feel tension between their strong cool conscience and their love of possibility. They tend to be less troubled by the tension, perhaps since Thinking is the undisputed King of the mind. They are interested in revolutionary ideas, but they don't usually spend time on ones that conflict with their moral sense. That's a good reason for their primary contribution to be in mathematics, where imagination can travel forever without meeting moral conflicts. When a moral question captures their attention, they have firm opinions about it and can be stridently vocal.

There's another inner tension that comes out more in their behavior. With Introverted Thinking's idealistic logic at their core, they are not usually lawbreakers. But cool conscience includes Extroverted Feeling, which is more pragmatic about relationships with people; combined with exploring Intuition, INTPs can be tempted to reserve zones of life for less conscience and more hijinks. In younger ages, they are famous for playing pranks. Tech schools with a large INTP and ENTP population are often hit by elaborate, nearly reality-defying pranks that may take in a whole building or the entire campus. Introverted Thinking matures some time after college, and usually older INTPs have better awareness of the potential rule-breaking nature of such pranks. But some INTPs on the internet remain detached from conscience and can become black-marketeers or enablers of theft.

INTPs are well suited to the Computer Age. Programming means taking many different tasks and ideas and breaking them into tiny pieces, each with a mathematical or logical routine that can make it happen. Most programming breakthroughs were discovered by INTPs, but few of them have become famous except in their own zones of influence. The open source computer culture is thoroughly ruled by INTP strengths and values. Although big corporations like Microsoft employ thousands of INTPs to make their products, corporate control and profit make these same INTPs uneasy. They love Linux programming and anything that the user can modify and improve. Open source software always has an INTP in the background, as does every forward step in file-sharing. BitTorrent, a computer code protocol that runs much of the internet's downloads, was invented by Bram Cohen, an INTP who wanted to see information control decentralized.

Even before the Computer Age, INTP inventors have tended to devalue the money-making side of invention, that is, patenting and marketing. Alexander Graham Bell had a lifelong obsession with machines to create sound, making him one of the most prolific inventors of his time. But he had to be pushed to patent anything, since he considered nothing completed or ready. He didn't file any patents between 1886 and 1903 (when his wife filled out the paperwork for him). During that time, he invented an automated telephone switchboard, but refused to patent it, since it might put human operators out of work. A century later, Steve Wozniak invented some crucial early steps in personal computing, but he planned to give computers away for free. Apple Computer couldn't have been founded by INTP Wozniak alone, because he simply didn't think about patents and money.

Introverted Sensing, the third function, adds to the INTP's sense of perfectionism. Music may be the most common (and perhaps the only typical) outlet for direct INTP participation in sensation. Albert Einstein was a gifted violinist who impulsively joined in, if he heard a pianist playing Mozart or Schubert. A less positive presentation of Introverted Sensing may be irritation with the intrusive, imperfect outside world. Alexander Graham Bell was easily irritated (and even made ill) by sudden noises and depended on his wife and assistants to maintain a precise and sheltered environment. Anything that didn't fit his exact ideas of what life should look or sound like might distract his mind from work.

Introverted Sensing also gives INTPs a preference for archetypal social roles, even if it's mostly an artistic sense. We see this very clearly in comic books, where there are heroes and villains who fulfill mythical archetypes in literal ways. The INTP worldview is perhaps most clearly illustrated in comic books: anything is possible, but right and wrong never change. You can invent anything, but it has to be used to stop the bad guys with black hats.

Extroverted Feeling, the fourth function, gives most INTPs some motivation to fit into society, though it may be fairly weak. They are reserved and never effusive, but they care about what people think. Although they can be unconventional and go their own way intellectually, INTPs don't choose to offend if they can help it. They can be sharply critical of the world around them, but they are not prone to sarcasm like INTJs. Perhaps for the same reason, they are less likely to be involved with the outside world; they aren't commonly found trying to solve local problems by running for school board or town council. Always aware of the deeper reasons behind every problem, INTPs don't see easy fixes for anything. Interpersonally, they tend to be gentle and tolerant.

INTPs can struggle in marriage and family, since they need a great deal of understanding as they strive to influence the hard reality of life outside a computer. They are non-confrontational, humble mates and parents. As parents, they have difficulty relating to their children in an authoritative, hierarchical way, since they prefer to explore the world with their children almost as equals. They may have blind spots, especially in realizing that they need to act, not just observe and understand. A good spouse is usually well-organized and outgoing, able to care for the shy INTP. He or she also has to see the INTP's blind spots and help compensate for them, perhaps distracting from work or finding settings where the INTP can interact with people more.

ENFP

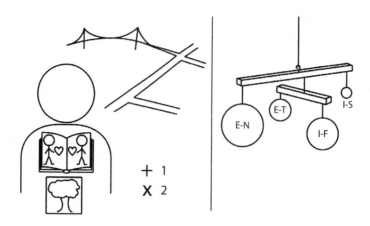

Fig. 12-15

#1: Extroverted Intuition
#2: Introverted Feeling
6.4% of men, 9.7% of women

ENFPs live in a world where anything seems possible. More than any other personality, they are geared to see potential without skeptical restraint. Their top function, Extroverted Intuition, scans the world to find endless room for improvement in building and connecting. The second function that acts as Intuition's teammate, Introverted Feeling, focuses them on people, not on machines or rules. To an ENFP, people are beautiful and every new possibility is the best ever. Where ENTPs see innovation in things, ENFPs see innovation in people; they are inventors with human material.

ENFPs may be found in nearly any line of work, as long as it allows them to work with people. They are more likely to go into work that lets them meet many new people, or form new groups, or try out new ideas. For example, ENFP teachers are likely to head for magnet schools, where they can meet students from disparate backgrounds, or for charter schools experimenting with a new model. ENFP doctors focus a lot on getting to know patients during office visits; ENFP salesmen create new ad pitches. They like to launch demonstrations, lead discussions, and form bands or book groups.

ENFPs have one typical danger with new ideas: the messy process of making ideas happen in real life can ruin their appeal. As soon as the idea begins to exist on a construction site or on paper, it isn't as perfect as it was when it was just an idea. In the process of becoming real, an idea must also close out many potential alternatives. ENFPs are usually uncomfortable with these stages. They are happiest when they can be involved in the first stages of brainstorming and planning, and then find a way to exit and leave the details and troubleshooting to other people.

Similarly, they are happiest when meeting new people who allow them to imagine ideal possibilities. In later years of friendship, these same people may really let them down or push them to the limits of their empathy, but ENFPs rarely see this coming. Their strong Introverted Feeling directs imagination to predict that ideals will finally come true. In literature, the character of Anne of Green Gables put the ENFP motto best: "I just know you're a kindred spirit!"

ENFPs are comfortable with leadership as long as it is limited in place and time, and even more importantly, as long as they are leading in some sphere of their own ideas. There are some projects that would never happen if an ENFP did not see the opportunity that other eyes missed. However, the details of leadership are even worse than the process of moving an idea into reality, since they are usually both impatient with routine and uncomfortable with conflict. It's best if there's a natural limit on ENFP responsibility.

ENFPs are drawn to music, art, psychology and writing. When they write, they are often drawn to the theatrical possibilities of poetry, fiction, or prose. Robert Browning, a famous ENFP poet from the 19th century, wrote in the voices of different people. Instead of creating poetry that looked inward at his own emotions, his works always portrayed what it would be like to be someone else, especially if they were very much unlike himself (such as psychopathic killers or madmen). Another ENFP writer, Charles Dickens, focused most on bringing a large number of characters to life in his sprawling novels. Dickens loved reading his work out loud to audiences, playing to their emotions and getting immediate live feedback. There are ENFP actors, like Robin Williams, who can create complete characters instantly as possibilities occur to them. Some ENFP writers lean toward cartooning, a form that quickly creates stories for large audiences. ENFPs are also enthusiastic social media users and bloggers; the internet is a sort of magic carpet that allows ENFPs to meet people across distance barriers.

The ENFP's third function is Extroverted Thinking; many ENFPs are very good at academic tasks. They are typically bright (but absent-minded) students who do especially well with verbal tasks. Extroverted Thinking and Extroverted Intuition make the world of science a particularly compelling playground for an ENFP in search of new things to learn. Extroverted Thinking also contributes to verbal wit, as exemplified by Oscar Wilde, another famous ENFP. From a young age, he was able to see many verbal possibilities and liked to ask his friends puzzling philosophical questions. He was able to use logic to demolish all religious beliefs and moral principles. His sense of humor prized the sort of statement that sounds very serious but can't possibly be taken at face value.

ENFPs with very strong Extroverted Thinking can do well in verbal tasks like law and government. President Bill Clinton may be the most famous ENFP in the United States. While he was in office, he delighted in ENFP-typical spontaneous conversations that brainstormed new ideas. At the same time, his Extroverted Thinking had to be under constant pressure to keep up with the rapid flow of information coming into the White House.

The two extroverted functions can make an ENFP seem casual about morality and rules. In a mind oriented first to endless possibilities, and also to amoral logic, most rules seem pointless. They will go to great lengths not to hurt someone, but punishment and peer pressure may not mean much. It's hard for them to believe that it won't all somehow work out fine.

The weakest function, Introverted Sensing, helps some ENFPs understand symbolism in literature. ENFPs can be accomplished poets and very imaginative writers, completely at home in the world of abstract thought. They have a latent romantic sense about historical archetypal roles, but they are not likely to conform to contemporary archetypes, such as kinds of work requiring uniforms. Archetypal roles are only weakly linked with good and evil; ENFPs would rather see a story that discovered hidden good potential in villains. Perhaps for some of the same reasons, ENFPs may also be drawn to comic-strip illustration.

With only weak and idealistic Sensing, ENFPs are rarely focused on physical exercise and fun; they would enjoy a party for the people, not for the dancing or food. They are not likely to become fanatics about exercise for its own sake, since they may feel a bit detached from the physical world. They may not be susceptible to natural beauty as much as those who enjoy Sensing in an extroverted way, but they do tend to form strong ties to particular places that are associated with personal emotions.

In family life, ENFPs are best at talking about feelings, smoothing over conflicts by creating mutual understanding. They like to see the individual talents in children and help bring these forward. Often absent-minded, they are generally happy to ignore a schedule and do something spontaneous. They are particularly drawn to fun activities that promote a sense of family harmony, as well as to activities that are new and different.

Some ENFPs are not good at keeping house, while others maintain an orderly environment to be in harmony with Introverted Sensing and Feeling. They may not be good at keeping up family traditions, since as a general principle, they are oriented to the present mainly as it merges into the all-important future; they are not closely linked to memory and the past.

Of all of the personality types, ENFPs may be the most likely to marry someone who isn't very compatible in the long term. Many ENFPs fall in love easily and each time they believe that it's the Best Love Ever; they recover relatively quickly from break-ups. Julia Roberts, an actress who appears to fit the ENFP profile, was at times ridiculed for her tendency to say of each short-lived romance that she was "born to love" this man. Although they have good instincts about people, ENFPs see the best potential in everyone; they aren't as good at seeing non-potential and negativity. Also, they may be quick to assume that everything in the other person could change, since change and variation are so easy for ENFPs to imagine.

INFP

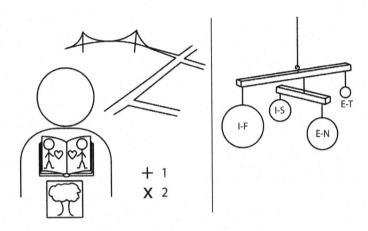

Fig. 12-16

#1: Introverted Feeling
#2: Extroverted Intuition
4.1% of men, 4.6% of women

The abstract battle between Good and Evil is often terribly real to an INFP, whose primary life is rooted in the invisible realm of the soul. With Introverted Feeling as the most dominant function, the INFP's mental make-up has few close ties to the pragmatic real world. Extroverted Intuition, the second function, is used most in exploring connections and imagining possibilities. While Feeling makes values judgments readily, its lack of pragmatism can cause great inner stress when the INFP has to live in the world.

INFPs can be found in many work roles, like ENFPs. This may be due to the impractical nature of their imaginative strengths. Only a few people can make a living on poetry, novels, music or languages, so INFPs usually earn money at something else. They are most comfortable in higher education, teaching the same things they love: literature, psychology, music, and languages. They are very good counselors, since they listen empathetically and try to shift everything toward inner harmony. Harmony and empathy are such strong motivators that no matter what field an INFP is found in, even in administration or law enforcement, the work will somehow get tilted toward values and peace.

Imagination is a key trait and perhaps the best escape from the dilemmas of world imperfection. However, Intuition and Feeling combine to make it almost an obsession for INFPs to imagine other points of view, other voices, even ones that are hostile to the INFP himself. This trait can make managing conflict very difficult. INFPs are at risk for falling into abusive relationships, because it's so natural for the INFP to feel the abuser's point of view as equally valid with their own. Most INFPs will never stand up for themselves unless they feel that an idealistic principle is at stake. They'll face conflict for truth, but not for self, because the truth may be clear to Introverted Feeling at the same time that Extroverted Intuition is muddying the waters with walking in everyone's shoes.

While most people can justify aggression, or at least compartmentalize it away from the rest of their inner life, INFPs find it nearly impossible to be aggressive and maintain inner peace. Audrey Hepburn, an INFP actress, found that she could not even muster enough aggression to drive her own car. It was easier to hire drivers or let her husband manage the car than to find ways to push back against others on the road. INFPs without the financial option of hiring others to do their aggression end up with many internal conflicts. They internalize most problems and hold themselves responsible for all imperfection, even unrealistically.

INFPs rarely care much about money and don't mind if others make decisions about food, schedule, and purchases. Little sacrifices are made without a ripple showing on the surface, because "what I want" is not a strong impulse. This may not be all for the best, although it's convenient for friends or family to take advantage of how easy it is for them to give things up. Over time, an INFP may suddenly find that too much has been given up, and it's no longer okay. When that happens, it's often too late to repair the situation.

Introverted Sensing is the INFP's third function. It's particularly important because it blurs with Intuition's imagination, making it an adjunct of the INFP's main way of relating to the world. When Introverted Sensing blends thoroughly with Extroverted Intuition, the world becomes animated like a Disney movie. Introverted Feeling colors it with emotional idealism, so that every object has a personal life of its own. Living and non-living are not distinct categories, as they are for most other people. Many INFPs struggle with a confused sense of compassion toward worn-out things in the trash, while INFP children may grieve deeply over a broken toy.

Introverted Sensing also brings in both romanticism and symbolism. INFPs are invariably and strongly drawn to historical archetypes like princesses, knights, and heroes. They read and write about these things, but the fascination may run into external life, with costumes, re-enacting, or a touch of romanticism in daily dress. Symbolism is a normal way of thinking, since things seem somewhat alive already. Of course, things stand for or in some sense already inhabit layers of other meanings. INFP poetry and other writing is strongly centered around figurative speech, partly because it's not merely words to them. But even when they're dealing only with words as sound or spelling, INFPs are innately attached. They have a natural gift for foreign language partly because words seem alive and colorful. J. R. R. Tolkien, an INFP writer whose main career was in languages, chose which languages to study based only on the way their visual surface appealed to him (he loved the look of Finnish and Welsh).

The external world is often a confusing place for someone with these traits, and that is probably why INFPs are so often driven to write novels. Stories allow the writer to create a limited world in which a narrator's voice can explain why things happen. INFPs are able to step into many points of view, from their own to those of inanimate objects or of their worst enemies; they care much more about why people do things than about judging whether the action was right or wrong. Their stories tend to be very strong statements of warm conscience values.

The list of famous INFP writers is both long and forever incomplete, since there are so many of them: Jane Austen, George Eliot, A. A. Milne, Isak Dinesen, C. S. Lewis, J. R. R. Tolkien, and J. K. Rowling. Stephen King, master of horror stories with a comic twist, may also be an INFP; his stories explore the nature of evil, which can be a strong INFP preoccupation. Characters in literature are often INFPs, since writers may base a main point-of-view character on themselves. Lucy in the Narnia series, Sara Crewe in *A Little Princess*, Dostoyevsky's third Karamazov brother Alyosha, Dorothea Brooke in *Middlemarch*, and Jane Bennet in *Pride and Prejudice* seem to be clear INFPs.

Extroverted Thinking, the fourth and weakest function, is often the only link to any sort of pragmatism, and it provides one of the INFP's few defenses. Being so empathetic, they can easily be drawn into unusual situations and charitable giving that others would not tolerate. They need logic to draw boundaries around what they're willing to do, and they need logic and wit to defend themselves verbally. INFPs can be carried away on clouds of impossible idealism, so pragmatic Thinking permits occasionally breaking rules as a needed escape from self-repression.

Extroverted Thinking can come out as a surprisingly critical or even amoral sense of humor, which may seem at odds in an otherwise unaggressive, gentle person. Jane Austen's writing is a good example; she was herself gentle and kind, but her narration can be as sharply critical as satire. Although many of her characters are deeply moral in an Introverted Thinking way, Austen's narrating voice is very different. She is able to joke about situations that were, at the time, shocking and unthinkable.

INFPs take love and family life very seriously. With Introverted Feeling as their primary identity, they do not get over romantic break-ups quickly, and many INFPs feel that even when a relationship is over or there has been some breach, their ability to continue loving someone is unchanged. Introverted Feeling also assists long-term memory to be both clear and central, so INFPs are usually good at family traditions.

Disciplining children is not a strength for INFPs, though their idealism about how to treat people means they hold their children to very high standards of interpersonal behavior. They are more likely to talk and teach, trying to reach consensus and help children see what's right for themselves. They are reluctant to impose punishments and readily listen to a child's point of view about what happened. Children may find it easy to talk an INFP parent out of punishment, but they can't ever reduce the parent's high expectations of forgiveness and generosity. Above all, INFP parents and spouses demand absolute truth. Verbal truth, the highest value of warm conscience, is the INFP's best and perhaps only defense, so they usually insist and resist on this point, if on no other.

Please check the Appendix's list of biographies, for further reading.

CHAPTER 13

Variations and Imbalance

As you read the profiles, you may find yourself recognizing yourself, people you know well, or even characters from movies and books. Some people fit these ideal, balanced descriptions amazingly well. On the other hand, a lot of people nearly fit a description, but miss in just a few ways. They may be able to do things that the profile suggests they probably can't do, or the other way around. They may have similarities to two types so that it's unclear which one is the right match.

We could look at personality type as a set of boxes that everyone must fit into. But theory based on living systems tells us to expect variations. For one thing, if we take seriously the parallels between human personality and a brain function such as the way a rabbit remembers smells, we can see that some variation is necessary and good. The organized system of strengths and weaknesses is efficient by always handling things in a routine way. However, there is always a disrupting energy that constantly prepares to handle things in new ways if needed. It's efficient to do things automatically, but it's also efficient to survive in times of change. Inconsistency is a type of flexibility.

Even beyond this, it's in the variations that we start to find real human beings. A strikingly high number of people fit into the "boxes" of type profiles, but even among the ones who appear to fit well, there are always slight differences. Sometimes, the ways that they are different from the paradigm can help explain why they're feeling tired, anxious, or defeated. This is where the dynamic personality model starts to become a useful tool. It provides an ideal model that's close enough to who you actually are that you can recognize it, and then you can start to examine how you're different. Are these differences positive ones in your life? Sometimes they are, though most of the time they're felt as negative. But even positive differences change the balance of personality, perhaps shifting weakness to an apparently unrelated part of who you are.

Variations can be inborn. When we talk about a function like Thinking, we're grouping together a lot of different brain processing loops. Some are specifically for math or spatial reasoning, others for logical propositions, others connecting logic to sacred values and ideals, and so on. Each person with Thinking as one of the top two parts of personality might use one or another of these skills more than the others. Thinkers can be poor at academic mathematics, if they have learning disabilities in that area; they're still Thinkers in the way they approach life and they may still use mathematical reasoning in other ways. Thinkers might also be weak in logic, although this sounds like a contradiction. The personality can be organized around Thinking, not around relationships, but without educated facts for logic to operate on, or without clear logical control over emotions. When this happens, you're probably looking at an explosive temper.

It's easy to generalize that people with Extroverted Sensing organize their lives around sports or art, but talent can be unpredictable. There are some who have Extroverted Sensing in their personality, but with poor or average coordination, they never quite make the team. So what do they do with Sensing? It might draw some people into constant danger, like police work or storm-chasing, while pulling others toward sensory experiences like dance or working with food. There can be socially anxious people whose Extroverted Sensing, while real, does not stand out in the quiet ways they live. We can say the same things about Feeling and Intuition. Each one is the sum of many parts, and certain parts might be more prominent, changing the way the personality presents itself.

Another kind of inborn variation we may see is that people can have additional gifts, as though we're hanging extra little balls on the mobile. Harry Houdini, the escape artist whose personality seems to fit the ENTP pattern, was clearly also very gifted with Extroverted Sensing. It's not easy to tell if we should call him an ESTP who was very interested in ideas and inventions, or an ENTP with really good body control. The best way to capture Houdini, who was clearly an extraordinary man, is to allow that he may have had unusual gifts of Perceiving, so that putting him into a "box" isn't useful. We may have to call him an E(S/N)TP or something like that.

On the other hand, since the brain can't be good at everything at once, we'd expect to see some losses in ability with Judging functions. There may be some evidence that Houdini had difficulty with emotional processing. Houdini remained so deeply attached to his mother that when she died at a ripe old age, he was nearly incapacitated by grief. His brain's organization may have invested so heavily in Perceiving that it left other areas somewhat isolated and under-connected. It's a common pattern with people who appear gifted in multiple areas; the brain can't be super-connected in all areas, so unusual gifting in one area means a loss in another.

Environment plays a huge role in determining what sort of balance our personalities end up with. The ideal childhood for developing personality type provides first, complete freedom to be oneself with opportunities to experiment, and second, a parent who has the same personality type. Between modeling on the parent's example and having no pressures to become someone else, the result is an adult who comes as close as possible to matching the ideal paradigm of personality type. Minimal brain energy is used for difficult, unproductive mental processes. The adult of this type feels confident in identity and ability to succeed in tasks and challenges.

Very few people had this ideal childhood. Some had a happy childhood free of pressures to be someone else, but without a role model to copy. Others had a role model, but this advantage came with many pressures to measure up and conform. Others had a parent who modeled the personality type, but in dysfunctional ways that they don't want to copy. It's hard for them to pick apart the real type from the alcoholism, depression, or whatever else interfered with the parent's ability to function. And of course, there are many people who lost one of their parents or suffered other family crises that put many pressures on them.

When a child lives in a situation that makes him uncertain of survival, and the situation goes on for a long time, it begins to imbalance personality. For a child, of course, parental acceptance is part of the meaning of survival, so "survival" must be considered very broadly when we look at its impact on personality.

Let's go back to the original concept of inborn knowledge. Like animals, we have some innate templates of what the world should look like. Following Jung, I've divided these templates into four kinds, with each showing us a different aspect of how the world ought to be. Each personality balance includes two of these, one in a strong dominant position, the other as a background part. Together, they form the template of safety and danger. When the template is violated, we feel deep fear at an unconscious level. That is, sometimes we're conscious of it too, we know we're afraid. But there are many times, particularly in young children, when the fear is truly unconscious.

The effect of frequent, chronic unconscious fear is much greater than the effect of conscious fears, like fear of zombies or the dog next door. Unconscious fear happens at the level that can shape personality; conscious fears generally can't. Of course, fears aren't always separable; if a child lives through a natural disaster, the fear is both conscious and unconscious. But any therapist will agree that it's the unconscious one that persists, long after the child has moved far away from the ocean, the volcano, or whatever caused the disaster. We should never be surprised to see an unusual personality balance in someone whose early life included violence, death, or other kinds of severe losses, like becoming a refugee or surviving a natural disaster. Such sudden traumas may create attractor and repeller points that we can't see easily, ones that push the personality to adapt to very misshapen landscapes.

Some of the different effects of family stress on children may trace to what sort of danger template they're working with. Siblings put under the same pressure could turn out very different, as their brains adapt to handle the powerful repeller force of fear. Fear may chiefly affect how freely we can use our Introverted functions, since they are the ones keyed to idealism and danger.

Children whose danger templates are shaped by Feeling are very sensitive to any disturbance in parental love and acceptance. Parents who cause chronic stress to children with Introverted Feeling are often unaware of what they're doing, but to the child with Introverted Feeling, there's daily danger. A sibling with Introverted Thinking might handle it differently, perhaps better able to brush off purely emotional events. Similarly, unconventional or chaotic families may have a different effect on children whose Perceiving template is Introverted

Sensing or Introverted Intuition. Children with Introverted Sensing may respond by seeking safety in physical order and tradition, for example, becoming compulsive about cleanliness and neatness. Those with Introverted Intuition might respond by withdrawing from the Sensing world as much as possible, retreating into the mind to understand what's safe.

Additionally, stressful situations usually have some kind of reward, an attractor point, built into the wrong place. For example, a child might be led to ignore physical dangers if tolerating them means feeling safe in a parent's love. How far outside of normal safety a child will go depends on the inner templates, and on the strength of the dangers and rewards. Most children will go through fire to feel warmth and acceptance even for a short time. The reward of love shouldn't be so rare and conditional, but in stressful childhoods, it usually is. Some adults can look back and remember only one way to earn a mother's or father's approval, for example winning at something, needing care for being sick, making people laugh, or being friendly with people who made them uneasy. This reward might increase the brain's use of an Extroverted function, the optimistic, risk-taking part that takes on challenges.

The neural patterns set during childhood are very hard to change in adulthood. There are millions of adults whose personalities adapted to chronic stress in childhood. Sometimes, they live with the same stresses in adulthood without any concern, because it's what they're used to. They may be either too cautious or too hardened to danger. Alternatively, they may live in a situation with very different stresses and rewards, but their brains are still organized around the childhood situation. Feeling unloved, they exaggerate sickness, unconsciously expecting the old reward of attention. Feeling unsafe, they retreat into secrecy or compulsively clean the house. Feeling insecure, they put all energy into competing or they pick a fight. These actions were rewarded in childhood, but now they may not be. In fact, now these same actions might be harmful to others while not achieving that feeling of safety for self.

In this general description of how personality can adapt to stresses, we find the roots of many problems in adult life. While we can't change the way our personalities are organized, we can often make things much better by coming to see exactly how our personalities shifted. There's one basic truth that may guide us back to better management, and that is the knowledge that the ideal balance of personality is still present and relevant. Within the bounds of normal personality imbalances, the original "type" balance is still trying to function. It may respond well to conscious attempts to recreate the rewards and safety that it originally needed.

Personality can also be put under stress in adult years, although during childhood it successfully balanced in a typical way. The stresses are similar and have the same effect, but stress in adult years does not usually change us permanently. Instead, it changes us for a time, and we often feel it consciously. We know that we're anxious, angry, frustrated or defeated. In these cases, the key question is what needs to be changed to allow personality to go back to its state of rest. Sometimes the answer is obvious. If you're working 60+ hours a week, we don't need to search for a "hidden" cause of stress. But other times, the answer isn't obvious. Personality type can become a useful tool. Once you know your best match type, you may be able to see which parts of you are not in balance.

PATTERNS OF IMBALANCE

The scope of possible imbalances is almost infinite, since each family is a unique combination of certain personality types, multiplied by each brain's individual ways and the external challenges life brings. But we can look at some basic patterns that can be illustrated with the mobile. I'll demonstrate some different kinds of imbalance and how they might influence various personality types. In each case, we could be talking about either a formative childhood stress or a passing one in adult years. The type of imbalance is the same.

Let's look first at what can happen when the strongest function becomes even more important than it should be. In a way, it's the paradigm for other kinds of imbalance, and it's also the one type of imbalance that Carl Jung wrote about directly. As he explained each type of mental function, he talked about what could go wrong when it was out of control. I'm not going to quote Jung here but will continue instead to discuss imbalance in my own terms and observations, but if you're interested, those sections[89] in *Psychological Types* are insightful and easier to understand than some other chapters.

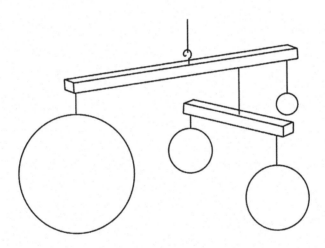

Fig. 13-1

We haven't labeled this mobile for any particular personality balances yet. The axis that's not balanced could be Judging or Perceiving; the too-large #1 ball could be Extroverted or Introverted. The effect of the imbalance will be significantly different, depending on

89: Carl Jung, "General Descriptions of the Types," *Psychological Types* (Princeton: Princeton/Bollingen, 1971), 577-665. After each section where he describes a mental function, he describes its "type," that is, what it would look like if it were swelled into such importance that it has taken over the personality. Jung used the word to describe imbalance (the opposite of how modern writers use it).

which balanced type we're talking about. When the top function is Extroverted and it becomes overly important, the effect on personality is always some loss of moral anchoring and predictability. When it's Introverted, the effects vary widely. I'll go through all of the possibilities, starting with ones where the imbalanced axis is Judging, and when the top function is Extroverted.

When Extroverted Thinking becomes too dominant in an ESTJ or ENTJ, its balancing function, Introverted Feeling, loses mental energy. Extroverted Thinking is the amoral, optimistic "green light" of logic; if it becomes overweening, then it does not permit Introverted Feeling to point out that some competition is cruel and some numbers will leave people hurting. It says "yes" to every way to win with numbers. Warm conscience goes silent, leaving only its permissive half.

It's not uncommon to see ESTJs or ENTJs with this balance problem. We usually view it as being a workaholic, because Extroverted Thinking is generally competing in earning money. Thinking may be so intent on building an organization that the person stops paying much attention to family and friends. Further, the ESTJ or ENTJ with out-of-control Thinking can't discern when the organization's goals need to be held back, not pressed forward. The end justifies the means, while self gets blurred with the project or cause. Introverted Feeling can't speak up for mercy or making exceptions to the rule.

ESFJs and ENFJs can fall into the opposite extreme, in which Extroverted Feeling takes energy from Introverted Thinking, which ought to be balancing it. Extroverted Feeling sees only green lights for social climbing. A mind imbalanced in this way probably knows, technically, that it's breaking rules. But Introverted Thinking is not creating the stab of fear that we know as conscience. Breaking the rule seems justified by the overwhelming value of getting ahead or pushing back an enemy.

Winning in Extroverted Feeling means gaining status and influence among people, which may involve money, but it may not. The Extroverted Feeler sees winning as an issue that's larger than self. He or she is probably the leader of a faction, one that believes terrible will things happen if the other side wins. Staying at the head of this faction means winning at all costs, elbowing out rivals and crushing enemies. Followers who don't obey must be punished. Without Introverted Thinking setting moral limits on numbers, this leader may end up involved in bribery, embezzling, blackmail, or slander.

On the other extreme, the Judging axis could be out of balance with an Introverted top function. When Introverted Judging becomes overly important, there is loss in flexible coping skills, since the Extroverted half of Judging is needed to deal with change and opportunity. Each personality balance presents a little different picture.

In the ISTP and INTP personalities, Introverted Thinking is supposed to be the King, but balanced by Extroverted Feeling. Extroverted Feeling's role is to understand the plain realities of social interaction, what's reasonable to expect from people.

Two things happen when Extroverted Feeling's balancing power is minimized by over-growth in Introverted Thinking. First, the ISTP or INTP has poor social skills. ISTPs become as silent as they can get away with, while INTPs may be silent or, on the other hand, talk obsessively about Thinking topics without regard for another's interest. Second, Introverted Thinking can become more judgmental than is typical in the ISTP's or INTP's personality.

Since it is an Introverted King, Thinking is not usually managing contact with the outside world. When it does, it gets angry. Its balancing side, Extroverted Feeling, is not strong enough to make compelling (and pragmatic) excuses about how people are just like this. Instead, Thinking condemns their mistakes and rule-breaking. The personality can't stop focusing on how wrong so many things are. It can also become perfectionist against itself.

In the ISFP and INFP personalities, Introverted Feeling is King, but if it takes too much energy away from Extroverted Thinking, there is a similar imbalance. Extroverted Thinking is able to be un-emotional, such as in managing money or time. Introverted Feeling, on the other hand, is not only emotional, it's deeply about identity. When Introverted Feeling tries to manage money, it becomes frightened because it can only think about numbers in terms of relationships and self-worth. If there isn't enough money, maybe it's because you aren't loved or failed to love someone else well enough.

In these extreme Introverted F types, Extroverted Thinking is the problem-solving engine for logical problems. When Introverted Feeling takes over logistics, every decision and plan is about relationships. Confronting a problem feels like not showing love, while saying "no" may lead to not being loved. Failure to manage a logistical problem means failure toward a person. Nothing is neutral. ISFPs and INFPs can both become deeply pessimistic about getting impersonal things to work out. They can also become self-critical, experiencing every problem in life as proof that they didn't love someone enough.

The same kind of imbalance can happen when the top function is a kind of Perceiving. The results are parallel to the imbalances seen in Judging. This isn't because Perceiving is about morality, but because any Introverted function, whether it's about decisions or process, is rooted in instinctive danger detection. Imbalanced Perceiving can still see and hear the world, but its sense of danger and opportunity gets skewed.

For example, ESTP and ESFP personalities both have Extroverted Sensing as the top function. Introverted Intuition is its balance; working together, they are supposed to evaluate opportunities and actions not just in the optimistic, positive way that an Extroverted function does. Introverted Intuition looks for the meaning of actions, trying to hold them together in a cohesive way, and it also evaluates for risk. Without this balance, Extroverted Sensing can get lost in opportunities for action without long-term plans. Such an imbalanced personality might answer an ad to teach overseas, come back and get a long-distance trucking license, then choose to train dogs. Each thing in itself has value, but there's little Intuition at work connecting them into a meaningful narrative. Previous ideas about the direction of career and life were made irrelevant by exploring each new opportunity. Living like this can work out, but it can also add up to a patchwork career with little to show at the end.

Relationships, too, can suffer from too much optimism about opportunity and too little sense of caution and meaning. Someone like this makes friends too easily, because the new avenues opened up by the friendship are so compelling. Old friends have shown their weaknesses and old opportunities have been tried. New opportunity can become almost an addiction. It feels very good to slip into the optimistic, expansive parts of who we are. The Introverted half of Perceiving might be still functioning a little bit, but its arguments for caution, research and screening aren't compelling, compared to the reckless optimism of imbalance.

Extroverted Intuition can go out of balance to very similar effect. Its reckless optimism is less about exploring places, jobs, and activities, but heedlessly dashing toward new ideas can lead to the same things. It should be balanced not only by Judging conscience, but also by Introverted Sensing, the other half of Perceiving. Introverted Sensing should at least narrow down options by making some of them seem out of place or just not right for that person. Ideally, Introverted Sensing creates a firm sense of self, one that can't just do or think literally anything. When it doesn't, too many doors stay open. Whenever we choose to go through one door, we have to accept closing others.

So ENTPs and ENFPs, who both have Extroverted Intuition as their dominant function, can become either indecisive or heedlessly decisive when this imbalance happens. They will trust new people too easily, or maybe enter on new ventures without considering the downside. Operating entirely in the optimistic, expansive, can-do arena of Extroverted Perceiving is a little bit like being manic. If the Judging conscience isn't doing its work, ENFPs and ENTPs might both wander into doing unethical or unkind things. But even without moral mistakes, out of control Intuition may campaign for philosophies, theories, candidates, friends, new fields of study and new inventions without any ballast.

Introverted Sensing is the top function for ISTJs and ISFJs. If it becomes even more important than it should be, then the Extroverted Intuition that acts as its balance loses influence. As we just discussed, Extroverted Intuition is optimistic and expansive; it tries to solve problems. If it loses its proper role, optimism is gone. Introverted Sensing is tied to a template of safety and danger, so it's very alert to things being out of place. It doesn't generate possibilities, but instead it compares things to an ideal that is rarely satisfied. So when it takes over even more of personality than it's supposed to have, it causes a general negativity.

Introverted Sensing is also supposed to be balanced by either Thinking or Feeling in its Extroverted form. If Introverted Sensing is completely overwhelming this too, the personality may sink into anxiety and withdrawal from society. The parts that are supposed to be confident, outgoing and practical are drowned out by incessant note-taking of what's wrong: things don't look right, people are acting strange, and we're on the edge of danger. An over-active Introverted Sensing might look like compulsive or obsessive behavior. Where true OCD causes compulsive, meaningless actions like re-washing hands too many times, the compulsive negative observation of Introverted Sensing remains basically meaningful, but overblown. The person expects the worst, flinches from change, and finds nothing good enough.

Introverted Intuition can also be a top function, though in a small number of personalities. When an INTJ or INFJ sinks into too much use of Introverted Intuition, there is a similar look of obsessive and compulsive thinking. In each personality balance, Extroverted Sensing is supposed to be balancing Intuition, and so is an Extroverted form of Thinking or Feeling. If Introverted Intuition is out of balance, it loses sight of opportunity, possibility and optimism. It knows only that there may be some hidden danger. Finding this hidden danger means studying and pondering, carefully examining all sides of some situation. Every appearance is mistrusted as a false front or mask.

Introverted Intuition can fall into a cycle of regression that strays toward mental illness. Since it is so keenly aware of ideals and dangers, it is also aware that it's out of balance. It can detect that the personality is too anxious, withdrawn, pensive and circumspect; so it sets out to solve the problem. Unfortunately, it has only one strategy, which is more study and pondering. It's really unable to rescue the personality by itself; the more it tries, the worse things get. After a while, the vicious cycle has Introverted Intuition questioning absolutely everything, including obvious facts and even reality itself.

All of these imbalance problems stem from the top function becoming too strong. It needs to be decisively strong, but in these cases it's handling work it isn't meant to handle. Life problems begin to pile up; they're caused by rash decisions or indecision, being too trusting or too cynical, and so on. The personality can't see how to solve these problems, because it's probably looking at them with that same strongest function. Extroverted Sensing wants to solve its problems by rushing into another venture, Introverted Feeling wants to solve them by being more and more idealistic and obsessive about perfect love, and Extroverted Thinking tries to solve them by cooking the financial books and competing harder. Each strongest function can become isolated in problems of its own making, unable to see how to change.

What does this look like on the outside? It could look like legal problems, up to and including arrest warrants and jail time. It could look like depression and anxiety; chronic indecision leads to repeated failure, which is depressing. Chronic negativity could lead someone toward divorce or family divisions. Unbounded exploration could involve serious betrayals of family and friends. In other words, personality imbalance could come to your attention as big, serious, insoluble problems, just as much as it might look like smaller stresses and foibles.

Personality imbalance may be somewhat fixable. It depends; there are cases when the imbalance seems to be part of the permanent brain wiring, and in those cases the label "personality disorder" may apply. But let's look at the people who have an underlying proper balance, but for various reasons got pushed out of using it properly. The balancing function is present, it's just minimized. What should they do?

The first step is to be sure of the right match with a balanced personality type. You may need to look at behavior and feelings that aren't part of daily life to find evidence of an underlying type. Look at how the person behaved in childhood, in case the imbalance got worse later. Look at how they behave in extreme stress and, by contrast, in times of no stress or duties at all. Look also at times when they recall being happy or peaceful; what was different at that time, in terms of experiencing and reacting to the world? Once you know that you're looking at a certain personality type, but imbalanced, of course you also need to see what the imbalance is. Is it in an Extroverted zone, causing risk-taking and shallow decisions? Or is it more Introverted, causing anxiety and caution? Is it in relationships, logic, actions in the world, or understanding meaning?

When you know what the problem is, there are two ways to approach a solution. It can help the imbalanced person to see why the imbalance is happening. What's pushing and pressuring him or her to over-use or under-use some of their strengths? When does it happen? What triggers it? This is part of traditional talk therapy, and it's clearly the first step. But second, how can this person begin to rebalance personality? There is probably some concrete action that he or she could take. Usually, in fact, there's pressure to make a decision right now, and the decision has this imbalance tied into it. Going with the imbalance means one decision, while going against it, trying to rebalance, means another completely different one.

Let's start with the last example, when Introverted Intuition has spun out of control. It's in a vicious cycle, trying to think its way out of the problem. This probably looks like reading a lot of self-help, philosophy or religion books. Intuition is looking for a theory that will connect all the dots. The harder it searches for the right theory, the more flaws it sees in every single one, until it concludes that life has no meaning at all. Only Extroverted Sensing can save this personality by drawing energy away from frenetic Intuition. Instead of seeking a better theory, the person needs to find ways to move and Sense in the world.

With a routine of physical movement and sensation, the brain begins to rebalance its Perceiving abilities. More sensory data is pouring in; energy is shifted away from introspective pondering. It's important to add that there's nothing wrong with introspective pondering, but here we're talking about its having been locked into a self-defeating cycle of negativity. It won't shrivel up and go away; it's still such a strong part of personality that even if it's deliberately drowned out by music, dance, karate and pottery-making, it will still be assertive and try to see meaning.

When an Introverted function has gone out of control, the solution is in the Extroverted functions that balance it. There is one that's on the same axis, both are Perceiving or both are Judging; there's another that's the opposite. This person who's trying to use Sensing to stop runaway Intuition can also lean on Extroverted Thinking or Feeling, whichever one is a strength. If it's Feeling, probably negative Intuition has been suggesting that group dynamics are not safe, optimistic opportunities, but instead they're just mistakes waiting to be made. If it's Thinking, Intuition sees danger in competing and trusting logic. So to help rebalance, this person needs to find some simple steps toward using the Extroverted part more. Join a group and push back against the anxiety until it gets better. Take a programming class or some other Thinking kind of thing, and give the search for meaning a rest. It won't go away, it will remain assertive; the worst you can do to it is just rebalancing it back into its correct size.

Very similar things can be said about Introverted Sensing, which goes out of control by compulsive criticism of how things look. To fix this, the Extroverted sides need more exercise. Extroverted Intuition should solve puzzles or read about new ideas; pick up a history of some faraway place and culture or read about science discoveries. Whichever Judging function is strongest, it too should be exercised consciously. It's Extroverted, so it is oriented to solving problems, not hiding from them.

When the Extroverted function spins out of control, we see rash decisions, randomness, and sometimes a lack of ethical behavior. The remedy isn't within the overgrown Extroverted strength, but instead it's in the two Introverted balances. Extroverted Feeling is balanced by Introverted Thinking's moral care of rules and numbers, and also by one of the Introverted Perceiving modes (Sensing or Intuition). The Introverted functions feel that there's one best way that things ought to look, mean, feel or add up to. An imbalanced Extroverted mind has to find ways to exercise them.

We tend to look for ways to rebalance personality and solve the original problem at the same time. This is great, but it may not be realistic. Rebalancing personality may call for smaller steps that aren't immediately connected to the looming issues. Rebalancing may be relatively simple or it may take several years.

Our minds want to be balanced. Imbalance happens when we're under chronic stress; it doesn't feel good even if it helped us survive the stress. Moving back toward balance may feel "wrong" or dangerous, but it usually feels secretly right, too. Sometimes it's pure relief to realize that the "right answer" according to a personality system is actually the one you wanted to do all along, but thought you shouldn't or couldn't.

CASE STUDIES OF NORMAL IMBALANCE

Let's look at some case studies, based on real life examples. All of the five personalities presented here are normal. They're able to take care of life, but they feel anxious, sad, or under-rewarded. They feel like something is wrong, but it's not clear what needs to change. When we compare each person to the theoretical balanced type, we can gain some insight on how life stresses pushed them into just enough imbalance to make life more difficult than it needs to be. I've based these studies on stories and people I've known, but all names (which begin with letters A-E) and circumstances have been changed.

1. The Controller, the Pleaser and the Gamer

Linda, a mother in her 60s, has three adult children. Her life has been marked by hardship, beginning with the death of her children's father in a highway accident when they were young. She moved back to the rural New England town where her grandparents could help out, and after a few years, she married an old high school acquaintance. He has been a fireman and trucker, but the poor rural economy disrupts his career, sometimes forcing him to work out of the area. They live in a small house with appliances frequently broken. After a few years of recurring depression, Linda developed physical symptoms and was diagnosed with Multiple Sclerosis. Her progression is slow and she is still able to do most things, but forgetfulness and depression limit her life even where walking doesn't. We're going to look at the differing ways that her children's personalities were influenced by these difficulties.

Annie, the oldest, is now 32; her baseline personality type is ENTJ. In early childhood, when her father was alive and they lived in the city, Annie was strong-willed and argumentative. She was tested for gifted programming, but in the summer before second grade, Annie was injured in the same accident that killed her father. When the family moved to the country, Annie slowly recovered, but she had difficulty concentrating, possibly from a slow-healing head injury. The rural school didn't have gifted programming anyway.

As she went through her school years, Annie had to pick up a large share of chores in addition to schoolwork. Her original argumentativeness grew quiet, internalized as determination to figure out a way to get out of the poverty cycle. Introverted Intuition, her second function, grew very strong. When her mother was sick and her stepfather was out of the area, Annie picked up a lot of the housework, but as a Thinker, she did not know how to cope with her mother's depression. She insulated herself with homework and began planning how to make her own life free from financial instability. When she was 16, the family's only car for a while was a borrowed truck with a snowplow attached. Determined to get a driver's license without taking such a monster vehicle into the niceties of parallel parking, she persuaded a teacher to lend her his car for the test.

As soon as Annie graduated from high school, she used her babysitting savings to start at a state university. Freed from chores by living away from home, she got good grades and finished college on scholarships. She became a teacher, with an eye to the financial stability of tenure, but also partly because some of her best role models had been teachers, like the one who lent his car. When she got a Master's degree and was hired by a large district in the city, Annie felt she had made it. She married a fellow teacher and for a few years, they saved money to buy a nice house.

Annie's first and only child was diagnosed with cerebral palsy. Annie had to stop working, since her daughter's needs were more severe than day care could manage. She hoped to get back into her tenure track as Elizabeth got older, but when Elizabeth was school-age, Annie found that all of her energy was taken up fighting a school district that expected Elizabeth to cope with a mainstream classroom. Elizabeth's IQ was within normal as far as anyone could tell, but she had vision and hearing problems that were hard to define, in addition to her limited motor control. The school claimed that Elizabeth's needs were met by sitting in the front row of a classroom and going to special ed pull-out classes half the time. Annie wanted the district to send Elizabeth to a special-needs school on the other side of the city, but the district refused to spend the money as long as Annie could not prove that Elizabeth's needs were not met, legally.

Annie's home is highly organized; she keeps all meetings and records in a planning book. After school, Elizabeth's time is equally organized as her mother tries various therapies to keep her muscles as toned as possible. Friends remind Annie to "take time for yourself," but Annie replies that there really isn't time. She is working with two outside agencies to prove that Elizabeth's needs aren't being met, and there is always paperwork to file for Medicaid, special needs summer camp scholarships, and the endless round of testing and evaluations. Life is like a detective novel that never ends; teachers, aides and agencies must be constantly checked and cross-checked.

Annie feels unfulfilled in this life. She loves her daughter and tries to maintain a good relationship with her husband, but she is usually tensed for the next crisis. She is afraid that her planning for financial stability was all for nothing. If her husband lost his job, as her stepfather so often did, they would lose their house. If Elizabeth could get into the special school, Annie might be able to work again, so when she feels most anxious about financial instability, she redoubles her efforts to battle the school.

Annie's original ENTJ personality was meant to have competitive Extroverted Thinking in a leading position, with Introverted Intuition acting as an assistant detective. Her personality type has not changed, but in the hardships of her childhood, Extroverted Sensing and Introverted Intuition had to determine most of what she did. She worked hard at chores, using her senses and movement to move faster and lift heavy objects without hesitation. Introverted Intuition studied the people around her, looking for any small tweaks she could make to her life so that she'd be a little bit ahead. Intuition successfully found helpers at key times, like for getting her driver's license, and it continues to be her mainstay in studying her daughter's needs. Extroverted Thinking does not have a leading role in her life, but it's still an element in her personality.

Friends, and especially her sister Brooke, consider Annie much too aggressive. They call her "controlling" and sometimes say they pity poor Elizabeth, always being worked on by therapists. They are uncomfortable with how Annie schemes to get every possible agency and scholarship for Elizabeth. Annie's just a 7th grade math teacher, and now a full-time mom, but she acts like she's competing against the entire world for the last scrap of bread. They worry that she "needs help."

Extroverted Thinking's competitive spirit was suppressed and diverted by the hardships of Annie's life, but it comes out when she is fighting the school. If Annie's father had lived and her mother had been well, if they had lived in the city with competitive school programs, Annie could have become a lawyer or banker. In her current life, her competitive, strategic abilities seem too aggressive, and she doesn't have them backed up by a law degree or wealth.

Introverted Intuition, which should be her second mental function, has always been her rescuer, first identifying the dangers of poverty, then planning a way out, and now working to recover her own career independence by defeating the school district's budget caution. Annie isn't really happy, because Intuition isn't actually her strongest part. Her personality was geared to rejoice in winning, just as in early childhood she loved winning arguments. Instead, she is surviving and constantly scanning for danger. She's doing okay, but she doesn't feel good about her accomplishments. Somewhere in her brain, it's still hard-wired that she should have been negotiating bank mergers.

Brooke is 29 and generally can't deal with her sister Annie. She lives just a few miles from Linda and spends a lot of time helping her mother. Brooke's underlying personality type is INFJ. She did very well in school and for a while she wanted to go to college and major in English or psychology. But during childhood, her chief role in the family was to comfort and understand her mother. Brooke's top personality function is Introverted Intuition, which was very pained by perceiving the depth of Linda's sorrows. Her second mental function is Extroverted Feeling, which came to the rescue. Extroverted Feeling allowed Brooke to be the perfect child, one who seemed older than her years. She knew exactly what to say to everyone.

When Brooke's stepfather seemed distant and impatient with Linda's fragility, Brooke found ways to smooth things over so that he eased back on his criticism. When Annie seemed coldly efficient, Brooke picked up that their mother felt guilty for not being well enough to work. She set aside her own homework for later and helped Linda work on a craft project that she could feel good about, something Linda would have been too tired or depressed to keep up without Brooke's help. Brooke's peace of mind came from seeing her mother's sadness or pain relieved.

Brooke's friends at school loved having someone they could lean on. She was very popular because she never offended anyone. Although her Introverted Intuition and Thinking secretly found fault with many of the silly or short-sighted things the other kids did, Extroverted Feeling kept her from ever letting on. When Annie went away to college, Brooke did most of the work that their mother could not keep up with, but even so, Brooke always found time to listen and counsel friends over their problems with boys or with each other.

Brooke went away to college for one year. During that year, Linda's MS symptoms grew worse, and Brooke felt horribly guilty for not being there to help. She didn't return in the fall; there wasn't spare money anyway. Working part-time, she did manage to get a Licensed Practical Nurse certificate. The LPN skills helped her care for her mother, and she worked at a nearby nursing home, mainly nights. Brooke's boyfriend graduated from college, married her and found work in the county government.

If you asked Brooke if her life is happy, she would immediately say yes. Everything is great and everyone is wonderful. On the other hand, if you were yourself unhappy and frustrated, she would depict herself as also unhappy, in a sympathetic way. If you say that having kids is wonderful, she'll sigh and say that someday soon she'll start a family; if you say it's better not to have kids, she'll agree that now just isn't the time and her job is plenty. If you ask her to help with a church project, she will agree to it. But she's very likely to call you the day before and apologize profusely for not making it, because her mother is having a bad spell. When her husband talks about moving to the state capital for a promotion, she says this would be wonderful and agrees with whatever he says. However, she takes on some extra nursing care for a neighbor's relative and tells her husband that she really can't leave the area quite yet, not until things are easier.

Basically, Brooke never says "no." Secretly, she may sometimes think "no," because Introverted Intuition is still watching the world with often critical eyes. Introverted Intuition is aware that sometimes the inner Brooke doesn't quite agree with the outer one. But in childhood, she perceived her mother's depression as a serious threat to family life. Extroverted Feeling allowed her to please everyone at once, merely at the cost of her own inner integrity. It was a small price to pay at the time; she didn't even notice the cost, because Intuition was intent on strategic social behavior that would neutralize the dangers.

Now, placating everyone with Extroverted Feeling is not only habit but also her established social identity, which her friendships and even her marriage are based on. Above all, her relationship with her mother is still based on constant emotional companionship and soothing. If she's aware of the loss of self now, she feels guilty because it seems like not loving her mother enough. Her mother is used to leaning on Brooke, so without realizing it, sometimes she reinforces Brooke's sense of guilt. When Brooke's husband persuaded her to take a vacation out of state, Linda was so anxious about her absence that Brooke inwardly vowed not to let that happen again.

If Brooke's natural personality balance placed Extroverted Feeling first, she would probably see her mother's challenges as something she needs to conquer and control, not serve. Extroverted Feeling can make someone into a social leader, but for Brooke, it acts only to compensate for Introverted Intuition's perception of danger and loss. Instead of becoming a social leader who uses her resources to placate her mother or get other people to help, she stays in the subordinate position of continual servant. She feels best about herself when her mother or her friends say they would be lost without her. Brooke may go on for a number of years like this without any real change, but eventually, something will happen to challenge her need to say yes to everyone.

The youngest of Linda's children is a son named Cody, now 26. Cody's baseline personality is INTP, and in early school years he was a whiz kid. He learned everything quickly and sometimes got called "the smart one." Of course, this wasn't quite fair since his older sisters were using their intelligence to survive academically and socially, but people aren't fair. But Cody was born late enough in the 1990s that computer games became a big part of his life. His reaction to the stress of home life was not to survive by striving harder or pleasing people, but to escape into a world where stress could always be overcome by beating the boss and leveling up.

By the time Cody was in high school, he did only enough homework to get by. He was bright enough to keep his grades up at first, but by late high school, there were problems. Cody didn't seem to notice; he was impatient if anyone tried to talk to him about school. He had joined an online games team and spent most of his evenings (and well into the night) on "TeamSpeak," discussing skills and strategy. After he graduated from high school, he tried to go to college, but he didn't pay much attention to his class schedule. He completely forgot to attend one of the classes, and for the others, he forgot about half the time. Eventually he had to go home.

Cody's most dominant mental function should be Introverted Thinking; he's definitely competitive and logical in games, and at times he has been good at programming and math. His personality type isn't really in question, but it doesn't appear that he's applying Introverted Thinking to his own life. Now that he's 26, he does get to work on time, but he has been careless with many numerical issues in real life, from time to money to grade points. He's highly accurate concerning numbers in games.

Extroverted Intuition, his second function, has invested heavily in the online experience. Earlier in childhood, he was often worried by the disorder and inabilities at home. When he lived in his imagination, playing a game, all that vanished. In his Extroverted Intuition, he felt optimistic and powerful. Introverted Thinking made him very good at games, and its competitive sense was satisfied by each game's many rewards. Leaving the computer, he had to face his mother's growing disability and his father's current employment problems. When he was facing the real world, Thinking sternly showed him his own problems, but they were too overwhelming. Invariably, he returned to the imaginary world as soon as possible. By his 20s, it was a settled habit, and it also formed his conscious identity. If anyone criticized him, he had logical arguments for why computer games weren't bad, and sometimes he started to prove that he could still be smart by taking a college course or starting to learn a new programming language. But so far, in his early adult years, Introverted Thinking has not been able to steer him into the hard discipline of improving life for real. When he faces his real-world problems, he finds them very depressing. The soaring freedom of being a winner with Extroverted Intuition could be described as addictive. After any frustration or defeat, he turns to his games to "feel better."

Annie, Brooke and Cody are ordinary people without serious problems, but they are all unhappy. All of the siblings have an imbalance problem in common, although it's seen in quite different personality types. Their sense of insecurity in childhood made them all lean more on their second function. In each case, it's something they're good at; Annie is good at using her intuitive strategy to get around intimidating problems, Brooke is good at reading and helping people, and Cody is good at imagination and exploration of ideas. But all three imbalances were shaped by stress and fear.

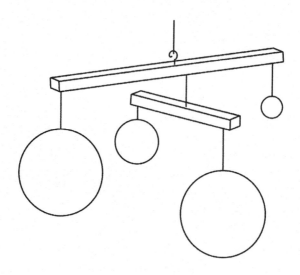

Fig. 13-2

Annie the ENTJ was most ambitious, but too many problems in life conspired to pull her down. In a perfect life, she could have been aware of strategy and danger while using optimistic Extroverted Thinking to take risks and compete. Instead, she survived by elevating cautious Introverted Intuition to a survival skill; now her mind feels the heavy burden of caution and negativity. Brooke the INFJ internalized her mother's depression and guilt at being sick, so that her primary function, Introverted Intuition, grew overwhelmed at the burden. She survived by bringing Extroverted Feeling's optimistic, pragmatic skills to the fore, so that she spends most of her time telling people what they want to hear. Cody the INTP avoided the uncomfortable logic of Introverted Thinking, instead using his optimistic, exploring Extroverted Intuition to create a happy world where success came easily.

Anyone who has lived among people knows that Annie, Brooke and Cody may never solve their problems. They could turn to substance abuse or getting other people to shore them up. However, let's imagine that all three of them become aware of the ways in which their personalities have become imbalanced. Give them five or six years to use this information, because change takes time.

Annie is finally able to get her daughter into the special school, and instead of going back to teaching, she takes a risk. Using a one-time inheritance, she gets a law degree. It feels terribly risky, but she actually loves the work. Even in law school, the training in adversarial argument comes easily to her; it makes her feel happy. As an attorney, she works for a non-profit that represents disabled people.

Brooke made a really hard decision; she finally agreed to move away from her mother. In their new location, she trains as a Physician's Assistant, then works in a doctor's office. She is still very much involved with people, but now Introverted Intuition is evaluating when it's time to deliver bad news, even if it's just the word "no." She and Annie are able to hire a part-time carer for Linda's needs, and on her stepfather's retirement, their life seems to settle into a routine. When there are problems back at home, Brooke struggles and then remembers that not everything is her fault.

Cody began dating a local girl, but just when his external life seemed to compete with the computer world, they went through a painful break-up. For a few weeks, everyone worried about Cody. It seemed like ten years of avoided bad news all fell on him at once. He stayed in his room and spent a lot of time staring at the wall. But this painful period was fruitful; Cody accepted the worst news that Introverted Thinking was able to deliver, while Extroverted Intuition cheerfully pointed out that he could change. This time, Intuition's optimistic good ideas weren't driven by needing to avoid Introverted Thinking. Looking around at opportunities, he went to stay with Annie for a few semesters, helping with Elizabeth before school. He wasn't very keen on disabled child care, but Elizabeth's needs forced him to stay in the real world. He succeeded by getting her on the bus, not beating a boss. He got a technical degree and moved out on his own. He still plays games, but the addictive edge is gone.

2. The Tired Architect and the Anxious Soprano

Dinesh and Eryka don't know each other, but they share an important life stress. They are both from minority families that are very conscious of the disastrous effects of failure. They both needed to be more capable than they actually were, sort of larger than life. In doing so, they developed not only skills but reactions and processes that don't belong to their natural personalities. As they get into middle age, both are beginning to wear out.

Dinesh's parents were immigrants whose families gambled their savings on establishing the next generation in a new country . His older sister succeeded easily at school and became a doctor. As he grew up, he felt a little detached from the family's ambitions. He was interested in the poetry of his parents' native language, and he learned to play the guitar. His one big academic success in early years was placing fourth at the regional spelling bee, which he found easy since he was good with words. Dinesh's personality is INFP; if he had been born to money and leisure, he would have become a poet or, in modern terms, a singer-songwriter.

Dinesh was too sensitive and squeamish to go into medicine, and although he got good grades in math, he knew he did not want to be an engineer. He liked to draw, and he loved beautiful buildings, so a guidance counselor suggested he try architecture. That was an acceptable choice in his family, so he quickly went through college and then got a Master's degree. He was not as keen on buildings as some of his fellow students, but he did well. He used his two Extroverted parts, Intuition and Thinking, for the technical work. Thinking had always been the academic work-horse, carrying him through math, physics and the basic engineering courses required for architecture. His Extroverted strengths became like an alternative personality, the "manly" one that won praise and earned money.

Dinesh's early years at work were often spent out of doors, at construction sites, as the supervisor on duty. In order to be good at this work, he had to develop abilities in Extroverted Sensing, to go with his Extroverted Intuition and Thinking. Sensing is part of everyone's abilities, to a point, since we all use our senses; Dinesh just trained his senses in particular ways. He learned to tolerate a great deal of noise, which used to bother his more perfectionist Introverted Sensing, and he became an expert in concrete.

By his mid-career, Dinesh was an excellent architect: imaginative, intuitive, logical, accurate, and "hands on" with the materials. He had a family of his own by now, in addition to supporting his grandmother who helped with the children. Everything really looked like it was going well. His father was glad that he deterred his boy from studying poetry and ending up as a poorly-paid academic, or worse, a starving musician.

The problem is that Dinesh is growing deeply tired. His wife suggested that perhaps he is depressed, so he talked to a doctor and tried an anti-depressant. It made him feel somewhat better, but he still feels increasingly impatient, resentful, and just tired. He finds himself reluctant to go to bed early, the way he always did. It's been especially bad since he made a trip back to the old country, where he took a number of close-up photos of ancient architecture details and materials. The slideshow delighted his family and colleagues, but for some reason, it made him melancholy. He made an ink sketch of some fancy ironwork and felt compelled to complete the sketch into a finished piece that might be used for a card. He made a few more, then set them aside. He also began playing not just the guitar, but also a vintage ethnic stringed instrument from a village. He's been buying poetry books, too.

There's nothing wrong with any of these things, but Dinesh finds that when he indulges his taste for beauty in music or art, he feels deeply and strangely resistant to the concrete and steel side of his profession. He complains about trends in architecture today, looking at the old Art Deco and Gilded Age buildings that spared no expense on carved marble or patterned bricks. But the fact is inescapable: somehow he's just tired of his profession. He spends a few years in a cycle of losing interest, then suddenly feeling stung by looming failure and guilt, setting aside his hobbies and pushing himself back into the old Dinesh. It works for a while, but every time it wears out again. He's also lonely; he feels like people don't really know him. His life has little use for the Introverted Feeling that is actually the largest part of his personality. He has children, but they are busy with school and only know him as their busy father.

Eryka's problem is parallel in a technical way, but it looks very different. It began when she went to college, the first person in her family to do so. Her singing talent was so outstanding that although her parents were afraid of the expense and risk involved in higher education, they could not deny that she was special. They often reminded her not to plan for a "musician" career, but instead to add something sensible, like teaching, so that she could pay back her student loans and be secure. The family stretched itself to get her through college, and Eryka repaid her parents by taking their advice. Her voice was trained for classical music, in addition to the pop and Gospel she'd grown up with. She got a secondary teaching certificate, too, and not long out of college, she landed a coveted job at a magnet arts school.

Eryka's personality type is ESTP, virtually the opposite of Dinesh's. Her two Extroverted parts are Sensing and Feeling, giving her a natural place in all social music activities. She loves to sing for large crowds and feels caught up in the music, as if it's something bigger than herself. In college, she auditioned for some opera roles and tried out some voice competitions, and she always did well, a natural competitor due to her cool Introverted Thinking.

But the pressure to get a good teaching position and then hold onto it against all rivals has pushed Eryka to develop another side that isn't natural to ESTPs. Her mother was a naturally neat, organized person and used to nag Eryka to do better. During student teaching, Eryka realized that being super organized made her a better teacher. Her grade books took hours to put together; everything is perfectly in order, perfectly updated, so that at any moment's notice she can give a detailed report on each student. In addition to this skill, of course she is also still so talented in her own singing that her students all try to emulate her. Her Extroverted people skills make her a classroom natural; she manages kids with skill and humor. Her teacher evaluations are always outstanding and in a few years, she moves up to Vocal Director for the whole school.

The problem is completely hidden from her work colleagues, because it comes out at home. Eryka married her college boyfriend and they have two small children. While their home also looks perfect, Eryka finds that when she's at home, everyone is stepping on her last nerve. She yells at her children, although she would never yell at her students. She's critical and tense around her husband, which surprises him because the girl he knew in college was fun-loving and nonjudgmental. She begins to be a worrier.

After a few more years, Eryka is given a chance to spend some time giving vocal concerts and touring with some other singers. Her husband's work is providing a stable income and benefits, so she decides to take the chance and do it. It's a pay cut, but her teaching career will benefit from some more high-profile concerts. The plain truth is that she loves being back in performing. When the concerts are going well, she can't quite remember why she ever became a teacher, apart from the reliability of the pay. When she's doing concerts in her own area or has returned from a short regional tour, Eryka is more easy-going at home. She thinks maybe it's because the kids are school age now, but they don't seem to try her patience the way they used to. Her husband finds her happier and more interested in both doing fun things and having sex.

But then Eryka's husband is laid off, and while he is having to find a new career path, she must go back to teaching. She becomes the vocal director at a prep school, working with a talented children's choir and preparing juniors and seniors for college auditions. She throws herself into the work, which is fun and rewarding. At the private school, her perfect gradebook and polished manners are even more important. Eryka becomes larger than life; she can sing, touch people's emotions while reading them intuitively, teach effectively, and maintain high standards that the school is proud of. Several local colleges are putting out feelers for possible interest in working for them.

At home, she is back to being critical and impatient. Worse, she has started to suffer from panic attacks, sometimes waking up in the night with irrational terrors. As the anxiety becomes a more crippling problem, a pattern starts to emerge. When school is out and Eryka only schedules some concerts for herself, she stops having panic attacks for the most part. They return when she's teaching. Anxiety medication is a losing battle because higher doses make her sleepy, which makes her a much less effective teacher.

What's going on here? Under intense pressure to succeed, Eryka has developed a fifth personality strength. Her mother was naturally organized and neat, with Introverted Sensing. Following her mother's role model, Eryka develops Introverted Sensing as an add-on to her

ESTP personality. It isn't naturally there, but she could imitate her mother, and that trait was highly rewarded in teaching.

Introverted Sensing is directly competing with Extroverted Sensing for mental energy. It turns out that she can really only use one of them at a time. When she teaches, it's the Introverted one, which forms a sort of voting block with Introverted Thinking and Intuition. Together, they notice everything that isn't ideal. It's useful in teaching, since it helps her to see what's wrong in a student's approach, or to set high standards in her own organizing. But it's really too much negativity and idealism.

Extroverted Sensing, her natural strength, loses energy to Introverted Sensing as if a switch is being flipped from one to the other. The switch can flip the other way, too. When she sings in a concert, the intense experience of becoming a musical instrument, feeling every breath, muscle tone and vibration, turns off Introverted Sensing. She becomes like her younger self, the talented singer but not the accomplished teacher. As soon as she gets out the grade book and faces a student, Extroverted Sensing switches off as Introverted Sensing takes over. She again becomes a perfectionist.

Extroverted Sensing and Feeling are the optimistic, expansive, can-do sides of her personality. When she's at work, Extroverted Feeling is still active because she is in a group of people. It's when she is alone at home, or with just her family, that the negative, critical, worrying Introverted voting block takes over. Her natural Introverted parts of Thinking and Intuition are joined by the unnatural one, Sensing, which is still on duty from a day of teaching. With three mental functions scanning life for flaws and dangers, she is overwhelmed with anxiety.

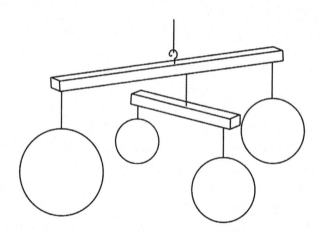

Fig. 13-3

Dinesh and Eryka are not in the early stages of life, as Annie, Brooke and Cody were. For the younger people, learning about personality imbalances led to changing career directions. Maybe Dinesh and Eryka, both now in their late 40s, will be able to make radical changes, but it's not likely. They need to find solutions within the choices they have already made. Let's say they both become aware of what the issues are. They can see their underlying balanced personality type, and they both recognize that their happiest times have been when they lived most in harmony with it. Now what?

Dinesh has about 15 years until retirement, and he doesn't feel there is an option to stop his career. There is, however, a basic decision he can make, to expand or to cut back a little. He understands that the profound fatigue comes from having lived mainly out of his Extroverted strengths, and not only that, but having developed Extroverted Sensing abilities that aren't really natural to him. He decides to cut back a little, instead of the more "sensible" choice to keep pushing forward and expanding his role in the partnership.

Dinesh needs to find a way to bring Introverted Feeling and Introverted Sensing into a more central role. With this insight, he realizes that one of his children is very much like him. His middle son, who is in early high school, gets good grades but is only motivated by art, music and stories. The family has already been warning the boy not to indulge those tastes, because they can't be financially successful. Dinesh realizes that while he has no answers to that conundrum, he can at least befriend his ENFP son in a way that he hasn't done before, and in a way that nobody did for him, when he was that age. He offers to spend several evenings a week helping his son study the family's native language, especially the poetry that once fascinated him. Studying poetry leads to talking about other things, and they become friends.

His wife and other children see a side of Dinesh that they were only distantly aware of. He continues to work at his career, but he no longer invests his identity in it. The family plans a trip to the old country to take photographs of its classic architecture, which had originally made him love buildings. His son asks if they can publish a book about what they find. And somewhere in that process, Dinesh does not feel so alone or weary. He is now using both Introverted Feeling and Introverted Sensing in integrated ways.

Eryka and her husband decide to focus on freeing her from teaching, even if it takes a year or two. She is still anxious and critical, but she starts to see it happening and can sometimes pull out of the tailspin. She realizes that every time she invests in her own vocal practice, it activates Extroverted Sensing. After an hour of singing, she feels confident that life will work out okay. Instead of working harder on teaching and slighting her own practice time, she begins to book more special concerts that force her to sing.

Her husband takes a job offer that moves them closer to the ocean. After suffering some anxiety attacks over quitting her teaching track, Eryka accepts the change with relief. It is difficult to manage financially with the uncertainty of concert gigs, but she soon realizes that she was more at the end of her rope than she knew. Change had to come, one way or the other. This way, she has made decisions with her eyes open, knowing she was trying to take care of her own mind and personality so that she could still be a loving friend and mother. She lives in a more spontaneous, less perfect way, more in tune with expansive, pragmatic, in-the-moment Sensing, and the panic attacks have become a memory.

ABNORMAL PERSONALITY

Not all stories of personality imbalance can be resolved. It's important to recognize that personality can be not only imbalanced temporarily but actually abnormal and malfunctioning. Psychiatry uses the term "personality disorder" to refer to a cluster of apparent mental illnesses that are chronic and severe, and which don't respond to medication. It's not clear that they are actually illnesses with progression or possible treatment. People who have them don't feel ill and may think they're fine.

"Normal" is a word that many people fear because it seems like a tool that will be used to exclude them for being different. The way I use it, I am not at all talking about people who are eccentric or don't fit in easily. "Normal" personality isn't about intellectual or social disabilities, either. There are people with mental retardation and treatable mental illnesses who have normal personalities. Autism as a social impairment stops the person from managing life in a normal, typical way, but this too is not what is meant by abnormal personality.

At this time, psychiatric writing about personality disorders does not really explain how or why they are disorders of "personality." It describes, instead, syndromes of behavior that stands out as problematic or maladaptive compared to normal, typical behavior. Since the 1990s, studies of these syndromes, using neuropsychological (paper and pencil) testing as well as neurological (EEG or imaging studies) data, have begun to sketch out some of the brain malfunctions that cause the syndromes.

Personality is a set of habitual ways that we process and respond to the world, and that includes maintaining our own identity and ideals while loving and caring for others. Personality disorder is a set of habitually problematic ways to respond to the world. Problems with identity and how to relate to others seem to be the core location of the disorder. There are a number of syndromes, each with particular features of inadequate coping methods and bad behavior. They each have a slightly different set of brain-problem features, including emotional regulation, memory and empathy.

There's no absolute line between imbalanced personality that can improve and abnormal personality that probably won't change. Still, sometimes we really need to know the difference, especially if we need to make a decision based on it. Should we invest more time and energy into helping this person improve, or should we cut our losses, whatever that means in the situation? There are many times when it matters tremendously to discern the difference between the many shades of normal and the much darker, often startling, mode of abnormal.

I suggest two tests to help distinguish normal from abnormal imbalance. First, has the person always had this problem, or has it been either later-developing or intermittent? If the problem was once not in existence, there's more chance that it can be nudged into improvement. (If you're looking at a child or teenager, err on the side of assuming that he or she might improve and use ideas about personality balance to help better the odds of improvement.) Lifelong patterns are less likely to change; for one thing, the person who has the problem is less likely to even know that it's a "problem," if things have never been different.

Second, is the problem profound enough to stop the person from being able to handle the basic tasks of life? There are three main tasks that our personalities have to manage across a lifetime.

1. Do or make something of value (i.e. work) to trade with the rest of society.
2. Form lasting ties of attachment within their age group, and with older and younger generations.
3. Ward off social danger and repair broken relationships.

A normal personality is one that can find ways to manage the tasks, perhaps forming alliances with other people who are better at earning money, playing with little children, taking care of the elderly, or managing defense or forgiveness. However the tasks are handled, they must be done. A newborn baby survives by smiling, forming bonds with adults. The elderly survive based on their history of caring for others, who now care for them. The sick survive by having worked hard and saved money to pay for care, or by having given love to those who give back. We survive economic hardships by maintaining bonds with extended family who can help us in a crisis, and those bonds are only maintained by years of gifts, holiday events, helping, and especially forgiving. People who can't work, give, share or forgive are likely to find survival difficult in hard times.

All of these tasks are about relating to people. The tasks of bonding across generations and both protecting from, and healing after, harm are obviously related to relationships. At first it may sound like holding down a job to support yourself and others is only a skill, but in fact it's profoundly about relationship, too. When we work, we accept a reciprocal way of relating to people. When they give, we give back. We don't just take things from them, and we recognize that we need to keep trades either exactly even (in a store) or mostly even (helping neighbors). It's a simple form of empathy, of being all equal and human together. We work because we are related as humans.

Each of the sixteen balanced personality types can be seen as a set of strategies to manage relationships and work. Strategies can be widely different, but as a balanced set, each personality can manage. When personality is merely imbalanced, that's still true. In my case studies of imbalanced but normal personality, it's clear that all five of these people are able to handle these tasks. They may be doing them badly (like not working up to potential or not spending enough time with the kids), but they are basically managing them. That's normal.

Personality disorders, on the other hand, are notable for blocking these fundamental tasks. Personality relies on the Introverted functions for its stoplights and red lines, and that's where abnormal personality mostly falls short. Introverted functions also provide our inner continuity, a sense of who we are; the inner self is at least partly defined by our moral ideals. These ideals define inner security; even if nobody likes me, I know that I've stood up for my ideals, so I feel okay about myself.

Abnormal personality syndromes involve uncertainty and insecurity about identity and a shifting sense of moral ideals and how to apply them. Extroverted skills are often intact, so that the abnormality does not show up in public. There may be subtle signs of trouble, but by and large, most people can ignore them most of the time. It's at home, and in private, that abnormality really comes out. When we are interacting with first-degree relatives (parent, sibling, child) or a spouse, we have to draw most on our Introverted stability and ideals. If Introverted functions are not working properly, that's where it will be visible.

The Introverted functions depend on brain structures that regulate fear and stress so that we can tell how big certain problems or issues are. Here's one place where all personality disorders break down in some way. Some syndromes, like Borderline Personality Disorder, cause easily-triggered panic that leaves the personality with a strong impression of danger. This sense can be very mistaken, but the internal impression can't be undone. Instead of correctly and appropriately sizing up dangers like betrayal, abandonment, and oppression, someone with the Borderline syndrome sees an exaggerated need to attack, defend or flee.

There's also a syndrome named Paranoid Personality Disorder. It's characterized by chronic misperceptions of danger and inability to sense when it's okay to trust anyone. The "paranoia" in its name probably isn't caused by hallucinations, as it is in paranoid schizophrenia. Instead, it indicates a serious, persistent breakdown of empathy mechanisms that should be reassuring the person of being loved and cared for. Missing these cues, the personality's Introverted functions stay locked on fearful scanning. Similarly, Avoidant Personality Disorder makes human interaction seem too difficult, though it appears to focus less on covert aggression and more on the person's own inadequacy. It is like a pervasive, disabling form of shyness.

Other PD syndromes make the personality less sensitive to dangers posed by other people. Borderline Personality Disorder syndrome itself can have this opposite side, since its problem is inaccuracy, which can go either way. Someone with BPD may flee conflict, but may just as likely charge into it recklessly. In particular, men with BPD are often violent; they account for many domestic abuse situations.

Psychopathy is the syndrome with a clearest lack of fear; one reason criminal-minded psychopaths take such risks is that they don't perceive the risks in the way a normal person would. When they do fear some kind of human loss, it may be in some odd way, prompting them to take an action we wouldn't predict. For example, in losing a human relationship they might process it as loss of property and react by imprisoning the person.

It's worth briefly noting that the *Diagnosing Standard Manual,* psychiatry's official reference book, does not list "psychopathy." Instead, it provides Anti-Social Personality Disorder, which is defined by aggression and law-breaking. Forensic researchers have noted some differences between prisoners who fit the profile for ASPD and others who meet criteria for psychopathy. If the two syndromes are different, those who fit Anti-Social Personality Disorder are more likely to feel anxiety (even panic) than psychopaths.[90] It's possible that they both over-estimate and under-estimate danger from others, with violent results.

Introverted functions manage who we are when we're with other people, especially when nobody is watching. They manage long-term relationships by scanning for signs that maybe we're taking more than we're giving; inborn knowledge understands how lethal it is to let this state go on for too long. But personality disorders are generally broken here, too. Narcissistic Personality Disorder most clearly gets it wrong, since its sense of self appears to be exclusive of the rights of others. Normal selfish people can go pretty far in taking more than their share, but they can sense red lines not to cross, or they'll try to make it up later. Narcissistic-disordered personalities don't have any sense of these lines.

Deficits like these make it impossible for such people to manage long-term relationships,

---

90: James Blair, Derek Mitchel and Katrina Blair, *The Psychopath: Emotion and the Brain,* (Malden, MA: Blackwell Publishing, 2005), 6-17.

especially across generations. They make many damaging mistakes when they are too aggressive, defensive, unpredictable, or unforgiving. They take more than they give and get angry when people challenge them on it. They may be able to work, they may even be very talented and good at what they do, but some personality-disordered people still make mistakes there about just what is the nature of work reciprocity.

The disorders that are most impaired in empathy are most likely to break out into visibly impaired work ethic. Narcissistic-disordered personalities seem to feel so fundamentally entitled that they have a distorted sense of how much work they ought to do for their money. They want to be paid very well for relatively light work, and they want other people to pitch in with most dull or dirty tasks. Narcissistic Personality Disorder doesn't prevent a career, but it usually creates a lot of unhappy colleagues and maybe some lawsuits.

Psychopathy takes this problem one step farther; psychopaths seem to lack any feeling of needing to work as part of the human race. They see work as painful, dull, and thoroughly unreasonable, so they will actually work very hard at non-work scams like false car sales on the internet. "Work" is what other people want them to do; sitting up late listing hundreds of false car ads is just a way to get the money they're entitled to have from fools. When a psychopathic personality gets a job, most of the "work" time is spent doing nothing and taking credit for the work of others. Psychopathy in its full-syndrome form usually blocks any kind of career, except that of a con man.

For all these reasons, people with real personality disorders simply cannot maintain the basic three tasks of life. They may be able to work, but they are not likely to preserve bonds across the generations or keep the peace with others. Their behavior is often deeply puzzling to the normal personalities around them.

Most people have normal personalities, but there are enough personality disorders that we can't turn away and assume we'll never meet them. The National Institute of Mental Health (NIMH) studied the prevalence of three personality disorders, choosing to focus on Avoidant Personality Disorder (extreme shyness), Borderline Personality Disorder and Anti-Social Personality Disorder. Taken together, they accounted for as much as 9% of the adult population.[91] Different studies, looking at other syndromes or using other criteria, have found even higher numbers.

Defining normal and abnormal problems matters because many of the world's toughest problems occur right at their intersection. When we can make more accurate predictions about what can change and improve, and what can't, we can manage these very difficult problems better. There may be no good answers, but all accurate answers are better than unrealistic ones.

91: National Institute of Mental Health website, "Statistics." http://www.nimh.nih.gov/health/statistics/index.shtml

PART FOUR:
RELATIONSHIPS IN BALANCE

CHAPTER 14

Temperament Columns

FOR THE LAST SECTION, LET'S turn to a more external view again. We've been doing personality brain surgery, and now we'll snap shut the skull and begin looking at the outside. How do personalities work in balance with each other? How do personality types influence relationships at work, in the family, and in marriage?

When we look at personality from the outside, we can ask whether there are visual cues to help us know what sort of personalities people have. We only get to know a limited number of people well enough to know how they process life on the inside. Everyone else is visible on the outside, with just a few clues from things they say or do.

I'm going to present a chart that organizes the sixteen types into columns and rows. The columns group them by an overall shared viewpoint and way of living that could be called worldview, personality style or temperament. The rows, which I'll discuss in Chapter 15, are about interpersonal dominance. If you are trying to understand the personality type of someone you know, you can use observations of temperament and dominance to guess which personality type might fit. If you're still not sure about yourself, this will give you another way to guess and check.

The chart is like the game "Battleship," where location of ships is described by row and column. Knowing only a little about someone, you can guess by row and column that meet at the square of one personality type. This may or may not be your friend's correct personality type, but it starts you out with a reasonable guess. From there, it becomes like a game of "Clue," in which you look for evidence for or against your guess until you feel sure.

WHAT IS TEMPERAMENT?

Ancient ideas about types of people have always sorted them into three, four or five groups based on body type, facial appearance, and emotional tendencies. The Indian Ayurvedic system uses three groups, while Chinese traditional medicine uses five. European philosophy and medicine has always seen four types. In Greek, Roman and medieval medicine, people's body temperaments were thought to produce primarily one of four fluids. Personalities were based on the fluids, for example, a sanguine man produced more blood and was more optimistic. In all of these ancient systems, medical treatment coordinated with personality type.

The Ayurvedic and Chinese traditional systems are still used today, while the Western system based on four has fallen out of mainstream medical use. It remains much in use with popular psychology, though. There are several four-based systems of classifying people, outside this book. They all seem to be describing essentially the same four groups of people, using different angles and terms, but recognizing same patterns. The best-known set of terms comes from the work of David Keirsey, a counselor and child psychologist.

Dr. Keirsey began working in counseling in 1950, around when Isabel Myers was trying to gain acceptance for the Myers-Briggs Type Indicator test. He used personality type in his work for many years, and gradually he developed his own take on it. Looking at the history of so many philosophers and writers who discussed four kinds of people, he believed that an important truth was embedded in this group of four. He agreed with Isabel Myers' personality types, but he organized them into four groups of four. He still used her letter-code names, but he felt that the four temperament groups were their own layer of reality, not just groupings of Jung's ideas. His book, published with co-author Marilyn Bates in 1978, was called *Please Understand Me: Four Temperament Types*.

Keirsey focused on "temperament" instead of personality. "One's temperament," he wrote, "is that which places a signature or thumbprint on each of one's actions, making it recognizably one's own." In other words, people have certain mental temperaments that influence the way they see the world in all settings. He believed that this was the primary layer of personality. Keirsey's first and second editions used different labeling systems for the four groups he proposed. In the first edition, he borrowed names from Greek mythology; Jung had been interested in the same myths, so he had also written about them in *Psychological Types*. These names were too difficult for modern readers, so in the second edition, Keirsey used names drawn from Plato's Republic: Guardians, Artisans, Rationals and Idealists.[92]

A similar four-group system was set up by Helen Fisher for the dating website Chemistry. com. She based her thinking on four hormones that could be mainly dominant in someone's temperament. The hormone-based system suits the basic meaning of "temperament" in neuroscience studies. There, it means something like reactivity, whether you startle easily into either flight or fight, or remain calm, perhaps freezing like a rabbit. Fisher's system is general, not an laboratory diagnosis of which hormones are most active in individuals, but

---

92: David Keirsey, *Please Understand Me II: Temperament, Character, Intelligence*. (Del Mar, CA: Prometheus Nemesis Book Co., 1998), 31.

her terminology is much in use at dating websites. Her four groups are Builders, Explorers, Directors and Negotiators.[93]

Both Keirsey's and Fisher's systems describe such similar groups that I consider them equivalent. Two of the groups correspond to some factors that I've already discussed, particularly in Chapter 9. Builders/Guardians are the traditional, decisive people with Introverted Sensing; their type of Perceiving shapes life into a Hollywood classic movie. Explorers/Artisans are the athletic, artistic people with Extroverted Sensing; their worldview is like an action or adventure movie.

Two of the groups are divided a little bit differently from how I discussed them in Chapter 9. Introverted and Extroverted Intuition are not split up here; N personality types are divided instead by the Judging function. When Intuition is paired with some kind of Thinking, it leads toward invention, logical criticism, and competition. Keirsey calls them Rationals, while Fisher calls them Directors. They make up 15% of men and only 6% of women. On the other hand, when ideas and connections are handled with the Feeling function, the ideas will gravitate toward ethics, humanitarian ideals, romance and imagination. They are Keirsey's Idealists and Fisher's Negotiators. Significantly more women appear in this column; they are 13% of men and 19% of women.[94]

I've placed the sixteen personality types into a chart, with the Intuitives (Ns) grouped by Thinking and Feeling. Sensing (S) personalities are divided as in Chapter 9. Above each column, see first Fisher's classifying name, then Keirsey's. Within each column, notice that all of the letter code names have two letters in common. To help make the letter code names more memorable, I'll refer to these columns by the two-letter pair that's shown in boldface.

Guardians Builders	Artisans Explorers	Rationals Directors	Idealists Negotiators
ESTJ	ESTP	ENTJ	ENFJ
ESFJ	ESFP	ENTP	ENFP
ISTJ	ISTP	INTJ	INFJ
ISFJ	ISFP	INTP	INFP

Fig. 14-1

The four "temperament" columns are useful because, as Keirsey predicted, they are sometimes more quickly evident than finer distinctions of personality. They may be an easier key to knowledge of your own personality and others', like sorting animals first into mammals, birds and reptiles. If you got a glimpse of an animal, but you aren't sure what it was, you can usually at least know if it was a hopping or flying bird, a crawling or running animal with fur, or something like a snake or lizard. These classes of animals have distinctive ways of moving and reflecting light, as well as characteristic colors. So using the temperament columns, we can make similar generalizations about groups of personalities.

93: Helen Fisher, *Why Him? Why Her?* (New York: Henry Holt, 2009), 8.
94: *MBTI® Manual, A Guide to the Development and Use of the Myers-Briggs Type Indicator*, 3rd edition (Mountain View, CA: CPP, 2003), 156-158.

FIELD GUIDE TO TEMPERAMENT TRAITS

The first column's letter names all include S and J: ESTJ, ESFJ, ISTJ, and ISFJ. We've discussed their interior view of the world as Introverted Sensing shapes what they perceive. Now, what do SJ types look like on the outside? How do they dress, and what attitudes do they usually have toward life? What sort of things do they often say?

SJs (Guardians, Builders) like to dress in a way that lets you know they mean business. If casual wear is appropriate, their clothes are casual but neat; but if they should wear skirts or suits, they absolutely do. SJ men are neatly groomed and don't hesitate to wear ties and formal shoes. Their ties are usually hung neatly, and they may give some brief thought to choosing the right tie to send a message for an occasion: bold, understated, serious, or respectful. It's not so much about the personal message they want to convey, but about what would be expected and fitting in the situation.

SJ women wear conservative make-up and if they color their hair, they usually maintain its natural hue or at least stay with the same color for many years. They use traditional, matching accessories. Following mainstream fashion, still they avoid fads and instant trends. They are always conscious of their appearance and the message it sends; again, it's less about a personal statement and more about fitting into what's expected. They want to be clearly identified as part of a group, not just any group but the one they feel part of.

They believe that society's rules are mostly good, and that even if some rules are unnecessary, rules are still so beneficial that they should all be followed. They are not likely to park in a no-parking zone and leave flashers on, hoping for the best. They assume that rules have reasons, even if those reasons aren't apparent at this moment. If everyone ignored rules when they felt like it, SJs reason, society would fall apart. They value few things more than the basic social contract. Certainly, a little personal inconvenience can't be compared to the value of maintaining social order.

Most proverbs suit SJs well, and it's likely that they were coined by SJs in the past. "Honesty is the best policy," "A stitch in time saves nine," and "Look before you leap" are all SJ sentiments. These sayings refer to caution and planning, two very high SJ values. Clocks, calendars and planning books are never far away. Mistakes happen, but all SJs feel that mistakes are inherently dangerous. They are highly concerned about their own mistakes, which they try to avoid (and perhaps cover up), but they are equally concerned about the mistakes of other people. It's worth a great deal of advance planning and trouble to keep mistakes from occurring at all.

Even at young ages, SJs have an eye out to see what other people are doing; they warn, object or block someone who may be about to make a mistake or break a rule. They are often drawn to careers that consist mainly of enforcing rules, such as teachers, managers, accountants and judges. While medical doctors can be from any of these groups, traditional medicine appeals very much to SJs, because it helps them enforce rules of health, while requiring them to make rapid decisions.

They impose rules on others, but first and foremost on themselves. If an SJ promises to help monitor or clean up from an event but she has a fever, she will be there anyway. If he's on a schedule to referee kids' sports and it's pouring rain, even if nobody shows up, the SJ will be there just in case the game hasn't been cancelled. SJs tend to be early to events because if they are right on time, they perceive it as almost late. Being on time means being there early so that other people aren't left wondering whether or not you'll show up; it shows respect. SJs feel a personal responsibility to the social order that amounts to devotion to schedules and events simply because they exist: if these events stopped, if people were late or didn't show up to sweep floors, social ties and morals would not be upheld. They believe that everyone has this responsibility, and that if others don't feel it, there is something wrong with them.

The second column's letter names all include S and P: ESTP, ESFP, ISTP, and ISFP. Keirsey called them Artisans after the craftsmen in Plato's ideal city, because they are compelled to use their hands, feet and whole bodies in their work. Fisher's term, Explorers, captures the exploring Extroverted Sensing that SPs all have in common.

SPs like to dress casually and stay in motion. They generally follow rules, but they frequently resent them. They don't hesitate to skirt a rule if nobody is looking and they're sure that no danger or harm will be incurred. They are more likely to trust their own sense of danger than someone else's, too. If firecrackers are illegal, but the SP is sure he can set them off without danger, he is likely to do so. They seriously dislike rules that seem needless and fussy, like dress codes. They like things to justify themselves in a functional way, including clothes.

SP women may like to dress sexy or formally, but if so, it's because they feel that the fuss of the clothing is justified for the event or that the clothes are fun. Young SP women can be counted on for the flashiest jewelry, the shortest skirts, and the brightest colors. When they color their hair, they may change its color every few years. As they get older, they often go for a practical, non-fussy casual look. They can be tomboys, especially if they are of a Thinking type. For them, clothes are not about what society expects, they're about fun, whether that means blue jeans or lime green high heels.

SP men rarely dress up. They believe that if clothing covers the body well enough for the weather, it's nobody's business what it looks like. For casual wear (which is pretty much always), they like t-shirts and caps with the names of sports teams or sponsors. They dislike peer pressure to dress in ways that seem fussy and pointless. On the other hand, they are more likely to wear Halloween costumes as adults or pick up some shirt that's fun and a bit crazy.

SPs value spontaneity and fun more than plans and duty. They don't tend to be judgmental if other people skip their duties from time to time, and they expect to be excused when they do. If it's a nice day, and an SP can go off to enjoy a hobby, he or she may well skip a minor duty. Of course, it varies from person to person as to which duties are "minor" enough to skip when golfing or surfing calls. They may consider quite a few meetings, weddings, showers, parties and other events to be optional on a sunny day.

SPs live by the rule to mind your own business. Although they love to tell and hear stories, they are not deeply interested in what their neighbors are doing, so they don't tend to gossip. They believe that you should have as much freedom and fun as possible in your life. "Dance like nobody is watching, and sing like nobody is listening," they say. A favorite SP saying on the internet is about living life so fully that at the end, the person will slide into the grave as into home plate, "chocolate in one hand, wine in the other, body thoroughly used up, totally worn out, and screaming 'WOO HOO, what a ride!'" But above all, the favorite proverb is, "Live and let live."

When SPs do pay attention to rules and laws, they usually have traditional values. When they don't, they may be rebels and hippies. An SP with traditional values is often personally close (sibling, friend or spouse) to an SJ, and it's their shared identity that most shapes the SP's views. This is especially true when they are actively religious. SPs are most drawn to religious services with excitement and emotion, and if they volunteer, they are most likely to volunteer to work with teens or children. They are more interested in finding acceptable activities within the group than thinking deeply about its philosophy or theology. But they take the general consensus of belief to be true, and they rarely challenge it. Their behavior may skirt these religious rules as much as any other rules, but they do not hesitate to defend the group's values. They may even join in criticizing a rule-breaker, but they are not as keenly interested in the topic as their SJ friends. Live and let live.

Moving to the third column, we encounter the personalities that all include N and T: ENTJ, ENTP, INTJ, and INTP. Keirsey's Plato-borrowed name Rationals is apt, since logic is something they're all keenly interested in. Fisher's term Directors is a little less generally appropriate, since only some of these personalities want to give orders or directions.

NTs usually have a distinctive appearance because they are deeply uninterested in the subject. Men and women alike, their clothes are practical, usually more or less appropriate, but often unvarying. Like SPs, they believe that clothes just need to cover the body, but unlike them, they avoid sports logos. Young NTs' t-shirts are more likely to have witty sayings or math jokes. Older NTs just avoid all branding slogans and choose plain shirts, whether t-shirts or buttoned shirts with collars. Gender marking isn't popular with NT; men may wear their hair long (pony-tailed physics professor), while women may keep short hair and avoid dresses.

They always maintain an appearance that does not call attention to itself, because they believe that what really matters is what they can do and how they think. They are offended by judgments based on appearance. Michael Crichton's *Jurassic Park* character Dr. Ian Malcolm speaks for all NTs when he explains why he wears only black and grey: "These colors are always appropriate, and they go well together… I find it liberating [to limit colors]. I believe my life has value, and I don't want to waste it thinking about clothing."[95]

NTs believe that they have a right to determine rules for themselves; they want autonomy. A Constitutional Convention would be an intellectual playground for these philosophical Thinkers, but they can also find enjoyment in writing contracts and by-laws. They are often drawn to study law, even if they don't become practicing lawyers. At the very least, they always make sure to know laws, penalties, rules and exceptions, because they dislike being dependent on others to tell them.

Even as children, they argue a lot. "That may be true for you, Mommy," argues the young NT, "but it's not true for me, and I shouldn't have to do what you say." Folk proverbs rarely capture their values, though they do believe in the foresight that proverbs recommend. They tend to be law-abiding and reliable. Many of them will say that they've rejected traditional morality, but you'll find that they have created their own rule system that meshes reasonably

95: Michael Crichton, *Jurassic Park* (New York: Knopf, 1990), 74.

well with society's rules. They usually include some quirk just to prove that it's their own system, not society's.

NTs do not like enforcing rules on other people, unless they are in a competition or negotiation. No NT can resist enforcing (to the letter) the provisions of a contract that both parties agreed to. As parent, an NT may make an agreement with a child and hold the child to those terms, whether the terms work out to reward or punishment. If the child chooses to break the contract, the NT parent feels comfortable meting out a punishment, but he does not think less of the child, and he may even admire or agree with him. Obedience by itself is not a high value.

NTs reserve the right to determine their own beliefs and actions without anyone judging them, and they give the same right to others: even if others don't want it. They do not like to pass judgments or give personal advice, even when they have definite views and opinions. They tend to have little respect for politics or any other system that depends on winning approval from many people. Who cares what the majority approves? They're probably wrong.

An NT's second highest value, after autonomy, is mastery of skills in order to win competitions. If an NT does not appear to be competitive, it may be because he is caught up in a competition with his own mind; he is solving a math problem or designing a killer graph. But many NTs feel compelled to compete and some try to turn daily life into competitions. They don't like to compete for the fun of it; they like to win. They may not value sports, unless they were blessed with some talent that they like to exercise.

Luck and chance have no appeal. NTs prefer to stack the deck in their own favor by becoming awesome at whatever they do. They can spend many years building up difficult or obscure skills just for the final moment of triumph when they can crush the competition. Their favorite relationship to sports is often prediction. They like to memorize so much information that they can correctly predict outcomes; it doesn't matter which team wins since the "horse in the race" is the NT's own triumph in superior knowledge.

The fourth column's letter names all include N and F: ENFJ, ENFP, INFJ, and INFP. Keirsey calls them Idealists while Fisher evokes a more business-oriented image of Negotiators. Either way, they are interested in ideas and harmony among people.

NFs do not have a distinctive culture of clothing, but they tend to use clothing to convey a message, like the SJ. However, their message is about personal identity, not about role or group identity. Unlike the NTs, who reject the idea that clothing defines them, most NF women, and some NF men, embrace clothing. They want their look to tell the world who they are; clothing is the bridge between the interior, hidden self and the visible world. It's an ambassador sent to tell the world who is inside.

Some NFs become very individualistic in their style; older women may still wear long hair, perhaps in braids or some other romantic, even historic, style. Men and women tend to wear hats, scarves or other signature accessories. Some NFs may appear shabby or mismatched, like the NTs, because they are more concerned with spiritual matters than with fashion. They are enthusiastic about ethnic folk styles and about vintage clothing from thrift and antique stores.

NFs believe in ideals, not rules. They feel that rules may help people remember right and wrong, but goodness and truth, not written rules or social customs, define right and wrong. Rules may be well-intentioned, but in some circumstances, a rule might cause a cruel or unjust result. They believe that exceptions should be made by looking at how the highest ideals apply. Not only that, they believe that rules often fall short of the best morality. Idealists feel that they are born knowing the nature of Truth, Justice and Goodness, and they freely compare laws and rules to these ideals. Instead of following a law or rule, an NF may ignore or break it to do what he feels is truly best.

NFs are the original conscientious objectors and pioneers of civil disobedience. Both of these concepts lean on the individual's right to choose punishment in order to live by a higher law and bring attention to a systematic injustice. Where an SP may break a law for fun or out of carelessness, or an NT may argue with the law, the NF will always invoke a higher principle than the law. The higher principle may turn into a frequent topic of conversation as the NF tries to persuade others to see it.

NFs live by the saying, "Love conquers all." They are not very fond of traditional proverbs, but they love inspirational quotes; metaphors of darkness and light are dominant. "Darkness cannot drive out darkness; only light can do that. Hate cannot drive out hate; only love can do that," wrote Martin Luther King, Jr.[96] From St. Francis of Assisi, "All the darkness in the world cannot extinguish the light of a single candle." (The quote is unverified but enduringly popular, whoever said it.) If your Facebook friend posts quotes from the poet Rumi, she's probably an NF. When the Dalai Lama said, "My religion is kindness," he spoke for all NFs; so did Gandhi: "My life is my message."

In fact, every NF is on a special quest to find out what that life message is, and who he or she is. NFs of every age are always fascinated by discovering a new way to compare and contrast themselves with others. They are usually interested in psychology; most books on personality types are written by Idealists. Many of the foundational psychologists were NFs, and their outlook shaped what they taught about people. For example, Abraham Maslow believed that everyone must reach a high level of self-knowledge that he called "actualization." Carl Rogers believed that a therapist must use empathy to help the client know himself. The strong emphasis on self-knowledge is typical of NFs. Self-knowledge is their lifelong quest, and it may not be easy for them to understand that other types aren't on the same quest.

NFs aren't reliable in the way that SJs (and even NTs) are, because they tend to be absent-minded; but they believe in setting everything aside to help someone who has an emotional problem. After their basic ideals, their most important values are intimacy and self-knowledge, and deep conversations are the best vehicle for both goals. They are drawn to work involving ideals or intimacy; they are often found in non-profits, counseling centers and religious ministry. Literature, too, draws them, since literature is a way to study relationships and the human condition. NFs personalities form a majority among professional musicians, both classical and as songwriters.

A simple joke memorializes each temperament group with one characteristic word:
Getting up in the morning, the SJ says, "Today I will do the **right** thing."
The SP says, "C'mon, let's just **do** something."
The NT says, "What does 'right' **mean**?"
The NF asks, "But who am **I**?"

96: Martin Luther King, Jr., at Dexter Avenue Baptist Church, Montgomery, Alabama, December 25, 1957.

TEMPERAMENTS INTERACT AND BALANCE

The "Field Guide" descriptions are probably enough to start slotting any mystery person, but we can also look at how the temperament columns interact. Individuals of these groups may get along splendidly with each other, or not at all. Obviously, generalizations have limits when humanity has been reduced to four categories already. There is always so much variation among unique people that no single rule can be adduced. However, here are some basic principles to guide your observation.

First, each temperament column has the greatest respect for its own values system. At any given time, each group has some kind of criticism of the failings of the other three groups. They gravitate to making friends within their temperament category because friendship is so often about discovering similar values and enthusiasms. SJs respect other SJs for being reliable and polite, and for always having appropriate behavior and responses. SPs have tremendous fun together because they can count on other SPs to be spontaneous and full of energy. NTs form competition teams, spar with each other intellectually, and judge each other's reading taste. NFs become instant best friends when they find each other, because they often feel misunderstood by the rest of the world. They can spend hours discussing relationships, memories and feelings.

While each temperament group likes its own values best, of course they spend a lot of time interacting with other types. Some combinations work better than others. SPs generally get along with nearly everyone because they are easy-going and focused on their work. In their non-judgmental attitude, they may get along well with NFs who believe that it's wrong to judge people. On the other hand, their casual attitude to rules, may offend NFs when the rules represented real values. But although SPs may not feel like obeying the rules, they rarely challenge them. In that attitude, they get along well with SJs and can form lasting partnerships with them. At work, SPs can get along well with NTs, since both are pragmatic about finding solutions. NTs want to innovate to find a better way of doing things, and SPs are often able to spot practical solutions based on observation. They both agree on getting things done without fuss.

SJs can be very good friends with SPs; they form natural partnerships (as illustrated in Chapter 9's example of "Ed" and "Ivan"). SJ parents often have SP children, and typically they develop a stern but fond attitude toward the child's rule-breaking. They view the behavior as naughtiness, but as long as they don't sense any real malice, they trust that sports will teach their SP children to play by rules. At work, SJs can get along very well with NTs, as long as they do not have the NTs' aloofness from social morality pushed in their faces. It helps if the NT is technically competent and, above all, reliable to finish things on time. SJs who work in non-profits may find themselves paired with NFs, and although they may be on the same side, real clashes can occur. NFs seem like nice people, but SJs can find them dangerous, because they challenge the foundations of the system. If SJs detect revolutionary challenge, they move quickly to use their authority to stop it.

NTs work most often with SJs, because they gravitate to business, law and science. An NT lawyer probably has at least one SJ associate and paralegal, and usually many more. NTs often sit on the board of corporations, so they must work closely with SJs in top management.

They work peacefully until there's a clash of vision, usually sparked by change. SJs want to do things the way they are usually done, but NTs believe that this time, something different must happen or there will be a disaster. If an NT has an SP employee, they probably get along well; they both value flexibility and results, and both like to ignore formalities. NTs usually have very strong feelings about NFs; there are great love affairs between them, if they share the same goals in life. On the other hand, NTs and NFs may clash badly. NTs insist on logical principles while NFs insist on their value judgments, and neither temperament type likes to give in. However, these two temperament types usually have a lot to say to each other, and they have a general understanding and respect.

NFs and SJs are both interested in goodness, but they approach morality in different ways. If NFs and SJs are forced to work together closely on anything that isn't perfectly routine, they are likely to disagree. When they clash, the NF often comes out of it puzzled and hurt, because he cannot understand why the SJ, whom he considered a good person, has suddenly turned punitive. The SJ may consider the issue so clear that it doesn't need further comment, while the NF would rather have talked it out more. When NFs conflict with NTs, the result is always an argument, since both are interested in the intellectual train of thought. Often, this intellectual clash results in compromise, learning and friendship. When NFs and NTs can form partnerships, they may create powerful non-profits or political movements. Finally, NFs generally get along with SPs, especially for doing fun activities. Close friendships may be challenging, since the SPs are soon tired of the NFs' wish to sit still and have long conversations. If the balance of activity and talk can be worked out, there are few problems.

In families, it's possible to have all four temperament types born into close quarters. This is probably the most taxing for everyone's frustration tolerance, since family life has so little privacy and so many inter-related decisions. People in families may look so similar that it's hard to really understand just how different they are. We often look to family patterns like birth order or the effect of a shared stress, trying to figure out why certain people just can't get along. These factors can be the root problem, but sometimes they turn up few solid explanations.

It can be very helpful just to realize that the other temperament groups are not on the same life missions. Each human being, born inside the world of his or her own mind, tends to imagine that everyone else is living by the same values. Since it's clear that other people make different choices, most of us believe that they are trying to do what we are trying to do, but they're failing at it (sometimes pretty badly). It can help to realize that in actuality, these people are not trying to do what we're doing. They are on a different mission, and if it's judged by their values and standards, it might turn out that they are doing a pretty good job.

The real challenge is to find a way to admit that these other goals and values are as good as ours. Nobody really thinks so; each temperament column fervently believes that its goals and values are the best. But if each of us can learn to admit that other goals are valid in their own way, or that other values might mean something to other people, it's a big step to acceptance and love.

CHAPTER 15

Dominance Rows

S OME PEOPLE SEEM TO HAVE an intense need to dominate their environment and everyone in it. Other people remain quiet when they don't get their way; they take for granted that other people will make their own decisions and they don't try to control what is going on. While our comfort with being dominant may vary with situations, there seems to be a general level that's inborn and stable over time.

Dominance is implicit in many books about personality, but it is rarely singled out and made explicit. This could be due to the uneasiness that a democratic, egalitarian society feels with the idea that some people are born to lead. We recognize this in a half-hearted way, but mostly in formal situations like politics and the military.

We prefer to view leadership as an attitude or set of habits that can be learned by practice or training. In this view anyone, properly taught or motivated, can lead. And yet personal experience often contradicts this view, because all of us have seen people who were trained in leadership but lacked the personality traits to support it. The results are often worse than no leadership at all; without the proper supporting personality traits, such leaders can inadvertently destroy the whole enterprise.

Dominance, as I use it, means the wish to make what's in your mind become real. We all experience a moment when, just before doing something, we briefly picture what we expect doing it to be like. It's a way to organize and prepare the actions we'll take: walking into a room, getting out a glass, reaching into the refrigerator to take a pitcher of tea, pouring a drink, and drinking it. "I'd like some iced tea" prompts this involuntary visualization, which primes motor neurons.

But what happens when things don't go as visualized? You walk into the kitchen and the glasses are all dirty. You open the refrigerator and there's only a small bit of tea left; someone else drank most of it. You could become very angry at the person who was supposed to leave tea for you or wash glasses; you could make or go buy iced tea and wash a glass; or you could take a mug or plastic cup and just get a drink of water. Your reaction depends on just how much it *mattered* to you that what you visualized (and anticipated tasting) would happen in exactly the way it was supposed to.

People with higher dominance get more annoyed when external life doesn't match their visions and expectations. They put more effort into making people and things conform to their visions. Not everyone cares the same about little things like a drink of tea, but in general, meeting expectations *matters* to higher-dominance personalities. With lower dominance, the effort goes into making peace with the way the external world is. There's much less effort expended to make the outside world conform. On the other hand, using "higher" and "lower" for dominance is misleading because it sounds like dominance is a substance that we can have more or less of. Instead, dominance is like light, which can be focused widely or narrowly.

Think of a strong outdoor spotlight. When it's shining down from a great height, it can light up a large area. The light may not be enough to read a book, but it's enough to cast shadows, see easily and play soccer. Imagine the light is on a crane that lets us lower it down to about 2/3 of its previous height. The light no longer lights up most of the field, but it still bathes many people in its light. The intensity is greater; shadows are crisper and seem darker, and you could easily read a book. Now swing the crane down to about the height of an ordinary traffic light. The spotlight covers a very defined circle, and it's too intensely bright. The people standing in its space have to shade their eyes. Last, let's move the light down to the height of a man's head. Its tiny circle is intensely, hotly bright; it may be dangerously hot.

The desire to control seems to be like this. Those who want to control large areas end up like the spotlight, spread thinly over a field, influencing everything but without detail. Those who want to control nothing but their own minds have a fiercer, more intense grip on tiny details in that small territory. In my observation, personalities seem to have a built-in sense of where they fit in this spectrum of control. Natural dominance is not related to actual skills, talents or experience, though of course we need these things to do well. One's inborn desire for dominance seems, instead, to be hard-wired into personality. Our achievements are driven, not led, by how much it matters to see our expectations met. We work harder on certain things in order to quiet the discomfort of unhappy, dissatisfied dominance.

The personality framework offers some support for why dominance might be inborn. As you know, every balanced personality type has two top mental functions; the Introverted one is idealistic, perfectionist and a bit negative, while the Extroverted one is pragmatic, realistic and optimistic. In half of the balanced types, the Introverted function is helping to shape worldview, but it's not the primary way of processing life. It shapes the goal we're aiming at, but not as much what we do. So when an Introverted part is in control, it is frequently disappointed. Its ideals are rarely met, its lovely images rarely seen. On the other hand, Extroverted parts often get what they want, because Extroversion is willing to make a few adjustments, but it's also willing to take external action to make things happen.

The eight personality types that begin with "E" usually have a stronger sense of wanting to make the world suit their mental images than the "I" types. They are like the spotlight set at sufficient height to light a large area. Since childhood, they've learned the lesson that some smart, pragmatic actions and words will probably set them up to get what they want. These might be their own actions, but probably other people are involved. "E" personalities usually figure out how to get Mom to buy the cereal they wanted, or can manage to have the family go out for their choice of restaurant food. Getting other people to do what you want is a precise set of skills, if "what you want" doesn't include having those people resentful or shouting in response. "E" types may try slamming doors or holding their breath when they're very young, but by adulthood, normal balanced "E" personalities have many ways to get what they want without unpleasantness.

The eight personality types that begin with "I" can have some of these skills, but they've usually spent those same years learning to manage disappointment. By teenage years, many of them realize that the mental image of how things ought to be is just not realistic. It's too expensive in some way; it could be too expensive quite literally, or it could cost too much in other ways. The "I" person could get what he or she wants, but it would mean violating some ideal. People would be left hurt (F), or the result would be unfair (T). It would mean acting against the role-ideal of correct behavior (S), or it would mean pitching a fit over something that, in the scope of philosophy, is actually trivial (N). When the idealized, Introverted form of T, F, S or N is the controlling part of personality, violating this ideal to get—what, just a glass of tea?—is not worth it.

So between early childhood and adulthood, the "E" types put most of their hearts into learning how to make what they want come true. On the contrary, the "I" types put most of their hearts into learning how to control their own actions to make ideals come true in a limited way, and otherwise to be philosophical about the imperfection that life always dishes out. "E" types, by this measure, are more likely to develop leadership skills.

There's a big difference between leadership and just telling people what to do. A bully or pirate can tell people what to do, using physical threats (implied or explicit). A leader knows that this sort of trick will only work once or twice. It's a lot of work to keep waving a gun around, and some may resent the use of force (or grab the gun). For a "leader" with a personality disorder, maybe this situation is acceptable. Double the bodyguard, execute anyone suspicious, and hide in a bunker. But for any normal dominant personality, it's not only way too much work, it's simply not what they want. Become hated just to get iced tea on time? Why do that, when with more skill, you could get someone to be happy to make everything the way you want?

Real, skilled leadership based in natural dominance can be very low-key, and almost nobody resents being told what to do in the right way. Natural dominance motivates people to spend years on trial and error, observation, and maybe even book research on just how to do it. It also harnesses the personality's Intuition reserves for this purpose. There are strong gut feelings about intangibles like how quickly to ask a question, when to back off, when to turn away, when to barter up or down, and how to react to an emotional signal.

It's important to understand levels of dominance because this subject is one of the great overlooked sources of despondency and depression among middle-aged adults. People who have a natural desire for dominance may not develop the skills to use it successfully, and they may not find their way into a place in life that allows them to use it. On the other hand, there are people who do not want high dominance, but whose career or social track has forced them to act it out. Having to be dominant when you dislike it can be just as much a source of despondency as being denied dominance that you want.

Dominance is important not only in the public sphere. In personal relationships, there is always a balance of power. There are many people who reach middle age and find that the marriage relationship they chose when they were young is a bad fit in terms of dominance. Perhaps both spouses want to be dominant over each other, so that they fight constantly. Perhaps each one has a zone of life in which he or she wants the other to be dominant, and they constantly negotiate. Perhaps neither wants to be dominant, and they take turns hiding from problems and trying to push each other into the place of power.

FOUR LEVELS OF DOMINANCE

I've named four levels of natural, inborn dominance implicit in personality type. Each one is defined by how large a territory the personality is comfortable controlling, and also by the intensity with which it wants to control that space. Like the spotlight, dominance in personality grows more intense as its space shrinks.

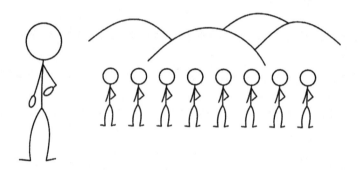

Fig. 15-1

Horizon Dominance is the desire and need to influence everything within this person's vision. There is no internal boundary that says "whoa, that's too much, I can't influence this whole territory." The territory might be literally vast, like Russia or an international corporation. It might have no geographical space but consist of many minds or souls. It could even be a stretch of time, such as to the end of one's lifetime or beyond.

How far away is a horizon? That depends on where you're standing. Literally, if you are standing at the bottom of a deep valley surrounded by mountains, or in a narrow city street surrounded by buildings, you see only a small piece of sky and your horizon does not reach far. If you're standing on an open plain, the horizon reaches out in a wide circle, taking in the whole half-bowl of sky. If you are, on the other hand, at the top of a tower or mountain, or in an airplane, your horizon is even larger.

Horizon Dominance means that wherever your personality "stands" in life, you feel no internal check on trying to dominate all that you can see. If you live in a tiny village in the

Alps, both literally and figuratively this may not be a very large space. Some people are born into families that are already located at the "top" of some social or political mountain. Their horizons are much larger than most people's.

Horizon Dominance also means giving up detail control. If you are the Tsar, you can't determine what color people paint their houses in Ryazan or Novosibirsk. You can decide what uniforms workers or soldiers must wear, but you have no control over how well each person cleans it, let alone whether anyone likes it. You could pass a law placing a certain book in every home, but you can't really enforce it and you certainly can't make everyone read it—or care. Horizon Dominant people always delegate the details. Like the spotlight, it can cover a wide area but not intensely.

Fig. 15-2

Room Dominance means that the horizon seems too large a boundary. Internally, in order to feel comfortable and confident, someone with Room Dominance needs to see a wall that defines "this much space and no more." It can be a literal wall, like the wall of a classroom or factory floor. It can be a political or social wall, counting "this many people and no more" who are under your control. It may be a time-limit wall, so that the Room Dominant person is in command of a large territory but only for a week—or a year—or until someone else is ready to take over.

Within the "room," this personality is confident and happy getting everything and everyone to be as envisioned. Room Dominant people have no desire to control anything outside their boundaries, although they can criticize problems on the other side of the fence. They know that they have the skills and energy to be dominant in the chosen space, no more. Within this limit, they can make sure the physical details are right and get people to cooperate. Outside that limit, their skills may not be enough and their energy will get drained from trying.

As with Horizon Dominance, someone can be born into a family that wields both Horizon and Room Dominance on a routine basis. That person's "room" boundary is probably going to be larger than some others'. Some other Room Dominant people may have outstanding talents that prepared them to lead larger rooms, and their comfort with room size usually grows to its largest possible size when they're around age 50.

One person's "room" may look like another's "horizon," in terms of real size. The distinction is internal. The Room Dominant person can see farther than the boundaries, and feels an aversion to extending control to the horizon. If influence extended beyond the visible boundaries, he or she would lose control over quality. Room Dominance is a compromise between quality and quantity; it's the most space someone can control without delegating important details to someone else.

Fig. 15-3

Bubble Dominance begins with strong Introverted ideals. Things really ought to look, feel, or mean a certain way, and the vision is detailed. It feels imperative. As all perfectionists know, if you're going to make sure something is done right, you must do it yourself. Bubble Dominance means intense control over one's own work and life, including influence and even command over the people who are intimately connected.

"Bubble" here refers to the "personal space bubble" we each have. It's usually about 18 inches, or we could think of it as approximately the space we need to put our arms straight out and spin around. A Bubble Dominant person wants absolute, detailed control over this space. It isn't just literally the space defined by outstretched arms, it's also whatever those arms need to touch, use, grow or make. Bubble Dominance is over the self and its immediate neighborhood.

Other people enter the bubble, sometimes permanently. When a Bubble Dominant person gets married, the spouse steps into the bubble. Children born to the marriage are inside the bubble until they grow up and break away. Co-workers who share a project are also inside the bubble. People hired to do single jobs, like painting the house, have also stepped into the bubble. On the other hand, people painting other houses, other people's kids, and co-workers who are on different projects are all outside the bubble.

Inside the bubble, little is delegated. The Bubble Dominant person knows that within this space carved by his arms or tools, he or she is confident to make sure that ideals are met as closely as possible. If it takes extra time to do a job right, so be it. The world outside the bubble is usually in violation of all ideals, but inside the bubble, things are safe. Introverted ideals tell us what's safe: keeping things neat, doing the math right, reading extra books to find truer meaning, meeting a high moral standard, and checking twice for errors. Meeting these ideas, whichever ones are built into the personality, means feeling safe and confident.

Soul Dominance means a degree of personal dominance that focuses on just the person alone, excluding everything else in the world. Someone standing nearby is merely that: nearby, not included in the zone of dominance at all. It's like in the spotlight analogy, when the powerful light held six feet above the ground made a dangerously hot, bright circle just big enough for one.

Soul Dominance is the exact inverse of Horizon Dominance in every way. It does not wish to enforce its vision on anything or anyone outside the self. It does not delegate any choices within its tiny sphere. It maintains perfect control over the personal zone of idealism. It is controlling not "as far as the eye can see," but the eye itself.

Fig. 15-4

Nobody else can enter this zone of dominance. The Soul Dominant person does not command or control. He or she may influence, but only as the other person comes alongside to observe. "What are you doing?" you may ask the Soul Dominant person, and you'll get a detailed answer. You can watch closely to see the perfection of detail in executing each inner wish. If you're influenced, it's because you recognized, yourself, the goodness of what the Soul Dominant person is doing. You chose, on your own, to do the same. Your reward may be a radiant smile or acceptance as a rare companion and peer, but you will never hear a command.

On the other hand, it's very hard or impossible to command a Soul Dominant person concerning those inner-zone things. You can command him or her to move, work or play; the turtle's shell comes along. You can't command the Soul Dominant person to think differently inside or stop caring about the perfection of what he or she is making. You can limit their time or stop their work, but there's no inner compliance and the person is left upset. If you challenge the ideals that rule their inner zone, you will meet with sudden, stark reb4ellion.

We can correlate these four levels of dominance with the sixteen balanced personality types. Each row represents, roughly and in general, one of these types of dominance. Horizon and Room Dominance correlate with the "E" personality types, while Bubble and Soul Dominance belong to the "I" types.

Within the E types, I've separated Horizon and Room Dominance along two general principles. ESFJ and ESFP are placed in the Room Dominant row because they care about relationships. When they are leading a class or group, they still want to be liked, and their personality supports the skills for handling leadership while being likable. They know instinctively that Horizon Dominance means making some people unhappy. ESTJ and ESTP personalities are much less troubled about having made someone unhappy by a rule or command, as long as the order was logically correct. ESFJs and ESFPs need to keep their boundaries visible and clear so that they can control the damage. If they make enemies, it's within the scope of what they can manage, perhaps isolating the foe or later making peace. In a Horizon territory, that's not going to be possible.

Horizon	ESTJ	ESTP	ENTJ	ENFJ
Room	ESFJ	ESFP	ENTP	ENFP
Bubble	ISTJ	ISTP	INTJ	INFJ
Soul	ISFJ	ISFP	INTP	INFP

Fig. 15-5

The same principle places ISFJ and ISFP in the Soul Dominance row, as compared to the Bubble Dominance of ISTJ and ISTP. Enforcing perfection in even a small zone will mean correcting, criticizing and perhaps punishing people who are nearby. That's very uncomfortable for the F types.

Among the Ns, the row divisions are by whether Intuition is Introverted or Extroverted. When it's Introverted, Film Noir skepticism rules out a number of possible options. Introverted Ns feel that they know with certainty what needs to be done, said or believed. When it's Extroverted, Intuition remains open and even uncertain about which option is the best. Extroverted Ns would like to see some limited trials in order to get more information or perhaps to try a few different approaches at the same time. So in both the E rows and the I rows, the Introverted Ns are relatively more comfortable with command.

We can get a sense of how common the levels of dominance are by looking at the personality types in each row. The MBTI National Sample sorted people for personality type and also by sex. They weren't directly asking about dominance, so my use of their numbers to talk about dominance is by inference.

Among men, the four rows are relatively even in distribution. About 21% of men have a Horizon Dominant personality, compared to 25% for both Room and Soul Dominance. Bubble Dominance forms the largest cluster, about 30%. By contrast, women are grouped more unevenly. In the largest group, 39% of women have personalities that fall into the Room Dominance row. Almost as many, 36%, are in the bottom row for Soul Dominance. Just 14% have Horizon personalities, while only 12% have Bubble Dominance.[97] Women's clustering in Room and Soul Dominance personalities is due to their being overwhelmingly more likely to be Feeling than Thinking types.

These four levels of dominance are all normal, healthy modes that can fit well into life. Of course, we also know people who have imbalanced problems with dominance. Soul Dominance is not the same as being a doormat or yes-man, nor are Horizon or Room Dominance the same as bullying or dictating. The Soul Dominant must have appropriate

---

97: *MBTI® Manual, A Guide to the Development and Use of the Myers-Briggs Type Indicator*, 3rd edition (Mountain View, CA: CPP, 2003), 156-158.

courage to stand up for their own selves. Leaders, at either of the top levels, must have the courage to listen and be patient. Even Horizon Dominance recognizes boundaries; while it controls what it can see, it doesn't control what's outside of its vision. It does not try to control what's outside its view, and it must delegate or pass over details. When people are misusing their power to over-control, that's not Horizon Dominance, that's a problem.

As a general rule, higher dominance takes more time to learn to do well. It takes no skill to get angry at not getting your way, but most people learn by mid-childhood that anger is a terrible strategy. Horizon Dominant people who aren't born into powerful families (and probably lack role models) may not learn all of the skills they need until they are into their 30s. At younger ages, they must work in positions of low power. How well they handle this frustration has a lot to do with how high they'll climb. If they can learn to leverage a little more influence than they're supposed to have, at each level of education and employment, they'll arrive in their late 20s with a lot of verbal and nonverbal influencing skills. Until then, the main outward sign of skills to come may be a lot of frustration and anger.

Room, Bubble and Soul Dominance also have sets of skills, some of them easily learned, some of them not. Soul Dominance may be second hardest to learn, next to Horizon Dominance, because it is nearly invisible and there aren't many mentors to pattern yourself after. How does a Soul Dominant person learn when to say no? Room and Bubble Dominance personalities seem to blossom earlier, perhaps in teenage or even childhood years. It's more likely that they've seen role models, especially in school. Most teachers are one of those two types; the best teachers are Room Dominant. Many children also see a lot of skilled workers, who typically have Bubble Dominance. Of course, perfecting dominance skills is always a lifetime process.

Sometimes, early life places someone in the happy path of rising to the correct dominance match. This is probably most likely with traditional work roles, like teachers or carpenters. But we see wrong dominance matches just as often as good matches, because the first steps of a long road may not be recognizable at the right stage of life. People can arrive in mid-life mismatched either higher or lower than they want to be in dominance. This may be one of the biggest reasons that people start new businesses, where they can determine their dominance at their own risk.

Frequently, a very competent Bubble Dominant personality gets promoted to managing a Room, or a Room Dominant manager is moved up into a Horizon position. Competency in one level is mistaken to mean competency in any level. When this happens, the individual is often keenly aware of struggling with despondency, even if things look okay on the outside. Conversely, someone with natural Room or even Horizon Dominance may not find the lower steps of the ladder, for whatever reason. Problems with health, family, the local economy, or just plain bad advice means that the critical early years weren't spent starting to climb. As a result, the person with natural high dominance is spending middle years in low-dominance work situations.

Dominance is so inborn that its skills are coded into body movements, voice, and attention span. When natural dominance is mismatched to workplace authority, it's often easy to see. The over-promoted manager has a soft voice and minimal movements, and his or her attention is never focused on the brewing conflicts that other employees see.

The under-promoted (but more naturally dominant) worker has a firmer declarative voice, larger body movements, and chronic consciousness of workplace conflicts that need to be solved. We try to address these problems as things that can be taught through management seminars, and of course some leadership skills can be both taught and learned. The kernel, though, is innate.

THE EXTROVERTS: HORIZON AND ROOM DOMINANCE

If you're not sure what someone's personality type is, you might be using observations of dominance to locate them on the chart, as in Battleship. Each of the four temperament columns has a different set of ambitions and values, and these too influence the type of dominance they seek. If you're looking for the wrong sort of dominance, you may miss out on accurate observations. So let's talk about how each temperament column works out in dominance.

Horizon	ESTJ	ESTP	ENTJ	ENFJ
Room	ESFJ	ESFP	ETNP	ENFP

Fig. 15-7

ESTJs, the most dominant of the SJ column, tend to seek power in traditional organizations. Extroverted Thinking's logic is confident; ESTJs don't usually second-guess their decisions, and they aren't afraid of their decisions becoming law for others. From Introverted Sensing, they have a firm bias in favor of laws, customs and traditions, and against exceptions and weakness. ESTJs can be found at the top of many official organizations; they account for most state governors, legislators, college presidents, and executive officers. They are judges, sheriffs, board members, and school principals. Their path to the horizon might be easiest to map out, since many ESTJs before them have modeled and planned the career-building steps.

ESTPs seek Horizon Dominance in physical zones. Extroverted Sensing works well in a role that requires constant rapid transitions. They tend to handle decisions as part of transitioning from task to task, focusing less on complex decision-making. ESTPs rise to the top in traditional organizations that most value action and movement, such as the military and sports. They also can be found leading rebellions and revolutions, not necessarily because they are thinking far in advance, but because they have the confidence to build and destroy in pursuit of their goals. Many Presidential candidates are ESTPs; they are happier on the campaign trail than most ESTJs.

On the other hand, the ESTP's dominance may not extend as readily to big organizations as the ESTJ's. While they make decisions quickly and confidently, Introverted Thinking isn't as driven to extend its judgments to wide horizons, and Extroverted Sensing is aware of the practical limits of any decision. Individual ESTPs may feel more comfort and resonance with Room Dominance. They may only rise into recognizable Horizon roles when there's a particularly good match of talent, opportunity, and even need. Until and unless that happens, they can be content with influencing within boundaries.

The Horizon Dominant N personalities, ENTJ and ENFJ, have to stay closely in touch with Introverted Intuition, which requires time spent alone. This trait alone makes it less likely for either to rise to power within a traditional structure. Introverted Intuition's mistrust of appearances and roles pushes them into avenues that come at power from another angle. As Ns, they find their way most easily during times of rapid change, like the eras of civil rights marches or internet technology development.

ENTJs rise to prominence in law and business, like ESTJs, but more often cluster where there is significant risk. They are particularly drawn to investment banking and high-tech start-ups, where innovative leadership can turn a disaster into a triumph. If an ENTJ gets into politics, he is most likely to be found leading a new movement (like Lincoln) or a small, at-risk country (like Israel). They are also the most far-sighted "big picture" thinkers and can be found at the top of the largest international corporations, where key decisions must reach into several decades of the future.

ENFJs feel Horizon Dominance in a spiritual zone. While an ENFJ may become a therapist or a teacher, the limits of small groups are frustrating. Especially as an ENFJ gets older and more skilled, he or she will reach for higher levels of influence. ENFJs can be found preaching to huge churches and stadiums, going on motivational speaking circuits, and starting television shows. When they work in smaller contexts, ENFJs are still comfortable with almost unlimited dominance over what they have. They don't hesitate to influence the lives of their employees and families. They may also be comfortable with a high level of dominance in company management, but usually they seek out some kind of idealistic higher good to serve.

Room Dominance means dominance over a literal room full of people, but it also refers to "rooms" of time, space and projects. Among the SJs, the ESFJ is best known for being a classroom teacher. This is literal Room Dominance, since she (or he) has a defined space with a door and windows, walls and display boards, desks and chairs. Every aspect of the room reflects a selection and limitation process. The people who belong in this classroom, whether children or adults, are enrolled members who selected or were assigned to this room. The classroom functions for a period of time: for certain hours, certain days, and a portion of the year. People and things enter and exit that space only with the teacher's permission. Within the room, the teacher sets and enforces rules, offers emotional comfort, and gives instruction. The limit serves to enforce authority.

ESFJs feel confident about what the room ought to look and feel like, because Introverted Sensing has this inborn confidence. Extroverted Feeling is actually the leading mental function, so that managing people in groups comes naturally. It may act somewhat as a limit on dominance, since ESFJs are happiest when they can get direct feedback as to how they're doing in a group. When the group gets so large that it vanishes into the horizon, that feedback stops. So they're generally happy leaving Horizon management to someone else.

Literal classrooms are just a place to start understanding how room limits work. ESFJs are glad to work with less visible walls and limits, as long as people are involved. They are happy as clergymen in a parish, supervising nurses in a hospital, office managers, head librarians, and club presidents or secretaries. When they start out in a low position, they will assiduously seek experience and skills to rise to Room Dominance. This level of dominance is so comfortable for them that not having it can be actively painful.

ESFPs do many of the same things, and they can be found in many of the same roles. The sheer energy of Extroverted Sensing still wants to influence the people and space around them, but with Introverted Feeling, they are less comfortable than ESFJs with managing groups. They can work well as leaders of a smaller "room" zone that's overseen by an ESFJ, for example, a nursing team but not the whole department. Time limits are also welcome; ESFPs are more likely to tackle a bigger zone if they know that dedication to the cause won't need to go on past a certain date. They're also happiest dominating a physical space with action. Organizing for an event, like a wedding reception or family reunion party, is a great match with their motivations. They like to be visible in whatever human field they are in, and they are usually unhappy if they feel overshadowed, pushed out or forgotten. On the other hand, being released from visible influence by the limit of time or space matters just as much.

ENTPs and ENFPs are the Room Dominant Ns, but unlike the Horizon Dominant Ns, they are using Extroverted Intuition. It is their strongest function, and it is pragmatic, inquisitive and optimistic. It functions well when it's plunged into the middle of activity, so they may not feel the same intense need for time alone. On the other hand, the expansive nature of Extroverted Intuition meets the same limits that the ESFP meets with Extroverted Sensing. The actual boundaries of the room zone mean a lot, because expending boundless Extroverted energy would be too draining.

ENTPs may consciously seek limits of both authority and time, specifically because they are aware of how much they can handle with competency and skill. Quality control matters; they do not want to be pushed beyond what they know they can do well. ENTP children like to be team competition leaders, and as they grow up and gain experience, they consciously work on leadership skills. An ENTP who works in a laboratory or university is an enthusiastic project leader. ENTPs who are inventors in some field may build their own team, rather than waiting to be appointed to one within an organization. In that case, they have set their own defined limits and can inform their new employees or team members where they fit into these limits. ENTPs may also share the ESFP's enthusiasm for leadership in parties and social events, especially if there is an inventive twist like a theme party. They may be enthusiastic teachers or lecturers, but again, they prefer to be in charge of a term class or a lecture series.

ENFPs are Room Dominant with all of the same things (classrooms, parties, events, projects), but they are particularly drawn to building teams of people. Their greatest enjoyment may be in building the team (not leading it), so they have a keen interest in being the originator of the idea, not just the person delegated to sit in the head chair. They are firm about the temporary nature of whatever they take on, since the originating steps are the ones they like best and do most successfully. When an ENFP is filling a job that was already defined by someone else, he is happiest developing mini-projects and teams within it. He likes to do one-time lectures and seminars that place him at the microphone, dominating a room that he may never see again. He loves to influence the people at each event, but his interest in maintaining dominance for a longer term drops off fast.

Horizon Dominant and Room Dominant people usually work well together, if they are in the positions they like and have good skills. Their zones of dominance don't compete as much as it might seem, because Horizon types are generally not much interested in managing at the Room level. Part of their Horizon job is to select the right Room types to work under them and then hand off the details. Most of the time, too, Room types are happy not to be at the top. If they managed a wider zone, they would have less control over how things went in their territory. The principal of a school can't care much how the classrooms look, but each teacher takes pride in the room's details. People with natural Horizon Dominance feel it as a penance if they must manage the details of a room, while those with Room Dominance feel deprived if they can't.

As discussed earlier, it can cause serious problems in a workplace if someone with naturally higher dominance is in a lower position. It's so easy for this to happen, because promotion is usually attached to seniority, credentials and having done well at a lower level. For example, if a Room Dominant person gets promoted to a position that's so large as to feel like a horizon, he can be an insecure boss. He knows it's important to maintain influence, but doesn't have the natural desire and skills to do it. He may make mistakes because his skills and force of will are more appropriate for a more limited territory. He may engage in symbolic power battles intended to show employees where the boundaries are. Natural Horizon Dominance is better at understanding how to deal with invisible or uncertain limits, with skills to enforce them without open battles.

A Horizon Dominant employee is this manager's worst nightmare. If he is managing a business with entry-level employees, and an ambitious young Horizon employee comes in and starts observing the manager's errors, that kid could become a target for serious personal dislike. The same can happen to a Room Dominant person who's in a starting position, if there's no clear promotion path upward. Managers who have natural Horizon or Room skills can recognize the skills in a younger person without feeling threatened, but very often, the more dominant younger person just gets in trouble.

THE INTROVERTS: BUBBLE AND SOUL DOMINANCE

Bubble	ISTJ	ISTP	INTJ	INFJ
Soul	ISFJ	ISFP	INTP	INFP

Fig. 15-8

The higher-dominance SJs had Introverted Sensing as a second function, so that their Extroverted Thinking or Feeling reached out to influence the world. But for the ISTJ, Introverted Sensing is strongly primary, leading to Bubble Dominance. In the immediate area around her, the ISTJ needs to exert absolute quality control. This means first her own hands and feet in their workspace; Bubble Dominance goes completely berserk if not permitted that much absolute control. Second, it means anything that people might interpret to be part of the ISTJ's personal space. This is tied to social roles, so that as a husband or wife, the ISTJ feels responsibility for the spouse. The ISTJ parent must have control over the child's appearance, actions and (to some extent anyway) outcomes. The ISTJ's car is part of the bubble, and so are particular rooms at home and work.

ISTJs typically have no interest in managing departments, schools, clubs, churches or large extended families. It's really obvious to them that, if they were promoted to these leadership roles, they'd find themselves stuck with responsibility for other people's careless work. Even with high standards personally, they couldn't enforce them on everyone. It would be like lending out the car for a month to random strangers, since of course you'd expect to find papers, crumbs, sand and sticky slime on things when it came back. This is not how an ISTJ wants the car to look, nor anything else.

However, most ISTJs make very good managers of very small groups, for example, a head volunteer who maintains the contact list and sets up schedules. They are orderly and good with details, so they can be in charge of one part of an event, or of monitoring a few people for a longer term. The ISTJ's greatest leadership skill is setting a good example and asking or prompting others to follow. ISTJs get frustrated if they're expected to enforce the example beyond a few people or a short time. Where some people with higher dominance don't actually want to live out their work or religious ideals when they're "off duty," ISTJs are usually happy to keep up consistency. An ISTJ's office, bedroom, home, refrigerator, garage, car and yard are well-kept. An ISTJ's family observes holiday and religious traditions. It is very important to them that these zones of their close environment remain as orderly as they choose, under their dominance.

ISTPs relate to the outside world through Sensing, but orderly Introverted Thinking is most important. Bubble Dominance means having complete logical control over their own work and workspace. Quality control matters a lot, but it's not about appearances, it's about the actual product. The ISTP mechanic maintains dominance over his garage, tools, quality level and choice of work type. An ISTP chiropractor runs his office with confidence; he is firm about the type of techniques he uses, his office policies, his hours and other details of his personal business. ISTPs are also very good at planning trips in the outdoors, where the focus of planning is on time and space, not people.

Bubble Dominance makes most ISTPs skeptical and a bit resentful of unsolicited advice. It's one thing if the advice is needed, for example if the ISTP is still young and learning, or if she just began a new kind of venture. But when Introverted Thinking is confident of facts and experience, there's a strong sense of competency within the bubble zone. ISTPs may prefer to teach themselves from videos or books, when they need to learn something. That way, they know that their own standards for skill competency have been met. There's nothing an ISTP hates more than to be ripped off by poor teaching when he's intent on learning how to improve his own work.

The two N types in the Bubble Dominance row are both using their primary mental function, Introverted Intuition. This kind of Intuition is focused on spotting mistakes not only in current work but in future planning and comprehension. It's best exercised alone or in very small groups, where Intuition has time to process the facts and make connections. Like the ISTJ, the Introverted Ns care intensely about taking responsibility for, and only for, their own work.

INTJs are most often found in science, engineering and law, where their Bubble Dominant zones are their laboratories, projects and cases. Like the ISTP in his workshop, an INTJ in his lab or office does not invite second-guessing or criticism. His strongest sense of dominance is over how his ideas are carried out. INTJs have a wide imagination about how life could be, but when they have solved a problem a certain way, they can be stubborn about seeing their solution carried out. They are perfectionists, a trait which can be great when they're truly in a Bubble Dominant position. It's not such a good trait if they are promoted to Room or Horizon Dominance, which can happen easily in the tech world.

An INTJ will voluntarily take control of a department or give crowd directions during a disaster if he must. He does it as a larger Bubble Dominance activity, though; if he takes charge for a while, it is because his competency will benefit people by being temporarily extended, like extending his arms. He won't wait for an official time limit to come around, but will quit his temporary leadership as soon as the emergency appears to be over.

The INFJ's "workshop" is often an abstract mental one. INFJs are drawn to situations where they can be of great influence one on one. If they teach (music, yoga, writing), they prefer to give private or small group lessons in a studio. If they go into psychology or ministry, they are happiest in a counseling office, influencing one or two people in a profound way. As parents, they are very focused on each relationship in the family and want to have maximum moral influence. They may be qualified to teach larger groups, and they may be asked to do it, but most INFJs are reluctant because their dominance is watered down in a group. They are not able to have maximum influence with each individual, and that is the really strong zone of their Bubble Dominance. INFJs can also make very courageous Bubble Dominance decisions that place them in prisons for conscience's sake. When they end up leading moral crusades, their focus is always on their own actions and the people nearest to them.

People who are Bubble Dominant can form good teams with others who are Room Dominant. Imagine a teaching team in which one partner naturally leads a room, and the other naturally leads individual sessions, like tutoring. A Room Dominant person loves to start a new program, but it may take a Bubble Dominant partner to examine the details like by-laws, enrollment and personnel. Room Dominant people have an instinct to seek out really competent Bubble Dominants so they can delegate perfection without having to carry it out personally.

Of course, they can also clash, if they are not in their natural roles. When a Bubble Dominant personality winds up managing a room, and a true Room Dominant person becomes a subordinate, the Room Dominant person instinctively finds ways to dominate the room (or team or project) for periods of time. A good Bubble Dominant manager can recognize and use this, but one who is insecure in his position may not be able to. A good Room Dominant employee can find supportive ways to use his dominance, but often it doesn't work that way. The Room Dominant person becomes more popular and can subvert the manager.

Soul Dominance is easy to mistake for Bubble Dominance, and in some individuals there may not be a clear line. The dividing line may be clearest in cases where outsiders have some opinion. Bubble Dominant people care, though they may spurn advice and go their own way. Still, part of having a personal space bubble is that some people are in, and some out, of its boundaries, so other people do have a role. But for strong Soul Dominance, the opinion of other people can come as somewhat of a surprise, in a sort of "I'm sorry, I didn't even see you standing there" way. The real dominance is so deeply internal that decisions and standards were set long before outsiders even noticed.

ISFJs are perhaps least likely to run afoul of what other people think, since they are strongly traditional in their Introverted Sensing. However, they have a strong personal zone of conscience that stands on its own more than may appear. Soul Dominance is about how to use the ISFJ's own resources of time, money and energy. ISFJs may choose to help people or animals that other people consider a waste of time. While others choose luxuries and entertainment, the ISFJ feels right denying herself (or himself) some of these games or clothes in order to give more to others. She is unlikely to ask others to deny themselves, but she considers it her complete right to deny herself.

Many of the most heroic nurses in history have been ISFJs, probably including many of the workers in Mother Theresa's ministry to the dying. Convents and monasteries have always drawn ISFJs, too. While not exercising dominance over the world around them, they exercise an unusual degree of dominance over their own lives and consciences. In this way they are often extremely influential, but only on a personal scale. If they lead at all, it's by personal example and not at all by choice. Rather than wanting to inspire crowds to follow, an ISFJ is likely to warn people off, concerned that the narrow path of conscience may get trampled.

ISFPs express Soul Dominance most often through some kind of aesthetic medium, as an artist's or craftsman's vision. Extroverted Sensing is managing contact with the outside world, while Introverted Feeling is actually the strongest, most idealistic mental function. The Soul must be dominant through what it sees and does with eyes and hands. An ISFP artist, whether visual or performance, often has a personal vision that remains strong in the face of society's rejection. ISFPs are generally responsible for experimental performances of dance, theater, painting and sculpture.

ISFPs who aren't artists find other ways to use their own eyes and hands to express an individual space. They are drawn to quiet work that doesn't require a lot of conversation, but does require a strong sense of personal standards that are only evaluated in their own mind. Massage therapy, for example, draws heavily on the therapist's sense of what ought to be done. The workspace is minimal; it is only the massage therapist's own hands and the physical body she is working on, but only as perceived by her own senses. The workspace is, in a sense, just in the mind.

Both of the Soul Dominant S types can easily fall into not exerting enough dominance in their worlds. The ISFJ's intense focus on taking care of people may take on care projects that are overwhelming or unhealthy in some way, like trying to "fix" an addict. The ISFP's need for quiet harmony can be stronger than the need or desire to stand up for Soul Dominant values. Both of them can fall into relationships with abusive people or get into draining situations that just go on and on. When this happens, there is probably some other part of Soul Dominance that isn't being given enough power. Learning to manage this balance is a big part of the process of learning how to be not just Soul Dominant, but good at being that way. It's easier to see the skills that high dominance people need to learn, but the skills of people with intensely-focused dominance are just as important and can be as hard to learn.

The two Soul Dominant N types both have Extroverted Intuition as a second function, while their real psychological energy is concentrated in Introverted Thinking or Feeling. Extroverted Intuition manages contact with the outside world by generating questions and potentials, not by comparing with other people. This leaves Introverted Judging free to consult nobody but its own idealism. These two personalities may be the ones least influenced by others, which can be good or bad.

INTPs are focused on Soul Dominance of the intellect. They are fiercely autonomous in their beliefs, such as in religion and politics; they are more likely to form a belief in silence from reading a book than from talking to anyone. Peer pressure means nothing, it even must become really stridently obvious for the INTP even to notice that it's there.

Mistakes bother the INTP deeply, because they disturb the internal dominance of his mind; to have errors in a thought process means not being fully in charge of his head. If INTPs are forced into greater dominance because they are very good at something, they find it stressful. Perfectionism is the only way they know to live, but as soon as other people are involved in a task, perfection isn't possible. When INTPs really must be in charge, for example when the project has a high intellectual purpose, they try very hard to do the work by looking at each management task as part of a personal project. To compensate for the stress of living with an imprecise world and sometimes having more oversight duty than he likes, the INTP tends to pick up hobbies that require quiet, concentration, and accuracy. These hobbies might exist only in the mind, where perfection may feel possible.

Soul Dominance in the INFP means maintaining absolute control over his or her imagination and values. INFPs may be reluctant to watch movies that introduce ugly or evil images. They want to be in control of the mind's private kingdom. INFP poets and writers resist being told how or what to write, because they have a vision of an imaginary world already. On the other hand, INFPs greatly dislike telling anyone what to do and may go out of their way to avoid influence. INFP writers can be very uncomfortable with having a public status, even if their work receives popular acclaim. The compliment they want to hear is along the lines of, "I read what you wrote, and then *on my own*, I agreed."

INFPs can be the least stubborn and most stubborn of people, because it all depends on whether the decision at hand has to do with an area of ideological dominance or not. They can take moral positions that are opposed to everyone around them, positions that scandalize more traditional people. At the same time, the inner idealist world is so dominant that, at times, it overwhelms even the INFP. An INFP is able to spend years in a state of guilt or regret over having been forced to do something he or she considers wrong, even if it was truly necessary. Soul Dominance insists that nothing outside of its immaterial kingdom should have had any influence, no matter if it was a question of life or death.

Where do Soul Dominant people fit into balance with other levels? This is a difficult question and it can't be answered in quite the same way as other dominance levels. We could see clearly how the first and second levels, or the second and third, could form partnerships. It's not as easy here. Bubble Dominant people may have difficulty getting along with the Soul Dominant, instead of forming pragmatic teams with them. Bubble Dominant people may expect the Soul Dominant ones to follow their example by controlling their families or work teams, which the lower dominance types are very unwilling to do. So to the Bubble Dominant, they may seem weak. On the flip side, if they appear to stand within a personal space bubble, they're expected to submit to influence—and they may suddenly refuse. Similarly, Room Dominant people understand matters in terms of groups and territories, a system that the Soul Dominant person feels no connection to. It's all good if the rules of the room are suitable, but Soul Dominant people can only be a cog in the machine for so long before they bust out and do something unexpected.

Horizon Dominance may be the easiest fit for teaming with Soul Dominance. At this level of dominance, they're used to experiencing frequent or chronic power challenges, and the Soul Dominant person simply does not make such challenges. Nor is Soul Dominance impressed with organizational power. A Horizon Dominant person may find this refreshing, and she or he may also find better personal acceptance through lack of conflict. It can be hard for a Horizon Dominant person to accept or seek advice, but sometimes the humble (but independent) low-dominance person is able to fill this role. Soul Dominance also brings a unique kind of wisdom, since these people have learned to give up many things they wanted in pursuit of their ideals or inner vision. We often see partnerships of the Horizon and the Soul in the art world, where artistic vision stays true only because of a protector who can manage financial and legal battles for the artist. The stubborn independence of the Soul Dominant person may be easier for the most dominant people to understand.

If you're trying to understand someone's personality, think about his or her work frustrations. Is this person at the right level of dominance? Does he have the right skills (especially in listening and taking blame) for his territory? Does she appear to chafe at management decisions, feeling she could do it better? What goals does this person set? Does he become happier or more stressed with promotion?

It's important to understand what someone's natural dominance level is, because each type of dominance requires a different life philosophy, skills and experiences. If your personality is mismatched with your life in its dominance requirements, it is not likely that you are happy. You may be able to function at one level higher or lower than your natural one, but if you are pushed beyond that, it will be stressful. If an INTP professor is appointed Dean of his college, he may be very unhappy before long. Similarly, an ESTJ kept at a low level of power by prejudice or bad luck may become very depressed. It's also important to understand that exercise of dominance is not a bad thing, in itself. The people around you have different needs and skills in dominance, and it's important to value them for what they can do and who they are. Dominance that is handled well helps everyone.

In a personal relationship, ask yourself how much zeal and zest your friend has for getting her way. If she convinces you to buy something you weren't interested in before, does it make her happy or uncomfortable? Does he handle disappointment well when things don't work out as he had imagined? How does he deal with this disappointment; does he make plans so that next time it won't happen, or just calm himself into not caring? Do you notice your friend reacting in a more dominating way when fewer people are present, or when a room is crowded? How much does she convey detailed expectations to you, or to the family? How much does she care about their exact fulfillment, and how much is she willing to do in order to make it work?

Naturally dominant people usually put a lot of effort into making sure their expectations will be fulfilled if possible, including teaching someone else the needed skills. When they learn lessons from experience, the lessons aren't just internal. They make note of what they can do differently so that others will do differently—and the second part, getting others to change, is the real focus. People in the lower dominance zones naturally turn to internal lessons: how they should respond or react differently. They don't usually anticipate much change in others.

You may also need to factor in life difficulties that make high dominance more difficult. For example, in a time of grief or anxiety, we all retreat from responsibility if possible. If you are evaluating a friend who suffers from clinical depression or anxiety, think carefully about dominance. A Room Dominant person with anxiety may act Bubble Dominant, but with dissatisfaction. Similarly, a depressed or anxious Horizon Dominant person can only handle a room. Since that's not the personality's natural zone, the Horizon person resents the details of managing a room and criticizes higher management. If you asked, he or she would say "oh no, I don't want to be in charge," but that may only be anxiety speaking.

We all have biases when we guess at someone's underlying personality type. We tend to assume that men are Thinkers and women are Feelers and it's easy to find evidence to confirm this bias. Most people seem to over-estimate the effect of Intuition in personality, noticing how important intuition (in the usual sense of the word) is and assuming that this means it's a dominant feature of personality. It's particularly easy to be biased toward your own personality's traits. Make your guesses in pencil, take notes, keep the case open, and be ready to erase.

CHAPTER 16

Marriage in Balance

There's one key relationship in which personalities have to work together in balance. Like a friendship, it is freely chosen. Like family, it's a relationship you can't easily opt out of when things are hard. It's financially managed like a business, but at its heart is the unpredictable energy of sex. Marriage is probably the single hardest task that people attempt, but civilization depends on it. The stakes are very high when children are involved, and yet betrayal can happen in small, barely noticeable details. The wrong decision could create life or death situations, but when it's successful, this relationship can be a lifelong source of comfort, happiness, and fulfillment.

Marriage involves two key lifetime decisions. First, are you going to marry this person? Second, if you're now married, can you go on with life in the partnership or do you need to make the decision to dissolve it legally? We have to make such decisions with so many factors to consider, and ultimately, we have to gamble on what's in another person's mind.

However well you know the person you're going to marry, or have married, there is some chance that you've overlooked or misunderstood some part of who they are. Even if you completely understand them now, time may bring changes. How can you predict someone's response to life? It goes without saying that you really can't. However, there are some ways to use personality balance to get a more realistic grip on which issues are most important and how changes are likely to develop.

Whatever is a natural response to your personality is what you're likely to keep doing as you get older, and do more when you're under stress. When we're young, we can learn alternative ways to manage our feelings, and these ways can appear to suit us. But when some disaster settles in, when life becomes a matter of caring for a severely disabled child or struggling in unremitting poverty, it becomes too hard to live in ways that aren't natural.

Your own personality patterns will reassert themselves. When this happens, you may be a better or worse partner in the marriage. It depends on the combination of personalities.

Life can be very difficult; it can put insurmountable barriers in front of you. You can't stop that from happening. But you can, with some planning, try to make marriage as easy as possible so that as a couple, you will have less difficulty facing the barriers. If you haven't yet chosen someone to marry, you can try to use your understanding of personality to put your own personality, and the other person's, to work in passive ways so that half the work is done without effort. It's like choosing the right breed of dog for some kind of work; you're halfway there if the dog's instincts are already on board.

If you've already married, you already have a sense of whether you're finding it easy or difficult to manage life tasks together. This outline of how personality can help with marriage balance may clarify why things are going well or badly. Personality notes can't tell you what you should do about divorce, if that's in your mind. Analysis can only help you see what's likely to change with time, and what's permanent. You may be able to develop some thoughts about how to nudge joint personality balance a little bit, or you may be able to spot some options for change that hadn't been visible before.

I'll discuss three areas in which we can predict the consistent ways someone will react and behave: decisions and conscience; priorities and attention; and interpersonal dominance. Decisions are shaped by Judging functions. For convenient shorthand, I'll use the abbreviations T and F to mean personality types with that letter in the name—or, in other words, personalities that have Thinking or Feeling as one of the top two functions. Priorities and attention are shaped by Perceiving, and when discussing them, I'll use the same shorthand, S and N for personality types with that letter in the name (and that function in the top two). It's much easier to drop the full words and just refer to people as Ts, Fs, Ss or Ns. Doing so brings a broader level of generalization, since the distinctions made in past chapters are only sometimes important in this context. The distinctions are not less important overall, but to talk about marriage in general, we need to look at the large trends among groups of people.

DECISIONS AND CONSCIENCE

Whenever we talk about decisions, the focus is typically on the outcome: how to make the *right* decision. But in the context of discussing marriage, I want to throw away the question of "right" outcome. Outcome of a decision concerns the future, especially a future we think we can control. The character of a marriage is often about the past, about memories and decisions that can't be altered since time has moved on. Decisions may have worked out badly, but they are now historical events. We must live with the past, changing (perhaps) only how we view it or feel about it.

Furthermore, marriage is part of a journey through life without any actual control over the future. None of us can really control what happens in the next hour. Some people are acutely aware of this fact, having survived a terror attack or other sudden tragedy. After Joan Didion's husband died instantly of a heart attack, she wrote, "You sit down to dinner and life as you know it ends."[98] Isn't this true each day, every day, even if some people's lives have run smoothly enough to permit them to feel like they have control? We can't plan for how our decisions, or the other person's, work out.

What we do control is the way we've evaluated decisions, which usually remains stable over a lifetime. Your life story is a blend of outcomes you like and don't like, but the way you made each decision shapes how you *feel* about the outcome. You can still feel good about a bad outcome if your own choices were and are consistent with your values. You can console yourself that we all win some and lose some, and at least you were true to yourself or did your best.

So when we talk about decisions and conscience in marriage, we're looking not at how things turned out, but at how you feel, together, about the process. When you share life with someone, including financial and legal responsibility, you may find decisions made for you. To remain happy in marriage while life goes through ups and downs, husbands and wives need to have confidence and empathy. In a nutshell: whatever happens, you can't blame each other. You have to know that both of you did your best. How do we improve the odds of this kind of understanding?

Husband and wife need to know that they considered all possible facts and didn't carelessly overlook something important. If they are opposite in dominant Judging, one T and one F, they are more likely to see and consider all facts and options. That's a basic teamwork principle: don't duplicate the same strengths and weaknesses in each member. Ts and Fs are better set to make the best pragmatic decision when they can offer alternative facts and debate opinions with each other.

On the other side, husband and wife need to have a shared sense of moral priorities. So many key decisions are made without any opportunity to have a conference, and sometimes they're made on gut instinct in a split second. Some decisions don't even clearly show up as decisions; they are actions we take, but with choices built into them. We may not even have time to think them out, let alone have a conference. We're going by the moral steering of Introverted Thinking or Introverted Feeling at those moments, perhaps unable to articulate why we turned right or left at the critical moment. It's very easy to be a Monday morning quarterback about such decisions, and when they turn out badly, criticism is compelling and maybe impossible to avoid.

Imagine a horrible "Sophie's Choice" moment, in which a parent must choose to save only one child. It can't be avoided, the choice must be made, and it might be a decision made by a nonverbal process like speed or muscle strength. Afterward, the choice must be lived with—by both parents. It's crucially important to have deep empathy for the way the decision was made when its outcome brings grief and guilt. Husband and wife must be able to say "In his or her place, I would have done the same thing," at least as closely as possible. If not, there's going to be serious trouble even if the "Sophie's Choice" was not the full-bore drama of life and death.

Even when parents must choose in a matter as small as which child to help with homework, they may be critical of each other's choices. There's an important difference between conscious and unconscious criticism, too. Refraining from active criticism is

98: Joan Didion, *The Year of Magical Thinking* (New York: Knopf, 2005), 3.

a choice you can make, but if your inner heart and mind feel that "I would have done something different," you're critical whether you choose it or not. This deeper unconscious criticism comes out in nonverbal ways: facial expressions, hesitation or reluctance to act, and apparently unrelated decisions that stem from those deep feelings. The person who feels guilty usually knows pretty accurately whether his or her spouse is unconsciously critical.

Unconscious, nonverbal decisions come from inborn, idealistic, instinctive knowledge. So it's usually easier for a married couple to share the same root of conscience, Feeling or Thinking. Two warm or two cool consciences understand each other. If you've ever faced a really hard moral dilemma or painful choice, you know that some people innately understand your decision, while others don't understand no matter how much you explain. Those who "get" what you did usually turn out to have the same conscience orientation, even if they have quite different personality types.

So one factor for harmony in making decisions is that both husband and wife have the same type of conscience. Warm and cool conscience form a checkerboard pattern on the personality type chart:

ESTJ	ESTP	ENTJ	ENFJ
ESFJ	ESFP	ENTP	ENFP
ISTJ	ISTP	INTJ	INFJ
ISFJ	ISFP	INTP	INFP

Fig. 16-1

In theory, we learn whether we have this type of compatibility during the time we're friends and dating, before marriage. In practice, it's very easy to overlook moral decisions or project our own framework where it doesn't belong. It's very hard to observe with complete objectivity and be able to tell with confidence which kind of conscience we see in a loved one. It's certainly worth the time spent studying this factor by itself, deliberately, to understand unconscious moral choices before we make those choices part of our permanent history.

Let's go back to the idea of teamwork to make pragmatic decisions. In these choices, although we can't control the outcome, we're doing our best to get the results we prefer. There may be moral dimensions, but we're focused on gathering all facts and options. A good decision means one that didn't overlook some range of known options; when its outcome is adverse, it's because the good decision gets derailed mainly by unknown, uncontrollable factors. That's when we feel that we did our best, even in losing. We know we did all we could.

Whenever people form a team, they try to choose members or partners who represent a wide array of skills and experience. For marriage to use this principle, it's better for husband and wife to have opposite Judging strengths. In shorthand, Ts are better off marrying Fs. Fs should marry Ts.

This is not the rule you'll find in some other books and articles about personality matches. It's much more common to suggest that we eliminate potential disagreement with Ts marrying Ts, and Fs marrying Fs. The idea is that the closer you can come to marrying someone just like yourself, the less arguing you'll have. I've already agreed with this principle concerning moral conscience, because disagreement about nonverbal, unconscious life-and-death values is corrosive. However, when the arguing can be done as pragmatic debating or delegating, it's not harmful.

When the marriage faces the world in economic competition, the team needs to have all skills, strengths and facts available. We get and change jobs, buy and sell houses, move our kids into different schools, and many more things. Such pragmatic decisions are really supposed to work out in the "right" ways, and we try to make them with the best information. Ts and Fs often start by disagreeing about these decisions. Obviously, Ts are probably talking about numbers (usually time and money), while Fs are talking about human needs in the family. Both sides need to be considered.

In Chapter 13, I presented a short list of basic tasks that every personality must handle across a lifetime. This list also applies to married couples and families, though in different ways.

1. Do or make something of value (i.e. work) to trade with the rest of society.

2. Form lasting ties of attachment within their age group, and with older and younger generations.

3. Ward off social danger and repair broken relationships.

A team must be able to manage these tasks with the outside world while, at the same time, managing them with each other. Do or make something of value to trade with the world, but also value to trade with each other. Form lasting ties with our parents and our children (and helping each other to do so) while maintaining ties together. Ward off danger from the world and between each other, repair damage with the world but also, very importantly, between each other.

A T and F team is best equipped to take on these tasks facing the outside world. Their contributions may not be similar or parallel. T personalities respond well to competition, so overall they are more likely to be good at earning money for the team. F personalities are much more likely to be good at generational bonding. Both T and F personalities have ways to defend against danger, but they're often keyed to different types of danger. Fs in general are much more attuned to the need to repair damaged relationships. That's what they excel in, as Ts excel in competition.

There are certainly happy marriages of Ts to Ts, and Fs to Fs. None of my personality analysis should be construed to criticize a functioning, happy marriage. There's no better test than what actually works. However, there are some risks in forming same-Judging teams (that is, same in strengths and relative importance, not in kind of conscience). The greatest risk comes in the last category: defending against aggression and repairing damage afterward.

Ts tend to see number-oriented danger and overlook social danger, while Fs go the other way. Fs are very concerned about subtle social attacks that will make them lose friends or community status. They look for hostility within the extended family and usually fret a lot about signs of danger among cousins and in-laws. Ts, on the other hand, usually focus on danger inherent in transactions with money and the law. Both Ts and Fs can see the other type of danger once it's pointed out, but they're likely to miss early signs.

When two Fs are married, they may not be able to defend themselves effectively against hard-edged dangers like lawsuits and violence. It may be that neither of them knows how to assess vulnerability. Also, perhaps neither of them has enough competitiveness and aggression to follow through the process of defense. When the problem hangs on, they grow emotionally tired and want to find a relationship solution. "Let's just ask them to drop the lawsuit." This sounds like a perfectly good idea to both Fs, whereas a T could recognize that signaling weakness is a big mistake. They may both lack the determination to stand up to unruly children, especially if those children are competitive Ts. Although the F spouses treat each other with warmth and kindness, as time goes by they suffer as a team from the damages of the world. Eventually, the losses may be so great that their personal harmony gets more difficult. At least one of them probably feels strongly that the other should have done something, should have seen the danger or had the right skills.

Two Ts are generally good at defending against logical and numerical dangers. They both read contracts carefully and negotiate lower fees, and they both know how to watch for that moment when benign competition turns into aggression. They both see the need to put these objective issues ahead of relationships, easily keeping secrets from friends when it's necessary. Sometimes, two Ts become a formal team to compete with the world, such as a political candidate and his T wife who acts as campaign manager. As long as they're focused on the external threats, it can work out well.

Repairing damage may be more difficult. Even in competing with and defending against the world, two Ts may lose relationships by coming off as hard-edged and unapologetic. Not seeing a logical reason to take action, they assume someone's hurt feelings will go away over time. But it's between each other that the worst damage usually accumulates. Both T spouses are focused on schedule, duties, and success; at the same time, both of them have emotions that notice slights, failures, and betrayals. Ts generally handle their hurt feelings by "putting them in a box" to deal with later. Their experience with emotion has been that feelings come and go, so they expect benign neglect to take care of it. Unfortunately, sometimes this doesn't work.

Over the years, two T spouses can both build up a deep base of resentment that neither of them can really process. They may both feel like the actual issues are trivial or already dealt with, since their framework of logic and numbers thinks this is true. The emotional measuring scale is completely different and quite unrelated to the size of the event. A tiny event can represent a very large wound. Ts are most likely to come to this understanding if one or both goes into therapy, because talk therapy is the domain of Fs. F observers quickly see the magnitude of damage.

Two T spouses can also have a problem with neglect of emotional needs. Every T has emotional needs, but most cannot see them even in themselves. Even when they can see the emotional needs of the other, they may not be able to help. So between not seeing and not meeting needs, they can both become isolated and deeply lonely. Talk therapy with an F counselor can help to understand the problem, but even then, it's not possible to magically transform T personalities into something else. The inability to meet these needs may be as genuine as the inability of a cow to lay eggs. Both spouses tend to seek solutions to emotional needs in other people, usually trying to keep these ties in safe categories: friends, therapists, co-workers. There is great danger that one or both T will become overwhelmed with emotion, falling in love or otherwise going out of bounds.

There's a simple and compelling reason why many Ts marry Ts, and Fs marry Fs. When we're young, there's a fairly long period when we're working hard to develop our own strengths. It's a longer period when there's no role model at hand, especially a role model of the same sex. A boy who's just like his father, or a girl just like her mother, learns confidence earlier. The years in which we're consciously trying hard to become good at our strengths can comprise much of our 20s. We tend to admire people who are good at the same things we are, and we're often deeply uncomfortable with or even offended by people who are bad at those things and good at very different ones, things we don't value. So in their 20s, Ts are likely to find each other's rationality a relief after a few bad experiences with emotional Fs. Fs, on the other hand, may find most Ts cold and unforgiving compared to warmer, kinder Fs. In our 20s, like attracts like. It's only over time, perhaps throughout the decade of 30s, that people face the shortcomings of their own strengths and learn to value what they don't have.

Ts may find chronic problems deeply stressful because they can't solve it, which feels like failure. Money, time, and logic can't always solve a chronic illness, for example, nor can they resolve events that are already past. T solutions can try to solve a problem like infertility, but the solutions may not work. When logical and number approaches fail consistently, Ts become very dejected. That's what they've got, and it didn't work. They are extremely dependent on an F partner to bring hope, to create emotional solutions that they can't see. An F might see feelings where a T sees only facts and numbers; the feelings perhaps can be solved, but only with emotional and relationship solutions.

Two Feeling type personalities can be trapped together in a very different sort of problem. Disagreement often brings in conflict, even if it leads to a solution. Most F personalities are uneasy about conflict because the decision is less important to them than the relationship. Fs are easily flooded by anxiety that's out of proportion to the disagreement. Two Fs can both be flooded by fears of how much they may be hurting the other one's feelings. Often this state leads to avoiding the discussion entirely, trying instead to finesse a solution without direct negotiation. It may also lead to a roller-coaster of emotion, as each sees the other's emotion and becomes upset and worried. When a Thinking personality is included in the conflict, the dynamics don't usually go the same way. Fs slowly realize that Ts aren't getting "hurt" in the way they expect. The Thinking purpose of a conflict is to air facts and opinions, and even if the T type seems angry, the anger is quickly gone. This is a relief to the Feeler.

It's perhaps easiest to see the advantage of Ts and Fs marrying across type when we look at their children's needs. Children of parents who are both Ts or both Fs may receive less balance in discipline. To take a historical example, the ENFP poet Robert Browning married INFP poetess Elizabeth Barrett Browning. They had one child, a son who was raised entirely by Feeling values and decisions. They made sure that he would never wake up at night and find himself alone. He was expected to be beautiful and sensitive, not tough. They gave him whatever he wanted, if they could afford it. Neither parent could model or encourage competition or unemotionality; it's not surprising that the boy grew into a pretty hapless adult.

Children of two T parents usually find both of them tough disciplinarians. Results and numbers matter most. This can be very good for achievement in the outside world, but the child may have emotional things that neither parents can detect. After an apparently problem-free childhood, a teenager or young adult may suddenly turn complicated, to the bewilderment of both parents. Unresolved anger and unseen needs can grow into a rejection nightmare. Sometimes the situation is rescued by an F sibling or grandparent who steps in to buffer the unrelenting focus on rationality and achievement.

Criticizing someone's marriage is a very high-risk gamble, so I want to repeat again that if you are in a marriage like this, two Ts or two Fs, and it's working, that's great. If one spouse has cool conscience and the other warm, and you're able to "get" each other, that's great too. My suggested principles are most useful to those who are making future decisions about marriage, or to those who know that married life is not going smoothly and need to know why. There are many times when just understanding why something has happened goes a long way toward forgiving or adapting.

PRIORITIES AND ATTENTION

In addition to moral and pragmatic decisions, there are many ongoing decisions about how to spend our time and where to focus our energies. Choices that we make in actions and attention come from Perceiving more than from Judging. We may call them decisions, but they're more like preferences, talents or even possibilities. Our Perceiving strengths show us the world as our eyes can see it, and we can't see it any other way. We focus on what we see. We pay attention to what we're able to process quickly. We're happy when we're doing what we're good at, and everyone tries to spend as much time in that happiness zone as possible.

Some of the same teamwork concerns about skills and blind spots apply to the balance of Perceiving in marriage. Ss have the best vision and attention for real, material things and the present time. Ns have better vision and attention for potential things, invisible connections and the future time. They have very different blind spots and an ideal group would definitely include both Ss and Ns. Including both types of Perceiving strength matters a lot for survival, since Ss and Ns see different kinds of dangers and solutions. To the extent that marriage is that kind of team, it clearly benefits from having one S and one N.

On the other hand, marriage is a very stripped-down, minimalist team. It can't employ more than two people. It's also a uniquely vulnerable one; if a team member needs to be replaced, life as we know it ends. Most other teams, for work or adventure, can take on extra members or replacements, but marriage cannot. It's also a team with an open-ended mission, one that the team can define. Search and rescue teams *must* go out into the field, and political teams *must* campaign, but a husband and wife can determine their projects to fit their preferences. If they both prefer to live in the real, concrete world or in the world of ideas, they can usually find a way to support themselves. It's not quite the same as with Thinking and Feeling, where life will force the issues we'd rather steer around.

Experience shows that it's easier for two S or two N spouses to make marriage work. The two different ways of Perceiving can create such different mindsets that it's as though a canyon is fixed between two people. Bridging the canyon requires so much work that it uses up energy for solving external problems. I think this is true most of the time; but as with any human issues, there's a large minority exception. S and N personalities who grew up in families with a mix are better at relating to each other, for example. Some S personalities use Intuition in ways that make them very comfortable around Ns, and the same is true of some Ns who have good Sensing ability, so these individuals may be natural bridges. When you read this section, please keep in mind the way that your individual personality balance might make some parts more relevant than others.

A married couple can also have so much else in common that their Perceiving orientation does not feel like more of a difference than any other. Life in common is particularly strong as a unifier in a subculture within the larger culture, such as a church community, an immigrant or ethnic community, or some close-knit schools or other groups. So if readers have not experienced such a divide between S and N personalities, I don't mean to project a canyon onto their lives when it doesn't exist. My own parents were different in Perceiving orientation, but they did not feel that it caused any sort of wall, canyon or other barrier between them.

However, most often, the S and N difference is experienced as a canyon that leaves two souls calling out across a distance and unable to get close enough to see what life looks like to each other. The canyon can exist between parents and children, siblings, and friends. It's only a greater problem in marriage because of the way marriage combines elements of family and friendship, voluntary choice and involuntary duty. That high-stakes mix of emotional dependence and practical decisions magnifies any sense of isolation or non-comprehension. When Perceiving differences are among friends or working partners, we can use the personality framework to just understand and respect each other. That's usually enough for non-marital relationships, including siblings and other family relationships. But for marriage, with its unique stresses, we need more than general respect for differences. There are some really difficult conflicts caused by S and N differences in outlook. By looking at them as caused by personalities, not situations, readers may find insight for resolving them.

The simplest surface problem is in daily attention span: what do we put our time and energy into, what do we talk about, what do we aim for? S personalities focus on the concrete things that need to be done, and this is true for both Introverted S and Extroverted S types. As noted in Chapter 9, Introverted and Extroverted Sensing have very different strengths, but they usually work together in close, happy cooperation. They agree on the importance of getting things done: fixing, making, buying, and many other actions.

N personalities, by contrast, are often a little bit resentful of the need for concrete actions in daily life. Even when "resentful" is an overstatement, they're usually trying to bring another layer into the tasks. When gardening, they're incorporating what they've read about organic methods, insects, hybrids, or comparative ideas of irrigation. S personalities can be equally interested in such things; it's hard to out-geek an ISTP or ISTJ who's on a research bender. However, there's often a difference in emphasis. For an S personality, research is for improving our skills, tools and outcomes. For most N personalities, research is for bringing in a layer of meaning that's otherwise lacking. N personalities usually feel that the tasks themselves need further motivational tie-ins.

Ns bring this attitude to every part of daily life. What they do has more meaning if it's tied to something they're thinking or reading about. Improving what they're doing is important, but the *meaning* of it all is *more* important. The ultimate meaning of everything is tied into mankind's quest for innovation and new ideas. Basically, N personalities accept daily life with more enthusiasm, the more it's tied to ideas and generalizations. Generalizing your own gardening to an idea like "what it means to produce food," or "taking care of the earth," is what gives gardening its meaning. It's the meaning that matters, and it's often the generalized meaning that Ns want to talk about.

At one level, this isn't a problem at all. If a husband and wife are working together on gardening, they're both interested in doing it well. If one of them has an N personality and likes to read philosophical works on gardening, or books on plant biology, or accounts of irrigation and pest control around the world, it's fine. They'll both enjoy talking about it over dinner. That's when the gain in teamwork is most visible, when they both care about what they're doing and what it means.

But N personalities have two other traits that cause problems. First, they are interested in all ideas about meaning, whether the ideas have relevance to daily personal life, or not. Second, they assume that everyone close to them must be equally interested. Ns try to talk about whatever they're reading, even if they know that the subject isn't of particular interest to the listener. They believe and hope that the ideas are interesting by themselves. To an N, it's not only polite but really kind to offer book reports as dinner table chat. Since other Ns all feel a bit chafed about the routine of daily life, they appreciate hearing scraps of ideas from other people's books. They may not have time to read the book, but they can ponder the interesting ideas while washing dishes or mowing the lawn.

Some Ns already know that book report conversations won't work for most people. Others blithely do it anyway. Sometimes it works out okay, but often an S listener feels that the N talker is being inconsiderate. To the N talking about a book, the information seems funny, unusual or significant, therefore it's perfectly polite to share. But to many S listeners, it's never polite to talk for more than a minute or two about a book that isn't interesting to both people. It may keep the listener from getting things done, or it may just put a claim on his attention span. Most Ns have very long attention spans for talking about books, even ones they haven't read. Most Ss don't, so they start to feel resentment building when their polite (but unenthusiastic) comments fail as hints to stop. The N talker is paying close attention to memory and ideas, so anything short of walking away may be taken as interest and encouragement. When the conversation finally ends, the N is still thinking about the book, rejoicing in having something so interesting to offer, while the S is thinking, "what a self-centered talker."

The mirror image of this problem happens when the N listener must spend long periods of time around small talk, which is usually centered around universal concrete topics like weather, seasons, traffic and prices. Perhaps outnumbered, the N listener can't turn the conversation to an N interest like something with science or history that might be related to the small talk. The conversation's purpose is to help people feel accepted and included, not to bring in new ideas or facts. Not all Ns, but many, become frustrated and bored.

In a marriage, conversational differences like this can turn into conflicts about extended family. If an N and S spouse need to spend time with each other's families, they could feel isolated with the in-law family. "Your family is so self-centered, talking on about what nobody cares about," and "I can't bear to spend time with your mom, who only talks about prices," could be signs of Perceiving differences. Instead of calling others self-centered or boring, we should understand that this is just how Ns and Ss show caring. However, sometimes the differences could be too great to overcome easily this way, and people stop accepting each other's families (or the families can't accept the spouses).

The same difference in attention can make it harder for Ss and Ns to find things they really enjoy doing together. As a general rule, Ns are happier reading and talking, while Ss are happier doing things like walking, dancing, or traveling. Each type of Perceiving relaxes best when it's focusing only one what it likes best: for Ns, ideas and talking, for Ss, things and actions. On the other hand, there are many reasons to enjoy things, so the Perceiving difference may not present insurmountable barriers. Some Ns like to hike, dance and travel; some Ss love to read. If you do have real problems finding things to enjoy in common, it's worth considering if Perceiving is the reason.

The difference in attention becomes a more serious problem in handling conflict. There are certainly exceptions to this rule, but on average most Ns want to figure out why the conflict happened. Most Ss prefer to settle it in some way and not talk about it again. Many Ss have a strong sense of moving forward through time and do not want to revisit even the recent past. Others care about the past, but they don't find it intriguing or useful to know why things happened; the past may be mainly a source of anger that's better forgotten. Still others care about why a conflict happened, but once the question is answered, it's over.

Most Ns care more about why the conflict happened than about what its outcome was. They also care a lot about how the conflict played out, how the process went. Ns are keen to observe patterns that put many different incidents into a meaningful order. When they discuss what conflicts mean, they may pull up a long-past incident or one that seems trivial compared to what's at stake now. They may want to compare personal events with historical or literary (fictional) ones, because they see a pattern. Some Ns, particularly in the NF temperament column, want to discuss conflict patterns until absolutely everything is understood by both people. Others, particularly NTs, are glad to discuss an incident, but they reach a comfortable level of understanding faster and feel ready to dismiss it as a problem solved. On average, Ns have a significantly longer attention span for hashing over past relationship problems than most Ss.

The N habit of discussing conflicts until patterns are clear may be okay with an S spouse. The purpose of talking out a conflict is to understand how to keep it from happening again, and some S husbands and wives appreciate this effort. Very often, though, the habit becomes a real irritation. When an S personality does not share this need, the constant discussions feel like unforgiveness, manipulation, punishment, or just obsessive focus on something that's done and over. Digging up the past seems dangerous; buried hurts could be re-activated. Maybe the S had accepted a benign idea of what the conflict had been about, and the N's bringing it up again disturbs this settlement and makes the conflict feel worse than she remembered. Maybe the conflict had an emotional facet that the S is not yet ready to face and really prefers to bury. For S personalities, the discussion process that Ns need really might turn sour. It suits them better to "just move on," a phrase they often use. Let the past be past, just move on and do better.

There's wisdom in moving on and letting the past be past; sometimes it's the best way to handle past conflict. The problem is that Ns actually need the clarity that discussion brings. Many lack the *ability* to "move on" without coming to inner harmony. They can try to "move on" externally, but internally the conflict is never really over. Worse, some Ns may have a greater need to understand the conflict than they're even aware of. NFs are usually keenly aware of the need, but NTs may have the need without feeling it. When conflicts end without clarity, they may "move on," but they may also draw wrong conclusions about what it meant. As Ns, they are incapable of letting it go without drawing some kind of conclusion. Without a partner in understanding the meaning, they may form an inaccurate sense of how they relate to people. Very typically, NTs may grow much worse at recognizing their own fault in the matter and turn into people who never see any reason to apologize.

N spouses who don't have a partner in hashing out the meaning of conflict may find friends or therapists who can help. With outside help, they can at least form a sense of what happened and what it means. But then there's an obvious problem: the N's sense of meaning isn't shared by the S spouse. This may be a benign problem if the S spouse has a fairly similar sense of things, achieved without talking. But it can also set them on a collision course such that after a few years, they live together but in different mental worlds. Everything that happens fits into the N's mental pattern, confirming and developing meaning, but the S spouse may have a completely different interpretation.

The need to know what things mean is usually as urgent for Ns as the need to exercise, or the need to get things done, is for their S spouses. It isn't an option that can be switched off. If daily life goes along without serious problems, the N spouse may be okay. However, if some tragedy happens (serious illness, death in the family, severe financial loss), the meaning of conflict can become the most important thing in the N's world. If an S spouse is not able to find common understanding, it will become very hard for the two to maintain a peaceful marriage. Instead, grief isolates and estranges them.

Another key difference between Ns and Ss is their tendency to view daily events as ordinary or unusual. Unusual events call for unusual or new solutions, instead of the traditional and customary ones. Ns serve as the innovators in society, always standing ready to offer ideas or take charge when customary action isn't working. Because this is their hard-wired worldview, they often rush to assume that many or most things are unusual, disturbing, or signs of change to come.

Most Ss, on the other hand, are hard-wired to see events as fitting into the flow of time. What has happened before is what's happening now, and we should do what has been done before. It worked before, so it will work now. Trying out something new is risky, since we already know what worked before. Why improve on success? Why take risks? Everyone agrees on what is customary, so if it somehow doesn't work, other Ss will not blame them for sticking with the tried and true.

All people have a strong bias toward seeing confirmation of their ideas as events play out. They tend to remember the times they were right. If an S personality has a strong tendency to assume that everything is going as usual and will turn out okay, he generally remembers all of the many times when it was true. For the times when this assumption was wrong, either there's a way to explain it or it's just forgotten. If an N personality has a strong tendency the opposite way, the same confirmation bias makes him remember every time when his insistence saved the day. So although sometimes things are ordinary and will be okay, and other times they are unusual and will not be okay without unusual action, both Ss and Ns find confirmation that their approach is right.

If one way of assessing the world was always better, it would be simpler to judge between them. Instead, either one could be right, depending on the actual facts. Let's say the baby wakes up crying in the night and starts really screaming. One parent assumes that the problem is ordinary and can wait till morning, when the doctor's office is open and it's easy to check in. Not only that, but in an ordinary case, some typical comforts will help and the baby will feel better. The other parent believes that this crying is a sign of some emergency condition coming on. The baby needs to go straight to the hospital, no matter how much trouble or cost it occasions.

Of course, we can't really say that the "it's okay" parent is an S and the "we have an emergency" parent is an N. It could be that one knows a lot more about sickness or babies, or that one is depressed or tends to be anxious. However, this type of dilemma is typical of the S and N approaches for many things, not just sick babies. Ns always have a radar scanning for change. Their detectors for change are set to register the smallest rumbles; after detecting a few signs that maybe things are different this time, the N's "software" begins calculating how to use the small, early signs to predict just how big the change is going to be. Long before the S spouse is ready to act, an N has concluded that something must be done. It may be heading for the hospital, or it may be some even more drastic action that will burn bridges.

Furthermore, Ns have a strong tendency to prefer alternative medicine, while Ss have the same tendency to feel safer within the network of traditional, officially-certified doctors. Again, this may be different in some cases, and there are certainly SP types who love alternative medicine (probably because of their Introverted Intuition, which provides a "Film Noir" suspicion of authorities). However, by and large, the field of alternative medicine is dominated by Ns. They're more likely to use the remedies, leave traditional careers and become alternative practitioners, write books to promote alternative approaches, and feel comfortable in the alternative medicine milieu (which is often crowded with other Ns).

So when a married couple, one S and one N, face symptoms of serious illness, they may get locked in conflict. By itself, that's okay. Disagreement and conflict are how we look at all options and make better decisions. Just as with Ts and Fs bringing their viewpoints to a decision, Ns and Ss can also prevent blind spots. The problem comes when the N and S worldviews function as a sort of conscience, not a true moral one, but a sense of how things should be. When a decision works out badly, can such different worldviews maintain sympathy, not blaming the other for the outcome?

It's possible, but it's difficult. Let's take the simple example of the sick baby. Suppose that the N spouse wants to jump up immediately and take the baby to the hospital, while the S spouse wants to wait, try ordinary remedies, and see if the problem goes away. As a couple, they will come to a decision one way or the other, whether they argue or handle it peaceably. So let's say they take the baby straight to the hospital. After an hour of driving and waiting has passed, the baby seems fine; examination and bloodwork prove that it was probably just a passing pain. Now let's say that the family has to pay a pretty large bill for the visit, and this turns into an ongoing dispute with the insurance company. Three months later, when the dispute goes to appeal, the S spouse (whose view proved to be correct, the baby was fine) probably resents what happened. He or she feels that next time the N spouse makes a big deal out of something, it's important not to give in.

On the other hand, perhaps the baby really was rapidly developing meningitis. If the S spouse chose to wait the extra hours until it was convenient to get a routine appointment, the baby may pass a critical point in worsening sickness. If the baby's life is lost, both spouses will grieve and feel guilty. The N spouse who wanted to assume it was an unusual emergency can't help feeling deep resentment. Married couples must not blame each other when things go wrong, but in such a case, forgiveness from the heart is going to be difficult to impossible.

There are times when Ns insist not only on immediate action, but on some unusual action. Let's say the N spouse wants to rub the baby down with an Essential Oil remedy, instead of using aspirin. This works out fine if it helps, or if the baby is okay anyway. But if the case turns out badly, the S spouse may not be able to forgive. The criticism, "you are always making a big deal out of everything" can become even worse, moving to "your crazy ideas stopped us from getting real help."

So while it's good to talk to someone with a very different point of view to avoid blind spots, husbands and wives who have widely differing ideas of what's right may not be able to forgive each other. It's much easier to forgive if we feel that the mistake is one we could have made. Two Ss who lean on traditional medicine are less likely to blame each other for a poor outcome. Two Ns who agree that all options, even nutty ones, are on the table are also less likely to blame each other.

The same principle applies to many things, not just medical decisions. Marriages face discipline problems with young kids, legal problems with older kids, changes in careers and school, and financial stress. Most S personalities want to try first the traditional ways of handling the problem. They ask what is customary, or what their family and friends have done. Many Ns, though not all, dislike tradition, custom and habit. They are always looking for reasons to change what's been done before. They're sure that this time is an exception or that these symptoms and events presage dramatic change. Their sense of humor often reflects this underlying belief, with sarcasm or other irreverence. When the S spouse sees clearly that they're really in a time of rapid change or unusual events, the N's bold approach is a welcome rescue. When the new ideas work, everyone is happy. But in daily life, such wide differences in Perceiving cause chronic friction and sometimes corrosive disagreement and blame.

These S and N differences may also be among the most accurate predictors of how someone will change over a lifetime. In early life, the differences may already be visible, but they also may not. Young people are flexible and every experience is new, so their preferred ways of sizing up life aren't as settled. All personalities tend to lose this flexibility in the middle years. Ns who accepted tradition in their 20s may want to challenge it in their 40s. Ss who were patient with changes and exceptions may fall back on rules and habits, weary of never knowing what to expect. When they meet with crises, their ways of managing problems confirm their biases. So S and N spouses who didn't have difficulty navigating life in younger years can be at an impasse at later ages. The years in between can help them understand each other more, but often it doesn't work that way.

We may have more realistic visions of the future if we can understand how someone's personality is going to react over time. Trends that seem small now can become large and insurmountable. If you're already in the middle of this process, use the framework of personality to do your best to understand. If you're at a point of decision, choosing whether or not to join your life to someone else's, considering Perceiving and Judging tendencies could help you forecast and decide well.

RELATIONSHIP DOMINANCE

In Chapter 15, I make a case that dominance is a permanent aspect of personality, based in the balance of Introversion and Extroversion. Although someone's ability to put dominance into practice changes over time and in different settings, the fundamental desire to control in a certain way seems to be stable. We rarely see it clearly when we're young, but it's there. Few people take it into account when they choose who to marry, but clearly it's a key predictive factor. Dominance and control may become increasingly bigger issues as adults age into the decades when they are typically in power, and then into the later times when they lose power.

When we come to talk about dominance in the context of marriage, it's especially important to keep firmly in mind that high dominance is not a "male" thing, it's a personality thing. Both men and women can have Horizon Dominance or Soul Dominance, as well as the levels in between. High dominance is more common in men (whether for innate or socially-primed reasons) but there's no simple correlation between dominance level and gender.

On the other hand, many of the problems of marriage are tightly connected to how men and women relate. Sex is a biologically determined act that results (or may result) in the conception of a child, who can only be developed and birthed by a woman. Only the woman can breast-feed the baby, and typically women do most infant care. But there's a distinction here, as to what's biologically determined and what's socially typical. A man cannot bear a child without medical innovation that's not yet available in 2015. But a man can feed a baby with a bottle and do all other care; a father may do more care of babies than the mother. So biological gender roles are fixed in some ways, and not in others. Men's and women's personalities may fit easily with the biological roles, but they also may not. There is always a tension between innate personality and the roles we must play.

Similarly, the psychology of the sex act itself puts the man in an apparently dominant role, the woman in an apparently non-dominant one. Our hormone systems support and encourage those roles, switching even dominant women into feeling like it would be "sexy" to be non-dominant. But at the same time, our personalities need to integrate sexual behavior with other attitudes. Some men and women are not comfortable with the dominance roles that biology hands them; they look for ways to shift the experience and its relationships into a dominance framework that works better. So this is another area where just the facts of being male and female appear to impose structures that may not fit.

When roles fit easily, advice is less necessary, so I'll focus more on how personality may not fit typical norms. It's not to suggest that these cases are the majority; instead, they are a significant minority, significant not only in numbers, but also in what we can learn about personality from their struggles.

When we talk about dominance problems, if we talk about them at all, we generally start with the assumption that everyone wants to be in control. We look at clashes between two people who both want control: somebody has to win or lose. But in the way I've laid out inborn personality dominance, this assumption doesn't hold. Each kind of dominance requires control of some zone, large or small, but at the same time, it rejects control of other zones. Normal personalities, who can maintain relationships and don't want to be in excessive conflict, don't want to control too much. Need for dominance and rejection of another kind of dominance always go together. It's quite possible for a marriage to have problems with dominance balance because there are zones of life that neither husband or wife really wants to control. It may be a less visible problem, but it can be just as profoundly troubling as flat-out power struggles.

The four levels of dominance fit into two quite different models of relating. One roughly correlates to the preferred patterns of Room and Bubble Dominance, while the other may be a better fit for Horizon and Soul Dominance. Early life experiences and individual balance influence which model some real person actually prefers, so I can't be dogmatic about what will work in theory for a real person.

In the more familiar model, life is a checkerboard of defined territories. Each spouse is dominant in the black or red squares, as negotiated. Most arguments are actually negotiating sessions; there's a new territory or someone is unhappy with the way territories have been divided, and the friction is a test of wills to find room to change.

Checkerboard territories can be fairly large, as in the traditional division where the kitchen and most of the house are strictly the wife's territory and the husband isn't allowed to change anything. In this traditional form, the husband usually has his own large zone, such as everything tended by motors and tools: garage, workshop, yard. When husbands and wives work long hours in different places, territories tend to be larger and with clearer boundaries, just as a practical matter.

Territories can also be small, co-existing ones that appear to overlap at first view. Maybe one spouse handles homework with the kids, and the other handles emotional upheavals. Maybe one child is more the territory of one than the other. There are many variations, some of them not traditional at all, such as marriages in which the husband handles all cooking or the wife manages tools. Work may be diced finely into territories, such that one buys food while the other manages how it's stored. Handling money could be the territory of one spouse, or it could be divided into tasks, such as one handles monthly budgeting while the other does long-term financial planning.

The key to territorial division is that both spouses recognize that the division exists and understand that if they meddle in the other's territory, it won't go over well. Life is governed by an unspoken but multi-part agreement stipulating who has what kind of say in which things. Living in peace means remembering the agreement at all times and not only leaving the other spouse to control his or her territory, but managing one's own. No slacking off, and no trespassing.

Limiting each person's territorial command is a way to contain the mess of human fallibility. Most of us are aware that we don't even want wide responsibility because we might make mistakes. When territories are more finely divided, there are more checks and balances. If one spouse helps kids with homework, and the other makes sure the right things are in the backpack, they share the blame if something important is left undone. Or if one buys food while the other stores it, and one cooks while the other washes up, then both know what's in the kitchen.

The checkerboard model works very well with Room and Bubble Dominance, since these personalities have definite ideas about what they want to control. They may not be aware of differences in how they wish to be dominant, because at the daily life level, they meet in negotiations for zones: house, schedule, kids, car, and specific rooms, tools and events. On the ground, it adds up to who cares most about which things, so it appears to be about preferences, specialty knowledge, and how touchy someone can be when crossed. But probably one of them prefers a larger territory with less detailed control, the other wanting greater control over a smaller zone. The split in dominance vision helps them divide areas of contention, even if it's not clear that this is what's going on.

Many children have grown up under the checkerboard model: a Room Dominant parent is generally in charge of schedule, style and religious tone, while the parent with Bubble Dominance tends to be in charge of some more intensive aspects of family life, like teaching the kids to think or to work hard. Children always learn which parent to ask first about which sort of things; if the territories aren't clearly visible to outsiders, they are very clear to the children.

Checkerboard power-sharing isn't only about physical territories. In a happy marriage where the spouses know each other well, they are also attentive to emotional strengths and vulnerabilities. Anxieties, kinds of stress, affections, and what makes us happy form another invisible checkerboard. Each spouse wants more dominance in areas of emotional strength, less dominance in vulnerable patches. We show love by organizing life so that those we love are most sheltered when they need it, most exposed when they're strong and happy.

When the couple needs to make a decision that crosses territorial lines, they make it collaboratively, often with a lot of arguing in the run-up to the decision. The arguing can be heated and unpleasant or just a persistent negotiation that runs until there's a settlement. Often, the spouse whose territory is most affected by the decision wins the argument. If the higher-dominance spouse has to give in, there may be a fair bit of argument from that side.

However, the fundamental principle is that neither of them wants to have sole responsibility for the decision. It may look at first like one or both of them just wants to win, but in reality, the argument serves the purpose of genuine persuasion. When one spouse finally agrees to do it the other one's way, it's only after all of the pros and cons have been laid out. Even if the "losing" spouse is still not happy with the decision, he or she has negotiated and finally acquiesced. If the decision doesn't go well, both of them share responsibility.

In an unhappy marriage of this kind, there may still be recriminations and "I told you so, but you wouldn't listen" statements. That's less about the model and more about imbalance, because in the best-working cases of the model, both spouses do accept that the decision was fairly negotiated. They both had a chance at persuasion, and the reluctant one could have refused to budge. If he or she didn't do that, it means acceptance of the other set of persuasions, and acceptance means responsibility.

There are cases when persuasion doesn't work, but the decision deadline still comes up. The "winner" will be the one whose territory is most affected, or the one who insists most fiercely. Winning in these decisions, however, is loaded with danger. If one of them just acts unilaterally to settle the question (signing papers to buy a house, enrolling a child in school), it's a serious blow to the checkerboard model. If it doesn't work out well, the other spouse may find it unforgivable. The other way to refuse to give in, while admitting defeat, is to say something like, "Fine, do whatever you want, but I don't agree." This means, "I will not take any responsibility for the decision if it goes wrong. I reserve the right to say 'I told you so,' and if that's the way it goes down, you will never again have the right to 'win' one of these arguments by just insisting, because I will remind you of this bad outcome every time." Most often, this possibility is enough to make the other spouse reluctant to barge ahead. He or she has to be extremely sure of being right, because there is such real potential loss of future negotiation power.

Neither a Room Dominant nor a Bubble Dominant personality actually wants full responsibility over something outside natural boundaries. Both dominance styles really want the other to come around to full agreement, because shared responsibility is vastly preferred. However the couple manages it, given their personality tolerance for voices raised in heated argument, they almost always come to shared responsibility at the end. It's usually a true negotiation with concessions on each side.

If we had to create one model to suit all, this one is the clear choice. It's flexible, and it distributes responsibility evenly. A more introverted person can focus on smaller territories that he can maintain to his Bubble Dominant satisfaction, while a Room Dominant spouse can oversee the general household, knowing that those small zones are going to be managed well. And when things are not going well, it limits damage. Many marriages are not peaceful, and spouses do not agree well on how things should be. The checkerboard model allows them to negotiate boundaries and maintain their own standards and rules in whatever they care about the most, giving up control of what they care about less. It's not as good as perfect peace from the heart, but it's often as good as this not-ideal world gets. It allows the family to get on with the business of life, with fights coming up only at predictable flashpoints or in times of change (like when Mom gets a job or Dad retires). Predictability is almost as good as peace, and it's certainly better than constant war.

The model is more stressful for people who have very high or very low dominance. Horizon Dominant people want complete authority and oversight over the largest view of the family: who we will be in the world, how we will look, how we will spend our time, where we will live, how much status and money we will pursue. They can be drawn into the power-sharing checkerboard model, but they're usually reluctant and even recalcitrant about actually letting the spouse control what he or she cares about most. Whatever it may be, it's still inside the horizon, so natural dominance prompts them to try to control some of it, at least a little. This can cause a lot of fights.

Before looking at the other model, I want to note in passing that there's one match of high dominance that seems to work reasonably well with the checkerboard model. I call it the "power couple," because what unites them most strongly is their joint mission to organize, rule and influence others. The match is an ESTJ with an ESFJ; the ESTJ has Horizon Dominance, while the ESFJ exercises more limited, but more personal, Room Dominance. The ESFJ spouse, who is most often the wife, definitely wants to control what goes on in the family, but the ESTJ husband is not content to focus on just a workshop and the checkbook. Instead, he controls something outside the family, while the ESFJ wife runs the family in a way that fits with his vision. They may move in corporate business/social circles, or they could be on a university faculty. They could be the pastor and pastor's wife at a church. What might divide them, such as arguments over money, is smaller and weaker than what unites them: a vision of themselves setting an example, guiding others, and getting it right.

Most personalities who are clearly Horizon or Soul Dominant are not entirely comfortable with checkerboard power-sharing. As mentioned above, Horizon Dominant people see the logic of the territorial model, but it doesn't feel right to them. A Horizon Dominant father who's in the traditional role of a full-time salaried worker has to leave the kids to his wife's care, because he isn't home most of the time. But Horizon Dominant men usually want some say in the general tone of what's happening at home. They disapprove of some activities and encourage others. They don't feel "hands off." It's not just a trait of men; Horizon Dominant women feel the same way. There's not the same sense of "this is your business, that is mine," but rather, they want to be sure things are "right" in *all* zones of life.

Soul Dominant personalities find the checkerboard model difficult for the opposite reason. While they can manage a territory competently, their natural inclination is to be the arbiter of inner identity issues, not external ones. The important questions that present to their minds are things like "who will we be in the world, when will we take a moral stand, how will we shape our characters, how will we stay authentic?" When they find themselves in a checkerboard marriage, they too see the logic of it; but their natural inclination feels like the other person should be making more of the big decisions about where to live, how much money to make, or what sort of car to drive. These "important" decisions feel unimportant to most Soul Dominant personalities. What feels crucial is, once we've chosen where to live, what will our home be like? Can we find careers that allow us to make adequate money while not selling out to wrong values?

So both Horizon and Soul Dominant personalities can be pushed and negotiated into maintaining territories of the traditional kind, but both feel uncomfortable. When they are married to Room and Bubble Dominant spouses, they probably have to buck up and just deal with it. Territorial power-sharing is safest, simplest and what most people want. Horizon personalities must practice patience in taking their hands off what their spouses care about most, biting their tongues and saying "it's great" instead of offering controlling suggestions. Soul Dominant personalities must force themselves to make decisions and keep up a territory, doing their part to keep zones like the kitchen or garage neat.

If a Horizon Dominant man or woman marries a Soul Dominant spouse, however, they can shift into a second, very different model. I call it feudal, because it's similar to how power was organized in medieval kingdoms. The king (or queen) owned all of the land, without limits; but the land was too vast to actually maintain in a defensible way. So the monarch delegated a smaller territory to a count or baron, who had complete control like a king within the county or barony. A count or baron could do literally anything, with one exception: he could not be disloyal to the king or queen. In a medieval kingdom, this was mainly applied to raising an army for defense. Each count or baron was responsible for a certain number of men, horses and swords, and it was non-negotiable that when the king called, they came. The king, on his side, must come to the count or baron's defense. The count or baron couldn't build a castle to start a rebellion against the king, but with the monarch's permission, the castle could be built and ruled any way they liked.

So how does this historical analogy apply to a modern marriage? In a feudal marriage, the Horizon Dominant personality is monarch over all, while the Soul Dominant personality has absolute power in exactly those things it cares about. In daily life, it may not look much different from a checkerboard territorial arrangement, since it still takes two (at least) to get all the work done. But when decisions are made, they are not negotiated in the same way. If the decision is about external horizon issues, the Horizon Dominant spouse makes it, unilaterally. If the decision is about internal soul issues, the Soul Dominant spouse has it. When they discuss a decision jointly, they are really just checking to see if the "horizon" issue has any "soul" points that need to be considered, or vice versa.

In the feudal model, children know that every decision goes primarily to the Horizon Dominant parent. That's where the direct yes or no answer comes, perhaps with questioning about cost, time and risk. If the child would rather talk at length about the decision first, the Soul Dominant parent is a better bet. Soul Dominance is mostly interested in helping the child come to a unified, peaceful internal position, not in giving permission or even in seeing the parent's own wishes fulfilled. In a balanced feudal marriage, the Horizon Dominant parent checks first to see if the Soul Dominant parent has already provided his or her quiet influence.

In this model, decisions that affect the whole family can be made unilaterally by either spouse, as long as the grounds for decision are solidly in the Horizon or Soul zone. More often, there's collaboration in an "advise and consent" style. Skipping the advise and consent stage is not unforgivable, but there needs to be a reason why it was bypassed. There wasn't time, the deadline loomed suddenly, or perhaps the deciding spouse honestly thought he or she already knew what the other would say. The "losing" spouse can forgive the trespass if either of those conditions is genuine (even if mistaken).

Both spouses are comfortable, at some level, with deciding unilaterally and accepting full responsibility. The Horizon Dominant spouse is particularly comfortable with taking full responsibility, since that's one of the driving motivations of Horizon Dominance. He or she is certain of being right, but at the same time, ready to take the blame if not. The reason a Horizon spouse wants to go through the advise and consent process is to show love and do one last double-check on being right. If the Soul Dominant spouse has an objection that the Horizon one had not considered, the decision might change. That's important, because Horizon Dominance, when it's done well by a mature person, cares a lot about not missing an important facet of a decision. Soul Dominant spouses often see what's in the Horizon blind spot.

Soul Dominant spouses are less likely to make unilateral decisions, but when they feel that a non-negotiable value is at stake, they do it without hesitation. What makes the feudal model work is that the Horizon Dominant spouse trusts the Soul Dominant one to be right. Soul Dominant spouses are very unlikely to skip the advise and consent stage; if they do, it's because there was no opportunity. But while seeking input and consent, they make it very plain if the decision is, essentially, non-negotiable. In a balanced marriage, the Horizon spouse accepts this. Probably he or she offers one proviso or modification that addresses some external danger that the Soul Dominant spouse wasn't considering. Consent is then given, not even because the persuasion was successful, but because in a balanced feudal model, the Soul Dominant spouse has the right to insist on soul values.

At first glance, the feudal model may sound like the patriarchal model that modern society has rejected. There are points of similarity, but the key difference is that when I talk about a feudal model for personalities, I am not talking about men being in charge. In both my models, men might have Soul or Bubble Dominance and prefer to control small territories or only set moral and spiritual priorities. Women might have better high dominance skills, due to personality and experience. So it's simply not about men and women, though in some marriages, the man might have higher dominance.

Another difference is that I'm not prescribing what the Horizon spouse should be controlling. An ENFJ wife married to an INTP husband is going to care about running many things, but financial investment is probably not among them. Money math would be left to the INTP's Soul Dominant perfectionist research. An ENTJ wife, on the other hand, would care very much about financial planning, as would the other two high-dominance T personalities, ESTJ and ESTP. So the zone of life that's being controlled is, in my model, dependent not on the sex (male) or role (husband) but on the skills and strengths of each personality.

Clearly, the feudal model is much riskier. It's not a good model for imbalanced personalities to get into, because the potential for abuse is much greater. That's why, on average, the checkerboard model is superior. It allows both people to keep an eye on what the other is doing, since their territories are small and sometimes interlaced. The feudal model is not recommended in a prescribed way, but I want to talk about how it works, because when Horizon and Soul people get together, this model happens whether we like it or not. It can be stressful for them if people say they're doing it wrong. Perhaps the wife has Horizon Dominance and some people hint that the husband is being passive or unimportant; or the husband has Horizon Dominance and everyone tells the wife to take back her power.

When the model works well, it works because the power truly is balanced. It's not balanced in a daily way, it's balanced between them *as personalities*. The Soul Dominant spouse has more power than outsiders can see, because he or she is primarily the safekeeper of the Horizon spouse's soul secrets. People who exercise high dominance can't appear vulnerable in public, although they may use self-deprecation as armor. Their real vulnerabilities are never admitted, but of course that doesn't make the weaknesses go away. Home has to be the place where it's safe to be vulnerable. A Soul Dominant spouse is usually a specialist at understanding this truth, and at least in theory, he or she does not have an instinct to use those vulnerabilities as weapons later.

When the model works well, the Horizon Dominant spouse is grateful for a safe place to store secrets and fears. The fastest way to spoil this safety would be to abuse power, wounding the Soul Dominant person. Horizon Dominance is exercised well when it watches out to restrain itself, asking "what matters most to my loved one (even if I think everything is within my horizon)?" and not overstepping those bounds. The Soul Dominant spouse acts as a restraint on power by speaking up about issues of values, authenticity, and truth. As long as the higher-dominance spouse listens, the lower-dominance spouse can go for long periods of time without making any particular objections or requests. For the Horizon person, the price of having his or her own way most of the time is that when the Soul Dominant person speaks up, it's time to listen, or life as he knows it will end. The sun will go behind a dark cloud; the safe zone may still be safe, but it won't be as warm.

It's easy to see how many things could go wrong. I don't want to take time describing dictatorial or abusive marriages, because we can find them in any movie or novel, as well as all around us. It's more important to explain the ideal, so that we can see how the model itself isn't the whole problem. The model can work, if personalities are balanced, and if they balance each other. If men and women, by numbers, were evenly distributed among these four levels of dominance preference, it might be a simple matter to match them up neatly. We'd have figured it out long ago. It's not so simple; nothing with real human beings is simple.

First, there are fewer women with either Horizon or Bubble Dominance. (For numbers, see Chapter 15.) Most married women want to be in charge of the family's general tone and daily decisions (Room), or else they prefer to focus mainly on matters of heart and conscience (Soul). Men are more evenly distributed, about one-quarter in each category. There are more men with Soul Dominant personalities than there are Horizon Dominant women who could live with them in balanced peace. There are more men with Room Dominance than there are Bubble Dominant women who'd be content to let them run most of family life. Mismatches are inevitable.

The most common mismatch may pair a Horizon Dominant man with a wife who doesn't want to give him unlimited power over the family's style. The Horizon Dominant man has an instinctive expectation that he'll set the tone on all major decisions. The children need to look basically the way he wants them to look; today's shirt color isn't important, but the everyday level of formality or expensiveness matters a lot. The house needs to look basically the way he envisions, with room for small decisions by others. He'll choose the cars and tell her which one is hers to drive. Naturally, his career comes first. He doesn't even need to be specially self-centered; it's just how Horizon Dominance works.

He doesn't think he's making any impossible demands, but to a Room Dominant wife, he's often impossible. He agrees to move the family to another state without asking her; he trades in the car and just brings home a new one. She's expected to be flexible, and she often isn't. Her "Room" is her job, her house, and her family, and she can't feel right with him assuming her life exists within his horizon. She makes it super clear that they sure aren't going to live this way. She tries to whittle him down to a territorial agreement. He sees the logic and the marriage counselor is totally on his wife's side: territorial agreements are good balances of power that leave neither party harmed. And yet he feels cheated and resentful when the marriage counselor persuades him to give up a career promotion to let her continue working at the same place. Yes, it's territory and it's fair. But it feels wrong, and he doesn't know why.

The other common mismatch happens when a Soul Dominant personality gets drawn into the checkerboard model. It puts pressure on the Soul Dominant person to be more decisive, active and assertive than he or she wants to be. This spouse's reluctance, in turn, puts pressure on the Room or Bubble Dominant spouse to be also more assertive. A Room person gets pushed to make Horizon decisions, which is almost okay but not quite. A Bubble Dominant person gets pushed to make broader decisions, room-sized, and he or she may push back against the Soul Dominant spouse. Everyone is a bit tired, sometimes one of them drops a ball, and it's unclear who is in charge. Sometimes, adverse circumstances such as illness or long absence forces a Soul or Bubble Dominant spouse to step up and take charge of everything. Society tells them that this is great, since everyone wants more control, right? But it's not great. It's tiring and over time, the introverted person forced to be in charge feels resentful and depressed.

In some personalities, Room and Bubble Dominance may encourage active competition for territory that comes out in criticism, harsh teasing, and little line-crossing tests. Soul Dominant personalities may find it very difficult to push back consistently over time, since they aren't primarily geared to defend unless they feel their mental or spiritual integrity demands it. In other words, they may put up with a lot of trespassing and jostling without much reaction, until it finally feels like a real threat. By then, a lot of love has been lost, and the conflict won't be jesting or brief; it will be real. In other words, it will be exactly what most Soul Dominant people dread.

Conflict avoidance is one reason why Soul Dominant personalities may end up in abusive situations more often. In many, perhaps especially the F types, there is also an unconscious need to be non-dominant or even submissive. This emotional need may be separate from what the person consciously intends or wants. It's not likely for someone in our time to think "I wish I could be submissive." It's more likely to be felt as fatigue: everything is too hard, why can't someone help me?

When this masked wish for non-dominance exists, it can allow people to become doormats or "enablers." Even the competitive razzing of a more dominant (but not ill-intentioned) personality can leave them with the impression of being at fault. If they're interacting with someone whose personality is imbalanced in unhappy ways, they can be drawn into really co-dependent behavior. It's even worse when the other person has a genuine problem, such as abnormal personality or addiction. Clear and deliberate abuse can be hard for a Soul Dominant person to guard against.

Much of married life consists of coping with the demands of our power expectations. Probably fewer than half of marriages are balanced in the way that's natural for both spouses' personalities. Most people have to negotiate and spend a certain amount of time feeling uncomfortable: curbed from doing this, pushed into doing that, listening to a conversation in the next room with mounting impatience. There's no perfect answer, and life will never be free of disagreements. However, taking personality dominance into account from the start can make long-term reactions more predictable. When possible, balancing dominance accurately can make life much easier.

GENERAL MODEL: RELATED OPPOSITES

If the world was ideal, we could match everyone up neatly. We can't do this, of course. It's not even an appealing idea, since life experience shapes all personalities into their own unique balances. Someone who's supposed to be Horizon Dominant might have individual differences that make Room Dominance a more comfortable fit. We aren't defined by our categories; warm and cool conscience are inborn, but our families influence most of us to have some affinity with both ways of thinking. Because real people are much more complex than the theoretical model can show, we can't ever make everything neat and simple.

On the other hand, for readers who aren't married and want to give the theory a real-life trial, we can unify all of the previous sections in one chart. Below, lines match the personalities who form what I call related opposite pairs.

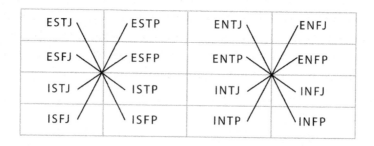

Fig. 16-2

The matching lines cross between temperament columns (Chapter 14) and dominance rows (Chapter 15). They connect personality types that have mostly different letters; in each case, the only letter that's the same is either S or N. All other letters are completely opposite. They have *opposite* skills and dominance needs, but *related* ideas of what life is about. They're a blend of the folk adages that "birds of a feather flock together," since they have similar values, and "opposites attract," since they have complementary dominance.

What I've observed is that related opposite pairs seem to have an affinity for each other, even amounting to synergy, something that goes beyond what theory could predict. They often find that they've arrived at the same conclusion from different angles. Related opposites may find they can finish each other's sentences, even if they recognize that the other person is choosing and doing things that they never would or could. Their degree of difference can't be papered over, but it doesn't seem to matter.

The related opposite relationship is particularly good for romantic relationships, because it matches dominance. But we can observe related opposite pairs in unique teams, like for songwriting. Paul McCartney seems to fit best as an ENTP personality, and he had two famously close relationships that both look like related opposites. One was with his wife Linda; she appears to have been easily able to understand him and yet different, very likely an INFJ. John Lennon was probably also an INFJ, and it's no wonder he felt isolated and misunderstood because INFJ men are some of the rarest personalities. When Lennon met McCartney, as teenagers, I think they experienced the instant synergy that often comes with related opposite pairs. Rare personalities, like Lennon, feel like it's a miracle when some new friend "gets" them. Lennon's second famously close relationship with Yoko Ono might have been another related opposite match. If I'm right about these musicians' personality types, then both of their lives (and much of our music) were shaped by related-opposite synergy.

In the chart, there are eight matches. Although it's important to observe that the pairs can produce creative teams, as in the Lennon-McCartney example above, I'll mostly discuss them as marriage pairs. Four of them are in the feudal model, and four share power via checkerboard territories. Each line crosses into a different, related temperament column, and each match pairs a Thinker with a Feeler.

Some of these pairs are not hard to observe, since they connect personality types that we run into frequently. The basic feel of such relationships is well known, and they are often depicted in books, movies and especially television shows. When I describe the basic nature of each match, you'll probably recognize yourself, people you have known well, or marriages you've seen depicted on TV. On the other hand, the couples we recognize most easily are usually following traditional male/female roles, but it's important to see that these matches also cross over traditional gender-role lines.

Taking the feudal matches first, there are two Sensing matches that we see very often, especially in politics: ESTJ marries ISFP, and ESTP marries ISFJ. Both Horizon types frequently occupy the White House, and both also frequently become famous through business success. The ESTJ is typically a restrained, dignified person whose ISFP spouse is a bit more Bohemian, or at least gentler and more artistic. A ballet dancer might marry someone on the dance company's Board of Directors; an artist marries a banker, who helps fund gallery shows. The classic movie *Citizen Kane* depicts one of these matches when Kane, a newspaper executive, marries a singer. That match doesn't work out so well, but other ESTJ-ISFP matches can and do work out. Many ESTJs who aren't famous, but who wield some middle level of power, are married to gentle, creative ISFP spouses.

ESTPs are usually the wilder half of their feudal marriages. They are comfortable with power, but they are less predictable and dignified, taking chances or making strident statements. Their ISFJ spouses are reliable, warm and nurturing; John McCain and George W. Bush both married women who fit this pattern. Hollywood ESTPs seem often to marry ISFPs, who are not quite related opposites, since they share the same temperament column. In such cases, neither spouse has SJ reliability, and the marriages usually don't last long. ESTPs need their related opposites, ISFJs, to guide and guard their consciences. ISFJs need protective, aggressive ESTPs to clear out external threats and give them greater space to be charitable and nurturing.

The N matches are less commonly seen, both in public and even in private. Since Ns are chronically outnumbered, they find it much harder to locate related opposites. In the ideal matches, charismatic ENFJ leaders marry perfectionist, reliable INTPs, while intensely competitive ENTJs marry daydreamy INFPs. One of the rarest happy couples I've observed was an ENFJ woman with an INTP man. She thought it was adorable that he was obsessed with math, keeping math notebooks stashed around their car and apartment. She viewed him as a lost puppy in some ways, but at the same time deeply admired his fierce intellectual independence. He didn't mind if she made many decisions, since it left him more time to work on math. I think ENFJ men rarely marry INTP women, partly because INTP women are scarce, partly because ENFJ men (and women) are generally confident that their charisma and insight can make any match work. When they do find a related opposite, they are probably less likely to become power-hungry, since INTPs are realistic ego-deflaters.

ENTJ women have a very hard time finding suitable lifetime mates because their competitive spirit seems "masculine" to many men. INFP men are often musicians and English professors, but they can be found in many lines of work, since they may have been forced to fall back on secondary skills to earn money. It's much easier to find ENTJ men in business and law, and they usually have easy success with women, at least in the short term. The idea that his conscience needs a poetic, idealistic keeper may be a hard sell to an ENTJ man. But there seems to be a very close affinity and synergy between ENTJs and INFPs when they do find each other. I have seen several cases of love at first sight.

There are four checkerboard, territorial matches between personalities who are in the middle ranks of dominance. The S matches are very frequently seen: ESFJ married to ISTP, and ISTJ married to ESFP. They form the basis of typical television stereotypes of marriage; any casting director for a sitcom knows the types. In real life, these two matches do seem to find each other often and with relative ease. The synergy is well known.

ESFJs are responsible, nurturing and stereotypically female; when they're cast on TV as women, their related opposites are usually ISTP tool guys. I have observed the ESFJ-ISTP match many times in real life, with both men and women in either role. An ESFJ pastor husband is married to an ISTP accountant wife; an ESFJ teacher is married to an ISTP mechanic husband. The ESFJ creates the social calendar, sets the moral tone and decorates for holidays, while the ISTP fixes things, goes on adventures, and gets into trouble now and then. ISTP women don't usually get into trouble, but they struggle with fitting into the traditional wife's role of housekeeper.

ESFPs burst onto the television screen with Lucille Ball. They're daffy, warm, and prone to mistakes because they are constantly innovating. In real life, they may not be quite as daffy or mistake-prone as their comedian TV counterparts. But they are funny, active, warm, and often sweet, in both male and female form. The personalities who find them irresistible are usually ISTJs. ISTJs have all the reliability, courage and realism that ESFPs need to feel secure. I've observed many of these matches, too: an ESFP engineer who loves to tell funny stories, married to an ISTJ teacher who keeps the calendar updated; an ESFP woman who loves to cook, married to an ISTJ bank manager.

The N checkerboard matches are numerically rarer, but they're not impossible to find when the T and F personalities match up with traditional sex roles. INTJ men are often found in science of all kinds, and often the scientists' wives are bright, warm and sociable— in a word, ENFPs. I have observed a reverse-role marriage of an INTJ woman with an ENFP man; the INTJ wife perceived her husband's emotional warmth as almost a miracle. INTJ women are one of the two rarest personalities, with INFJ men. If they find related opposites at a time when marriage is possible, it may be something like a miracle.

I've already spoken of my guess that Paul McCartney has an ENTP personality and found a related opposite in his first wife. I have not been able to observe many examples of the ENTP match with INFJs, perhaps because INFJs are so rare. Were some of history's famous INFJs able to find ENTP spouses? In theory, the match should be between a competitive, energetic scientist or inventor with a thoughtful yoga teacher or cellist. ENTPs are not good at self-knowledge and emotional regulation, but an INFJ's insight should help mediate and moderate. INFJs want to stir up revolution for the sake of justice and truth, but they need help assessing what can really be done, and how to make an impact among larger groups.

There are people who don't find the idea of a related opposite compelling or even appealing. In some cases, they knew or dated someone who was a related opposite, but who was imbalanced or immature. The experience was not pleasant for long, and they're left with a sense of danger about the type of closeness that can be easily engendered. It feels like possessiveness or smothering.

Many people are themselves not perfectly balanced, and they're never going to be the "gold standard" version of their personality type. Their unique balances make them better suited to matches that aren't related opposites. Perhaps a different personality type functions like a related opposite, while not being the theoretically "correct" type. Someone whose personality rates as Horizon Dominant, but who is not really comfortable with extensive influence, might well choose a related type with Bubble Dominance, someone who wants to share power more equally. A personality that I've classified as Soul Dominant might actually prefer to control more of their personal space bubble. Someone whose personality should have warm or cool conscience may be more comfortable dealing with the other conscience orientation, because various life experiences make it feel safer or more appropriate. Some Ns and Ss may like being around the opposite Perceiving type, even if theory says they don't. And sometimes people just fall in love and make it work.

The principle of related opposites is more important than the theoretical details. We need to pair up with people who complement and complete us, who are different and yet able to "get" who we are. Marriage becomes hard work when those conditions aren't met. For readers who are completely unattached, it might be worth the effort to learn how to see and know their related opposite types. Try dating some. Does it work? For readers who are already married, perhaps understanding the theory of related opposites can help you identify chronic conflicts. Understanding doesn't make them vanish, but it can suggest solutions that you might not have seen before. You can see what works and what doesn't work, and why. You can connect events that didn't seem related. If you've survived disasters together, you can see why and how.

We can use these all of these insights to understand how people's personalities balance each other. Each model shows how we can balance and help someone, or unknowingly get in their way. You can at least work smarter, not harder, on your relationships. Life is difficult, and it will never be anything but challenging. A personality framework allows us to see new ways to ease life's burdens where possible. It helps us understand and love each other, with greatest possible sympathy for differences. That's life at its best.

AFTERWORD

Each mortal thing does one thing and the same:
Deals out that being indoors each one dwells;
Selves—goes itself; **myself** *it speaks and spells,*
Crying **What I do is me: for that I came**.

—*Gerard Manley Hopkins, 1908*

Hopkins' verses capture the essence of personality theory: "indoors" of each one of us, something dwells. It's a way of being, it's our "I am" and "it is." When we go through each day, we live out that being; we "self" (to turn the pronoun into an active verb). We came into this world to be what we are, to live out our natures.

Poetry and science intersect on this point: if personality is based in our neurological organization, then "selving" is what we do, in fact the only thing we can do. If we try to be someone else, we're still *selving*, because it is self who tries to transform or act. We suffer imbalances in our own manner, and we try to correct them according to our own abilities. We see what we can see; we are blind to what we can't perceive. We act on what we perceive, and we marvel at others' mystifyingly different perceptions. How we process the world is who we are, and who we are becomes what we do.

I would have liked to present my balanced personality model as a proven fact, upheld by studies and science. But a model can't be proven true; it's not a fact that can be shown true or false. It can only be tried out and tested for being helpful as it organizes facts and suggests solutions. As an author, I'm equally comfortable with readers testing to see if the model resonates with their life experiences. I have Soul Dominance, so I like to point to a truth that I've seen and explain why I see it, instead of telling someone else what to think. The model has helped me understand some complicated, layered human problems in my own life, as well as in other people's stories. I hope that many readers will test and try it, finding out how well it holds up under other conditions.

319

For readers, the primary test is in our own personal lives. Does this framework help you understand chronic conflicts? Does it suggest productive directions for your looming decisions? Does it accurately describe your family and friends? Even more, when you feel you've learned how the model describes your friends, does it help you predict or explain parts of their behavior that used to seem like anomalies? Can it help you understand normal personalities under stress, and can it then help define emotion and behavior that fall outside of normal?

The principles I've outlined have many applications to how people behave in society, too. To select just one of the principles, I have often wondered if the different kinds of Perceiving can account for some of our "culture wars." Debates over culture and art raise many important questions. Is it a good thing to try out depicting terrorists as sympathetic human beings with a valid point of view? Is there inherent value in seeing religious images placed in shocking contexts? Or should moral considerations of right and wrong come before art in some cases? Our society has seen many demonstrations and debates over those questions, but we've never looked at people's responses to the issues in the framework of personality.

In these debates, each side usually calls the other side backward, philistine, oppressive, or just evil; but perhaps the truth is that different realities are perceived, literally via different Perceiving modes. Introverted Intuition considers it good and productive to poke holes in traditional archetypal images. Introverted Sensing, on the other hand, sees danger in tearing out foundational ideas and beliefs. Extroverted Intuition and Sensing generally want many possibilities to be explored, but with a keen moral sense of absolute right and wrong waiting in case things go too far. It's not much of a step to get from these personality-based worldviews to our controversies over provocative art and theater.

Some of the principles of warm and cool conscience may help interpret other culture wars. How far should we bend rules in pursuit of acceptance and kindness? Is there a point where each conscience type, warm or cool, should admit that its answers are incomplete? Instead of talking about absolute or relative morality, we may get better traction by looking at each speaker's sense of idealism. Where do our ideals overlap, and where do they differ? Can sympathy and understanding show us how to talk to each other?

Last, there is much room for academic study. Readers with advanced degrees in psychology or neuroscience are keenly aware of how little of this material qualifies as "proven." When a new model is proposed, the model's first qualification is to be consistent with underlying laws of nature, and second, to organize the existing facts with as few outlying anomalies as possible. In proposing my model, I've made many suggestions verging on claims, chiefly that certain types of mental organization result in thoughts that lead to external behavior. It's what I've observed, but can these ideas be tested by science? Can studies be structured to verify whether personality types follow the patterns I claim? Do they react to stress the way I suggest, do they make friends along my lines?

Further, what about my suggestion for using the sixteen personality balances as definitions of normal personality? I hope to write more about this idea in a second book. I believe that the "trophic cascades" of both mental illness and personality disorder start with a few limited changes, which form the core of the illness or disability. As dynamic, balanced personality adjusts to these losses, there's a chain reaction of compensatory changes. It's the combination of the original core losses with compensating changes and habits that produces each syndrome. Finding full solutions means looking at how personality has adapted, in addition to treating the brain's medical issues. We've never looked at mental illness in combination with personality type, so there would be much to study and test. We've also never defined personality disorders within a general personality theory, nor have we studied the blend of organic difference and learned compensation.

What can neuroscience tell us about inborn personality? This field of knowledge is growing so fast, there's no predicting how much we can or can't learn in the next five years. We can image many things, and we can study others with eye movements and EEGs. Can we form a reliable correlation between any of Jung's observed mental functions and structures in the brain? Can we measure physiological differences, such as speed of eye movement or skin conductivity, among groups defined by factors like dominance of Thinking, Feeling, Sensing and Intuition in personality? I believe we probably can, but studies have yet to look for the differences, let alone find them. If they were found, can we then show that such differences are consistently reliable and meaningful in human interactions?

For now, I hope that my suggested model will be as helpful for readers as it has been for me. I've gained much understanding of some very complex situations. The dynamic, balanced personality model allows me to see many layers of the mind's operation, separating innate personality from learned experience, and separating both from things like learning disabilities and illness. The more clearly we can see, the better we can decide and act. Above all, the more clearly we see, the more we can forgive and love.